THE DYNAMICS OF THE WEALTH OF NATIONS

Luigi Pasinetti
Drawing by Gino Arzuffi

The Dynamics of the Wealth of Nations

Growth, Distribution and Structural Change

Essays in Honour of Luigi Pasinetti

Edited by

Mauro Baranzini
*Professor of Economics,
Università di Verona*

and

G. C. Harcourt
*Reader in the History of Economic Theory,
University of Cambridge, Fellow of Jesus College, Cambridge, and
Professor Emeritus, University of Adelaide*

St. Martin's Press

© Mauro Baranzini and G. C. Harcourt 1993

All rights reserved. No reproduction, copy or transmission of this publication may be made without written permission.

No paragraph of this publication may be reproduced, copied or transmitted save with written permission or in accordance with the provisions of the Copyright, Designs and Patents Act 1988, or under the terms of any licence permitting limited copying issued by the Copyright Licensing Agency, 90 Tottenham Court Road, London W1P 9HE.

Any person who does any unauthorised act in relation to this publication may be liable to criminal prosecution and civil claims for damages.

First published in Great Britain 1993 by
THE MACMILLAN PRESS LTD
Houndmills, Basingstoke, Hampshire RG21 2XS
and London
Companies and representatives
throughout the world

A catalogue record for this book is available
from the British Library.

ISBN 0-333-57397-8

Reprinted and bound 1995
in Great Britain by
Antony Rowe Ltd, Chippenham, Wiltshire

First published in the United States of America 1993 by
Scholarly and Reference Division,
ST. MARTIN'S PRESS, INC.,
175 Fifth Avenue,
New York, N.Y. 10010

ISBN 0-312-09587-2

Library of Congress Cataloging-in-Publication Data
The Dynamics of the wealth of nations : growth, distribution, and structural change : essays in honour of Luigi Pasinetti / edited by Mauro Baranzini and G. C. Harcourt.
    p. cm.
Includes bibliographical references and index.
ISBN 0-312-09587-2
1. Economics. 2. Economic history. 3. Pasinetti, Luigi L.
i. Pasinetti, Luigi L. II. Baranzini, Mauro. III. Harcourt, Geoffrey Colin.
HB171.D97   1993
330—dc20   92-46517
                                                        CIP

Contents

List of Tables	vii
List of Figures	viii
Preface	x
List of Contributors	xii

Introduction
Mauro Baranzini and G. C. Harcourt — 1

PART I: RICARDO AND CLASSICAL POLITICAL ECONOMY — 43

1 Marshall on Ricardo
   Peter Groenewegen — 45

2 Physiocratic Dichotomy in Price Determination and its Ricardian Resolution
   Izumi Hishiyama — 71

3 The 'Standard commodity' and Ricardo's Search for an 'Invariable Measure of Value'
   Heinz D. Kurz and Neri Salvadori — 95

4 Ricardian Comparative Advantage and the Perils of the Stationary State
   Andrea Maneschi — 124

PART II: ON CAPITAL THEORY — 147

5 Samuelson and the 93% Scarcity Theory of Value
   Avi J. Cohen — 149

PART III: POST-KEYNESIAN INCOME DISTRIBUTION AND GROWTH THEORY — 173

6 The Method of the Pure Ratio in Economic Analysis
   Amit Bhaduri — 175

Contents

7 A Post-Keynesian Theory of Growth, Interest and Money
   Amitava K. Dutt and Edward J. Amadeo — 181

PART IV: STRUCTURAL DYNAMICS AND VERTICAL INTEGRATION — 207

8 Commodity Flows and Productive Subsystems: An Essay in the Analysis of Structural Change
   Michael A. Landesmann and Roberto Scazzieri — 209

9 On Economic Science, its Tools and Economic Reality
   Alberto Quadrio-Curzio — 246

PART V: DEVELOPMENT ECONOMICS AND MODELS OF UNSTABLE GROWTH — 273

10 Development Economics: Some Basic Issues
    Sukhamoy Chakravarty — 275

11 The Economy as a Chaotic Growth Oscillator
    Richard M. Goodwin — 300

12 Long-Run Changes in the Wage and Price Mechanisms and the Processes of Growth
    Paolo Sylos-Labini — 311

PART VI: INSTITUTIONS AND ECONOMIC STRUCTURE: HUMAN ACTIONS AND THE PURE LABOUR THEORY OF VALUE — 349

13 Reflections on the Significance of the Labour Theory of Value in Pasinetti's Natural System
    Heinrich Bortis — 351

14 Rationality and Economic Behaviour
    Siro Lombardini — 384

Bibliography of the Works of Luigi Pasinetti — 403
Name Index — 413
Subject Index — 419

List of Tables

Table 4.1: Possible stationary-state patterns of
            specialization   133
Table 7.1: [untitled]   187
Table 12.1: Trends of prices and wages, 1800–1989   312
Table 12.2: Public expenditure in the United States
            1903–87   329
Table 12.3: Italy: economic growth, public expenditure
            and fiscal receipts   333

List of Figures

Figure 4.1		131
Figure 4.2		134
Figure 4.3		136
Figure 4.4		137
Figure 7.1		191
Figure 7.2		192
Figure 7.3		195
Figure 7.4		198
Figure 11.1		303
Figure 11.2		305
Figure 11.3 (a)		305
Figure 11.3 (b)		305
Figure 11.4		305
Figure 11.5		306
Figure 11.6		306
Figure 11.7		307
Figure 11.8		307
Figure 11.9		308
Figure 11.10 (a)		308
Figure 11.10 (b)		308
Figure 12.1:	United Kingdom: industrial production and national income	323
Figure 12.2:	United States: national income	323
Figure 12.3 (a):	United Kingdom: industrial prices (P_i) and raw material prices ($\hat{RM}$) (rates of change): 1800–1913	339
Figure 12.3 (b):	United Kingdom: industrial prices (P_i) and raw material prices ($\hat{RM}$) (rates of change): 1923–39 and 1948–89	339
Figure 12.4:	United Kingdom: wages (rates of change) (W) and unemployment (U) three periods: 1861–1913, 1923–39, 1948–90	340
Figure 12.5:	United States: wages (rates of change) (W) and unemployment (U): three periods: 1890–93, 1923–39, 1948–89	341

Figure 12.6:	Raw material prices ($\hat{RM}$) and world industrial output (Y_i) (rates of change) 1956–89	342
Figure 12.7:	United States: industrial prices (P_i) and raw material prices ($\hat{RM}$) (rates of change) 1948–89	343

Preface

On 12 September 1990 Luigi Lodovico Pasinetti turned sixty, and it seemed fitting to mark this occasion by presenting him with a volume of essays specifically written by a number of his teachers, colleagues or former colleagues, pupils and fellow economists. The relatively young age of Pasinetti is witnessed to by the fact that this volume includes contributions by two of his teachers, Siro Lombardini (then at the Catholic University of Milan) and Richard Goodwin (then at the University of Cambridge). The year 1990 also marks the thirtieth anniversary of the publication of two early and most significant essays by Pasinetti: 'A Mathematical Formulation of the Ricardian System' and 'Cyclical Fluctuations and Economic Growth' appeared in *The Review of Economic Studies* and *Oxford Economic Papers* respectively (see the Bibliography of the Works of Luigi Pasinetti at the end of this volume). Finally, 1990 also represents the thirtieth anniversary of Pasinetti's election to a Fellowship at an 'Oxbridge' College (first at Nuffield College, Oxford and, one year later, at King's College, Cambridge) where he was to spend a long stretch of his scientific life and where he laid, precisely in those years, the foundations of his ambitious research programme on the 'dynamics of the wealth of nations'.

This volume of essays does not only represent a tribute to the scientific achievements of a distinguished scholar; it also represents a comprehensive and specifically planned assessment of the six most important lines of inquiry of Pasinetti's vast research programme, by evaluating his contributions and by giving new insights. Last, but not least, this volume provides a more general assessment of the significance of a number of issues of the 'pure' Post-Keynesian School of economic thought, which had and still has in the University of Cambridge its stronghold and of which Pasinetti has been the 'senior heir' since the deaths of its founding members Piero Sraffa, Joan Robinson, Nicholas Kaldor and Richard Kahn, in the 1980s.

The preparation of this volume has been made possible by a number of institutions and persons who have supported our project in different ways. First of all thanks are due to our present academic institutions, respectively the University of Verona (in particular the Institute of Economic Sciences) and the Faculty of Economics and Politics of the University of Cambridge and Jesus College, Cambridge. Mauro Baranzini would also like to thank the University of Fribourg, Switzerland, The Queen's College, Oxford, and the Catholic University of Milan (Centre for Research in Economic Analysis, CRANEC), for providing at various stages of the preparation of this volume, research facilities and an intellectual environment which has stimulated our work in an important way. Finally, research help has been provided through grants of the Swiss Science Foundation, the Italian National Research Council and the Italian Ministry for the University.

Mauro Baranzini
G. C. Harcourt

Notes on the Contributors

Edward J. Amadeo is Professor of Economics at Pontificia Universidade Catolica Do Rio de Janeiro, Brazil.

Mauro L. Baranzini is Professor of Economics at the University of Verona and Catholic University of Milan. He was formerly Lecturer and Tutor in Economics at The Queen's College, Oxford.

Amit Bhaduri is Professor of Economics at the Indian Institute of Management, Calcutta, India; he was formerly Professor of Economics at Jahwaharlal Nehru University, New Delhi, India.

Heinrich Bortis is Professor of Economics at the University of Fribourg, Switzerland.

Sukhamoy Chakravarty was Professor of Economics at the Delhi School of Economics and Chairman of the Indian Economic Advisory Council, New Delhi, India.

Avi J. Cohen is Professor of Economics at York University, Toronto, Canada, and Fellow of Clare Hall, Cambridge.

Amitava K. Dutt is Professor of Economics at the University of Notre Dame, Indiana, USA.

Richard M. Goodwin is Professor of Economics at the University of Siena, Italy; he was formerly Reader in Economics at the University of Cambridge and Fellow of Peterhouse, Cambridge.

Peter Groenewegen is Professor of Economics at the University of Sydney, Australia.

G. C. Harcourt is Reader in the History of Economic Theory at the University of Cambridge, Fellow and former President of Jesus College, Cambridge, and Professor Emeritus of the University of Adelaide, Australia.

Notes on the Contributors

Izumi Hishiyama is Emeritus Professor of Economics at the University of Kyoto and Professor of Economics at the Industrial University of Osaka, Japan.

Heinz D. Kurz is Professor of Economics at the University of Graz, Austria; he was formerly Professor of Economics at the University of Bremen, Germany.

Michael A. Landesmann is a Senior Research Officer in the Department of Applied Economics, University of Cambridge, and Fellow of Jesus College, Cambridge.

Siro Lombardini is Professor of Economics at the University of Turin; he was formerly Professor of Economics at the Catholic University of Milan, Italy.

Andrea Maneschi is Professor of Economics at Vanderbilt University, Nashville, Tennessee, USA.

Alberto Quadrio-Curzio is Professor of Economics and Chairman of the Faculty of Political Sciences at the Catholic University of Milan, Italy.

Neri Salvadori is Professor of Economics at the University of Pisa, Italy.

Roberto Scazzieri is Professor of Economics at the University of Bologna; he was formerly Professor of Economics at the University of Padua, Italy.

Paolo Sylos-Labini is Professor of Economics at the University of Rome, 'La Sapienza', Italy.

Introduction
Mauro Baranzini and G. C. Harcourt

LUIGI LODOVICO PASINETTI: A SHORT BIOGRAPHY

Luigi Pasinetti was born on 12 September 1930 at Zanica, near Bergamo, northern Italy. He was the eldest son of a small entrepreneur who got into considerable financial difficulties in the years of Luigi's adolescence, immediately after the war. This event undoubtedly influenced Luigi's decision to study economics as he moved from secondary education (at Bergamo) to university education (at Milan). He received his first university degree (*laurea, summa cum laude*) from the Catholic University of Milan in 1954 with a doctoral thesis on 'Econometric models and their application to trade cycle analysis'. He was subsequently awarded a British Council Scholarship and two Stringer Scholarships of the Bank of Italy for graduate studies at Gonville and Caius College, University of Cambridge, England (for the academic years 1956–7 and 1958–9) and at Harvard University in the USA (1957–8). He then went to Oxford University, where he spent a year (1959–60) as a research student and a second year (1960–1) as a research fellow of Nuffield College. In 1961 Richard Kahn called Pasinetti back to Cambridge where he was elected a Fellow of King's College; he remained there until 1976. The graduate work done at Cambridge, Harvard and Oxford allowed him to complete his PhD in economics at the University of Cambridge in 1962 with a well-known dissertation, 'A Multi-Sector Model of Economic Growth' (the dissertation itself was never published, but it formed the basis for a revised and expanded version, see Pasinetti, 1981).

As he was later to write, he came into close contact 'with that remarkable group of thinkers – Richard Kahn, Nicholas Kaldor, Joan Robinson and Piero Sraffa – whom I had the rare fortune of meeting, discussing with so often, and then being associated with, in Cambridge, which has been to me the most stimulating place I could possibly imagine for progressive thought in economic theory' (Pasinetti, 1974, p. x). Besides being Fellow of King's College, Pasinetti was, from 1961 to 1973, a University Lecturer in Economics and Politics in the Faculty of Economics and Politics in the University of Cambridge; in 1973 he became a University Reader in the same Faculty – a great distinction indeed since his predecessors were Piero Sraffa, Maurice Dobb, Joan Robinson, Nicholas Kaldor, David Champernowne and Richard Goodwin.

Pasinetti never severed his links with his *alma mater* in Italy during the two decades he spent mainly in Cambridge. In 1976 he returned to Italy to a chair (first of econometrics and eventually of economic analysis) at the Catholic University of Milan, where in quick succession he was chairman of the Faculty of Economics and Commerce (1980–3), Director of the Department of Economics (1983–6), and Director of the doctorate programme of the four Milanese universities (1986–).[1]

LUIGI LODOVICO PASINETTI: THE 'SENIOR' HEIR OF THE POST-KEYNESIAN SCHOOL

Luigi Pasinetti may be defined as a 'senior' representative of the Post-Keynesian School, both because of his acknowledged achievements and for his early involvement with the pupils of John Maynard Keynes, the founding members of the Cambridge School, in particular Richard Kahn, Nicholas Kaldor and Joan Robinson.[2] We should further point out that Pasinetti was also closely linked with a complementary line of research initiated in Cambridge in the fifties and much developed in the sixties, concerning in particular the disaggregated analysis of the economic systems, the structural dynamics and the economic cycle, whose main initiators were David Champernowne, Richard Goodwin, Piero Sraffa and Richard Stone. Pasinetti himself acknowledges that

> It was Richard Goodwin who skillfully directed my very first timid steps into research work. And later, when I began to write a great deal, Richard Kahn very patiently read, criticised and commented every single note I submitted to him. Through Kahn I came in contact with that unique mixture of radicalism, wisdom and social concern that was the distinct mark of Keynes' environment. Through Goodwin I was stimulated to open up my intellectual curiosity and interests towards tools of analysis that came from outside. At the same time, I also benefited from long discussions, and often from daily conversations, with Nicholas Kaldor, always

bubbling with new ideas, Joan Robinson, always hard as a rock on her theoretical conceptions, and Piero Sraffa, the real master of all critics. It is from them that I learnt that passionate critical attitude which has been the *conditio sine qua non* for starting and pursuing an investigation of this type. (Pasinetti, 1981, p. xiv)

One indication that Pasinetti is considered the 'senior' heir of the Post-Keynesian School may be found in the fact that he was asked to give the address at the memorial service of the late Richard Kahn as well as to write official biographies for the late Joan Robinson and the late Nicholas Kaldor. In the address given in honour of Lord Kahn, delivered in the Chapel of King's College in Cambridge on 21 October 1989, Pasinetti stated that:

This is the third time, over a short span of years, that the Congregation assembles in this Chapel to commemorate, and reflect upon the life of, a major contributor to that intellectual breakthrough that has become known in the world of economics and politics as 'the Keynesian Revolution'.

Pasinetti was referring to the previous commemorations of Joan Robinson and Nicholas Kaldor; he went on to say that

If one adds that another memorial service, shortly after that of Joan Robinson, was held in Cambridge, though in another Chapel, for yet another close associate of Keynes, Piero Sraffa, one cannot resist the impression that today's ceremony concludes a whole historical phase, almost an era, in the recent history of economic thought. This group of Cambridge economists has been protagonist of one of those extraordinary and unique events in the history of ideas that decisively pushed ahead and created a break with the past.

Pasinetti was one of the major contributors to the controversies on capital theory, income distribution and theory of value that were fought out between Cambridge, England, and Cambridge, Mass., during the 'raging' fifties, sixties and seventies. The battle was, as we shall see, won by Cambridge, England, but paradoxically the losing side was awarded, over the years, a number of Nobel prizes (while significantly none of the above mentioned Cambridge UK economists were awarded one). Notwithstanding the strength and the high analytical rigour of such a group of thinkers, as time passed, the 'Keynesian' and later the 'neo-Keynesian' schools have progressively become a 'minority' school of thinking, while the marginalist school has taken over and, numerically at least, has become the dominant school in most of the Western world. In a sense the first 'Keynesian Revolution', led by Keynes himself, Kahn and Joan Robinson, had been able to 'create a break with the past' and to convert most of the leading economists and fellow politicians of the thirties, forties and fifties; but when the time was ripe for a continuation of the 'Keynesian Programme' to problems concerning the long run, the majority of economists did not follow. The 'Keynesian Programme' suffered a halt and its leading members found themselves besieged mainly in Cambridge, England.

Pasinetti has an extraordinary clarity of mind and vision, so that he has been able to carry out a remarkably unified research programme, one which encompasses a great number of strands within its scope. (Because of the clarity and simplicity of his vision, unsympathetic critics have sometimes taken him to task, for example, Solow, 1970; Bliss, 1986. They have often confused clarity of vision, the concentration on fundamental, central, conceptual points, with undue simplification.)

In addition, Pasinetti's thirty-year-old research programme has followed a coherent pattern, first outlining the weaknesses of the marginalist model, and then laying step by step the foundations of the reconstruction, on mixed classical/'pure' Keynesian bases, of a 'more general theory' in order to identify, explain and analytically recompose the mechanisms and dynamics of modern economic systems. This has been carried out with powerful tools of analysis, in particular the method of vertical integration, so allowing the understanding of a number of very complicated phenomena taking place in economies, such as the unequal distribution and pace of technical progress, the non-linear variations in the composition of demand, the presence of a great variety of asymmetric behaviour and the complex role of institutions (although Pasinetti begins with a core model which is free from institutions).

Pasinetti's study on the 'long-term evolution of industrial economic systems' was originated, in his own words, by 'a combination of three factors – one factual and two theoretical' (Pasinetti, 1981, p. xi).

> The factual element was provided by the extremely uneven development – from sector to sector, from region to region – of the

environment in which I lived (post-war Europe) at the time I began my training in economics. The two theoretical factors are represented by the two types of theories – specifically the macro-dynamic models of economic growth and input-output analysis – ... Both the macro-dynamic growth models and input-output analysis impressed me at the time; but they left me profoundly dissatisfied when I tried to use them in order to understand what was going on in economic systems with a very high degree of dynamism, i.e. of technical progress. And I began to think that an attempt might be made to develop a theoretical scheme which, while retaining the analytical character of input-output analysis, could also deal with uneven increases in productivity, in the way the macro-dynamic models had begun to do, but only for the very simplified case of a one-commodity world. It was from this determination to look for new tools of analysis that the present work has come into being. (Pasinetti, 1981, p. xi)

Step by step Pasinetti's work became a 'theoretical essay on the dynamics of industrial systems'; its publication was held back by two elements, which account for the long time that has elapsed since it was first written for a PhD dissertation at Cambridge. The first of such elements is connected with the publication of Sraffa's *Production of Commodities by Means of Commodities* which brought attention back to the concept of 'circularity' in economic theory. Pasinetti's dynamic analysis had already the advantage of avoiding the fixity of coefficients which had forced inter-industry analysis 'into a strait-jacket'. A few years later Pasinetti (1973) was able to establish a link between Sraffa's analysis and to work out, without any loss of generality, all analytical inter-industry connections.

The second problem which held back Pasinetti's project is connected with a distinctive feature of his research programme, that of a 'level of investigation which is so fundamental as to be independent of the institutional set-up of society', the so-called 'natural' feature. The elaboration of this concept was refined in stages. In his well-known (1962) article 'Rate of Profit and Income Distribution in Relation to the Rate of Economic Growth', Pasinetti was able, starting from Kaldor's income distribution theory, to define a 'natural' rate of profit at the macro-economic level, determined by the natural rate of growth of the system and the propensity to save of the 'pure' capitalists' class. However, this type of 'natural system' was not satisfactory since, as Pasinetti himself (1981, p. xiii) points out, 'it did not take long to realise that introducing behavioural (savings) relations did not fit consistently into a theoretical framework which was basically conceived independently of institutions'.

A few years later, in a paper published in the *Journal of Post Keynesian Economics* (1980/81) with the title 'The Rate of Interest and the Distribution of Income in a Pure Labour Economy', Pasinetti was able to fix the concept of 'natural' at the industry or sector level (and hence no longer at the macro-level) where there logically exist a whole series of 'natural' rates of interest, at a stage which even precedes the process of capital accumulation. As a matter of fact in a pure labour economic system characterized by structural dynamics of technology and prices there exists a rate of interest on interpersonal loans that keeps 'labour commanded' equal to 'labour embodied' through time. This natural rate of interest, obtained independently of any institutional framework (as we shall explain below, pp. 20–1) allowed for the completion of Pasinetti's theoretical scheme, making it logical and complete.

Pasinetti (1981, p. xiii) rightly emphasizes the relevance of an institution-free scheme of inquiry: 'For the first, more fundamental, stage of analysis a complete and self-contained theoretical scheme has at least clearly emerged'; for these first important steps towards a full-scale reconstruction of political economy allow for a more comprehensive methodological approach. In fact alternative schemes of analysis provide a general rule (such as the equality between marginal productivities and factor payments) and successively are constrained to modify such a rule in order to take into account a number of exceptions (such as the presence of market imperfections, and so on). On the contrary, in the case of the 'natural' system approach the presence of a particular institutional set-up does not modify the basic framework, but simply provides additional information. And in the case of a modification of the institutional set-up the framework does not require modifications bound to alter its 'scope and method'. For instance, the 'natural' framework does not require the existence of 'symmetric' relations; rather it presupposes a world characterized by 'asymmetric' and cumulative behaviour, as in the case of stickiness of prices due to oligopolistic situations, mark-up pricing rules in manufacturing business, contractually fixed wage-rates, etc., and many other institutional factors continually evolving (on this point see, for instance, the contribution of Sylos-Labini in this volume).

In this way one obtains a sharp differentiation between those economic problems that have to be solved on the ground of logic alone – for which economic theory is entirely autonomous – and those economic issues that 'arise in connection with particular institutions, or with particular groups' or individuals' behaviour – for which economic theory is no longer autonomous and needs to be integrated with further hypotheses, which may well come from other social sciences' (Pasinetti, 1981, p. xiii). It is with this kind of issues that Pasinetti's life-long effort has been concerned; and a clear distinction between the two levels of inquiry (the first 'natural', the second 'institutional') is always kept in the foreground.

* * *

Pasinetti's scientific output consists, at the time of writing (1992), of some ninety papers mainly published in international journals; and of eight volumes (four of which are edited) published with the best presses and usually translated into several languages. To give some order to these contributions we shall discuss them under the headings of six different, yet strictly interconnected, partial research lines: (i) on Ricardo and classical political economy; (ii) on capital theory; (iii) on Post-Keynesian income distribution and growth theory; (iv) on structural dynamics and vertical integration; (v) on the pure labour theory of value: and (vi) on models of unstable growth, development economics and international trade. We review the above mentioned areas of research in some detail by linking them with the main controversies at the centre of which the contributions of Pasinetti have regularly found themselves.

ON RICARDO AND CLASSICAL POLITICAL ECONOMY

One of Pasinetti's earliest major contributions was published in February 1960 in *The Review of Economic Studies* under the title 'A Mathematical Formulation of the Ricardian System'.

Pasinetti's early work on Ricardo shows his superb theoretical skills, his mastery of the interconnections between value, distribution and growth which was to become a characteristic feature of all of his work. The principal object of the Ricardo paper was to show how an analytical model could capture the ingredients of Ricardo's system and produce his results. The model contained the essence of Ricardo's theory of value – that it was principally embodied labour which in practice determined the natural exchange ratios of reproducible commodities. It also highlighted Ricardo's own stress on persistent and permanent or dominant factors at work in the economy which expressed themselves in the forces which determined natural prices. The short-term factors associated with supply and demand and the determination of market prices were relegated to a secondary position. No more so was this the case than in Ricardo's theory of the natural wage and changes in population *cum* labour force, with which was associated his theory of accumulation. In Pasinetti's model of Ricardo's system, the Malthusian principle of population, which Ricardo adopted, is treated as though it works instantaneously so that the wage is *always* at its natural level even though accumulation is occurring. (As with Ricardo, Pasinetti does not suppose the natural wage to be a physiologically determined subsistence wage; habit and history also influence its size.) This simplification allows a much more clear-cut picture of the accumulation process and the approach to the stationary state (abstracting from the offsetting influence of technical progress) than later models were to allow.

The two and then n sector versions of the model are neatly presented and the results of the simple model are shown to be robust (n sector models for Pasinetti are also the crux of structural dynamic analysis). In the process, Pasinetti uses the theory of value in Ricardo to illustrate the dichotomy in value theories, as between the two dominant traditions, which has become a feature of all Pasinetti's work and which was to call forth such an ill-tempered response from Bliss (1986) when Pasinetti succintly stated this view many years later in Pasinetti (1986a). It seems that modern neoclassical economists find it impossible to accept that there *is* a distinction between the notion of price as an 'objective' index of reproducibility in the classical tradition and as a 'subjective' index of scarcity in the neoclassical tradition; and that this implies a difference between the surplus that is relevant for distribution and consumption theory, on the one hand, and for production theory, on the other. We find such a response mysterious. The factors which determine growth which Pasinetti through Ricardo captures create a process which still makes more sense of the world to us than that which emerges from the Fisherian model. In the former, it is decision-making by the entrepreneurial class which explicitly drives the system along (with landlords playing a more dominant role then than now, of course). Certainly this captures more of what the world is like than the notion that all activities and institutions in capitalism exist only as the agents who serve the purposes of utility maximizing consumers trying to allocate their consumption in an optimal manner over their life-cycle.

ON CAPITAL THEORY

Pasinetti's fundamental contribution in the capital theory controversy has often been erroneously labelled a 'paradox' – as has often been the case of the Kaldor/Pasinetti income distribution theorem considered below. Yet the significance of paradox may be better understood from the following passage:

> Economists sometimes tend to examine a large domain of economic phenomena by adapting theoretical concepts that had originally been devised for a much narrower range of special issues. The discoveries of 'paradoxical' relations derive from the fact that their process of generalization often turns out to be ill-conceived and misleading, if not entirely unwarranted. (Pasinetti and Scazzieri, 1987, pp. 363–7)

It was in the early 1960s that economists first came to doubt that it could no longer be taken for granted that there is a unique, unambiguous profitability ranking of production techniques in terms of physical capital intensity along the scale variation of the rate of profits. It was originally Paul A. Samuelson who, with a number of other, principally American, economists, started looking for the conditions that would ensure a strictly monotonic relation between the rate of profits and capital intensity (capital/labour ratio) even in the presence of a non-linear relation between the wage-rate and the rate of profits. This was claimed to be found by a pupil of Paul Samuelson, David Levhari, in an article published in 1965 in the *Quarterly Journal of Economics*; here Levhari claimed to have shown that while reswitching and capital-reversing (he was never clear with which phenomenon he was dealing, for he confused the Ruth Cohen curiosum, capital-reversing, with reswitching) could occur in an industry, they would not occur in the economy as a whole. The refutation of Levhari's thesis came promptly from Pasinetti (who was encouraged to do so by Piero Sraffa[3]) in a paper presented at the First World Congress of the Econometric Society held in Rome in 1965; that paper gave rise to a host of other papers (and to a discussion on both sides of the Atlantic among economists who had participated at the World Congress) gathered together in a 'Symposium on Capital Theory' of the *Quarterly Journal of Economics*, November 1966.

Paul Samuelson wrote his 'summing up' paper, as well as a note with Levhari (1966), in which they said that the reswitching theorem, but not the accompanying non-substitution theorem, was wrong. Samuelson apologized handsomely and gave some extremely useful examples which brought out why the possibility of capital-reversing and reswitching had been overlooked in the neoclassical tradition. Pasinetti, in his paper, rightly stressed the dominant importance of capital-reversing – it was this result which undermined the conceptual foundation of a well-behaved demand curve for capital within the neoclassical tradition. Pasinetti provided an example: on the wage-rate of profits envelope there is capital-reversing at every switch point except the last, but no reswitching at all (on the envelope, that is, beneath it we have to have reswitching for the main result to go through).

Though all these results were obtained in terms of comparisons of stationary states, in our view and, we believe, in Pasinetti's view, too, this is all that is needed to make the points involved. First, the stationary state is the simplest model within which could be included all the essential ingredients. If the intuitively appealing results of the 'parables' could not survive transition to this setting, it hardly seems necessary *in a doctrinal debate* to go further and become more complicated. Secondly, comparisons of long-period positions *were* the traditional setting in which these and earlier arguments were carried on when neoclassical theory was emerging as a challenge to classical political economy and Marx. Furthermore, in the view of Piero Sraffa and his immediate followers (but *not* Joan Robinson), it *is* the appropriate method to use in a theoretical argument. Of course, this has not stopped innumerable defenders of the faith wandering off into comparative dynamics and even more complicated settings in order to find the conditions under which capital reversing and reswitching cannot occur. Perhaps the one that sticks most in our mind (or gizzard) is Burmeister and Turnovsky (1972) on regular economies – those economies in which capital-reversing cannot occur, not, as might be thought, those economies in which the inhabitants have All Bran for breakfast.

Pasinetti shares this methodological view for his next major foray in capital theory was his 1969 *Economic Journal* article on the relevance of the 'new' results for Fisherian theory. The latter itself had

had a principal part to play in the modern debates when Solow (1963) used it as the means to get away – he claimed – from the aggregate production function, aggregate 'capital' and 'its' marginal product, preferring to pitch the analysis in terms of intertemporal prices and, in particular, to concentrate on the social rate of return on investment. Pasinetti reread Fisher in the light of the results of the controversy in capital theory and, he argued, unearthed as a consequence an 'unobtrusive postulate', to wit, no capital-reversing allowed by assumption in Fisher's and Fisherian analysis. Pasinetti interpreted the purpose of the postulate to be the means by which a rigorous meaning could be given to the scarcity view associated with one of the determinants of the rate of profits. This determinant was the marginal rate of return on sacrifice which was the productivity analogue of the psychological determinant, the marginal rate of time preference.

Pasinetti's argument is well known and we need only summarise it here. The argument contains essentially two steps. The first is to show that if the rate of return on investment in an aggregate or economy-wide sense can be defined independently of prices as a ratio of physical quantities, Irving Fisher's marginal rate of return over cost, a marginal concept in the full sense of the word, including its traditional association with continuity, emerges with the corollary that there is a downward sloping relationship between the quantity of 'capital' per man, on the one hand, and the size of the rate of return, on the other. Pasinetti illustrates this proposition with a 'corn as seed corn, corn as output' example within the context of a Ricardo-Sraffa circulating capital goods model. As the measure is independent of prices and the rate of profits, it could form the basis for the construction of an investment-opportunity curve with the 'right' shape.

The social rate of return on investment is essentially a concept of consumption foregone, consumption thus gained. At an aggregate level, the consumption foregone – saving – has to be invested: new capital goods have to be constructed in an out-of-equilibrium transition process – and the impact of this on the overall price level cannot be ignored. Moreover, more than a marginal change in the composition of the means of production before and after the transition may be involved. Pasinetti shows that if we assume malleability (no redundancy of commodities in the means of production because of the transition), infinite possibilities of substitution and the 'unobtrusive postulate' of no capital-reversing, then, even though the calculations of the rate of return at every level depend on arbitrarily chosen sets of prices yet, *in all essential respects*, the rate of return so calculated is akin to the corn rate of return above. It may be given a marginal interpretation, it is 'well-behaved', and it can act as a determinant of the rate of profits in the economy as a whole. Once we remove the 'unobtrusive postulate', i.e. allow for the possibilities of capital-reversing and reswitching, however, the (physical and value) marginal interpretations are no longer possible: 'continuity in the scale of variation of the rate of profits does not imply continuity in the change of amounts of capital per man' (Pasinetti, 1972, p. 1352). The social rate of return on investment ceases to have the relevant properties of the corn rate of return.

Pasinetti's paper brought a veritable barrage of criticism, especially from Solow (1970), Dougherty (1972), Craven (1977) (though his attack is on Harcourt (1976, 1982a)) and, certainly by implication, from Bliss (1975) and Dixit (1977). Solow was defending econometric procedure rather than theoretical purity. Bliss was annoyed with both of them – with Solow for talking as if there were only one rate of return on investment (and rate of profits?), and with Pasinetti for imputing to Fisher views which could not be found in his work (as they could be in J. B. Clark), an argument that Dougherty also emphasized.

The main point remains, however, the disjunction between the 'profit-wage rate' relationship and the 'technique of production-profit rate' relationship. More specifically slight changes in the rate of profits may lead to sharp variations in the choice of techniques of production in terms of capital intensity (per man). This is a property of our economic systems, first pointed out by Pasinetti, which has never been challenged. The implications are far-reaching: for the price system variations may be quite small, but for the choice of techniques and the distribution of income such variations will be much greater.

ON POST-KEYNESIAN INCOME DISTRIBUTION AND GROWTH THEORY

Pasinetti's most widely known contribution (although not necessarily most original) is surely in the field of income distribution, profit determination and growth theory: his works (about twenty papers and essays) in this field have generated at least 200 papers in scholarly journals, numerous books and a 'must' reference in a large number of textbooks on economic analysis. (For an exhaustive list see

Baranzini, 1991, and for an exposition of this topic see Harcourt, 1969; 1972, Ch. 5.)

In his seminal paper 'Rate of Profit and Income Distribution in Relation to the Rate of Economic Growth' (*The Review of Economic Studies*, 1962), starting as a critique of Kaldor's growth model where there exist two different saving rates, one for the workers and one for the capitalists, Pasinetti shows that the equilibrium rate of profits is totally independent of the saving behaviour of the working class; it is determined only by the saving rate of the pure capitalists (s_c) and by the rate of growth of the system (n). (The solution $P/K = n/s_c$ is known as Pasinetti's Theorem or the New Cambridge Equation.) Such a rate of profits is, however, independent of the production function and of the capital/output ratio. In this way the Cambridge (or Post-Keynesian) School was in a position to (i) provide a solution to the Harrod-Domar dilemma by specifying an aggregate saving ratio determined by the exogenously given rate of growth of population, capital/output and capitalists' propensity to save; (ii) determine the long-period equilibrium value of the rate of profits, the distribution of income between profits and wages, and the distribution of disposable income between the classes; (iii) allow for the existence of an income residual (very much in line with classical and neo-Ricardian models) namely the wages, consistent with the assumption of a relationship between the savings of that class of individuals (the capitalists or entrepreneurs) who determine the process of production and the patterns of capital accumulation; and (iv) give some insights into the process of accumulation of capital by specifying the equilibrium capital shares of the socio-economic classes. This range of results is obtained by Pasinetti (1962; 1974 Ch. VI) within a fairly simple framework and on the basis of relatively few assumptions, much less 'hybrid, opposite and extreme' than those of the neoclassical model.

Post-Keynesian distribution theory now occupies, thanks to the seminal contributions of Kalecki, Joan Robinson, Kaldor and Pasinetti – along with a number of other younger scholars – an undisputed place in most textbooks of modern economic analysis. Stemming from the Kaldor/Pasinetti model we find a very high number of subsequent contributions branching out in various directions and covering many aspects of the wider research programme relevant for the general topic of income distribution, profit determination and capital accumulation, both from a theoretical and applied point of view. Among the research lines grafted onto the Kaldor/Pasinetti model we may distinguish the following seven.[4]

The Introduction of a Differentiated Rate of Return on Savings for the Classes

This hypothesis has been first explored by Laing (1969), Harcourt (1972, p. 217) and Balestra and Baranzini (1971); it inspired a large literature. It was also taken up by Pasinetti (1974, pp. 139–41), who showed that under general conditions this hypothesis reinforces the validity of the Cambridge Equation. The implications of the assumption of a different rate of return for the accumulated savings are far-reaching. It affects directly the distribution of income between classes, and it affects the overall saving ratio and the patterns of wealth accumulation.

The Introduction of the Monetary Sector and of Portfolio Choice

The contributions in this field were first motivated by the desire to assess the neutrality of money in these caste-models of growth and distribution. Secondly, it was important to determine whether the equilibrium rate of interest, in a monetary context, would maintain the same characteristics as in the real world. The introduction of the monetary factor and of the portfolio choice (where groups of individuals or classes may choose among different assets with different rates of return and different variances) has the merit of bringing together the 'objectivist' and 'subjectivist' Keynesian research programme. Additionally, stochastic models including portfolio choice, under fairly general conditions, confirm the polarization of different socio-economic classes, with a very different rate of wealth accumulation (see Baranzini, 1976; 1990b, Ch. 7).

The Stability Analysis and the Long-Term Properties of the Model

Many authors have considered the adjustment time required for the economy to return to the steady-state situations from any initial disturbance, as well as the stability conditions in general. Not surprisingly, the adjustment time which is required to arrive at the steady-state solutions (or to return to them in the case of initial disturbances) is, in general, quite long. Taniguchi (1987) has recently shown that, in the specific case of the Kaldor/Pasinetti model, there exists a 'traverse' which from one steady-state equilibrium approaches asymptotically a new long-run equilibrium path provided that the rate of profits is constant in the long period.

The Introduction of a Public Sector

Another line of enquiry has been taken up by a number of authors who considered the implications of the introduction into the Post-Keynesian model, of a public sector with its own propensity to save, to consume and to run into deficits or surpluses. The starting point is Steedman (1972) who considers the case of a perfectly balanced government budget, and shows that the existence of government expenditure and taxes should not affect the validity of the Kaldor/Pasinetti theorem while, except for quite particular cases, it denies the possibility of the Meade-Samuelson-Modigliani's Dual Theorem. Furthermore, in the case of a government budget deficit or surplus, the Cambridge Equation maintains its relevance. Indeed, in this specific case (see Pasinetti, 1989, p. 11, replying to Fleck and Domenghino, 1987, and Domenghino, 1982; and see also Denicolò and Matteuzzi, 1990) it may be proved that the equilibrium rate of profits is determined by the natural rate of growth divided by the capitalists' propensities to save, here 'modified' by the effects of both taxation on profits and of government deficit (surplus) spending.

The Introduction of Micro-Foundations into the Model

The aim of this research is not exclusively that of providing some micro-foundations to the model of distribution and accumulation, but rather of providing a framework where the propensities to save of the various classes are not simply exogenously given, but are a function of economic, demographic and institutional parameters of the system. The results obtained in this framework provide us with new insights into the micro-mechanisms of the accumulation of savings and of the inter-generational transmission of wealth. This analysis may be carried out both in the original Post-Keynesian model of distribution, where there is not perfect substitutability among the factors of production, and without a neoclassical production function, and in the traditional neoclassical model. In this way the historical aspects of savings and capital accumulation are brought to the forefront.

The Analysis of the Long-Term Distribution of Wealth and of the Income Share of the Socio-Economic Classes

Still another area of research has been concerned with the determination of the share of income and wealth (both inter-generational and life-cycle) accruing to each class of the system. This aspect is important, since the seminal works mentioned above only focused on the distribution accruing to the factors of production on the basis of the value of the equilibrium rate of profits. The contributions in this area have in certain cases led to the formulation of models where the level of aggregate saving of the system is determined by the kind of income and not by the class status. This, of course, tends to weaken the hypothesis of constant propensities to save related to the existence of homogeneous socio-economic classes, and introduces the possibility of a more flexible approach to the treatment of savings.

Other General Aspects of the Kaldor/Pasinetti Model

In particular, we should mention the inclusion of other types of socio-economic classes and the applicability of the Meade-Samuelson and Modigliani's Dual Theorem. A large number of papers have considered the existence of other types of socio-economic classes, mainly stimulated by the contribution of Tobin (1960) where the Kaldor/Pasinetti model is generalized to include many sub-classes of capitalists and workers. Additionally the relevance of the Meade-Samuelson and Modigliani Dual Theorem (dubbed the 'Anti-Pasinetti' Theorem) has drawn increasing attention. (See, for instance, the April 1991 issue of the *Oxford Economic Papers*, with contributions by K. Miyazaki, P. A. Samuelson and M. Baranzini.) We should also mention the literature generated by the formulation of the 'neo-Pasinetti' theorem by Kaldor (1966, Appendix): see, for instance, Wood (1975), Harcourt and Kenyon (1976), Targetti (1991); and also Marris (1964) and Marglin (1984).

Summing up, we may stress that, over a span of more than three decades, the Kaldor/Pasinetti Post-Keynesian model has been developed and refined in order to include a number of issues associated with the distribution of income and wealth and with the determination of the rate of profits in a steady-state growth model. The historical, demographic and institutional aspects of these models have come under close scrutiny and a number of relevant questions seem to have received adequate answers. It is worth noting that Pasinetti himself has contributed, since 1962, a high number of papers, essays and parts of volumes to all of the seven research sub-programmes described above, by outlining new issues and by taking authoritative positions in the context of various controversies.

ON STRUCTURAL DYNAMICS AND VERTICAL INTEGRATION

The relevance of these topics was stressed by Pasinetti as early as 1962 in his Cambridge PhD dissertation (which was partly published in 1965 and finally completed in 1981). Pasinetti studies the conditions under which an economic system may reach and maintain full employment and full capacity utilization over the long period when it is subject to the main pressures leading to structural change, i.e. technical progress, non-uniform productivity increases and changes in the consumption structure (or consumers' preferences) according to Engel's law. This new approach, which leaves entirely aside the analytical tools of marginalist economics, faces technical change by giving up the input-output scheme and focusing instead on the 'vertically integrated sectors' approach. (On this point see, for instance, Baranzini and Scazzieri, 1990, pp. 1–130.) This approach allows Pasinetti to bring up to date the truth contained in the classical theory of value, to devise a tool with which to handle technical progress in a complex model, and to provide a bridge between a 'world' of production of commodities by means of commodities and the characteristics of the Keynesian system with its flows of final expenditure, production and incomes.

Pasinetti started from Sraffa's ingenious device of a sub-system whereby the total direct and indirect labour content of a particular commodity in a given production and technical situation may be obtained immediately. Suppose that we consider an economic system of circulating commodities, each one of which is produced in a single commodity industry, i.e. the model which underlies much of classical political economy. (The device is, nevertheless, a general one, applicable to joint production systems, including the case of fixed capital.) In the actual economic system we suppose there to be produced over a given production period, a gross product of such size and composition as to provide a net product. With this particular level of production will be associated a given amount of labour units, distributed in a technically determined way between each industry as its direct labour content. We wish to find, though, the direct and indirect labour content of each particular commodity in the net product. Therefore, we notionally construct a system in which the net product contains one (or more) units of the commodity that we are interested in *but no other*. The total amount of labour associated with the sub-system is the direct and indirect labour content of the commodity that constitutes its net product.

In a sub-system we may see immediately the total labour requirements, and Pasinetti demonstrates that we may see also the capital requirements in terms of a unit of (vertically integrated) productive capacity for each unit of final good. In this way we come to rearrange our way of looking at the production process so as to form a series of 'notional' vertically integrated activities, one for each commodity. We have also 'redistributed' the total labour force employed in the economy into its vertically integrated components, as obtained from the sub-system corresponding to each commodity in the original net product. The same process also may be repeated, as many times as we like, for the 'composite commodity' of each sub-system. It is this approach and variations on it that Pasinetti exploits in order to discuss the implications of the theoretical concept of vertical integration for value, distribution, capital accumulation and growth theory. (Interestingly enough, Pasinetti shows that the notion of vertical integration for labour and capital may be generalized to any higher order that may be necessary.)

In particular Pasinetti (1986b, pp. 11–14) is able to show that the concept of vertical integration results in a vertically integrated sector which may be represented by one physical unit of its final good, one physical unit of vertically integrated productive capacity for the final good, and one physical quantity of labour for the final good. Put this way, the components of the sector have the remarkable property (which a sub-system has not) of being unaffected by technical progress. This thus makes possible 'an economic analysis that may encompass, at the same time, the circular process of production and the evolution of the economic system through time' (Pasinetti, 1986b, p. 14). It has the added advantage, Pasinetti argues, of linking onto (long-period) Keynesian analysis, if we reclassify the final goods within that framework in terms of those associated with the Sraffian production interdependent model.

It is worth noting that the use of vertically integrated sectors permits the author to overlook the network of inter-industry transactions which may obscure the picture when we use the input-output approach. Additionally such an analytical formulation provides a logical framework in which both technological and demand conditions may be integrated in order to give a comprehensive interpretation of the dynamics of the 'wealth of a nation' both concerning its absolute level and possible changes in its composition. Finally, it must be mentioned that Pasinetti has chosen an analytical device that permits us to focus on the 'natural' properties of the economic system, leaving aside the institutional mechanisms, such as the tendency towards the equalization of the rate of profits in a competitive market economy.

ON THE PURE LABOUR THEORY OF VALUE

Starting from the analytical scheme described above, Pasinetti has more recently put forward a 'pure' labour theory of value and distribution, around which his more recent work has centered. Pasinetti (1986b, 1988) first introduced a set of 'newly defined sub-systems', much more comprehensive than those considered in Pasinetti 1973 and 1981, Ch. 7, since 'they include not only the labour and the means of production for the reproduction of each subsystem, but also the labour and the means of production necessary to its *expansion* at its particular rate of growth $(g + r_i)$' (Pasinetti, 1988, pp. 126–7).[5]

By additionally assuming that (a) the rate of growth of these 'newly defined sub-systems' may be different (due to a different rate of growth of technical progress and changes in the level and/or composition of demand), (b) there will be a particular natural rate of profits for each hyper sub-system (where a natural rate of profits is defined as a rate of profits which is equal to the rate of growth of demand for the corresponding consumption good), and (c) defining by $l^{(i)}$ the vector of the vertically hyper-integrated labour coefficient for commodity i, Pasinetti (1988, p. 129) obtains the specific set of natural prices $p^{(i)} = l^{(i)} \cdot w$, where w is the wage rate. This result is remarkable since, as Pasinetti himself points out, it is a complete generalization of the pure labour theory of value; in fact each physical quantity of any consumption good is shown to be unambiguously related to a physical quantity of labour. What is more important 'the two [i.e. physical quantities of consumption and of labour] have, between them, a physically self-replacing, and expanding, circular process' (Pasinetti, 1988, p. 130). Consequently the whole set (for the various industries) of natural prices of the means of production appear as performing in each hyper-subsystem 'a sort of ancillary role with respect to the corresponding price of the consumption good. Formal symmetry has been re-established perfectly between all aspects concerning physical quantities and all aspects concerning prices'. Once again Pasinetti's analysis reveals a strong intellectual sympathy with Adam Smith; first for the representation of the productive system as a set of vertically integrated sectors, and then for the associated concept (common to both Pasinetti and Smith) that labour may be considered as the ultimate source of wealth; the subtitle of Pasinetti's *opus magnum* (*A Theoretical Essay on the Dynamics of the Wealth of Nations*) published in 1981 is significant in this respect. Pasinetti is working at present on a further generalization of the above model which, besides introducing a full-fledged model of capital accumulation on the lines of his (1988) *Cambridge Journal of Economics* article, should also show how the analysis may be taken beyond the natural system to include relations referring to the institutional framework of the various economic systems and their relations with each other.

Linked with this issue we find another work of Pasinetti (1980-81) in which he shows that at a stage which precedes the introduction of capital accumulation and thus the emergence of any rate of profits, the theoretical scheme of a pure dynamic labour economy (see above) contains already a comprehensive theory of the rate of interest and hence a theory of income distribution which is not yet linked with the existence of profits. More specifically Pasinetti considers a simple economic system in which all goods are produced by labour alone (a pure labour economy) and proves that the theoretical scheme of such a simple economic system contains ('as had been known since Adam Smith') a pure labour theory of value. Additionally, such a simple theoretical model, by avoiding the complications relating to capital accumulation and hence the emergence of any rate of profits, logically contains both a 'pure theory of the rate of interest' and a 'pure labour theory of the distribution of income'. Pasinetti readily points out that these two theories 'necessarily follow from exactly the same postulate as that on which Adam Smith's pure labour theory of value is founded: namely, from the postulate that "labour commanded" be equal to "labour embodied"' (Pasinetti, 1980–81, p. 181). More specifically, in a pure labour economic system characterized by structural dynamics of technology and of prices, there exists a rate of interest on interpersonal loans – i.e. a rate of interest equal to the growth rate of the wage rate, which Pasinetti calls the 'natural' rate of interest – that keeps 'labour commanded' equal to 'labour embodied' through time. Hence there exists a level of interest on interpersonal loans (i.e. a 'natural' interest) which 'if paid annually by debtors to creditors, keeps income flowing to each single individual, through time as well as at any given point of time, in proportion to labour contributed to the production process' (Pasinetti, 1980–81, p. 181).

Finally, we may note that in a volume to be published soon by Cambridge University Press (*Structural Economic Dynamics – A Theory of the Economic Consequences of Human Learning*) Pasinetti offers a theoretical investigation of the development through time, as a consequence of human learning, of a 'pure labour economy', that is to say, an economy in which production activity is carried out by labour alone – 'labour unassisted by any intermediate commodity' (as the author himself defines it). The theory is simple; yet it is aimed at catching a number of basic features of our industrialized societies. Economists have known for a long time of two basic phenomena at the root of the long-term movements of our industrial societies: capital accumulation and technical progress. But, according to Pasinetti, the privileged position has always been given to capital accumulation. In Pasinetti's latest volume this approach is reversed and technical progress is assigned the central role. Within a multi-sector framework he first describes (against a background of 'natural relations') the structural dynamics of prices, of production and of employment (implied by differentiated rates of productivity growth and of expansion of demand); he then discusses a whole series of problems that arise at the institutional level. According to Pasinetti 'Individuals' and social learning, know-how and diffusion of information emerge as the fundamental factors accounting for the features and fate of industrial societies – the source of their trouble, and the source of their wealth. The pure labour theory of value allows Pasinetti to shift the theory of long-term economic development from a traditional framework based on capital accumulation to new foundations based on learning, technical progress, and diffusion of knowledge.

AT THE ROOTS OF POST-KEYNESIAN THOUGHT

At this point we may reassess the significance of Pasinetti's vast path-breaking research programme, which provides a comprehensive alternative to prevailing economic thought and which is based on alternative foundations of how modern economic systems work. We may indeed talk of 'new foundations' of economic analysis. More specifically, Pasinetti has provided, over a span of three decades, a new theoretical framework capable of synthesizing the works of Smith, Ricardo, Marx, Keynes, Sraffa and Kaldor, by appropriately modifying parts of their foundations and completing still other parts so as to arrive at a whole, coherent framework. The scheme itself is, however, so enormous that it is unrealistic to expect it to be completed by Pasinetti himself; for the final fruition to be reached the contribution of colleagues, pupils and other scholars will be necessary.

It has been often pointed out that Pasinetti has, among other original contributions, successfully achieved the difficult task of providing a bridge between two different levels of analysis, sharing the same scope but not the method, i.e. that of John Maynard Keynes and Nicholas Kaldor on one side and of Piero Sraffa on the other;[6] the former was characterized by a mainly macro-economic scheme built with the preoccupation of explaining the working of the actual economies and also founded on quite simple, though revolutionary, foundations. The latter was based instead on an aseptic and extremely refined system of inter-industry relations, not so much directly concerned with the most pressing problems of the modern economic systems, but more with the construction of a lucid and self-contained model within which the oldest questions of our science may find adequate answers. (Even at the personal level we find passion on one side, and coolness on the other.)

The tentative bringing together of the two complementary schemes may, among other things, be connected with the following three basic features of Pasinetti's theory:

(i) The use of vertically integrated sectors permits us to focus on the input requirements for producing any given vector of final commodities (and so overlooking the network of interindustry transactions that may obscure the picture when we choose the input/output approach). Additionally it shows that there is no need for Keynesian analysis to be carried out exclusively in full macroeconomic terms; actually the vertically integrated approach, besides the consideration of different socio-economic classes of savers (see Pasinetti's (1962) model of distribution) provides a first step towards the construction of the micro-foundations of the model, where the dynamics may be much more easily described and understood. Clearly the full disaggregation of the Post-Keynesian model will require necessary additional information and assumptions about consumers' allocation of income between consumption, savings and inter-generational bequest, consumers' choice of goods and producers' choice of techniques. (On this point see Pasinetti, 1962, 268–9).

(ii) The theory of economic dynamics outlined by Pasinetti is an original and important effort to study how an economic system may maintain full employment and full capacity utilization through time and in presence of uneven technical progress, growing population and changes in consumption patterns, according to Engel's law. Short-run difficulties – unemployment, spare productive capacity and rapid rise or fall of particular industries – have hence to be considered as necessary conditions for long-run growth in which there is a continuous modification of the productive structure. For what concerns the linkage between growth and the system of prices (i.e. distribution), Pasinetti (1965, pp. 692–3) maintains that:

> In the theoretical scheme I am proposing (a theoretical scheme for the long period), relative prices are determined by technology. Demand (i.e. consumers' preferences) then determine the relative quantities to be produced. Prices, therefore, emerge as a sort of indexes of *relative efforts* that society is obliged to put into each single unit of the various commodities.

(This is quite different from what happens in the 'pure' marginalist scheme with scarce goods, where endowments are accepted as given by nature and prices emerge as a sort of indexes of scarcity with respect to consumers' preferences.) Hence the relationship between the uneven dynamics of technology on the one hand, and the non-linear evolution of consumers' preferences on the other hand becomes crucial. There from the difficulty of maintaining, in the course of time, a productive structure compatible with the structure of demand: which explains both the short-run problems, such as the alternation of booms and recessions, and the fact that the movement of an industrial economy must follow a long-run development path along which structural change is necessary.

(iii) The focus is on the natural properties of an economic system, allowing the analysis to reach beyond certain institutional mechanisms, such as the tendency towards the equalization of the rate of profits in a competitive market economy. Indeed, as Pasinetti has repeatedly pointed out, the introduction of the concept of vertically integrated sectors implies a radical change in the meaning of the rate of profits with respect to a standard multisector model. However, the complex link between institutional set-up and economic dynamics requires further inquiry. (Pasinetti is writing an essay on this topic, to be included in a forthcoming volume.) More specifically, as Scazzieri (1983, p. 87) has pointed out, the interpretation of the overall historical dynamics of an economic system leaves space for a full-scale analysis of those patterns of expansion that are to be expected as a result of the interaction between the fundamental factors of change (common to all industrial systems) and the special behavioural principles characteristic of each particular institutional and technological set up. The role of the 'natural rate of profit' had already been stressed by Pasinetti as early as in 1962, when he brought to a close his masterly essay on income distribution and profit determination by saying that:

> In a full employment economic system in which all net revenues that accrue to the organizers of the process of production are saved, there exists one particular rate of profit, which we may indeed call the *natural rate of profit* – since it turns out to be equal to the rate of growth – which [. . .] if it is applied both in the process of pricing and in the payment of interest on loans, it causes the system, *whatever the individual decisions to save may be*, to produce a total amount of savings which is exactly equal to the amount of investment needed to cope with technical progress and population growth.'

Pasinetti's contribution remains fundamentally (and 'passionately') 'at the roots' of post-Keynesian economics, or rather at the roots of that work of Keynes which started his 'revolutionary' approach to economic thinking. Pasinetti (1990) has recently returned to this point by quoting a passage from Keynes's well-known letter to

George Bernard Shaw, dated 1 January 1935 (a year before the publication of *The General Theory of Employment, Interest and Money*):

> To understand my state of mind, however, you have to know that I believe myself to be writing a book on economic theory which will largely revolutionise – not, I suppose, at once but in the course of the next ten years – the way the world thinks about economic problems. (Keynes, 1973, vol. XIII, p. 492)

Post-Keynesian economics – according to Pasinetti – starts when the 'revolutionary' change – i.e. the switch from the old to new foundations – has already taken place. And Post-Keynesianism inherits all the problems that a revolutionary change implies. Provided that Keynes had perceived 'very clearly that the centre of the new foundations were those of an advanced *monetary theory of production*' Post-Keynesians were faced with two distinctive tasks:

> Firstly, there was the task of putting together a coherent 'production model', that the earlier literature had proposed but rather sketchily singled out. This was the task of so to speak completing the foundations. Secondly, there was the task of 'shifting', on to a new basis, what may be called a 'superstructure' of arguments that had been constructed during years of solid work, but had been laid on what now appeared a shaky, weak and deficient foundations. In so doing, it could not be immediately clear which elements of the 'superstructure' also had to go and which elements could be kept, and made use of. (Pasinetti, 1990, p. 7)

According to Pasinetti the contribution of Piero Sraffa has clearly been concerned with the first task and that of Kaldor mainly, though not exclusively, with the second one, while Richard Kahn, Joan Robinson and Richard Goodwin have been concerned with both. To the latter list we must undoubtedly add the name of Luigi Pasinetti himself.

We would like to bring to a close this introduction to the volume in honour of Luigi Pasinetti by stressing the positive attitude that he has always demonstrated towards the 'reconstruction task' that he set himself at the early stages of his distinguished scientific career. It is also interesting to note that the message of hope and encouragement which he gave to his generation on the occasion of an inaugural lecture delivered at the Catholic University of Milan in 1964 (see Pasinetti, 1964/5) has now become a message for the younger generation:

> I should like to draw the attention of the young generation of scholars to the enormity of the work that has to be undertaken. Most of all I should like to draw attention to the positive attitude that a reconstruction work requires. [. . .] An enormous work is still waiting to be performed. Post-Keynesian economics is a grand, exciting research project, most of which is still to be carried out. (Pasinetti, 1990, p. 8)

THE ORGANIZATION OF THE VOLUME AND THE CONTRIBUTIONS

The contributions to this volume have been organized to comprise the six areas of research which have been covered by most of Pasinetti's work and which have been (except for the last one) considered in detail above. The area on *Ricardo and Classical Political Economy* contains four contributions: by Peter Groenewegen ('Marshall on Ricardo'), Izumi Hishiyama ('Physiocratic Dichotomy in Price Determination and its Ricardian Resolution'), Heinz D. Kurz and Neri Salvadori ('The "Standard commodity" and Ricardo's Search for an "Invariable Measure of Value"') and Andrea Maneschi ('Ricardian Comparative Advantage and the Perils of the Stationary State'). In his paper Peter Groenewegen confronts the Pasinetti-Sraffa interpretation of Ricardo with the perspective on Ricardo's economics by Alfred Marshall. As the author points out, such an evaluation is particularly important for the following two reasons. First, he focuses on the conflict inherent in the different approaches of classical as against marginalist economics (on this point see also Pasinetti, 1982 and 1986), differences that the contributions of Pasinetti have greatly elucidated. Secondly Marshall came to be seen as the marginalist economist who attempted 'a reconciliation with the classical economists because he was never really able to turn his attention away from production' (Pasinetti, 1981) and classical supply considerations.

After a review of what Marshall said about Ricardo in his writings, both in general and with respect to particular parts of his doctrines, Groenewegen assesses the operational significance of the classical-Ricardo heritage for Marshall's economics and attempts to explain

Marshall's emphasis on the continuity between his economics and that of Ricardo, and his profound admiration for the work of that economist. The analysis carried out by Groenewegen comes to reinforce, in his words, 'Pasinetti's perspective on Marshall and Ricardo in his theoretical essay on the dynamics of the wealth of nations'.

In his paper 'Physiocratic Dichotomy in Price Determination and its Ricardian Resolution' Izumi Hishiyama reconsiders the physiocratic dichotomy in the determination of price as between agriculture and industry (which has been the topic of his early works). Such a dichotomy is reassessed through its entire life-cycle 'that is to say, its birth in Quesnay's mind, its succession via Turgot and Smith, and its death as a result of Ricardo's fatal blow'. Hishiyama concludes that Ricardo's rejection of the physiocratic notion on prices inherited by Smith leads to an evaluation of agriculture as a 'trade' nondifferentiated from manufacturing; and with Ricardo it becomes evident that both agriculture and manufacture are 'governed by the same rule', that is, the principles of costs of production in the determination of prices. According to the author 'this clearly implies in Classical Political Economy the final resolution of the dichotomy in price-determination or, in short, the end of physiocracy'.

The next chapter is by Heinz D. Kurz and Neri Salvadori on 'The Standard commodity and Ricardo's Search for an "Invariable Measure of Value"'. Such a search, for the two authors, is initially concerned with a standard which would measure the value of commodities at different times and places, i.e. intertemporal and interspatial comparisons. This is a concern which is closely related to the time-honoured problem of distinguishing between 'value' and 'riches' (cf. *Works* I, ch. XX), which had already worried authors such as Petty and Smith. In this regard Ricardo's contribution is largely in line with the discussion of his time. While no single commodity may be considered as a perfect and thus permanent measure, it is Ricardo's contention that the prices of gold and silver are least subject to fluctuations and hence, for comparisons of periods which are not too distant from one another, they may reasonably be used as measures of value.

The problem of an invariable measure of value is dealt with in detail in Ricardo's *Principles*. In editions 1 and 2 *Ricardo* maintains that in order to be invariable in value a commodity should require 'at all times, and under all circumstances, precisely the same quantity of labour to obtain it' (*Works* I, p. 27n.). In edition 3, however, Ricardo concedes that the same difficulties encountered in determining relative prices also carried over to his attempt to define the essential properties of a correct standard. Whereas in his original approach to the problem of the standard of value Ricardo was exclusively concerned with intertemporal and interspatial comparisons, that is, measurement with respect to different technical environments, he is now in addition concerned with the different problem of measurement with respect to the same technical environment, and a changing distribution of income.

The second part of Kurz and Salvadori's paper concerns Sraffa's interpretation of Ricardo: according to them Sraffa emphasizes those aspects of Ricardo's thoughts which point in the direction of the Standard commodity and its role as an analytical device to simplify the investigation of the mathematical properties of the system of production prices. In his Introduction Sraffa focused his attention on those aspects of Ricardo's search for an invariable measure of value which concerned the theory of value and distribution with a given technological environment, whereas the intertemporal and interspatial aspect of Ricardo's problem were neglected. The last part of the paper turns to a detailed analysis of Sraffa's *Production of Commodities . . .* and the role of the Standard commodity in it. It is stressed that the main aim of Sraffa's Ch. III is to provide a 'preliminary survey' of price movements consequent upon changes in distribution on the assumption that the methods of production remain unchanged. The complete analysis of these movements is presented in Ch. VI. The comparison of the 'preliminary survey' with the complete analysis reveals that in order to obtain the results of Ch. VI Sraffa needed a number of propositions to hold. These propositions are proved by using the Standard commodity which is shown in this way to be, first of all, a tool of analysis. The paper stresses that Sraffa saw only a single analytical purpose for the Standard commodity, i.e. to simplify the analysis of the effects of changes in the division of the product between profits and wages on prices.

The final chapter of Part II is by Andrea Maneschi on the 'Ricardian Comparative Advantage and the Perils of the Stationary State'. This paper explores the open-economy implications of the dynamic Ricardian model; in fact while static gains have been considered by all textbooks on international economics, 'the dynamic gains have instead been neglected in most accounts of the open Ricardian system'. Ricardo expected such gains to accrue to a country like England if it were to abolish the Corn Laws and thus permit the free importation of a wage good like corn when this can be produced more cheaply abroad. The open version of the Ricardian system proposed by Maneschi is a modified version of the Pasinetti-Hicks-Casarosa-Hollander model (on this point see Pasinetti, 1982). After a brief review of the mathematical structure of the closed and open Ricardian system and the nature of the gains from trade enjoyed by the two open Ricardian economies, Maneschi analyses the types of adjustment which two such economies must undergo as they approach the stationary state and considers in detail the impact of trade on the equilibrium they attain (when the latter is reached). The results obtained by Maneschi are very interesting and their welfare implications are more complex than had previously been imagined. To the traditional static gains from trade we must add the more important dynamic gains as its trajectory towards the stationary state is either accelerated or slowed down. The final conclusion of Maneschi's analysis is worth quoting: 'The Heckscher-Ohlin model is in a sense stood on its head: instead of factor endowments determining trade, trade determines long-run factor endowments. This adds a third dimension to the gains or losses from trade experienced by open Ricardian economies: a long-run endowment-cum-diversification gain or loss.'

The third part of the volume is on *Capital Theory* and contains a contribution by Avi J. Cohen with the title 'Samuelson and the 93% Scarcity Theory of Value'. Cohen's paper starts from Stigler's essay written in 1958 ('Ricardo and the 93% Labour Theory of Value') with the aim of demonstrating that Ricardo's labour theory of value cannot be defended as an analytical proposition, but can be defended as an empirical proposition. In Cohen's paper Stigler's criteria for analytical and empirical theories are used to evaluate the Cambridge Capital Theory controversies and in particular Samuelson's contribution to this debate. Cohen's evaluation demonstrates that the neoclassical (or marginalist) scarcity theory of value (i.e. the conception of price as an index of resource scarcity relative to consumption demand) 'cannot be defended analytically but can be defended empirically'. In fact, the analytical deficiencies in both theories of value stem from capital-related problems. According to Cohen, within the neoclassical theory these problems are not eliminated at the general equilibrium level. Instead, the problems are sidestepped by abandoning the scarcity theory of value as an analytical proposition. By discussing the empirical implications of the issue Cohen concludes that 'only a hybrid analytical-empirical value theory has a future role in economic analysis'.

Part III is on *Post-Keynesian Income Distribution and Growth Theory*. It includes contributions by Amit Bhaduri ('The Method of the Pure Ratio in Economic Analysis'), and Amitava K. Dutt and Edward J. Amadeo ('A Post-Keynesian Theory of Growth, Interest and Money'). Bhaduri's paper starts from the method of the 'pure ratio' which was first formulated by Ricardo and later taken up by Sraffa; for instance, for the latter the rate of profit in agriculture may be defined as a pure ratio independent of relative prices, if corn is both the output and also the only input in the form of capital advanced. With corn as the sole basic product required both for its own production and for the production of all other commodities, Ricardo's conclusion is that 'it is the profits of the farmer that regulate the profits of all other trade'. As Bhaduri points out 'although devised in the context of the classical theory of value and distribution to show the emergence of profits as surplus, this method of the "pure ratio" can be generalized to yield powerful results in other areas of economic theory'. And in relation with this Bhaduri quotes Pasinetti's (1962) theory of income distribution, according to which only the propensity to save of the capitalist class may influence the distribution of income between capital and labour, irrespective of the behaviour of the other socio-economic classes (in particular the workers). Bhaduri points out that 'In essence, this apparently intriguing result can be seen to follow from an application of the method of the pure ratio' since the capitalists come to play a leading role in the process of income distribution and capital accumulation. This result applies also in the case in which the rate of profits is greater than the rate of interest (i) earned by the non-capitalists on their life-cycle savings. According to Bhaduri a common feature of the Ricardian-Sraffian-Kaldorian-Pasinettian models of distribution and accumulation is that 'whenever [. . .] an independently defined pure ratio describes the relevant property of a (basic) sector, it regulates the equilibrium properties of all other sectors as well'.

In their paper 'A Post-Keynesian Theory of Growth, Interest and Money', Amitava K. Dutt and Edward J. Amadeo examine the central features of the Post-Keynesian approach to growth, distribution, interest and money by discussing the implications of class distinctions and conflict, the pervasive influence of uncertainty, and the role of money and interest in the economy. Drawing on these issues Dutt and Amadeo develop a simple model along the lines of Pasinetti's two-class model and examine both the determination of the rates of accumulation and inflation and the distribution of income and wealth in capitalist economies. In particular the model highlights an aspect of capitalist economies which has not adequately captured the attention of Post-Keynesian theory, i.e. long-period effects of changes in the monetary policy, or more specifically the rate of interest. Dutt and Amadeo conclude that 'The central implication of our model is that changes in the interest rate affect the level of investment and the distribution of income and wealth between profit-receivers and wage-earners, and thus the level of consumption'.

Part IV is on *Structural Dynamics and Vertical Integration* and includes contributions by Michael A. Landesmann and Roberto Scazzieri ('Commodity Flows and Productive Subsystems: an Essay in the Analysis of Structural Change') and Alberto Quadrio-Curzio ('On Economic Science, its Tools and Economic Reality'). Landesmann and Scazzieri consider the alternative specifications of productive subsystems as the expression of distinct methods of economic dynamics. They first examine the utilization of non-overlapping subsystems as a tool for the analysis of non-proportional economic dynamics. Here certain features of Pasinetti's (1973, 1988) analytical contribution are considered; such as the reclassification of inter-industry commodity flows in terms of distinct vectors of intermediate products, or the identification of a one-way relationship between the quantity of labour directly and indirectly required to produce any given vector of final consumption goods and the utilization of such analytical tools for the investigation of paths of non-proportional dynamics. The authors also examine an alternative classification of commodity flows, which was proposed by Richard Goodwin, and which consists in the identification of hypothetical consumption baskets ('eigengoods') reflecting the consumption pattern associated with a given distribution of income (net output) between wages and profits. Such an analytical formulation is associated with separate cycles for each subsystem producing a particular 'eigengood' and it is possible to investigate the transmission mechanisms of these local dynamics to the overall economic system. Finally, Landesmann and Scazzieri outline a general framework for the consideration of the ways in which alternative specifications of productive sub-systems may lead to the analysis of different features of transitional paths from one position to another. In this connection three distinct models are discussed: the temporal integrated model originally presented in Hicks's *Capital and Time* (1973), the circular framework with horizontal inter-dependencies and structural bottlenecks (Baldone-Belloc) and the circular approach built upon non-overlapping sub-systems linked with one another by means of net product accumulation (Quadrio-Curzio). This contribution ends with the formulation of a general criterion by which distinct specifications of sub-systems may be related to each specific set of dynamic issues.

In his paper 'On Economic Science, Its Tools and Economic Reality', Alberto Quadrio-Curzio reconsiders the various stages through which economics has developed, via the phases of exchange, of production, and finally of the structural theories of economic dynamics. The argument carried out by the author focuses on the 'scope and method' of the various approaches and provides a precise evaluation of the contributions offered by a number of economists, ending with structural change approach put forward by Pasinetti in 1981. The description and evaluation of the theories of exchange and production, and of the way in which they have come to cover most fields of economics, is here reconsidered, by referring to a number of contributions of Quadrio-Curzio (jointly with R. Scazzieri) which appeared between 1978 and 1983. Of particular interest is the author's assessment of Pasinetti's approach 'which is fundamental for the methodologies of structural economic dynamics, because of the masterful application of formalized theory and stylized-historical theory'. Emphasis is also laid upon two characteristic features of Pasinetti's methodology, that is, his attention to the 'natural' vis-à-vis institutional character of any given economic system; and to the type of causal relationship most suitable for analyzing structural dynamics. In this connection Quadrio-Curzio considers the specific role of recursive causal processes, which allow us to cut through a complex system by identifying critical explanatory variables and simultaneous causality in which all variables depend on each other and are determined at the same time. Quadrio-Curzio ends his contribution with an analysis of the 'global method of economics': here the role of 'positive' and 'normative' economics is brought to the fore.

Part VI offers three contributions in the field of *Development Economics and Models of Unstable Growth*; the first is by the late Sukhamoy Chakravarty ('Development Economics in Perspective), the second by Richard Goodwin ('The Economy as a Chaotic Growth Oscillator') and the last one by Paolo Sylos-Labini ('Long-Run Changes in the Wage and Price Mechanisms and the Process of Growth').

In his paper Sukhamoy Chakravarty reconsidered a number of important issues linked with development economics, and recalled that 'development economics, in its initial formulation, was strongly interventionist, an important qualification in which it differed from major development theories such as Marx's and Schumpeter's which, despite their differences, were mostly occupied with processes of long-term change'. For this reason Chakravarty maintained that the work of Keynes was of fundamental significance in this context 'not because Keynes had something to say of direct significance to the development problem', but basically due to his successful redefinition of the agenda of the State, which was first expounded succinctly in his (1926) article 'The end of Laissez-Faire'. Secondly, according to Chakravarty, there has been a shift of interest from the process of capital accumulation to the issues of technology and knowledge, which may be studied in complete disjunction from their embodiment in capital goods. Finally, economists have now become much more aware of the 'fallacy of misplaced concreteness' in connection with issues relating to capital formation, 'a point which was perceptively discussed a long time ago by Veblen, who distinguished between different forms in which society may preserve unlimited capital'.

Richard Goodwin, in his paper 'The economy as a chaotic oscillator' considers the medium and long-term fluctuations of an unstable modern economic system, by first rejecting Frisch's statement according to which the economy must asymptotically be stable but kept in motion by exogenous shocks, since in his view 'the economy is highly unstable but confined with a limit by such things as full capacity and full employment'. With this aim in mind Goodwin then considers the theory of chaos, a term which he means to cover a wide range of phenomena from mild irregularity to unpredictable or totally formless behaviour. According to the author:

> The fundamentally new concept of chaos is important because it shows that a completely endogenous, deterministic system can produce any degree of irregularity and unpredictability. It is not that one can deny that there are random exogenous shocks to the economy; rather it is that there are two, rather than only one, sources of the pervasive irregularity of economic time series.

At this point Goodwin introduces the concept of 'chaotic attractor' first proposed by Rössler:

> instead of one or more simple closed curves, one finds an outer boundary and an inner boundary in the state space, which define a limit region within which the motion can fluctuate in a seemingly

more or less random fashion, although the motion is in fact completely deterministic. The equilibrium band may be large or small, but given the system structure, all motions, whether initially outside or inside, will in the limit be contained within the band. (Goodwin, pp. 301–2)

In the second part of his paper Goodwin develops a model for analyzing the eight to twelve years cycle and the longer one of about forty to sixty years, by assuming, among other things, a constant labour force and a wage-rate which depends on the ratio (v) of employment to the labour force and on a level (u) which leaves unit labour costs constant. (Both $\dot{v}$ and $\dot{u}$ vary above and below zero by small quantities.) To make the economy perform in a circumscribed region of phase space he introduces a third variable z, which will control the pair of u and v, so as to counteract their tendency to continuing expansion. (To conform to the Rössler specification z must have a small constant growth rate plus one which is proportional to the difference between v and c; and the constant c may be associated with an approach to full employment.) The results obtained by Goodwin are striking. In fact after a careful choice of the parameters and of the initial conditions, the author shows that 'this single system with only one nonlinearity can perform the remarkable feat of producing over a fifty-year period a Kondratieff in the form of four to five single (shorter) cycles, each different from the other'. Additionally the economy exhibits a succession of increasing vigorous expansions reaching a crescendo shortly after the twenty-fifth year and thereafter collapsing into relatively flat cycles. As the author points out 'only a chaotic attractor model could produce such a result, undisturbed by exogenous events'.

In his paper on 'Long-run changes in the wage and price mechanisms and the process of growth' Paolo Sylos-Labini critically examines the changes undergone by the wage and price mechanisms in the last two centuries; mechanisms which are relevant in determining the growth process of our industrial nations. The main conclusion drawn by Sylos-Labini is that 'it is quite unbelievable that a great number of economists still assume, as the most natural thing to do, full flexibility of wages and prices both in the short and in the long-run'. As a matter of fact while during the last century competition was the rule not only in the markets of agricultural and mineral products, but also in those of industrial products, in our century most prices are flexible upwards *but not* in the downward direction both in the short and long run (only rarely and in any case to a limited extent they do show downward flexibility in the short run). Sylos-Labini goes beyond these empirical results and considers the role of institutional changes and of monetary and fiscal policies in this process. He concludes that the change in wage and price mechanisms is just one aspect of a process of transformation that has affected the complex economic system of this century.

The transformations have been so radical as to make legitimate the question of whether there is much in common between the laissez-faire capitalism of the last century and the present-day system. The truth is that 'the end of laissez-faire' was prepared long before Keynes published the pamphlet with that title (Keynes, 1926).

The last part of the volume is on *Institutions and Economic Structure: Human Actions and the Pure Labour Theory of Value*. It includes contributions by Heinrich Bortis ('Reflections on the Significance of the Labour Theory of Value') and Siro Lombardini ('Rationality and Economic Behaviour'). In his paper Bortis stresses that Luigi Pasinetti's 'natural system' is, like Sraffa's *Production of Commodities by Means of Commodities*, an unfamiliar piece of 'highly' classical economic theory in a theoretical world dominated by the marginalist or neoclassical approach: hence the necessity to demonstrate the significance of Pasinetti's system with respect to its content and method and to put it into a wider context by comparing it with the Walrasian general equilibrium model. Three selected features of the natural system provide the starting-point for Bortis's discussion: the labour theory of value, the priority of production over exchange and the fact that the system is a 'natural' one. The labour theory of value which is at the heart of the natural system leads to sketching the theoretical content of Pasinetti's framework, particularly his theories of distribution and of employment. The fact that the starting point is production, not exchange, leads to a particularly classical way of tackling these great economic problems. Finally, the method put to use by Pasinetti may be revealed best by looking at the implications of the term 'natural'. The conclusion of these reflections is that, in elaborating the natural system, Luigi Pasinetti has laid the foundations for the bringing together of Ricardo and Keynes in a great synthesis of Post-Keynesian political economy, constituting thereby a superior alternative to the dominating neoclassical economics.

The final paper is by Siro Lombardini on 'Rationality and Economic Behaviour'; the author provides a critical assessment of the rationality assumption that is usually made about individuals' behaviour in micro-economics. In particular, it is shown why rationality criteria for the economic system as a whole cannot be reduced to individual rational criteria as they have been defined in the context of utilitarianism. From this specific point of view, the author moves alongside Pasinetti's main argument concerning the dichotomy between macro- and micro-foundations of economics; as a matter of fact for Pasinetti, and for all Post-Keynesians in general, macro-economic phenomena may not exclusively be explained in terms of micro-behaviour. Such a point of view is shared by Lombardini, who adds that: 'In other fields as well scientists are starting to realize that local laws do not allow us to understand the working of the global system. When the global system is studied as a whole, the need arises to study afresh the problem of how to explain the behaviour of the elements of the system itself.'

Lombardini first considers the issue of rationality and equilibrium, and introduces, at a later stage, a weaker definition of rationality. He then considers the complex process of decisions; and with reference to the issue of 'aggregation and rationality' he points out that rarely do economists apply their theories to forecast the behaviour of a single individual; instead they want to explain (and possibly predict) the behaviour of a sufficiently large set of individuals who are supposed to face similar decisions. Among other things Lombardini points out three main difficulties concerning aggregation: the first with reference to the fact that 'if we assume that the individual's tastes reflect his autonomy and apathy, namely that there is no envy nor philanthropy, the choice of any individual is independent from the choice made by other individuals'. Second, the production of public goods does not respond to the laws that are normally valid in the case of private goods (the case of environment is typical). For this reason, as the author points out, these two kinds of aggregation 'can no longer be considered separate from each other; there are inter-relations between them that cannot be ignored by economists'. Third, individuals (both consumers and entrepreneurs) by their choice may alter the conditions under which other individuals make their own. On the whole Lombardini's arguments are relevant for that line of the Post-Keynesian research programme which aims at providing the micro-foundations of the macro-model.

EPILOGUE

Taken in their unity the essays of this volume, which come from the four corners of the globe and which cover a number of specific areas of inquiry, offer an overview of the issues which have been raised by the contributions of Pasinetti during his lifelong theoretical investigation into the long-term evolution of modern economic systems. Additionally these contributions provide an assessment of the strength of the Post-Keynesian research programme, of which Luigi Pasinetti's own contribution represents a central foundation-stone.

The bibliography of Pasinetti's writings completes this volume. This includes all his books, articles in learned journals, and comments and discussions at conferences to date. This long list demonstrates the way in which an ambitious research programme requires a meticulous step-by-step building up of scientific knowledge using increasingly powerful tools of analysis in order to reach the final goal. It may also be noted that the more crucial each of such steps turns out to be, the more likely will it be to cause a 'controversy' in the scientific world; controversies at which Luigi Pasinetti, and the whole Cambridge School with him, have been regularly at the centre. These features, with the relatively young age of the scholar to whom this volume is dedicated, make us hope for the attainment of more ambitious frontiers of economic knowledge.

NOTES

1. Over the years Pasinetti has held a number of visiting appointments throughout the world: he was Wesley Clair Mitchell visiting research professor of economics, Columbia University, New York, Fall 1971 and Fall 1975; visiting research professor, Indian Statistical Institute, Calcutta and New Delhi, Spring 1979; visiting professor of economics, Carleton University, Ottawa, and Université d'Ottawa, Fall 1981; visiting professor of economics, Kyoto University, Fall 1984; visiting professor of economics, University of California, Los Angeles, Fall 1985; and visiting fellow, Gonville and Caius College, Cambridge, Lent and Easter Term 1989. Among his professional honours we may mention that Pasinetti has been editorial advisor to the *Review of Economic Studies* (1962–4) and patron or editor of the *Cambridge Journal of Economics* (1977–), *Journal of Post-Keynesian Economics* (1978–), *Kyklos* (1981–), *Political Economy: Studies in the Surplus Approach* (1986–), and *Structural Change and*

Economic Dynamics (1989–); member of the Executive Committee of the International Economic Association (1980–9), President of the Società Italiana degli Economisti (1986–9), Fellow of the Econometric Society (1978–), and Vice-President of the Confederation of European Economic Associations. Among his academic distinctions are the St Vincent Prize for Economics (1979); the Gold Medal, First Class Merits, in the field of 'Education, Culture and Arts' by Decree of the Italian President of the Republic (1982); a *doctorate honoris causa* of the Swiss University of Fribourg (1986); the membership of the prestigeous Accademia Nazionale dei Lincei of Rome (1986–) and 'La Madonnina' International Prize, Economic Section, Milan, 1987. (Additional biblio-biographical data on Pasinetti may be found in M. Blaug's *Great Economists since Keynes – An Introduction to the Lives and Works of One Hundred Modern Economists* (Brighton: Wheatsheaf, 1983 and 1986); *Who's Who in Western Europe*; *Who's Who in the World*; *International Who's Who*; *Who's Who in Economics*; *5,000 Personalities of the World*; *Men of Achievement*; *Dictionary of International Biography*; *Who's Who in Italy*; and P. Arestis and M. C. Sawyer (eds.) *Biographical Dictionary of Dissenting Economists*, Cheltenham: Edward Elgar, 1992.)
2. Following Hamouda and Harcourt (1988) we may distinguish between three different strands of Post-Keynesianism: (i) Keynesian fundamentalists (represented by Paul Davidson, Hyman Minsky and Sidney Weintraub); (ii) Robinsonians (represented by Joan Robinson, Richard Kahn and Michal Kalecki); (iii) neo-Ricardians (represented by Krishna Bharadwaj, John Eatwell, Pierangelo Garegnani and Murray Milgate). To these we may add a fourth one grouping together Nicholas Kaldor, Alfred Eichner, Robin Marris and Adrian Wood. Pasinetti himself has been explicitly withdrawn from this list.
3. If one of us (GCH) may be permitted to be self-indulgent, this is how it happened. I was the first person in Cambridge to read Levhari's article in the *Quarterly Journal of Economics*. I told Sraffa about it, i.e., that some chap in the *QJE* said his result was wrong for the economy. Piero Sraffa: 'He's wrong – and you show it.' Me: 'I can't do matrix algebra.' PS: 'Neither can I' so he asked Pasinetti.
4. All references concerning the various research lines are provided in Baranzini (1991, Ch. 2).
5. Note that g is the proportional rate of growth of the labour force (whether by natural growth or by immigration) and r_i (which may be positive or negative) is the per capita rate of growth of consumption demand for each commodity i.
6. This point was recently raised by Professor Michele Salvati during a meeting at the Catholic University of Milan.

REFERENCES

Arestis, P., and Sawyer, M. C. (eds) (1992) *Biographical Dictionary of Dissenting Economists* (Cheltenham: Edward Elgar).
Balestra, P., and Baranzini, M. (1971) 'Some Optimal Aspects in a Two Class Growth Model With a Differentiated Interest Rate', *Kyklos*, pp. 240–56.
Baranzini, M. (1975) 'The Pasinetti and Anti-Pasinetti Theorems: A Reconciliation', *Oxford Economic Papers*, pp. 470–3.
Baranzini, M. (1976) 'On the Distribution of Income in Two-Class Growth Models', DPhil. thesis, University of Oxford, The Queen's College.
Baranzini, M. (1987) 'Distribution Theories: Keynesian', *New Palgrave Dictionary*, vol. I (London: Macmillan) pp. 876–8.
Baranzini, M. (1991) *A Theory of Wealth Distribution and Accumulation* (Oxford: Oxford University Press).
Baranzini, M. (1992) 'Luigi Lodovico Pasinetti' in P. Arestis and M. C. Sawyer (eds) op. cit., pp. 417–25.
Baranzini, M., and Scazzieri, R. (1986) 'Knowledge in Economics: A Framework', in M. Baranzini and R. Scazzieri (eds) *Foundations of Economics. Structures of Inquiry and Economic Theory* (Oxford and New York: Basil Blackwell) pp. 1–87.
Baranzini, M., and Scazzieri, R. (1990) 'Economic Structure: Analytical Perspectives', in M. Baranzini and R. Scazzieri (eds) *The Economic Theory of Structure and Change* (Cambridge: Cambridge University Press) pp. 227–333.
Blaug, M. (1985) *Great Economists since Keynes. An Introduction to the Lives and Works of one Hundred Modern Economists* (Brighton: Wheatsheaf).
Bliss, C. J. (1975) *Capital Theory and the Distribution of Income* (Amsterdam/Oxford: North Holland).
Bliss, C. J. (1986) 'Progress and Anti-Progress in Economic Science', in M. Baranzini and R. Scazzieri (eds) *Foundations of Economics* (Oxford and New York: Basil Blackwell) pp. 363–76.
Burmeister, E., and Turnovsky, S. J. (1972) 'Capital Deepening Response in A Model with Many Capital Goods', *American Economic Review*, pp. 842–53.
Craven, J. (1977) 'On the Marginal Product of Capital', *Oxford Economic Papers*, pp. 472–8.
Denicolò, V., and Matteuzzi, M. (1990) 'Public Debt and the Pasinetti Paradox', *Cambridge Journal of Economics*, 14, pp. 339–44.
Dixit, A. (1977) 'The Accumulation of Capital Theory', *Oxford Economic Papers*, pp. 1–29.
Domenghino, C.-M. (1982) *Die Weiterentwicklung der postkeynesianischen Verteilungstheorie* (Europäische Hochschulschriften) (Berne: Peter Lang).
Fleck, F. H., and Domenghino, C.-M. (1987) 'Cambridge (U.K.) versus Cambridge (Mass.): A Keynesian Solution of "Pasinetti's Paradox"', *Journal of Post Keynesian Economics*, pp. 22–36.
Dougherty, C. R. S. (1972) 'On the Rate of Return and the Rate of Profit', *Economic Journal*, pp. 1324–50.

Dougherty, C. R. S. (1980) *Interest and Profit* (London: Methuen).
Hamouda, O. F., and Harcourt, G. C. (1988) 'Post-Keynesianism: From Criticism to Coherence?', *Bulletin of Economic Research*, pp. 1–33.
Harcourt, G. C. (1969) 'Some Cambridge Controversies in the Theory of Capital', *Journal of Economic Literature*, pp. 369–405.
Harcourt, G. C. (1972) *Some Cambridge Controversies in the Theory of Capital* (Cambridge: Cambridge University Press).
Harcourt, G. C. (1976) 'The Cambridge Controversies: Old Ways and New Horizons – or Dead End?', *Oxford Economic Papers*, pp. 25–65. Reprinted in Harcourt (1982), pp. 239–78.
Harcourt, G. C. (1982a) 'Post Keynesianism: Quite Wrong and/or Nothing New?', *Thames Papers in Political Economy*; reprinted in P. Arestis and T. Skouras (eds) (1985) *Post Keynesian Economic Theory* (Brighton: Wheatsheaf; Armonk, New York: M. E. Sharpe) pp. 125–45.
Harcourt, G. C. (1982b) *The Social Science Imperialists*, ed. by Prue Kerr (London: Routledge and Kegan Paul).
Harcourt, G. C., and Kenyon, P. (1976) 'Pricing and the Investment Decision' *Kyklos*, 29, pp. 449–77, reprinted in Harcourt (1982), pp. 104–26.
Kaldor, N. (1956) 'Alternative Theories of Distribution', *Review of Economic Studies*, pp. 83–100.
Kaldor, N. (1966) 'Marginal Productivity and the Macro-Economic Theories of Distribution', *Review of Economic Studies*, pp. 309–19.
Keynes, J. M. (1936) *The General Theory of Employment, Interest and Money*, (London: Macmillan).
Keynes, J. M. (1973–) *The Collected Writings of John Maynard Keynes*, ed. by Austin Robinson and D. E. Moggridge (London: Macmillan; Cambridge: Cambridge University Press).
Laing, N. F. (1969) 'Two Notes on Pasinetti's Theorem', *Economic Record*, pp. 373–85.
Levhari, D. (1965) 'A Nonsubstitution Theorem and Switching of Techniques', *Quarterly Journal of Economics*, pp. 98–105.
Levhari, D., and Samuelson, P. A. (1966) 'The Nonswitching Theorem is False', *Quarterly Journal of Economics*, pp. 518–19.
Marglin, S. A. (1984) *Growth, Distribution and Prices* (Cambridge, Mass.: Harvard University Press).
Marris, R. L. (1964) *The Economic Theory of Managerial Capitalism* (London: Macmillan).
Meade, J. E. (1963) 'The Rate of Profits in a Growing Economy', *The Economic Journal*, pp. 665–74.
Meade, J. E. (1966) 'The Outcome of the Pasinetti Process: A Note', *The Economic Journal*, pp. 161–5.
Moore, B. J. (1974) 'The Pasinetti Paradox Revisited', *Review of Economic Studies*, pp. 297–9.
Morishima, M. (1977) 'Pasinetti's Growth and Income Distribution Revisited', *Journal of Economic Literature*, pp. 56–61.
Morishima, M. (1989) *Ricardo's Economics* (Cambridge: Cambridge University Press).
Pasinetti, L. L. (1960) 'A Mathematical Formulation of the Ricardian System', *Review of Economic Studies*, pp. 78–98.

Pasinetti, L. L. (1962) 'Rate of Profit and Income Distribution in Relation to the Rate of Economic Growth', *Review of Economic Studies*, pp. 267–79.
Pasinetti, L. L. (1964/5) 'Causalità e interdipendenza nell'analisi economica', *Annuario dell'Università Cattolica*, Milan, pp. 233–50.
Pasinetti, L. L. (1965) 'A New Theoretical Approach to the Problems of Economic Growth', no. 28, Pontificiae Academiae Scientiarum Scripta Varia, Vatican City; reprinted in *Econometric Approach to Development Planning* (1965) (Amsterdam: North Holland) pp. 571–69.
Pasinetti, L. L. (1966) 'Changes in the Rate of Profit and Switches of Techniques', *Quarterly Journal of Economics*, pp. 503–17.
Pasinetti, L. L. (1969) 'Switches of Techniques and the "Rate of Return" in Capital Theory', *Economic Journal*, pp. 508–31.
Pasinetti, L. L. (1970) 'Again on Capital Theory and Solow's "Rate of Return"', *Economic Journal*, pp. 428–31.
Pasinetti, L. L. (1972) 'Reply to Mr. Dougherty', *Economic Journal*, pp. 1351–2.
Pasinetti, L. L. (1973) 'The Notion of Vertical Integration in Economic Analysis', *Metroeconomica*, pp. 1–29; reprinted in L. L. Pasinetti (ed.) *Essays on the Theory of Joint Production* (1980) (London: Macmillan; New York: Columbia University Press).
Pasinetti, L. L. (1974) *Growth and Income Distribution. Essays in Economic Theory* (Cambridge: Cambridge University Press).
Pasinetti, L. L. (1980/1) 'The Rate of Interest and the Distribution of Income in a Pure Labour Economy', *Journal of Post Keynesian Economics*, pp. 170–82.
Pasinetti, L. L. (1981) *Structural Change and Economic Growth. A Theoretical Essay on the Dynamics of the Wealth of Nations*, (Cambridge: Cambridge University Press).
Pasinetti, L. L. (1982) 'A Comment on the "New View" of the Ricardian Theory', in M. Baranzini (ed.) *Advances in Economic Theory*, (Oxford: Basil Blackwell; New York: St. Martin's Press) pp. 240–2.
Pasinetti, L. L. (1986a) 'Theory of Value – A Source of Alternative Paradigms in Economic Analysis', in M. Baranzini and R. Scazzieri (eds) *Foundations of Economics. Structures of Inquiry and Economic Theory* (Oxford and New York: Basil Blackwell) pp. 409–31.
Pasinetti, L. L. (1986b) 'Sraffa's Circular Process and the Concept of Vertical Integration', *Political Economy. Studies in the Surplus Approach*, pp. 3–16.
Pasinetti, L. L. (1988) 'Growing Sub-Systems, Vertically Hyper-Integrated Sectors and the Labour Theory of Value', *Cambridge Journal of Economics*, pp. 125–34.
Pasinetti, L. L. (1989) 'Ricardian Debt/Taxation Equivalence in the Kaldor Theory of Profits and Income Distribution', *Cambridge Journal of Economics*, pp. 25–36.
Pasinetti, L. L. (1990) 'At the Roots of Post-Keynesian Thought: Keynes' Break with Tradition', Tenth Annual Conference of the Association of Post-Keynesian Studies, Amsterdam, mimeo.
Pasinetti, L. L., and Scazzieri, R. (1987) 'Capital Theory: Paradoxes', in *The*

New Palgrave Dictionary of Economics, Vol. I (London: Macmillan) pp. 363–8.
Quadrio-Curzio, A. (1986) 'Technological Scarcity: An Essay on Production and Structural Change', in M. Baranzini and R. Scazzieri (eds) *Foundations of Economics* (Oxford and New York: Basil Blackwell) pp. 311–38.
Quadrio-Curzio, A., and Scazzieri, R. (eds) (1977–82) *Protagonisti del pensiero economico*, vols. 1–4 (Bologna: Il Mulino).
Samuelson, P. A. (1962) 'Parable and Realism in Capital Theory: the Surrogate Production Function', *Review of Economic Studies*, pp. 193–206.
Samuelson, P. A. (1966) 'A Summing Up', *Quarterly Journal of Economics*, pp. 568–83.
Samuelson, P. A., and Modigliani, F. (1966) 'The Pasinetti Paradox in Neo-Classical and More General Models', *Review of Economic Studies*, pp. 269–301.
Solow, R. M. (1956) 'The Production Function and the Theory of Capital', *Review of Economic Studies*, pp. 101–8.
Solow, R. M. (1963) 'Substitution and Fixed Proportions in the Theory of Capital', *Review of Economic Studies*, pp. 207–18.
Solow, R. M. (1970) *Growth Theory: An Exposition* (Oxford: Oxford University Press).
Scazzieri, R. (1983) 'Economic Dynamics and Structural Change: A Comment on Pasinetti', *Rivista Internazionale di Scienze Economiche e Commerciali*, pp. 73–90.
Scazzieri, R. (1990) 'Vertical Integration in Economic Theory', *Journal of Post Keynesian Economics*, pp. 1–15.
Steedman, I. (1972) 'The State and the Outcome of the Pasinetti Process', *Economic Journal*, pp. 1387–95.
Taniguchi, K. (1987) 'The Existence of Traverse in Pasinetti's Model of Growth and Distribution', mimeo.
Targetti, F. (1992) *Nicholas Kaldor* (Oxford: Oxford University Press).
Tobin, J. (1960) 'Towards a *General* Kaldorian Theory of Distribution', *Review of Economic Studies*, pp. 11–20.
Wood, A. (1975) *A Theory of Profits* (Cambridge: Cambridge University Press).
Wood, A. (1978) *A Theory of Pay* (Cambridge: Cambridge University Press).

Part I

Ricardo and Classical Political Economy

1 Marshall on Ricardo
Peter Groenewegen

INTRODUCTION: PASINETTI ON RICARDO

In spite of, or perhaps more precisely because of his many contributions to the economic theory of production, Luigi Pasinetti has written a number of interesting and important contributions to the history of the subject. These started with his very influential mathematical formulation of the Ricardian system (Pasinetti, 1960). By way of introduction to his major theoretical contributions, Pasinetti (1977, 1981) provided the historical background of the foundations on which he built his own analysis of production, structural change and economic growth. These introductions invariably contrast the classical tradition, in the main exemplified by the work of Ricardo, with the post-1870s marginalist tradition. In a more detailed historical framework, Pasinetti (1986) developed this theme further by examining the theory of value as a source of alternative paradigms in economic analysis. These alternative approaches are reflected in the classical labour model focussing on production, and the pure exchange or pure preference model which came into its own in the post-1870s marginalist period.

Basing itself in part on Pasinetti's interpretation of Ricardo and, more generally, the Sraffa-inspired interpretations, this chapter implicitly confronts such interpretations with the influential perspective on Ricardo's economics by Alfred Marshall, the founder of that Cambridge school of economics of which Pasinetti himself is such a distinguished product. For a number of reasons such an evaluation is particularly appropriate to a volume of essays in honour of Luigi Pasinetti. In the first place, because it focuses on the conflict inherent in the different approaches of classical as against marginalist economics, differences which Pasinetti's work has greatly elucidated. Secondly, Pasinetti himself has commented on the peculiar role played by Marshall in this context (Pasinetti, 1981, pp. 9 n.7, 139–42). There Marshall is correctly portrayed as a marginalist economist who attempted a 'reconciliation with the Classical economists' because 'he was never really able to turn his attention away from production' and classical supply considerations. This is the type of view that made Dobb, following Veblen, bestow the title of 'neo-classical economics' on the Marshall school (1931, p. 369) and Shove (1942, p. 295) to claim that Marshall's economics 'is of the true Ricardian stock, neither a cross-bred nor a sport'. It also explains what Stigler (1941, p. 63) described as the 'regrettable' tendency in Marshall of burdening his treatise with classical terminology or, as Schumpeter (1954, p. 837) put it more poetically, that the rooms in Marshall's new structure 'are unnecessarily cluttered up with Ricardian heirlooms, which receive emphasis quite out of proportion to their operational importance'.

The argument in this chapter is presented as follows. After a review of what Marshall said about Ricardo in his writings, both in general and with respect to particular parts of his doctrines, some conclusions are presented which comment on the operational significance of the classical-Ricardo heritage for Marshall's economics and which attempt to explain Marshall's emphasis on the continuity between his economics and that of Ricardo and his enormous admiration for the work of that economist. These corroborate in some respects Pasinetti's perspective on Marshall and Ricardo in his theoretical essay on the dynamics of the wealth of nations (Pasinetti, 1981).

MARSHALL'S VIEWS ON RICARDO

In his famous biographical memoir, Keynes traced the manner in which Marshall gradually switched to economics from mathematics and physics via a study of philosophy, theology, metaphysics and psychology (Keynes, 1925, pp. 2–12, see also Whitaker, 1975, I pp. 4–12). Much of this account was based on Marshall's own recollections supplemented by Keynes' conversations with Marshall's widow. These suggest that Marshall's serious reading of economics began in 1867 and included a careful study of Mill's *Principles of Political Economy*, then the dominant text on the subject.[1] In addition, they indicate that Marshall conducted his economic studies by translating the economics he was reading into mathematical form. The extent to which Ricardo was influential during Marshall's formative period as an economist is clearly of relevance to this discussion.

Keynes' account leaves little room for doubt on this score. On the basis of an autobiographical sketch by Marshall, he summarized the position as follows.

> Thus, when Marshall began, Mill and Ricardo still reigned supreme and unchallenged. Roscher . . . was the only other influence of importance. The notion of applying mathematical methods was in the air . . . This, and *the natural reaction of Ricardo on a Cambridge mathematician of that date* . . . were *all* that Marshall had to go upon in the first instance. (Keynes, 1925, p. 19 – my italics).[2]

The source for this statement by Keynes was Marshall's sketch of himself written for a projected collection of portraits and short lives of eminent economists.[3] The operative sentence from this text is that with which Keynes' quotation of it commences:

> While still giving private lessons in mathematics [i.e. in 1867] he [i.e. Marshall] translated as many as possible of Ricardo's reasonings into mathematics; and he endeavoured to make them more general. (Cited by Keynes, 1925, p. 20).

Earlier recollections by Marshall (but not published until after his death) place less emphasis on Ricardo and more on Mill. The more important of these contained in Marshall's correspondence with J. B. Clark (2/7/1900 and 24/3/1908 which are contained in Pigou, 1925, pp. 412, 416) and L. C. Colson (1908 or 1909 in Marshall, 1933, pp. 221-2) in fact suggest that J. S. Mill was the dominant influence on his early thinking on economic theory and not Ricardo. Internal evidence from Marshall's early economic writings supports the view that Mill rather than Ricardo was the person whose doctrines were being translated into mathematics. Mill's influence on Marshall has been well documented[4] and needs little further discussion, but some of the references to Ricardo in these early writings may be looked at more closely.

As edited and collected by Whitaker (1975), Marshall's earliest economic writings (dated between 1867 and 1874 by Whitaker) contain only a few references to Ricardo, all insubstantial. For example, Marshall's early essay on value refers to Ricardo on only two occasions. The first sees Ricardo's definition of supply and demand as inappropriate (Whitaker, 1975, I p. 129),[5] the second links his and

Malthus' theory of value to the long period (ibid. p. 144). Ricardo is referred to four times in early manuscript fragments on rent; three of these are highly critical of his views (ibid. pp. 238, 247, 249), the fourth brackets him with the Physiocrats and Smith in assuming that 'labourers are just on the limits of subsistence' (ibid. p. 153). None of these references suggest Marshall translated Ricardo's theories into mathematics in the late 1860s, as he subsequently claimed.

Likewise, there are only a few references to Ricardo in Marshall's writings of the later 1870s. Marshall's drafts for the uncompleted volume on international trade say little about Ricardo's views on the subject. The few references to his work, all either critical or non-substantial, include brief mentions of Ricardo's doctrine on gross and net revenue, fixed capital in foreign trade and its effect on employment as well as a historical comment portraying Quesnay and Ricardo as founders of the 'two first schools of abstract economics' (Whitaker, 1975, II pp. 61, 99, 85 respectively). Ricardo's views on 'sudden changes in the channels of trade' are used by Marshall to demonstrate that the classical economists were aware of the consequences of drastic policy switches such as a rapid transition to free trade, for example, (ibid., II p. 106). The only remarks on Ricardo in the privately printed pure theory of international trade are methodological and warn of the dangers of using arithmetical examples (ibid., II pp. 132–3).

Marshall's first book, *The Economics of Industry*, written jointly with his wife Mary Paley Marshall, also provides no support for the subsequent contention that Ricardo was a greater early influence on his economics than J. S. Mill. However, in Marshall's *Principles*, Ricardo seems to receive far greater notice than in the earlier works, a matter commented on by reviewers of the first edition of the *Principles*. This conforms with Marshall's increasing emphasis on Ricardo's influence in his personal recollections as he grew older.

Marshall's access to Ricardo's works should also be noted. From internal evidence it is clear that the edition of Ricardo he basically used was that edited by McCulloch, during Marshall's lifetime the standard edition of Ricardo's works. (See Marshall, 1961, I p. 835 n.1.) This edition gave Marshall not only access to the third edition of the *Principles*, but also to the *High Price of Bullion, Reply to Bosanquet, Essay on the Influence of a Low Price of Corn on the Profits of Stock, Proposals for an Economical and Secure Currency, On protection to Agriculture, Plan for a National Bank* and *Essay on the Funding System*. In his *Principles*, Marshall also cited Bonar's edition of Ricardo's letters to Malthus (Bonar, 1887; and see e.g. Marshall, 1961, p. 819). He owned copies of the letters to McCulloch and Trower, published in the 1890s (Hollander, 1895; Bonar and Hollander, 1899).[6] Compared to the Sraffa edition of Ricardo's works (Ricardo, 1951–73) the more notable items from Ricardo's writings not accessible to Marshall were the correspondence with James Mill and the final paper on absolute and exchangeable value.

Some general remarks on Ricardo by Marshall relating to Ricardo's method, the scope and objectives of Ricardo's *Principles* as Marshall saw them, and the place he assigned to Ricardo in the development of economics can also be recalled by way of introduction. Consideration of these aspects of Ricardo's work were essential to Marshall's defence of Ricardo against the hostile criticism of his work by both British and European economists. Such critics of Ricardo focused largely on two matters, separate from the Jevonian criticisms of Ricardo's theory of value and distribution. First, and most frequently, the critics focused on the inadequacies of Ricardo's 'abstract' method as compared with the advantages from using a historical (inductive) economics. Secondly, they emphasized the use which had been made of his views on value, wages and rent by socialist writers ranging from Marx to the land nationalization doctrines inspired by Henry George, the last being particularly virulent when Marshall was constructing his *Principles*. Marshall tended to implicitly link these criticisms, as shown by his reference quoted below to the 'evils' from crude applications of Ricardo's conclusions 'to real problems'. In short, Marshall's defence of Ricardo was not only directed at the marginalist critique of his work.

In early writings, Marshall had already described Ricardo's method as abstract, or deductive, and this view was maintained (Marshall, 1961, I, pp. 761 and n.1, 813; 1921, p. 674; 1923, p. 190).[7] Although this abstract method is praised because 'it can lead to new and unexpected results' (Marshall, 1961, I p. 761 n.1) warnings are given about its dangers. 'Great then is the usefulness of Ricardo's method. But even greater are the evils which may arise from a crude application of its suggestions to real problems. For that simplicity which makes it helpful, makes it also deficient and even treacherous' (Marshall, 1923, p. 190). However, Marshall (1961, I p. 761) suggested that these dangers were least when the method was applied to the 'theory of currency' and international trade, where 'pure deductive reasoning' was on more 'safe ground'. In addition, Marshall emphasized the pitfalls in using arithmetical examples which 'can as a rule be safely used only as illustrations and not as proofs: for it is generally more difficult to know whether the result has been implicitly assumed in the numbers shown for the special case than it is to determine independently whether the results be true or not' (Marshall, 1961, I p. 836; cf. Whitaker, 1975, II pp. 132–3).

As Hicks (1965, pp. 49–50) has pointed out, Marshall also saw considerable strengths in Ricardo's method. These cannot be directly inferred from the text of his *Principles*. In Appendix C of that book Marshall (1961, I p. 773) defined the function of 'analysis and deduction in economics' as the art of forging 'rightly many short chains and single connecting links'. This good methodological practice is ascribed to Ricardo in a rather negative manner; Appendix D only 'absolved' Ricardo from indulging 'in long chains of deductive reasoning without reference to direct observation' (Marshall, 1961, II pp. 770–1; cf. I p. 781). Marshall's half-hearted concession absolving Ricardo from indulging in long chains of reasoning is all the more strange because the procedure of arguing by 'separate logical stages' was in fact an important characteristic of classical political economy with Ricardo a leading practitioner, as Garegnani (1983, p. 312) has noted. Marshall's concession was also contradicted in Appendix I (Marshall, 1961, I p. 816 and see section II below).

Marshall's perceptions of Ricardo's purpose in writing the *Principles* are also worth noting. They not only shed further light on his views on Ricardo's method, but more importantly reveal an opinion on the background to Ricardo's writings which coloured his interpretation of Ricardo's work. Early editions of Marshall's *Principles* claimed that Ricardo's *Principles* were 'not originally designed for publication' but that they were 'terse notes, written for the benefit of himself and perhaps a few friends, on points of special difficulty' (Marshall, 1961, II pp. 757–8). From the fifth edition, this changed to the view that Ricardo wrote for 'men of affairs with a vast knowledge of the facts of life' (ibid., I p. 761 n.1). This description of the purpose of Ricardo's *Principles* varies little from the account given in what became Appendix I. Here Marshall (1961, I p. 813) said that Ricardo's:

> book makes no pretence to be systematic. He was with difficulty induced to publish it; and if in writing it he had in view any readers at all, they were chiefly those statesmen and businessmen with whom he associated. So he purposely omitted many things which were necessary for the logical completeness of his argument, but

which they would regard as obvious . . . further [Ricardo] was 'but a poor master of language.' His exposition is as confused as his thought is profound; he uses words in artificial senses which he does not explain, and to which he does not adhere; and he changes from one hypothesis to another without giving notice. If then we seek to understand him rightly, we must interpret him generously, more generously than he himself interpreted Adam Smith.

Marshall may have derived these views from Roscher's statement that 'in judging Ricardo, it must not be forgotten that it was not his intention to write a textbook . . . but only to communicate to those versed in [political economy] the result of his researches in as brief a manner as possible'. Marshall approvingly quoted this statement (1961, I p. 163, n.1; II pp. 179–80) probably because it so clearly matched his own method of interpreting Ricardo. Such an interpretation facilitated the argument that Ricardo's views were often incomplete, that some of his peculiar expression was due to careless writing and that he did not always list his assumptions clearly, hence supporting a plea for generous interpretation (Marshall, 1961, Appendix I; cf. Marshall, 1923, p. 323 n.1, and some fragments of early lecture notes on Ricardo possibly from the early 1870s in Whitaker, 1975, II pp. 253, 257, 160).[8]

Lastly, Marshall left some general comments on Ricardo's place in the history of economic thought. These give more emphasis to the 'shortcomings of Ricardo and his followers' than to their achievements, despite Marshall's frequently expressed admiration for Ricardo. Marshall's praise concerns their application of deductive reasoning to the theory of money and international trade, where such reasoning was most appropriate. However, 'their work' is criticized for 'a certain narrowness' because they neglected systematic comparative study and tended to generalize the human aspects of their theories from their experience with city men rather than ordinary people (Marshall, 1961, I p. 761, cf. p. 12; 154–5). This limited perspective led them into error when dealing with class relationships. Examples are their treatment 'of labour as a commodity' without discussing the human qualities of workers, and the fact that they 'attributed to the forces of supply and demand a much more mechanical and regular action than is to be found in real life: and they laid down laws with regard to profits and wages that did not really hold even for England in their own time' (Marshall, 1961, I pp. 762–3).

Marshall here seems to reject the theory of distribution, which

Ricardo himself regarded as the core of his *Principles* and the principal objective in the study of political economy. Lack of awareness of change in habits and institutions, combined with a neglect of reassessing their theoretical speculations in the light of such change, constitutes the 'most vital fault' of Ricardo and his contemporaries. Within the context of his only systematic writing on the history of economics, Marshall's praise of Ricardo is confined to contributions to monetary and foreign trade theory, and even here praise is muted because Marshall hardly ever mentions Ricardo directly by name. As shown subsequently, this probably reflects the fact that only in the area of monetary policy was Marshall directly and demonstrably indebted to Ricardo's opinions. Marshall's undoubted admiration for Ricardo appears founded on more general factors such as his 'brilliant originality' only approached by Jevons (Marshall, 1971, I p. 817), or 'the genius which enabled Ricardo to tread his way safely through the most slippery paths of mathematical reasoning, though he had no aid from mathematical training . . .' (Marshall, undated postscript to his review of Jevons, in Pigou, 1925, pp. 99–100). It is the form rather than the substance of Ricardo's economic reasoning that made him a classic author, as Marshall indicated in the letter to Bonar (referred to in note 2 above) where 'agreement with many, or even a single point in the argument' is counted as little relative to 'the form or the matter of his words or deeds' or the creation of immortal and original 'architectonic ideas in thought or sentiment . . . [which] are an existing yeast ceaselessly working in the cosmos'.[9]

THE OPERATIONAL SIGNIFICANCE OF THE CLASSICAL-RICARDO HERITAGE FOR MARSHALL'S ECONOMICS

As Shove (1942, pp. 295–6) explained in his centenary evaluation of Marshall, Marshall saw his task as completing the classical economists' theories, rather than correcting them. This aim is particularly clear in Marshall's famous discussion of Ricardo's theory of value. It is also visible in his more prolix analysis of Ricardo's views on rent and wages. Marshall's treatment of Ricardo's monetary theory is also discussed in some detail, for reasons suggested in the preceding section. Rather than dealing with all of Marshall's remarks in Ricardo's economics, therefore, the objective of this section is confined to illustrating aspects of Marshall's interpretation of Ricardo which highlight features of Marshall's enigmatic position on the work of this classical author in economics.

The most famous and controversial of Marshall's statements on Ricardo is Appendix I of the *Principles* on Ricardo's theory of value. Its text changed little between 1890 and 1920, though its position in the book was altered on three occasions (see Marshall, 1961, II pp. 813–16). Its origins go back to Marshall's earliest published piece on economics, the 1872 review of Jevons' *Theory*, of which a substantial part is incorporated in the Appendix (see Marshall, 1961, I pp. 817–19; Marshall, 1872, in Pigou, 1925, pp. 93–5). Appendix I is largely devoted to a defence of Ricardo against criticism attributed to Jevons and others (Macleod, Walras, Menger, Böhm-Bawerk and von Wieser). These critics, Marshall argued, were all confused on the *mutual* determination of value by the 'one all-ruling law of supply and demand', depicted by Marshall's colourful analogies like the 'blades of the scissors' and the 'balls in the bowl' (Marshall, 1961, I pp. 818, 820).

Marshall admits that Ricardo shared in such confusions about the mutual determination aspects of the theory of value. He nevertheless argued that Ricardo's theory required completion rather than reconstruction, because Ricardo was fully aware of the fact 'that demand played an essential part in governing value, but that he regarded its action as less obscure than that of cost of production, and therefore passed it lightly over in the notes which he made for the use of his friends, and himself; for he never essayed to write a formal treatise . . .' (Marshall, 1961, I p. 503, cf. pp. 85, 101 n.1, 525; Marshall, 1921, pp. 396–7; Marshall, 1923, p. 167). Marshall's position therefore depends in part on the characteristics he ascribed to Ricardo's *Principles*, which in the previous section were shown to be no longer sustainable on the current information about Ricardo's writing of that book. In addition, it relies substantially on quotations from the correspondence with Malthus, to demonstrate Ricardo's position with respect to supply and demand.[10] Last, Marshall demonstrates Ricardo's awareness of the role of demand and the nature of wants from textual evidence in Ricardo's *Principles*. Marshall correctly suggests that Ricardo believed utility to be absolutely essential to value though not to the measure of value. Evidence is then produced by Marshall to show that Ricardo introduced 'subjective' elements into his value theory when he referred to 'desires', 'wants' and 'wishes of the people', by way of introducing his well-known interpretation of Ricardo's chapter on value and riches in terms of marginal and total utility. Only Ricardo's lack of calculus and 'the right words in which to say it neatly', Marshall concluded, prevented him from stating the law of diminishing marginal utility. Both recognition of the importance of demand to value theory and preliminary investigation of its subjective foundations are ascribed to Ricardo by Marshall on the basis of this evidence.[11]

From the demand side, explicitly acknowledged to have been imperfectly developed by Ricardo, Marshall switches to what he calls the supply or cost of production side (Marshall, 1961, I p. 814). In this context, Marshall successively indicates a number of propositions which according to him can be attributed to Ricardo. First, it is claimed Ricardo was fully aware that commodities 'fall into three classes . . . of diminishing, of constant, or of increasing returns; yet he thought it best to ignore this distinction . . . [and to assume] provisionally that they all obeyed the law of constant returns' (ibid.). Marshall subsequently provides a reader's guide through Chapter 1 of Ricardo's *Principles*. A labour proportionality rule is ascribed to Ricardo in 'early stages of society' where capital is unimportant and labour can be assumed homogeneous, but these assumptions break down during 'later stages of civilization' in which 'the relation of value to cost of production is more complex' (Marshall, 1961, I pp. 814–15). Marshall then criticizes Ricardo for assuming, rather than analyzing, that under modern conditions variations in the reward for different types of labour 'cannot be great' and then discusses the qualifications to the labour proportionately value rule which Pasinetti (1960, p. 21) neatly summarized as variations in the relative time period of production. Although acknowledging that it is possible to interpret Ricardo as thinking that such modifications were slight, Marshall prefers to draw attention to Ricardo's identification of cost and value where cost of production includes profits, and to Ricardo's strong emphasis on the fact that 'time or waiting as well as labour is an element of cost of production' (ibid., p. 816).

Marshall's perspective on Ricardo's theory of value in relation to later developments follows from this characterization of its essentials. On the basis of a letter to Malthus (in Bonar, 1887, pp. 173–6), Ricardo's position is described to be 'more philosophic in principle and closer to the actual facts of life' than that of Jevons and some of the other marginalist critics. He can only be criticized for not stating his assumptions clearly (particularly with respect to the partial equilibrium and long-term nature of the argument), in being careless 'with regard to the element of time' and above all, for not clearly stating, perhaps from lack of complete or clear perception, 'how, in the problem of normal value, the various elements govern one another *mutually*, and *successively*, in a long chain of causation'. Methodologically he was therefore guilty of what Marshall most disliked in economic reasoning, 'the bad habit of endeavouring to express great economic doctrines in short sentences' (Marshall, 1961, I pp. 816, 819, 821).

Irrespective of the interpretation of Ricardo on value the reader may hold, Marshall's views on the subject can be criticized on several grounds. Above all, he can be charged with an anachronistic reading of Ricardo's text, which transforms Ricardo's notions into Marshallian terminology and thereby induces the resemblances Marshall desires his readers to find. Examples are Marshall's attribution to Ricardo of a threefold classification of commodities in terms of the laws of returns; the assumption of constant returns in his value theory; the identification of long-term normal value with Ricardo's natural price; as well as the attempted identification of Ricardo's utility notion with those Marshall held himself. Secondly, Marshall can be charged with interpreting Ricardo's value theory exclusively as an analysis of 'causes which govern the relative exchange values of different things'. He only casually noted its measurement role, and confined this to monetary questions rather than the question of distribution, which as the Mill-Ricardo correspondence so convincingly shows, was the basic motivation for Ricardo's search for an invariable standard of value. The measurement requirements of Ricardo's value theory were dismissed in the *Principles* (1961, I p. 821) as largely 'historical' but this view was at least partly contradicted in Marshall's later book on money (1923, pp. 21–2).[12]

Marshall's defence of Ricardo's theory of value was strongly criticized by Ashley (1891) a criticism to which Marshall briefly replied in the *Principles* (1961, I pp. 816–17 n.1; II p. 815). This reply largely concentrated on two issues. The first was Marshall's rejection of the widely-held view that Ricardo saw cost of production in terms of quantities of labour only, a proposition subject to only minor modifications on this view of Ricardo and the one most consistent with his writings as a whole. Secondly, Marshall strongly defended his own position on the subject, that is, that Ricardo had an incomplete theory, 'true as far as it went', hence the need for rehabilitation, 'i.e. clothing more fully his somewhat naked doctrines'. This does less than justice to Ashley, who had criticized Marshall for attempting to justify his substantial changes in economics by 'a new interpretation of an authoritative text' (1891, p. 474) and who, in this context, could depict Marshall as running the risk of the 'sympathetic theorist' in being 'unhistorical' for attempting to achieve that aim (1891, p. 489). Although Ashley conceded Marshall's attitude was a 'natural one, . . . it is not without its dangers', and in particular such dangers are great if the aim is to obtain a reasonable understanding of Ricardo's theory of value. Ashley's own exegetical standards, including his use of what contemporary writers judged Ricardo to mean in his theory of value, were far superior to the peculiar practice of Marshall in this regard. Similar criticism of Marshall's exegetical practices have been made by others.[13]

After value, rent is next in importance as a topic on which Marshall frequently mentioned Ricardo in his *Principles*. The thrust of Marshall's interpretation of Ricardo on rent is broadly similar to that on value theory. Marshall viewed Ricardo's theory of rent and associated topics 'correct as far as it goes' but it had to be generously interpreted by making due allowance for his careless use of language. This allows Marshall to infer that in the analysis and theory of rent, 'of which Ricardo was the chief builder, [there are] firm if often unseen foundations [for the present theory']. (Marshall, 1961, II p. 512, cf. II pp. 493, 495).

Marshall's general observations on Ricardo's rent analysis are well illustrated in Appendix L of the *Principles* on Ricardo's (and Mill's) doctrine on taxes on raw produce and improvements in agriculture. Marshall regarded Ricardo's analysis of the incidence of taxes on raw produce as perfectly correct, though his use of the assumption of 'zero elasticity of demand' for corn is criticized for its lack of realism. Ricardo is also criticized for his carelessness in failing to specify the time period assumed in the analysis. 'When appropriate interpreting clauses are supplied, very few of his reasonings will be found invalid' and a similar conclusion is drawn by Marshall for his analysis of the effects on rent of a capital saving improvement in corn production (Marshall, 1961, I pp. 833-4, 835-6).[14]

A study of Ricardo's text reveals that Marshall's interpreting clauses are inappropriate for understanding Ricardo's argument. Two examples suffice. First, Marshall is quite wrong in saying that Ricardo did not specify the time period under consideration with sufficient care; in fact, the chapter on taxes on raw produce shows Ricardo particularly careful to distinguish immediate from more long-term effects (Ricardo, 1951-73, I pp. 160-2). Secondly, and more importantly, Marshall's attribution to Ricardo of an 'absolutely inelastic' demand for produce suggests that Ricardo saw demand as a function of price and not, as Ricardo explicitly does in the chapter referred to, as influenced largely by changes in income (Ricardo, 1951–73, I pp. 162–4). Marshall's specific identification of classical demand theory with the marginalist view of the subject is a typical interpretative anachronism which does less than justice to Ricardo's text.

Other aspects of Marshall's evaluation of Ricardo's rent theory need less extensive treatment. For example, Ricardo's phrase, 'the original and indestructible powers of the soil' is favourably mentioned (Marshall, 1961, I p. 144 n.1) while the depiction of rent as a 'limitation of the bounty of nature' is a 'further truth' ascribed to Ricardo (ibid., p. 633). However, Marshall's claims that Ricardo treated rent basically as a 'scarcity price' and his occasional identification of Ricardo's rent analysis as one of 'producer surplus' (ibid., pp. 644 n.2; 834), are further instances of reading his own views into those of Ricardo.

Similar considerations can be shown to apply to Marshall's discussion of Ricardo on wages. In the first place, Marshall strongly disassociated Ricardo from his 'German socialist followers' on the so-called 'iron law of wages'. Ricardo had clearly argued that the natural price of labour depends on 'the habits and customs of the people' and is not 'absolutely fixed and constant' (Marshall, 1961, I p. 508). This part of Marshall's rehabilitation of Ricardo was also criticized by Ashley (1891, pp. 484–5) because Ricardo's subsistence wage theory 'led directly' to some of his 'most important doctrines' on profits and taxation. Whether Marshall or Ashley were right on this issue raises difficult problems in interpreting Ricardo's theory of wages. Operational significance of the subsistence wage for Ricardo was, however, implicitly denied by Marshall (1961, I p. 508 n.4) while it may also be noted that the detailed reference to the precise location of Ashley's criticism was deleted from the fifth edition onwards (Marshall, 1961, II pp. 552–3).[15]

Two further observations can be made on Marshall's interpretation of Ricardo's views on wages. In the first edition of his *Principles*, Marshall attempted to demonstrate that 'Ricardo and the able businessmen who followed in his wake were perfectly familiar with the practical working of the Law of Substitution. But, perhaps for that very reason, they did not emphasise it, did not make clear the important position which it really holds in their doctrines of wages . . .' (Marshall, 1961, II p. 592). This generous interpretation appears to have been even too much for the generosity of Marshall and the passage was transformed from the third edition onwards to refer to Ricardo's (and businessmen's) practical familiarity with the 'law of demand' in the context of the theory of value, for reasons not explained by Guillebaud. Later in the chapter on wages, there is a subtle attempt by Marshall in a rather long footnote (Marshall, 1961, I p. 550 n.1) to associate Ricardo with a productivity theory of wages. Although this footnote can be read to imply a concept of wages in terms of the total product going to labour, Marshall transforms Ricardo's aggregate concept of wages into an argument relating the individual labourer's wages to *his* product and consequently the profitability of *his* labour to *his* employer. When read in the context of the argument to which the footnote refers, this suggests that Ricardo's views on wages resemble Marshall's own productivity theory.[16]

Finally, Marshall's comments on Ricardo's monetary and trade theory must be briefly examined. Here it is possible to identify one subject where Ricardo clearly influenced the work of Marshall in a positive manner, as Marshall himself explicitly acknowledged. This is Marshall's strong support for a modified version of Ricardo's 1816 ingot plan (Ricardo, 1951–72, IV pp. 65–73, esp. 66–7), or, as Bonar (1923, pp. 298–9) called it, 'Professor Marshall's symmetalism . . . expressly based on Ricardo's Economical and Secure Currency'. (Cf. Keynes, 1925, p. 31.) Marshall put this scheme forward in 1886 in his written answers on currency and prices in connection with the Royal Commission on the Depression of Trade and Industry (Marshall, 1916, pp. 14–15). He developed it further in his written submission and oral evidence to the Royal Commission on the Values of Gold and Silver in 1887–8 (Marshall, 1926, pp. 18–31, 102–3, 165). The essentials from this evidence were incorporated into his *Money, Credit and Commerce* more than three decades later (Marshall, 1923, pp. 64–7, esp. p. 65). Marshall's version of Ricardo's ingot plan, in my opinion, is the one Marshallian proposition which can unambiguously be described as being 'of the true Ricardian stock, neither a cross-bred nor a sport' to use Shove's (1942, p. 295) phrase.

Marshall's evidence reveals detailed knowledge of Ricardo's monetary theory and policy writings so well represented in the McCulloch edition of Ricardo's works. Two points of his detailed knowledge of Ricardo's monetary proposals may be noted here.

The first relates to Ricardo's opinion as to whether a gold or a silver standard was the more appropriate. This led to a number of altercations during Marshall's appearances before the Gold and Silver Commission. At his second appearance he was asked by Mr Barbour (Q. 9838) whether Ricardo did not 'recommend silver as the standard of England' to which Marshall replied in the negative, referring to Ricardo's gold ingot plan based on gold bars of twenty ounces as the standard for a 'safe international currency'. A follow-up question quoting Ricardo on the advantages of silver as a standard elicited the reply from Marshall that he did not think that Ricardo's proposal provided for bars of silver (Marshall, 126, pp. 102–3).[17] Towards the end of this session, the matter was referred to again in the context of a reference to Lord Liverpool's opinion about a popular preference for gold coin, an opinion with which Ricardo had disagreed. In this discussion, Ricardo's remarks on Locke's preference for a silver standard were quoted, in which he had also argued that under a silver standard gold coin should be left to fluctuate according to the relative market values of gold and silver. Contrary to Locke, Ricardo believed that the guinea had been overvalued at 22 shillings and at 21s 6d and that this caused export of silver and the retention of gold coin (Ricardo, 1951–73, III pp. 202–3 and cf. 176–8 and III 65–6). Marshall agreed with this proposition of Ricardo and conceded that 'Ricardo would not have denied that the people had a great preference for gold' (Marshall, 1926, pp. 136–7).

At a subsequent hearing, there was another exchange on Ricardo's alleged preference for a silver standard as a sound basis for a paper currency. This time, reference was made to his *Principles*, Ch. 27, particularly to two paragraphs in which Ricardo praised the introduction of a domestic paper currency and restated his preference for a mono-metallic system based on either gold or silver rather than the dual standard criticized at the end of the seventeenth century by Locke (Ricardo, 1951–73, I pp. 361, 369; Marshall, 1926, pp. 143–4). Marshall once again indicated agreement with Ricardo's propositions on a 'national scheme of fixed-ratio-mintage' but added that he now also agreed with Mr Barbour's opinion that Ricardo's general preference had been for a silver rather than a gold standard.[18]

The second point of interest in Marshall's evidence is his opinion that for Ricardo bullion is only a commodity in international trade and that money is only a mechanism for facilitating what essentially are barter transactions. Marshall significantly described this as a sound proposition about permanent but not about temporary effects, a proposition with which Ricardo would not have disagreed (Marshall,

1926, pp. 115–16, 117–18, cf. 372). The remaining references to Ricardo in Marshall's official papers are non-substantial, referring to Ricardo's pioneering work in the foreign exchanges in relation to the direction of trade, a theory which Marshall appreciated because of its value for policy discussion (Marshall, 1926, pp. 170, 372). Marshall's opinions of Ricardo's monetary and trade doctrines conform with the high place he accorded them in his view of the development of economic thought, though Fay (1960, p. 35) reports a partial change of mind. By 1907–8, 'after long years of thought he [i.e. Marshall] had come to the conclusion that in the great currency controversy of Tooke versus Ricardo, Tooke was more right than Ricardo'.

Subsequent references to Ricardo's international trade theory by Marshall are not very important. Ricardo's work in trade theory, particularly the doctrine of comparative advantage, is praised in general terms (Marshall, 1923, pp. 108, 148; cf. 1921, p. 19 n.1) but these contributions are also criticized as over-simplifications of complex problems and as far too abstract (Marshall, 1923, pp. 158–321). On this subject Mill and Ricardo are invariably bracketed together as the pioneers, and it is particularly interesting to see that on one such occasion while it appears from the text that Ricardo's conclusion is being quoted, the actual quotation is from J. S. Mill (Marshall, 1923, p. 231 and n.1). As indicated earlier in note 4, Marshall was indebted to Mill on the subject of international trade. Apart from the ingot plan, it seems therefore not possible to speak of any appreciable direct Ricardo influence on Marshall.

CONCLUDING REMARKS

This examination of Marshall's views on Ricardo allows some further conclusions. These in part shed light on matters raised by Pasinetti in his identification of a dual approach to economic theory. They also afford an opportunity for comment on the use and abuse of methods of interpreting the work of a particular author, a matter of importance for historians of economic thought.

First, the previous sections permit judgement on the extent and nature of Marshall's admiration for Ricardo. They also assist an assessment of the importance of the 'Ricardian lineage' for Marshallian economics. There is little reason to doubt Marshall's admiration for Ricardo's genius as an economist, particularly with respect to his enormous logical powers in handling economic problems. However,

Marshall was rather circumspect in his praise of Ricardo's method and confined its suitable application to monetary theory. Marshall's later claims about substantial intellectual obligations to Ricardo (see Whitaker, 1975, II p. 249 n.5) are difficult to sustain on the available facts. Marshall's own recollections have to be regarded with considerable suspicion, because of a tendency as he got older to substitute Ricardo's influence for the real influence exerted by J. S. Mill. Marshall's early writings on economics, for example, reveal no strong Ricardo influence. Furthermore, there is no substantial theoretical matter in the core of Marshall's *Principles*, that is, the theory of value and distribution as set out by him in that and earlier work, which bears unmistakable signs of a Ricardo influence. Marshall's one genuine obligation to Ricardo which can be identified is his acceptance and modification of Ricardo's ingot plan for an 'economical and secure currency'.

Lack of influence has of course little to do with Marshall's genuine expressions of admiration for Ricardo's genius as a classical economist in the meaning he himself had given the term. Ricardo had clearly produced such immortal 'architectonic ideas in thought' which qualified him as a classical thinker; lack of agreement on Marshall's part with specific, if not with most points in Ricardo's doctrine, did nothing to destroy the basis for such a judgement, as Marshall had written on the subject to Bonar (in Pigou, 1925, p. 374). In addition, Marshall would have fully endorsed the thrust of Ashley's (1891, p. 475) judgement that 'English economists can hardly fail to be proud of Ricardo . . . [and that] it is a comfort for the staid and academic to feel that they are building on [his] foundations . . .' Admiration for genius, filial piety, plus a very strong sense of the desirability of continuity in doctrine (cf. Marshall, 1961, I p.v) explains much of the nature of Marshall's views on Ricardo expressed in later life. It does of course not explain all, as Pasinetti (1981, pp. 138–42, esp. p. 140) has explicitly noted. Elucidation of this permits further understanding of the extent of Marshall's Ricardian lineage.

A distinction can be made in this context between some of Marshall's classical heirlooms which, in Schumpeter's phrase, cluttered up the individual rooms of his new structure. A number of these, contrary to Schumpeter's view quoted at the start of this paper, have significant operational value in Marshall's system, though others clearly do not.[19] Pasinetti has identified the following features of Ricardian analysis which are important in Marshall's work. The first is his emphasis on reproducible rather than scarce commodities *per se*; the second his stress on the long run 'and the fundamental determinants, which make themselves felt in the long run' (Pasinetti, 1981, p. 140). In addition, though not unrelated to emphasis on the long run, is the dynamic treatment underlying Marshall's theory of value (cf. Loasby, 1978, esp. pp. 586–7; Dardi, 1984, esp. Ch. 4) and his never-ending quest to incorporate evolutionary changes in his system. His emphasis on the importance of the division of labour, external economies combined with his recognition of the difficulties they raise for marginalist theory (Marshall, 1961, I pp. 805–9) is another important classical heirloom, more associated with Smith than Ricardo. In this sense, Marshall fits the neo-classical label which Dobb (1931) bestowed on him. However, it may be noted that these are classical economics attributes rather than views attributable to Ricardo alone.

Given such considerations, Marshall's admiration for his classical predecessors becomes easier to understand. However, this does not absolve him from the ahistorical and anachronistic practices he used in his interpretation of Ricardo and which, at best, can be described as misleading. Marshall's interpretative rules have been described as 'personal exegesis' or a desire 'to ascertain what [an author] really meant' by interpreting ambiguous phrases in such a way that they conform with the meaning 'he would have wished us to give them' on the basis of other passages in his writings (Marshall, 1961, I p. 813).[20] When criticized, Marshall defended these rules as follows: 'each reader must decide for himself according to his temperament; *it does not lend itself to be solved by argument*' (Marshall, 1961, I p. 817 n. – my italics).

As indicated in the previous section, Marshall did not strictly apply these rules as he had originally stated them, that is, by defending the meanings he assigned to Ricardo's propositions through a careful textual exegesis of passages from his writings. The opposite is in fact true, since it was noted that Marshall was rather economical in quoting from Ricardo's text. His actual working rules for the interpretation appear quite different. He deliberately started from the premise that Ricardo's *Principles* was an incomplete and badly constructed book, where the author's intention was interpreted as deliberately omitting obvious material, defined as that which could be easily supplied by his specialist readers. From this opinion on the nature of Ricardo's *Principles*, the reader (including, of course, Marshall himself) was given licence to introduce any argument into the text which he considered Ricardo would have thought 'obvious' thereby 'completing' the book in an 'appropriate' manner. This makes a travesty of the scope and contents of Ricardo's *Principles* and of its serious textual interpretation. Sraffa's demonstration (in Ricardo, 1953–71, I pp. xii–xxx) of the importance for textual interpretation of 'arrangements and subdivisions' of contents can be usefully recalled here.

The basic thrust of Marshall's comments on Ricardo cannot therefore be accepted as accurate, nor can it be said, as Marshall himself suggested in his later years, that he owed a substantial intellectual obligation to Ricardo. Hence Marshall's lengthy, scattered and not very detailed commentary on Ricardo is a good illustration of 'the fact that each generation rewrites its own history of economics [and that] from this perspective an evaluation often tells us more about the commentator than the subject' (Hollander, 1979, p. 4). Contextual reading as a more appropriate approach to understanding a classical text like Ricardo's *Principles*, shows that Hollander's dictum need not necessarily apply. A contextual reading exacts higher standards of scholarship and greater historical knowledge from the author who is investigating the meaning of the text, but such practice is rewarded by a richer appreciation of the work studied. Pasinetti's historical contributions, particularly his discussion of the theory of value (Pasinetti, 1986, pp. 410–11) warns against 'straining' the meaning of a text in the manner Marshall did with Ricardo. Irrespective of the merits of Pasinetti's own contributions to interpreting Ricardo, and more generally, classical economics, this shows the fastidious nature of Pasinetti's judgement in this matter and the enormous value of his contributions for the practising historian of economic thought as well as economists as a whole.[21]

NOTES

1. Marshall's personal copy of the 1865 People's edition of J. S. Mill's *Principles* is in the Cambridge University Library (Marshall, d 61). It contains many annotations made at various periods of Marshall's life and on the basis of his handwriting, a considerable number of these appear to have been made in the late 1860s.
2. In the paragraph from which this quotation is taken, Keynes also refers to Cournot and Mill. Keynes' reference to Mill is surprising since it confines his influence on a Cambridge mathematician to 'some hints of

algebraic treatment in the arithmetical examples of Mill's Book III chapter XVIII on "International Values"' (Keynes, 1925, p. 19). Since these hints are generally regarded as the inspiration for Marshall's pioneering work on reciprocal demand curves, Keynes' downgrading of Mill's influence on Marshall is surprising. Keynes' remark may reflect precisely Marshall's views derived by him in conversations, on which much of the memoir is based.

3. This autobiographical sketch from which Keynes only quoted an extract has been reproduced in full with an introduction in Robinson (1972). See also Whitaker (1975, I p. 6, n.8) and Robinson (1973) which suggests that there are some difficulties in the precise dating of this fragment.

4. Mill's influence on Marshall was greatest on the theory of value, international (see Viner, 1937, pp. 535–46 and Haberler, 1936, esp. pp. 145–54) and domestic (Bharadwaj, 1978, pp. 254–8). See also Stigler (1965a, pp. 6–11) which suggests a wider range of influence. Marshall's views on Mill underwent considerable change, as is documented in his correspondence. In July and August 1883 he quarrelled on this subject with Foxwell, warning him not to 'vilify Mill', and though conceding that Mill 'is literary and therefore full of error . . . he and Ricardo contain their kernel of truth'. Fourteen years later, in 1897, Marshall was more conciliatory to Foxwell's critical views of Mill, agreeing 'with the tendency of all you say about him: but I do not go as far as you do. Even when I differ from him, he seems to keep my mind in a higher plane of thought than ordinary writers of economics'. In 1898 Marshall wrote to Bonar, with reference to Bonar's entry on classical political economy in Palgrave that 'I incline to regard Petty and Hermann and von Thunen and Jevons as classical, but not Mill . . .' (Marshall, in Pigou, 1925, p. 374). Marshall had written a careful defence of Mill's theory of value in 1876, which argued that much of that work had to be 'supplemented' but that much is 'in the main, sound as far as it goes' (Marshall, in Pigou, 1925, p. 121).

5. The reference is to Ch. 30 of the *Principles* where Ricardo is said to 'speak of the ratio between supply and demand as regulating prices in some cases', an erroneous statement which is corrected by Mill's remark that there 'cannot be ratio between such heterogeneous quantities as a supply and demand in Ricardo's sense' (Whitaker, 1975, I p. 129). It is interesting to note that Marshall marked this passage in his copy of Mill's *Principles* and noted, 'This is distinctly the position of Ricardo. See ch. XXX on Value (Ricardo)'.

6. Marshall's copy of Ricardo's *Works* as edited by McCulloch has not been preserved among his books held in the Marshall Library at the Faculty of Economics and Politics, University of Cambridge. This library does hold his copies of Ricardo's letters to McCulloch, Malthus and Trower as published in the 1880s and 1890s, the first being a presentation copy from its editor, Jacob Hollander, dated 10 May 1896. Marshall's copy of the Bonar edition of the Letters to Malthus bears 'annotations' largely in the form of pencil markings which emphasize passages and pages referred to in Marshall's *Principles* (1961, I pp. 813, 819). The holdings of early editions of Ricardo's *Principles* and others works held at the Cambridge University Library as part of the 'Marshall Collection' (Marshall c20, c30

and c31) did not belong to Marshall but to Sidgwick and Keynes respectively.
7. Marshall advanced no less than three reasons to explain Ricardo's predelictions for the abstract method. In the *Principles* he ascribed it both to Ricardo's semitic origins and to Bentham's influence on the economists of the early nineteenth century (Marshall, 1961, I pp. 760, 761 and c.f. his inaugural lecture, in Pigou, 1925, p. 153). The former argument is explicitly derived from Bagehot (1879, pp. 197–8), the second probably from Toynbee's essay on Ricardo (first edition 1884, 1913, pp. 142–3). The third and more curious reason is given by Marshall in a subsequent work (1921, p. 674) where the taste for abstract reasoning is ascribed without any explanation to the 'temporary return of Europe, between 1790 and 1820, to a reign of violence'. An explanation for this remark can be found in Marshall's manuscript draft preface for *Money, Credit and Commerce*, written in 1917 and rescued from the wastepaper basket by his wife. Keynes (1925, p. 10) quotes part of this, leaving out the part dealing with Ricardo as irrelevant for his purpose. This reads as follows:

> But yet the science seems to progress steadily. What is known of it now, though only a small part of what needs to be known, is yet large relative to that which was known a hundred years ago when Ricardo's vigorous and trenchant thought had given it unprecedented prestige. The success which he achieved was perhaps partly due to the extreme urgency of the practical problems, which had been brought to the front of grievous destructions of wealth during the Napoleonic wars, and by hopes that seemed to be justified by the rapid advances in the arts of agriculture and manufacture of the preceding generations. But, though he, and his great interpreter, John Stuart Mill, carried many of Adam Smith's best thoughts very far towards completion, they seem to have taken insufficient account of the difference between those truths which are valid only in regard to the stage of economic development in which they are made manifest, and those which are in great measure independent of time and circumstance. (Marshall Papers, Cabinet file 8, Miscellaneous Manuscripts, Marshall Library, Cambridge University.)

In spite of the peculiarities in Marshall's remarks on Ricardo's method, Marshall found this aspect of Ricardo's economics most attractive because it coincided with his own predilection in viewing economics as an engine to arrive at concrete truths.
8. Another potential source for this view of Ricardo's reluctance to publish is McCulloch (1853, p. 476), which was cited in Dunbar (1887, p. 474) to which Marshall (1961, I p. 813 n.2) referred in this context. Such an interpretation can now be refuted from Sraffa's research (Ricardo, 1951–73, I p. xx) and the Ricardo-James Mill correspondence not available to Marshall. Marshall's view that Ricardo wrote mainly for 'businessmen' and that this explains his shortcomings in exposition is repeated in *Money, Credit and Commerce* (Marshall, 1923, p. 167). See also Gonner (1890, p. 287).
9. Cf. Marshall to L. L. Price (19/8/1892) where Ricardo is described as an

exception to the general proposition that the substance of economic thought cannot be ascribed to the work of one man (in Pigou, 1925, p. 379).
10. Marshall's interest in this evidence is still visible in the pencil marks and comments he made in his personal copies of the Ricardo correspondence preserved in the Marshall Library, where passages relating to demand in isolation, or to supply and demand, are invariably marked. See note 6 above.
11. Marshall gathered his textual evidence from the first section of Chapter I of Ricardo's *Principles* and the second paragraph of Chapter IV (Ricardo, 1952–73, I pp. 11, 12, 88) but gives no detailed page references to the chapter on Value and Riches. This illustrates Hutchison's charge (1952, p. 423) that 'Marshall never quotes more than a couple of lines of Ricardo's words consecutively' though even this is an exaggeration. Apart from Marshall's quotes from Ricardo's correspondence with Malthus and passages from the *Principles* quoted in Appendix L, Marshall quotes *words* rather than lines from Ricardo. Marshall's argument on marginal and total utility in Ricardo is persuasively criticized by Stigler (1965a, pp. 75–7) who concludes that it 'should be added to the list of examples of [Marshall's] peculiar documentation and interpretation of predecessors'. Hollander (1979, p. 279 n. 25) argues that 'Stigler's reaction to Marshall's interpretation' is 'rather too harsh' because 'Marshall was not far from the truth is this matter' but his argument in support of his criticism of Stigler is not convincing.
12. While discussing the measurement of general purchasing power, Marshall argued in the passage referred to that labour and corn were considered reasonable measures for that purpose in the times of Smith and Ricardo. He added that 'it is necessary to interpret "classical" doctrines as to value by reference to it'. Support for the association between Ricardo's Chapter I and measurement of the purchasing power of money is implied in Hollander (1904), to which Marshall referred in the *Principles*. Marshall's comment was probably inspired by Cannan's (1898, pp. 305–6) argument that 'we are indebted to the Bullion controversy for the Ricardian theory of value ... and that therefore Ricardo's interests were as practical as those of Malthus'.
13. For example, Jacob Hollander (1904, p. 455) implied that 'Marshall's distinct reappreciation [as was the case with other contributions] ... in no small degree replaced textual study'. Hutchison (1952, p. 423) strongly implies that Marshall gives no hint of ever having studied Ricardo's preface to the *Principles* which states his objectives so clearly and which differentiates them so strikingly from Marshall's aims. (Cf. Gonner, 1890, p. 282, who highlights this objective of Ricardo's economics.) It may be noted that the Marshall papers contain a draft reply to Ashley, presumably prepared for submission to the *Economic Journal*. Its thrust is that Ashley concedes what Marshall considered to be his major points in the interpretation of Ricardo on value: that Ricardo included interest on capital in value as a matter of course and that Ricardo appreciated that his rule that 'exchange values will be proportionate to the amount of labour spent on them' is modified 'when there are differences in the

proportions of fixed capital [and] in the rapidity with which the capital returns'. To Ashley's charge that 'Ricardo did not think these modifications touched the essence of his doctrine', Marshall replied that he had always admitted that 'it was very ill-judged' of Ricardo not to 'make continuous reference' to these modifications. (Cabinet file 8, Miscellaneous documents).

14. Earlier work (for example, Marshall and Marshall, 1881, p. 85 n.1) had criticized both Mill and Ricardo on this subject, but in the *Principles* Ricardo is vindicated and J. S. Mill is not. Appendix L shows Mill's 'acute logical mind' to be 'unequal to the task' of correctly analyzing the effects of agricultural improvements on rent, a clear example of the elevation of Ricardo and the downgrading of Mill in Marshall's published evaluation of their work as he grew older.

15. Marshall's interpretation of Ricardo's wage theory is vindicated by Samuel Hollander (1979, pp. 555–7) but Hollander fails to note that Marshall never referred to Ricardo's doctrines of market wage determination and that, in general, he had a rather poor opinion of Ricardo's contributions to wage theory. See Marshall (1961, I p. 550 n.1 and cf. his letter to J. B. Clark, 2 July 1900, in Pigou, 1925, p. 413). In an earlier paper, Marshall (1961, II pp. 598–614) had stated that Ricardo 'had very little sympathy one way or the other with a desire to diminish the evils of poverty' and that he never acted as an 'earnest and fearless friend of the working class' (ibid., p. 599).

16. Sraffa (introduction to Ricardo, 1951–73, 1 p. liii) comments on this passage in Marshall as an indication that Malthus was not the only person annoyed with Ricardo's habit of giving special meanings to common words.

17. Interestingly, both Barbour and Marshall are correct. The passage from Ricardo cited by Barbour (Q. 9840) on the silver standard is from his 1816 Proposal, section III (Ricardo, 1951–73, IV, p. 73) in which Ricardo also argued that silver is preferred because of its more stable value. As Marshall correctly indicates, Ricardo's ingot plan proposed in the subsequent section was based on gold bullion in bars of 'not less than twenty ounces', though a footnote to this passage suggests that the weight is immaterial and there are good reasons for making them either ten or thirty ounces in weight (Ricardo, 1951–73, IV pp. 66–7 and note * on p. 66). In the Appendix to the fourth edition of his *High Price of Bullion*, 1811, which was also published as a separate pamphlet, Ricardo had first proposed his gold ingot plan (Ricardo, 1951–73, III p. 124).

18. Marshall conceded the point because he had found it in a footnote to Ricardo's 1816 proposal (Ricardo, 1951–73, IV p. 67 note *) which he had not previously noticed and which he had looked up in the interval. It is ironic to note that Ricardo changed his mind on the matter in his evidence to a later House of Lords Committee on the resumption of specie payments (24 March 1819, question 36) where he stated that he now preferred gold as the standard because it had become 'the more invariable metal' as a result of improvements in the production of silver through the introduction of better machinery (Ricardo, 1951–73, V p. 427). Neither Marshall nor the members of the Royal Commission

appear to have been aware of Ricardo's change of mind, though Marshall knew of the 1819 House of Lords Committee and referred to it (Marshall, 1923, pp. 67, 83, n.1).
19. An example of the latter is Marshall's discussion of productive and unproductive labour (Marshall, 1961, I pp. 65–67); another noted specifically by Stigler (1941, p. 63) is his 'unsatisfactory treatment of diminishing returns, . . . capital theory and the marginal productivity theory'.
20. With Marshall in mind, Stigler (1965b, p. 449) has dubbed this 'personal exegesis' to contrast it with scientific exegesis which relies on the consistency of an interpretation 'with the main analytical conclusion of the system of thought under consideration' (ibid, p. 448). It is interesting to note that in this paper Stigler illustrates these notions of exegesis by an example drawn from Marshall (1961, I, pp. 833–4, 836) on whether Ricardo customarily assumed zero elasticity of demand for corn (Stigler, 1965b, p. 447). As shown in the previous discussion of Marshall's Appendix L where such an assumption is made on Ricardo's behalf, in order to validate his conclusions as Marshall implies, the question is never raised whether Ricardo had made such an assumption or whether it was a meaningful one in the light of his theoretical conceptions. Hollander (1979, pp. 643–6) has defended personal exegesis à la Marshall.
21. In the various revisions of this chapter I have incurred debts to a large number of people, often at the various seminars at which a much earlier version was presented. I am indebted to the Librarian of the Marshall Library and the Faculty of Economics and Politics for permission to quote from unpublished Marshall manuscripts in their possession.

BIBLIOGRAPHY

Ashley, W. J. (1891) 'The Rehabilitation of Ricardo', *Economic Journal*, 1, pp. 474–89.

Bagehot, Walter (1879) 'Ricardo' in *Economic Studies*, third edition (London: Longmans, Green and Co.).

Bharadwaj, K. (1978) 'The Subversion of Classical Analysis: Alfred Marshall's Early Writings on Value', *Cambridge Journal of Economics*, 2, pp. 253–71.

Bonar, James (1887) *Letters of David Ricardo to Thomas Robert Malthus 1810–1823* (Oxford: Clarendon Press).

Bonar, James (1923) 'Ricardo's Ingot Plan: A Centenary Tribute', *Economic Journal*, 33, pp. 281–304.

Bonar, James and Hollander, Jacob (1899) *Letters of David Ricardo to Hutchess Trower and Others* (Oxford: Clarendon Press).

Cannan, Edwin (1898) *A History of the Theories of Production and Distribution from 1776 to 1848*, third edition (London: Staples, 1917).

Dardi, Marco (1984) *Il giovane Marshall: accumulazione e mercato* (Bologna: Il Mulino).

Dobb, M. H. (1931) 'The Cambridge School', part of the article 'Economics', *The Encyclopaedia of the Social Sciences* (New York: Macmillan) vol. 5, pp. 368–71.
Dunbar, C. F. (1887) 'Ricardo's Use of Facts', *Quarterly Journal of Economics*, 1, pp. 474–6.
Fay, C. R. (1960) *The World of Adam Smith* (Cambridge: Heffer).
Garegnani, P. (1983) 'The Classical Theory of Wages and the Role of Demand Schedules in the Determination of Relative Prices', *American Economic Review*, 73, pp. 309–13.
Gonner, E. C. K. (1890) 'Ricardo and his Critics', *Quarterly Journal of Economics*, 4, pp. 276–90.
Haberler, G. (1936) *The Theory of International Trade* (London: William Hodge and Co.).
Hicks, J. R. (1965) *Capital and Growth* (Oxford: Clarendon Press).
Hollander, Jacob (1895) *Letters of David Ricardo to John Ramsay McCulloch*, published for the American Economic Association (London: Swan, Sonnenschein and Co.).
Hollander, Jacob (1904) 'The Development of Ricardo's Theory of Value', *Quarterly Journal of Economics*, 18, pp. 455–91.
Hollander, Samuel (1979) *The Economics of David Ricardo* (London: Heinemann).
Hutchison, T. W. (1952) 'Some Questions about Ricardo', *Economica*, N. S. 19, pp. 415–32.
Keynes, J. M. (1925) 'Alfred Marshall 1842–1924', in Pigou (1925), pp. 1–65.
Loasby, B. J. (1978) 'Whatever Happened to Marshall's Theory of Value', *Scottish Journal of Political Economy*, 25, February, pp. 1–12, reprinted in *Alfred Marshall. Critical Assessments*, edited J. C. Wood (London: Croom Helm, 1983) vol. III, pp. 586–99.
McCulloch, J. R. (1853) *Treatises and Essays on Subjects Connected with Economical Policy with Biographical Sketches of Quesnay, Adam Smith and Ricardo* (Edinburgh: Adam and Charles Black).
Marshall, Alfred (1921) *Industry and Trade*, third edition (London: Macmillan).
Marshall, Alfred (1923) *Money, Credit and Commerce* (London: Macmillan).
Marshall, Alfred (1926) *Official Papers*, ed. J. M. Keynes (London: Macmillan).
Marshall, Alfred (1933) 'Alfred Marshall, the Mathematician, as seen by himself', *Econometrica*, 1, pp. 221–2.
Marshall, Alfred (1961) *Principles of Economics*, ninth (variorum) edition with annotations by C. W. Guillebaud (London: Macmillan).
Marshall, Alfred and Marshall, Mary P. (1879) *The Economics of Industry*, first edition (London: Macmillan and Co.).
Marshall, Alfred and Marshall, Mary P. (1881) *The Economics of Industry*, second edition (London: Macmillan and Co.).
Pasinetti, L. L. (1960) 'A Mathematical Formulation of the Ricardian System', *Review of Economic Studies*, 27, February, pp. 78–88, reprinted in L. L. Pasinetti, *Growth and Income Distribution* (Cambridge: Cambridge University Press, 1974) pp. 1–28.

Pasinetti, L. L. (1977) *Lectures on the Theory of Production* (London: Macmillan).
Pasinetti, L. L. (1981) *Structural Change and Economic Growth. A Theoretical Essay on the Dynamics of the Wealth of Nations* (Cambridge: Cambridge University Press).
Pasinetti, L. L. (1986) 'Theory of Value – a Source of Alternative Paradigms in Economic Analysis', in *Foundations of Economics*, edited Mauro Baranzini and Roberto Scazzieri (Oxford: Blackwell) pp. 409–31.
Pigou, A. C. (1925) *Memorials of Alfred Marshall* (London: Macmillan).
Ricardo, David (1951–73) *The Works and Correspondence of David Ricardo*, edited by Piero Sraffa with the collaboration of M. H. Dobb (Cambridge: Cambridge University Press).
Robinson, Austin (1972) 'Alfred Marshall', *History of Economic Thought Newsletter*, 8, Spring, pp. 14–17.
Robinson, Austin (1973) 'Alfred Marshall: A Further Note', *History of Economic Thought Newsletter*, 10, Spring, pp. 12–16.
Schumpeter, J. A. (1954) *History of Economic Analysis* (London: Allan and Unwin).
Shove, G. F. (1942) 'The Place of Marshall's *Principles* in the Development of Economic Theory', *Economic Journal*, 52, pp. 294–329.
Stigler, G. J. (1941) *Production and Distribution Theory. The Formative Period* (New York: The Macmillan Company).
Stigler, G. J. (1965a) *Essays in the History of Economics* (Chicago: Chicago University Press).
Stigler, G. J. (1965b) 'Textual Exegesis as a Scientific Problem', *Economica*, N. S. 32, pp. 446–50.
Toynbee, Arnold (1913) 'Ricardo and the Old Political Economy', in *Lectures on the Industrial Revolution of the Eighteenth Century in England, Popular Addresses, Notes and Other Fragments* (London: Longmans, Green and Co.).
Viner, Jacob (1937) *Studies in the Theory of International Trade* (New York: Harper and Brothers).
Whitaker, John (1975) *The Early Economic Writings of Alfred Marshall 1867–1890* (London: Macmillan).

2 Physiocratic Dichotomy in Price Determination and Its Ricardian Resolution*

Izumi Hishiyama

INTRODUCTION

I indicated and analyzed in my early works the physiocratic dichotomy in the determination of price, in criticizing chiefly A. Oncken's and A. Kubota's view of Quesnay's value theory.[1] Quite recently I was very impressed by G. Vaggi's argument about the point at issue in his interesting book on Quesnay's economics.[2] I want therefore to reconsider, in the following pages, that physiocratic dichotomy, particularly throwing light on the phases of its life cycle, that is to say, its birth in Quesnay's mind, its succession via Turgot and Smith, and its death as a result of Ricardo's fatal blow. I hope one facet of Ricardo's contribution to classical political economy will be clarified by this short attempt.

PHYSIOCRATIC DICHOTOMY IN PRICE DETERMINATION

A striking characteristic in Quesnay's physiocratic system is that there is a dichotomy between the determination of the price of agricultural products and that of manufactured goods, in accordance with another dichotomy, in which agriculture is considered to be productive in the sense of generating net product (*produit net*), namely surplus product, and manufacture to be unproductive, or rather sterile, in the sense of not generating net product. Consider the following excerpts quoted from Quesnay's controversial article.

> Les productions, indépendamment des frais de culture, ont leur prix réglé par leur quantité et par la concurrence des acheteurs,

dont les besoins surpassent toujours la masse de la reproduction. Donc l'épargne qu'on fait sur les dépenses du cultivateur, quoiqu'elle augmente la portion qui excède les frais, n'en diminue pas le prix, et par conséquent la reproduction n'en est *pas moins richesse*.

Au contraire, dans les ouvrages de l'artisan, il n'y a nul surcroît de richesses au-delà de ses dépenses, comme on l'a prouvé; ainsi plus on épargne sur ses dépenses, *moins ses ouvrages sont richesses*.

Ces observations, qui, sans doute vous sont familières, devaient, mon ami, vous faire remarquer la différence qu'il y a entre l'effet des dépenses de la culture, et celui des dépenses des artisans, et surtout entre la valeur des richesses que le travail de la culture fait naître et la valeur des ouvrages de l'artisan. (Quesnay, 1888, pp. 551–2; 1958, p. 910; author's italics)

In the above excerpts one can clearly see the dichotomy in the means of determining prices; the fundamental idea is that the price of manufactured goods is, under competitive conditions, regulated according to the cost of production, while the price of the agricultural products is, or should be, something above and independent of, the cost of production.

To clarify Quesnay's theory of price, we must first look for his peculiar terminology relating to the prices of commodities. First of all, it should be noticed that there exists, in Quesnay's writings, a clear definition of wealth; that is, the goods (*biens*) which have both use value (*valeur usuelle*) and market value (*valeur vénale*) are called wealth (*richesse*).[3] Here, we must proceed into the concept of market value (*valeur vénale*) more carefully. The *valeur vénale* does, above all, belong to the price of sellers at first hand (*le prix du vendeur de la première main*), i.e. the original producer's price, which is distinguished from the price of the purchaser-consumer (*le prix de l'acheteur-consommateur*).[4]

Moreover, price refers not to individual exchanges of commodities but to the circulation of products between the different expenditure classes which is termed the *circulation* in the *Tableau Economique*. In other words, Quesnay's *valeur vénale* is not a similar concept to Smith's 'value in exchange'; the latter means the power of purchasing other commodities which the possession of one commodity infers in *individual exchanges*, while the former means the value in exchange of one object at the point of sale by the original producer, more specifically, the value realized at the point of sale by the productive expenditure class under the *circulation*, assumed in the *Tableau Economique*. Hence, it may be useful to quote the following excerpts from the third edition of the *Tableau Economique*.

> Par *circulation*, on entend ici les achats de la première main, payés par le revenu qui se partage à toutes les classes d'hommes, distraction faite du *commerce*, qui multiplie les ventes et les achats, sans multiplier les choses, et qui n'est qu'un surcroît de dépenses stériles. (Quesnay, 1972, p. V; my italics)

It might be desirable at this stage to pay attention to Quesnay's methodological concept; Quesnay seems to prefer always to approach price formation from the macro or rather multi-sectorial background of circular process of annual reproduction with the aggregate sectors interconnected with one another,[5] although it is today taken for granted that the problem is considered from the conventional *general equilibrium* viewpoint in traditional economics. I think this methodological framing of Quesnay in face of price-formation phenomena should not be neglected even though he never brought it to fruition.[6]

Now, let us return to the main theme. Compared to market value (*valeur vénale*), there is, in Quesnay's works, the current price (*prix courant*) which is, I think, a rather treacherous concept; the current price may, at first sight, be regarded as a similar concept to Smith's 'market price' which is altered by temporary and accidental causes, but, in fact, it is emphasized by Quesnay that the 'current price' or 'actual price' (*prix actuel*) depends on general causes – which are concerned with the question of whether the products are abundant or not, and whether the competition between sellers and purchasers resulting from haggling is severe or not.[7] In short, Quesnay is chiefly interested in disclosing the logical and chronological priority of price formation in advance of the individual exchanges in the market. Thus, it would not necessarily be easy to distinguish among these expressions: *prix courant* (current price), *prix actuel* (actual price) and *prix absolu* (absolute price).[8]

It is supposed that even the market value (*valeur vénale*), as mentioned above, is expressed or computed in terms of 'absolute price', which is identified with the average price – a price arrived at by averaged higher prices in the years of bad harvests and lower prices in the years of good harvests.[9]

However, from the viewpoint of mainstream value theories

springing from Quesnay's thought, it should be stressed that we are analyzing the physiocratic relation between 'market value' and 'fundamental price' (*prix fondamental*), as seen in the next section.

PRICE OF AGRICULTURAL PRODUCTS AND THEIR COST OF PRODUCTION

The highest level, as far as possible, which the 'market value' (*valeur vénale*) of wheat will reach under free competition, is called *bon prix*, in Quesnay's terminology; this is sometimes termed *cherté* (dearness), or *haut prix* (high price). It should be noticed that these are all synonymous and assumed to be realized under competitive conditions.

Now, Quesnay regarded *bon prix* to be the alpha and omega of economic science (*la science économique*).[10] In other words, it should be more appropriate to state that the concept (*bon prix*) is the sheet anchor on which the Quesnay-type 'Essay on Prices' (*Essai sur les prix*)[11] is built.

Then let us enter in detail into the relation between the market value and the fundamental price (*le prix fondamental*) which means the cost of production in the annual production of corn. First of all, we may quote here, as it were, the *locus classicus* of the point at issue.

> Ce ne sont donc pas simplement les productions du territoire d'un royaume qui forment les revenus de la nation; il faut encore que ces productions aient une valeur vénale qui excède *le prix des frais de l'exploitation de la culture*. Il n'y a que cet excédent qui puisse fournir le revenu ou le produit net. Ainsi, plus cet excédent surpassera les frais, plus la nation aura de revenu. (Quesnay, 1958, pp. 691–2; my italics)

> Si le prix qu'on les vend n'est pas au-dessus du *prix fondamental*[12] qu'elles [*les productions*; my comment] coûtent, elles dégénèrent en perte pour les cultivateurs, elles ne produisent donc des revenus qu'autant que leurs prix surpassent les frais, ou les dépenses qu' elles exigent: ainsi le plus haut prix qu'elles peuvent acquérir constamment par le commerce avec l'étranger, profite à l'État, aux propriétaires, au peuple, à la population et à l'abondance. (ibid., pp. 534–5; my italics)

Dichotomy in Price Determination

Looking at manufactured goods, the price is, as mentioned above, considered to be ultimately regulated by the cost of production, which comprizes food and raw materials – consumed in the manufacturing process – for the master and artisans who work together. Thus, Quesnay has pointed out that '*dans les ventes de la classe stérile, cette classe ne vend que des valeurs de pures dépenses en frais*'.[13] In other words, the 'net product' is never *realized* at the sale of the manufactured goods; for, in manufacturing, it is considered net product, is never *produced* and, at the sale of goods, only the exact equivalent is realized.

In a striking contrast with manufacturing, the productive class, of which the representative is the cultivator, is not only able to replace the value of his annual expenditures, but also to produce 'net product' which is, or should be, in absolute freedom of trade, realized at the point of sale of the products. Moreover it goes without saying that the realized 'net product' comes to pass into the hand of the proprietor as his revenue.

It was frequently emphasized by Quesnay himself that net product or surplus product is never generated in the exchange process, since, according to Quesnay, an exchange is nothing but exchange between equivalents.[14] It may be said, therefore, that the problem concerning '*bon prix*', i.e. the highest market value which entails net product, that is, surplus value above the cost of production, is, in one sense, concerned with a so-called realization problem; i.e. the problem of whether or not the surplus products, generated in the (agricultural) production process, are realized in the market, more specifically, in the 'circulation' of annual reproduction as defined in *Tableau Economique*.[15]

A crucial point under discussion is, however, what can determine the *bon prix*, that is, the highest – exceeding the costs as far as possible under the free competition – market value (*valeur vénale*) of the products; whereas, in the *Tableau Economique*, to single out clearly the circular process of whole reproduction, the *bon prix* of the produce of land is assumed to be fixed as a constant, from beginning to end of the process, abstracting from the determination of market value.

In Quesnay's works emphasis is, quite often, placed upon the absolute freedom of foreign trade[16] as a condition indispensable to the maintenance of the constant level of *bon prix* in the transaction of the produce of land. It may be considered that two results are consequential to Quesnay-type free trade, equalization of prices and reduction of transaction costs.

At first, by means of the transference of the excess products from some nations (or provinces in the same nation) with good harvests to other nations (or provinces) with bad harvests, we can see common price, i.e. uniform price, coming into existence among the nations (provinces) in free transactions with one another.

We shall cite here the relevant quotations as follows:

> Par la liberté et la facilité du commerce extérieur d'exportation et d'importation, les grains ont constamment un prix plus égal, car le prix le plus égal est celui qui a cours entre les nations commerçantes. Ce commerce aplanit en tout temps l'inégalité annuelle des récoltes des nations en apportant tour à tour chez celles qui sont dans la pénurie le superflu de celles qui sont dans l'abondance, ce qui remet partout et toujours les productions et les prix à peu près au même niveau. (Quesnay, 1888, p. 352; 1958, p. 971)

Secondly, a merchant who is given monopoly power from the state will endeavour to obtain the maximum gain as far as possible by means of decreasing 'the price of seller at first hand' (*le prix du vendeur de la première main*) and increasing 'the price of the purchaser-consumer' (*le prix de l'acheteur-consommateur*); the former price will, however, be bidding up and on the other hand the latter price bidding down through Quesnay-type free trade, whether the sales and purchases can be effected through domestic or external trade.

It goes without saying that the merchants' gain implies the (transaction) costs from the standpoint of the original producers and of the final consumers; and, therefore, the reduction in the merchants' gain is nothing but a saving in the transaction costs. It may be added that Quesnay is entirely aware of those advantages which the regime of absolute free competition, if adopted, would make possible for the nation to obtain. Thus he puts it as follows:

> La nation ne doit donc avoir plus de prédilection pour les uns que pour les autres dans la concurrence de son commerce, qu'autant qu'elle ne préjudiciera point à cette concurrence générale, qui est toute à son avantage par l'épargne sur les frais du commerce et par la communication des prix entre les nations commerçantes. (Quesnay, 1888, p. 486; 1958, p. 851)

Dichotomy in Price Determination

Even though, according to Quesnay's assumption, the absolute freedom of trade would, as already seen above, make possible the establishment of a uniform price, which is called *le bon prix*, not only in one nation's market but also in all markets throughout the world. In other words, Quesnay's free trade would be a presumption of the coming into existence of *le bon prix*; it does not by any means imply the determining factor of the price. We are therefore not sure, up to this point, what kind of factors would determine the uniform price of wheat prevailing in every market, or, for what reason it would be considered to make the market value (*la valeur vénale*) normally exceed the costs of production (*le prix fondamental*) so as to generate constantly 'net product' (*produit net*). This is the main topic of the next section.

THE FACTORS THAT DETERMINE MARKET VALUE

If we look at the factors which determine or regulate the market value of *agricultural products*, it may be said that Quesnay would refrain from pinning down a single determining factor. Or rather, in short, he may be reluctant to single out for certain some basic factor that uniquely regulates the value. It seems to me, at first sight, that Quesnay would be ambiguous and even irresolute as to this point. To say the least, we may be sure that he has never achieved the complete 'Essay on Prices' (*Essai sur les prix*), although he could not refrain from expressing his hope to do so.[17]

Consider the following excerpts which, I think, hint at the subject.

> *Le prix est la valeur vénale des richesses commerçables.* Ainsi on ne doit pas confondre le prix des richesses commerçables avec leur valeur usuelle, car ces deux valeurs n'ont souvent aucune corespondance entre elles. La valeur usuelle est toujours la même, et toujours plus ou moins intéressante pour les hommes, selon les rapports qu'elle a avec leurs besoins, avec leur désir d'en jouir. Mais le prix au contraire varie, et dépend des différentes causes aussi inconstantes qu'indépendantes de la volonté des hommes: en sorte qu'il ne se règle point sur les besoins des hommes, et n'est point d'une valeur arbitraire ou de convention entre les commerçants! (Quesnay, 1958, p. 526; author's italics)

It seems to me that Quesnay, even if not explicitly, is about to propose the famous Smith's 'diamond and water' example; it is to be noted that he will prefer the non-subjective to the subjective view which rests ultimately on individual human desire and will, in a word, on man's preference.

It may be better to call the above-mentioned view on value, the objective rather than non-subjective view, although we may suggest the relativity of the use-value; for Quesnay regarded the market value (*la valeur vénale*) as a certain concept depending on the various and indefinite causes which are independent of man's will.

It is necessary to reconsider, though we have previously mentioned it as compared with Smith's 'value in exchange', that the market value of the products, more specifically, 'the market value in sales of the products at first hand' is 'the absolute price' (*le prix absolu*) which exists well before the circular process in Quesnay's *Tableau Economique* and which is realized at the '*circulation*' between the different classes required for society's annual reproduction.

Let us look at the following extracts in this context, that is, with respect to the features of the market value of *agricultural products*.

> De valeur, dis-je, qui existait d'un côté et de l'autre avant l'échange; ainsi, dans le fait, l'échange ne produit rien. (Quesnay, 1888, p. 389; 1958, p. 753)

My preliminary comment is this: to find out the determining factors of value, Quesnay would not enter the exchange market, for it appears to him that value is never to be determined in the exchange market but is something in advance of exchange and independent of man's volition regarding exchange, to use Smith's words, 'the propensity to exchange one thing for another'.[18]

Thus it may be said that in the attempt he would be forced to take a further step into the circular process of production as a whole in society; that is to say, as a physical mixture from which the values spring directly, he ought to have brought into his analysis the physical or objective and interindustrial complex -- that technological leviathan -- which operates absolutely independently of man's will as if, as he once put it, '*le monde va de lui-même*'.[19]

However, even though we have viewed his attempt in a favourable light, it should be said that he stopped before the gate of such an intricate construction and could not enter it; in short, he was unable to complete the theory of value. He was still less able to formulate a systematic and satisfactory view on the determining factors of market value, although he is in his *Tableau Economique* the first to postulate the system of annual reproduction as a circular process under the assumption of the *constant market value* in the produce of land.

Having been interested in the study of value so as to refute the utility theory of Condillac, Le Trosne, one of Quesnay's disciples, seems not to propose any more systematic view than that of Quesnay; or, in short, he only enumerates one by one the various causes seemingly relevant to value determination, i.e. utilities, fundamental prices (costs of production), scarcity or abundance, competition, and finally products in themselves.[20]

TURGOT'S VIEW ON MARKET VALUE

Let us, by way of an interlude, make an excursion. That is to say, we proceed to consider here Turgot's view on the market value in *the produce of land*, for he is commonly considered to be in one sense the reformer of Quesnay and at the same time the forerunner of Smith in the formation of modern economic thought.

It is, as in the case of Quesnay, a fundamental value (*une valeur fondamentale*) that implies the costs of production, i.e. '*les frais de la matière première, intérêt des avances, salaires du travail et de l'industrie*'[21] ('the costs consisting of raw materials, interests on advances, and salaries (or wages) of labour and industry'); and since the market value (*la valeur vénale*) implies '*le prix dont l'acheteur convient avec le vendeur*' ('the seller's price agreed by the purchaser'), there is no possibility of a difference between 'the price of the purchaser-consumer' and 'the price of the seller at first hand'. In other words, it is assumed that 'the price of the purchaser-consumer' is always equal to 'the price of the seller at first hand'. Thus it is in Turgot's case taken for granted that there is absolute free competition; that is a Quesnay-type free trade, as we have designated it in a previous section.[22]

How then, does he consider the relation between 'the market value' and 'the fundamental value' with regard to the pricing process in *the produce of land*? Turgot said that, although the fundamental value is a relatively fixed price, the market value is mainly regulated by demand and supply of the products.

Consider first the following quotations.

Elle [la valeur vénale, my comment] n'a pas une proportion nécessaire avec la valeur fondamentale, parce qu'elle dépend immédiatement d'un principe tout différent; mais *elle tend continuellement à s'en rapprocher, et ne peut guère s'en éloigner beaucoup d'une manière permanente.* (Turgot, 1844, p. 431, note 1; 1914, p. 656 note 1; my italics)

Turgot obviously grasps that there is a basic difference between the principle of supply and demand and that of costs of production; the market value is regulated by the former, but the fundamental value is regulated by the latter.

As I have shown above by my italics, Turgot seems to comprehend the relation between the fundamental value and the market value as being nearly the same as the classic relation between the natural price and the market price, clearly formalized in *The Wealth of Nations*.[23] That is to say, Smith's natural price is assumed to be, as it were, the central price towards which the ever fluctuating market price is, in the long run, attracted; and Turgot's fundamental price is situated in almost the same position as Smith's natural price, in the self-regulating system.

Let us now mention Turgot's words concerning the self-regulating price system:

Il est évident qu'elle [la valeur vénale, my comment] ne peut rester longtemps au-dessous; car, dès qu'une denrée ne peut se vendre qu'à perte, on cesse de la faire produire jusqu'à ce que la rareté l'ait ramenée à un prix au-dessus de la valeur fondamentale. Ce prix ne peut non plus être longtemps fort au-dessus de la valeur fondamentale, car le gros prix, offrant de gros profits, appellerait la denrée et ferait naître une vive concurrence entre les vendeurs. Or, l'effet naturel de cette concurrence serait de baisser les prix et de les rapprocher de la valeur fondamentale. (ibid., p. 656 note 1)

Concerning this, Quesnay's view is quite different from Turgot's. For the fundamental value is, in Quesnay's case, considered to be, as it were, the *floor* price below which the market value cannot fall for a long time; while, in Turgot's case, it is considered to be the *central* price as mentioned above; and therefore, the market value turns out ultimately to settle in and equal the fundamental value. As a result the Quesnay-type problem of realization of the net product disappears in this case.

It may be better to state in Quesnay's case that the market value is considered to rise, under the absolute freedom of trade, beyond the fundamental value and to maintain the level of '*le bon prix*' so as to realize constantly the net product (*produit net*). That is to say 'the market value' *does* in the case 'deviate considerably therefrom (from the fundamental price, my comment) on a long term basis'. Furthermore, it should be added that Quesnay assumes the situation to be desirable and natural.

SMITH'S VIEW ON PRICING OF PRODUCE OF LAND

Smith's view is very delicate regarding the price of wheat which is considered to be 'the principal produce of land' used in Europe as human food and regarding the continuity of rent which is afforded in corn production.[25]

In Smith's 'advanced or improved society' coming into existence *after* the accumulation of stock and the appropriation of land, rent, together with wages and profit, is one of the component parts in the price of the produce of land.

Therefore, as to the price of wheat, 'the whole price still resolves itself either immediately or ultimately into the *same* three parts of rent, labour [wages, my comment] and profit'.[26]

While the price of wheat resolves itself into the *undistinguished* or *homogeneous* component parts, it is also obtained by the adding-up of these three parts. It is to be noted that wages, profit, and rent are, in Smith's concept, considered not only to be the three component parts of the price of a separate commodity as mentioned above, but also to be the three sources of total national income.

To sum up, as far as Ch. VI 'Of the Component Parts of the Price of Commodities' in Book I is concerned,[27] Smith stated clearly that rent, together with wages and profit, plays a quite similar (that is, undistinguished or homogeneous) role, both as the component part of the price and as the source of the income. In short, the three component parts rank equally, each of them playing a quite similar role.

But, in contrast to this, looking at the role of each component part in the determination of the price of wheat, Smith seems to assume that rent plays a quite distinguished or heterogeneous role as opposed to the other component parts, i.e. wages and profit.

Consider the following relevant excerpts.

> Rent, it is to be observed, therefore, enters into the composition of the price of commodities in a different way from wages and profit.

High or low wages and profit are the causes of high or low price; high or low rent is the effect of it. It is because high or low wages and profit must be paid, in order to bring a particular commodity to market, that its price is high or low. But it is because its price is high or low; a great deal more, or very little more, or no more, than what is sufficient to pay those wages and profit, that it affords a high rent, or a low rent, or no rent at all. (Smith, 1950, p. 147)

Smith clarifies that, in the determination of the price of wheat, rent will occupy the opposite end to wages and profit in the causal nexus, because rent is the effect but wages and profit are the cause in the pricing process.

Thus, although rent is, together with wages and profit, the third part of the price, it is considered to play its role in a quite different way from others (wages and profit) in the pricing. Therefore, rent is, in one sense, assumed to be a purely passive element because its existence and extent will depend on whether or, if any, to what extent, the price is able to increase beyond the sum of wages and profit; in other words rent has no part in the determination of price.

Now let us consider how the price of wheat is determined; and what are regarded to be the determining factors of the price. Although, as I have already indicated, Quesnay did not make an unambiguous answer to these questions, we shall see what is considered to be Smith's response to them.

The following quotations appear relevant to the present topic.

Such parts only of the produce of land can commonly be brought to market of which *the ordinary price* is sufficient to replace the stock which must be employed in bringing them thither, together with its ordinary profits. If the ordinary price is more than this, the surplus part of it will naturally go to the rent of the land. If it is not more, though the commodity may be brought to market, it can afford no rent to the landlord. *Whether the price is, or is not more, depends upon the demand.* (Smith, ibid. p. 146; my italics)

Suppose now that Quesnay's 'market value' (*valeur vénale*) of the produce of land is a similar notion to Smith's 'ordinary price' and the costs of production[28] – suggested in the above quotations – which are replaced with ordinary profits correspond with Quesnay's *le prix fondamental* or *les frais*.

Simple comparison shows that the following two passages, the

Dichotomy in Price Determination

first by Adam Smith as quoted above, and the second by François Quesnay as I have already cited,[29] have a common logical construction.

> If the ordinary price is more than this, the surplus part of it will naturally go to the rent of the land. (Smith)

> Elles [les productions] ne produisent donc des revenus qu'autant que leurs prix surpassent les frais, ou les dépenses qu'elles exigent. (Quesnay)

To put it exactly, it is never completely clear in Quesnay's case whether the ordinary profits of capital employed by farmers are included in the costs of production i.e. *le prix fondamental* of their products; it is more difficult to say that Smithian uniform rate of profits in all trades is embraced in Quesnay's cost of production.[30]

But in so far as the *valeur vénale* (market value) of the produce of land may rise beyond the limits set by the costs of production (*le prix fondamental*), the 'net product' (*produit net*), that is, the excess value over costs, will be afforded. So, I think Quesnay's view is substantially similar to Smith's view on the origin of rent.

It should be noted, however, that in *The Wealth of Nations* Smith consistently insists upon the demand factor in the pricing of the produce of land. In other words, the *raison d'être* of excess value over costs, which will naturally go to rent, is obtained in the excess demand for the produce. Moreover it is assumed that there is not always such an excess demand for the produce of land in general, except for food, more specifically, for wheat. Thus he states: 'Human food seems to be the only produce of land which always and necessarily affords some rent to the landlord. Other sorts of produce sometimes may and sometimes may not, according to different circumstances'.[31]

Now, the principal produce of land which served then for human food in Europe was – as Smith points out – wheat; it is considered as a *specific* product which is distinguished from other produce of land. The reason is suggested in the following quotation:

> As men, like all other animals, naturally multiply in proportion to the means of their subsistence, food is always, more or less in demand. It can always purchase or command a greater or smaller quantity of labour ... (Smith, ibid. p. 147)

In short, food (or wheat), owing to its specific character, is, as it were, a demand-generating product.[32] Therefore, we shall always face a seller's market, that is, excess demand for wheat. That is why human food, or wheat, as Smith states, 'always and necessarily affords some rent to the landlord'. Since Quesnay, in the above cited excerpts,[33] states '*les besoins [des acheteurs] surpassent toujours la masse de la reproduction,*' it should be evident that he is thoroughly aware of the excess demand for wheat.

Nevertheless, as we have already seen, Quesnay does not pin down a single determining factor and he never attributes the permanent high price [over costs] (*la cherté permanente*) of wheat solely to such a demand factor – the excess demand in question.[34] At the same time, he always stresses universal free competition as a presupposition for *le bon prix*. It should be recalled here that he distinctly denies the notion that the market value [of wheat] is to be determined by man's requirements.[35]

RESOLUTION OF THE DICHOTOMY – THE MEANING OF RICARDO'S THEORY OF RENT

Everything becomes clear and distinct in a moment when we reach *The Principles*[36] of David Ricardo. It is Ricardo himself who ultimately resolves Quesnay's view on price which is echoed in *The Wealth of Nations*.

In contrast with Quesnay's view, Ricardo has adopted the notion that the exchange-values of all commodities, no matter whether they be manufactured or the produce of land, are always regulated by the same principle, that is the principle of costs of production.[37] As a result, Quesnay's dichotomy in the determination of prices, as considered in the preceding section, is definitely rejected by Ricardo in *The Principles*.

Now, what I have just called the principle of costs of production is clearly implied in Ricardo's statement that 'it is the cost of production which ultimately regulates price';[38] and 'the exchangeable value of all commodities' regulated by their costs is not an ever-fluctuating market price which depends on any temporary or accidental causes, but the central price, that is, the natural price.[39]

First, it should be noted that the necessity of having to consider the determination of price in the produce of land in the same way as the determination of price of manufactured goods implies the exclusion of rent from the component parts of the price. Since, according to Ricardo, it is the greatest quantity of labour, i.e. the greatest cost of production bestowed on the most inferior lands which pay no rent that regulates the price of the produce of land, rent cannot enter among the component parts of its price.[40]

Such an exclusion of rent from the component parts of the (natural) price, on the other hand, seems to have given rise to the establishment of what is called the Ricardian theory of differential rents of which the substance is briefly shown as follows: rent would always be equal to the difference between (lower) costs of wheat produced on superior lands and the greatest cost of the wheat produced on the most inferior land paying no rent and regulating its (natural) price.[41]

There is another aspect to be considered in the Ricardian theory of rent. The above-mentioned exclusion of rent from the component parts of price is inseparable from the purification of the Ricardian labour theory of value.

Now Ricardo's main theme 'On Rent' [Ch. II] is, it should be noticed, evident in the following quotation.

> It remains however to be considered, whether the appropriation of land, and the consequent creation of rent, will occasion any variation in the relative value of commodities, independent of the quantity of labour necessary for production. (Ricardo, *Works*, vol. 1, p. 67)

Ricardo, in relying on his own theory of rent, has given a negative answer to this question, in the sense that the labour principle of value can never be modified.[42] That is to say, although the establishment of the Ricardian theory of rent would, as may be perceived, accompany the resolution of the physiocratic dichotomy in the determination of price, it would also result in the verification of his labour principle of value.

Seen from a different angle, it might be said that the existence of the price of the produce of land which will be determined independently of its cost of production – the physiocratic dichotomy of price-determination which is echoed in Smith's view – seems to be, as it were, a black point which always disturbs attempts to single out or purify the principle of cost of production and, consequently, the labour principle of value.

Such a black point has been, it may be said, eradicated by means of the establishment of Ricardo's theory of differential rent; what is important in the accomplishment of the theory of rent in the Ricardian system is – though one may see in it a sort of predecessor of marginal theory – firstly, its genetic role of completing the labour theory of value and, secondly, its offensive role of resolving the physiocratic-Smithian dichotomy of price-determination.[43]

It should also be noticed that Ricardo definitely decides to reject the notion – which springs from physiocracy and develops with Smith – that rent is regarded as *'dons de la terre'* (gifts of the land).[44] Although such a notion was chiefly developed by Quesnay's disciple,[45] we cannot say that Quesnay is in no way responsible for the notion's development.

In considering, in any case, from Ricardo's viewpoint, it is not 'the gifts of land' but 'the niggardliness of nature' that is the genuine cause which will afford rent; in other words, a physical presupposition of affording rent is not inexhaustible productivity of land but diminishing returns of land;[46] and therefore it is not true that, agriculture, both in regard to its capacity to provide employment and in regard to the value-added productivity per unit of its productive labour – as Smith has indicated[47] – would be superior to manufacture.[48] Consequently, investment in agriculture is not considered necessarily and naturally to be the most advantageous to the public interest.

As may be seen, the essence of the Ricardian critique of Smith, or rather the physiocratic notion of rent is, interesting enough, explicitly suggested in the following passages – quoted from Ricardo's *Principles* – of David Buchanan, an early editor of *The Wealth of Nations*.

> The notion of agriculture yielding a produce, and a rent in consequence, because nature concurs with human industry in the process of cultivation, is a mere fancy. It is not from the produce, but from the price at which the produce is sold, that the rent is derived; and this price is got not because nature assists in the production, but because it is the price which suits the consumption to the supply. (Ricardo, vol. 1, p. 77)

Ricardo's rejection of the physiocratic notion inherited by Smith results in consideration of agriculture as a trade not distinguishable from manufacturing; and it becomes clear that both agriculture and manufacture are governed by the same rule, that is, the principle of costs of production in the determination of prices. Additionally Ricardo's rejection clearly implies in Classical Political Economy the final resolution of the dichotomy in price-determination or, in short, the end of physiocracy.

NOTES

* I should like to thank Haruo Hayashida, Ryûzô Kuroki, Tetsurô Kamiya and Masahiro Nei for their comments.
1. Cf. Hishiyama (1954), pp. 153–7; (1962), pp. 196–202, especially pp. 197–8. For Oncken's view see Oncken (1902), pp. 369–73, and for Kubota's view see Kubota, 1942, pp. 213–34.
2. Cf. Vaggi (1987), pp. 94–120 (Ch. 4: Capital, Competition and the origin of Surplus), especially pp. 101ff.
3. Cf. Quesnay (1888), p. 289 note (1); 1958, p. 652 note (11). See also, Quesnay (1888), p. 353; 1958, p. 972.
4. See Quesnay, (1888), p. 449; 1958, p. 816.
5. Marx would clarify the circulation assumed in the *Tableau Economique* ('*la Formule*') as follows: 'The innumerable individual acts of circulation are at once brought together in their characteristic social mass movement – the circulation between great functionally determined economic classes of society.' (Marx (1967), p. 363; 1963 b, p. 359).
6. According to Pasinetti's classification – a pure exchange versus a pure labour model – relating to the theory of value, the conventional general equilibrium theory seems to be reduced to 'a pure exchange, or pure preference model'. It may however be said that Quesnay's (albeit immature) theory of value would, if anything, point towards 'a pure labour model' or rather 'a pure production model' since his value theory seems ultimately to depend on the circular process in the *Tableau Economique*. See Pasinetti (1986), pp. 421–7; also (1981), pp. 23–5; (1977), pp. 1–32. This classification is ultimately based upon Pasinetti (1965), pp. 572–9.
7. A. Oncken appears to identify Quesnay's '*prix courant*' with Smith's 'market price' which is regulated by supply and demand and oscillates around its 'central price', i.e. the 'natural price'. See Oncken, 1902, p. 307:

> Hier ist zu unterscheiden zwischen dem natürlichen Preis (*prix naturel*) und dem laufenden Preis (*prix courant*). . . ., der letztere bewegt sich nach Angebot und Nachfrage und oscilliert beständig um das Niveau des natürlichen Preises.

It seems to me however that the exact definition of '*prix courant*' is shown in the following quotations: 'les prix constants qui *ont cours entre* les nations commerçantes, dans le cas où il y a constamment une libre concurrence de commerce . . .' (Quesnay (1888), p. 309; (1958), pp. 794–5, my italics). It is therefore better to state that current price (*prix courant*) is equal to natural price (*prix naturel*) because according to Quesnay

> l'effet de la communication du commerce par la libre concurrence est d'entretenir le niveau entre les prix chez les différentes nations qui commercent entre elles; cette compensation universelle des prix forme leur état naturel . . . Je dis que c'est l'état naturel des prix, parce que

la libre concurrence du commerce est une dépendance naturelle du commerce. (Quesnay (1888), pp. 463–4; (1958), pp. 829–30)

8. Cf. Quesnay (1888), p. 388; (1958), p. 752: 'Or c'est sur ce prix absolu, auquel la classe stérile elle-même est assujettie préalablement à ses achats, que sont établis dans le Tableau économique les calculs de la valeur vénale des productions que la classe productive fait naître.'
It follows that the market value (*la valeau vénale*) of the products is, after all, reduced to the absolute price, prior to purchase by the unproductive expenditure class.

9. Cf. Quesnay (1888), p. 388; (1958), p. 752. Notice the expression 'ce prix même, réduit en année commune', referring to the absolute price which is equal to the market value of products. See also Quesnay (1888), p. 323; (1958), p. 808: 'celles-ci [les richesses de la nation] ne peuvent s'étendre annuellement au-delà du débit de la reproduction annuelle de son territoire assujettie aux prix courants des ventes de la première main'.

10. Cf. Quesnay (1888), p. 458; (1958), p. 824.

11. Cf. Quesnay (1888), p. 385; (1958), p. 750: 'je désire ardemment que vous-même ou quelqu'autre entreprenne l'Essai sur les prix dont vous avez esquissé le plan dans vos réflexions, et que je crois indispensable pour terminer les contestations sur cette matière.'

12. The fundamental price (*prix fondamental*) of wheat includes the taxes and rent of land as follows: 'il faut comprendre dans le prix fondamental, les impositions et le fermage des terres' (Quesnay 1958, p. 555). All items which are paid from the cultivator's own pocket may be included in the expenses of production, that is the fundamental price from his farm administration (or exploitation) viewpoint, so that the concept does not correspond with the *reprises* (aggregate cost) of the whole annual advances in the *Formule* of *Tableau Economique*. The fundamental price seems, however, to function as a criterion determining whether the market value of wheat is *bon prix* (Hishiyama, 1962, p. 193). The commentator of Quesnay's works (Quesnay, 1958) indicates regarding this point the following note: 'le prix fondamental – le coût de production – ne comprend, en réalité, ni les impositions, ni le fermage. Mais Quesnay se place ici au plan national et non au plan de l'exploitation' (Quesnay, 1958, p. 555). In contrast with this interpretation, G. Vaggi appears to find the innovative aspect of Quesnay's value theory in the inclusion of an element of surplus rent, together with cost, in the fundamental price of foodstuffs (Vaggi, 1987, pp. 76–93).

13. Cf. Quesnay (1888), p. 389; (1958), p. 753.

14. Cf. Quesnay (1888), pp. 389, 458; (1958), pp. 753, 825, the following expression: '*échange de valeurs pour valeurs égales*' and '*des échanges assurés de valeurs pour valeurs égales sans perte ou bénéfice*'. It may be noted that the assumption of the exchange between equivalents is one of the basic ideas upon which is centered the controversy on trade, although that is something like a drama of Quesnay's own making and acting. See Quesnay (1888), pp. 446–93; (1958), pp. 815–58.

15. See above p. 72. Incidentally I should like to mention my paper on the

Tableau Economique which considers the problem of realization of 'net product' relating to Say's law. See Hishiyama (1960), pp. 25–34, 'The *Tableau Economique* and the Theory of Markets').

16. We shall call this 'Quesnay-type free trade'; its prerequisites seem to be as follows, namely (i) that there function thoroughly three kinds of free competition, namely, competitions among sellers, those among purchasers, and those between sellers and purchasers; (ii) that the triple competition will be applicable to external trade, that is, export, import, and mutual trade, and finally, (iii) that perfect equality of opportunity to participate in the trade of wheat should be guaranteed both to domestic and to foreign merchants.
17. Cf. above p. 74 and also note 11.
18. Smith (1950), p. 15. The commentator on Quesnay's works (1958) considers something which exists in advance of exchange to be a use-value, according to the subjective interpretation of Quesnay's value-theory. See Quesnay (1958), p. 753, note (5): 'Avant l'échange il y a une "valeur usuelle", mais non point une "valeur d'échange".' As a rule there are not a few economists who support subjective interpretation of the physiocratic theory of value. For example, Schumpeter states as follows: 'Barter and Pricing he [Quesnay] analyzed on strictly 'subjective' lines – basing his theory resolutely upon the fact of consumers' wants' (Schumpeter, 1954, p. 234). It is however better to notice again the following expression of Quesnay mentioned above (p. 77): 'Mais le prix [*le prix vénal*] . . . varie, et depend des différentes causes . . . indépendentes de la volonté des hommes: en sorte qu'il [le prix] ne se règle point sur les besoins des hommes'.
19. Quesnay (1958), p. 727.
20. Le Trosne (1846), pp. 889–97.
21. Turgot (1844), p. 431, note 1; (1914), p. 655, note 1.
22. See above p. 76 and note 16.
23. Cf. Smith (1950), ch. 7, pp. 57–65. See also Ricardo, *Works*, vol. 1, ch. 4, pp. 88–92.
24. Turgot's view is, however, that '[*la valeur vénale*] ne peut guère s'en éloigner beaucoup d'une manière permanente'. See above, p. 79–80.
25. Cf. Smith (1950), pp. 159–60, 162.
26. Smith, ibid. p. 52; my italics.
27. Ibid. pp. 49–56.
28. Smith, referring to the price of coals, considered their costs (or the lowest price) as follows: 'the price which is barely sufficient to replace, together with its ordinary profits, the stock which must be employed in bringing them to market.' (Smith, ibid. p. 168)
29. See above, p. 74.
30. It is, nevertheless, obvious that Quesnay, in his works, particularly his 'Grains, Econ. polit.', written earlier for *L'Encyclopédie*, vol. 7 (1757), assumes including 'the farmer's profits' (*les profits des fermiers*), together with 'the proprietor's revenue' (*les revenus des propriétaires*) and with the product of tithes, in 'the net product' (*le produit net*) from empirical investigation on the actual conditions of large-scale cultivation of wheat. We can see however that, in the same context, 'the farmer's profits' are

regarded as 'a gain for subsistence' (*un gain pour subsister*). Cf. Quesnay (1888), pp. 196-8, pp. 243-4, pp. 248-9; (1958), pp. 461-3, p. 505, p. 509. See also Smith (1950), p. 50.
31. Smith, ibid., p. 162.
32. However, Smith does not consider that there is unlimited demand for food (wheat). See the following quotation: 'the desire of food is limited in every man by the narrow capacity of the human stomach; but the desire of the conveniences and ornaments of building, dress, equipage, and household furniture, seems to have no limit or certain boundary' (Smith, ibid., p. 165)
33. See above, p. 71-2.
34. Needless to say, the above-mentioned excess demand for wheat is nothing but the demand which is sufficient to make the price of wheat increase beyond the floor set by its costs of production (no matter whether the farmer's ordinary profits are contained therein).
35. Notice the sentence cited above: 'il [*le prix*] ne se règle point sur les besoins des hommes.' See above, p. 77.
36. Ricardo, David, *On the Principles of Political Economy, and Taxation*, 1st ed. (London: John Murray, 1817).
37. Ricardo, *Works*, vol. 1, p. 73:

> The exchangeable value of *all* commodities, *whether they be manufactured, or the produce of the mines, or the produce of land*, is always regulated, . . . by the greater quantity of labour necessarily bestowed on their production by those who have no such facilities; by those who continue to produce them under the most unfavorable circumstances; meaning – by the most unfavorable circumstances, the most unfavorable under which the quantity of produce required, renders it necessary to carry on the production. (my italics).

38. Ricardo, ibid. p. 73, original note.
39. Ricardo, ibid. p. 92: 'In speaking then of the exchangeable value of commodities, or the power of purchasing possessed by any one commodity, I mean always that power which it would possess, if not disturbed by any temporary or accidental cause, and which is its natural price.'
40. Both Smith and Ricardo seem, at first reading, similar, in that rent is not the cause but the effect of the high price of wheat. (Concerning Smith, see above, p. 82.) The high price of wheat is, however, in Ricardo's case the consequence of the greatest quantity of labour or *the greatest cost of production* which is bestowed on producing the last portion of that wheat, while it is in Smith's case the consequence of *the excess demand* which makes the price rise beyond the lowest price only including ordinary profits and paying no rent on a permanent basis.
41. Cf. Ricardo, *Works*, vol. 2, p. 116:

> It is the expense of producing the last portion of corn [wheat] which regulates its value, and the value of all other corn that comes to market. Corn raised under more favorable circumstances, and on

more fertile land, will afford a rent in proportion to the difference of expense in raising it.

42. Ricardo's answer implies of course a critique of Smith's value theory. See Ricardo, *Works*, vol. 1, pp. 77–8:

> Adam Smith, therefore, cannot be correct in supposing that the original rule which regulated the exchangeable value of commodities, namely, the comparative quantity of labour by which they were produced, can be at all altered by the appropriation of land and the payment of rent.

43. We may here note Ricardo's confident statement: 'The clearly understanding this principle [relevant ultimately to rent, my comment] is, I am persuaded, of the utmost importance to the science of political economy' (Ricardo, ibid. p. 77, original note).
44. Cf. Quesnay (1888), p. 287; 1958, p. 650. See also, Quesnay (1888), p. 294, note (1); (1958), p. 656, note (12): 'les dons de la terre qui forment le revenu des propriétaires'. See also Smith (1950), vol. 1, p. 344: 'It [rent] is the work of nature which remains after deducting or compensating everything which can be regarded as the work of man.'
45. Cf. for example Le Trosne (1846), pp. 887–8, for his hypothesis of Nature and Man:

> elle [la terre] la [*cette faculté* i.e. *la fécondité*] tient de la puissance du créateur et de la bénédiction originaire, source inépuisable de la fécondité de la nature. L'homme trouve cette faculté existante, il ne fait que s'en servir. . . . Ce principe de production est toujours prêt à agir dès qu'il est sollicité, ou plutôt il est si efficace par lui-même, qu'il agit seul et indépendamment de tout secours. . . . Mais il [le créateur] associe en quelque sorte l'homme à cet acte de sa puissance, en exigeant le concours de son travail. . . . En lui-même son travail n'est qu'une action, un mouvement, une manière d'être dirigée par l'intelligence.

To sum up, the spontaneous, active and inexhaustible faculty (or productivity) of nature, i.e. land, constitutes the primary factor in the principle of production, or rather reproduction, whereas man's work is only the secondary factor which contributes like a servant to the reproduction of things, originating in the creator's power (*la puissance de créature*). In short, according to the physiocrats, '*ce travail, porté partout ailleurs que sur la terre, est absolument stérile, car l'homme n'est pas créateur*' (ibid., p. 942). Thus it may be such a nature-oriented model that Ricardo will, in effect, exclude from his man-oriented model.

46. Cf. Ricardo, *Works*, vol. 1, p. 75:

> Yet when land is most abundant, when most productive, and most fertile, it yields no rent; and it is only when its power decay, and less is yielded in return for labour, that a share of the original produce of the more fertile portions is set apart for rent.

47. Smith (1950), p. 344:

> The capital employed in agriculture, therefore, not only puts into motion a greater quantity of productive labour than any equal capital employed in manufactures, but in proportion to the quantity of productive labour which it employs, it adds a much greater value to the annual produce of the land and labour of the country, to the real wealth and revenue of its inhabitants. Of all the ways in which a capital can be employed, it is by far the most advantageous to the society.

48. What about Quesnay? See Quesnay (1888), p. 290, note (1); (1958), pp. 652–3 note (11):

> celles-ci [les richesses] ne sont qu'un flux de productions continuellement détruites par la consommation et continuellement renouvelées par les travaux des hommes, . . . mais une même quantité d'hommes n'est pas toujours nécessaire pour produire une même quantité de richesses; parce que la production des différentes richesses exige plus ou moins de travail d'hommes; par exemple, deux millions d'hommes peuvent faire naître par la culture des terres la valeur d'un milliard en productions: au lieu trois millions d'hommes ne produiront que la valeur de 700 millions en marchandises de main-d'œuvre; ainsi dans un royaume où l'on cultive la terre, les hommes pourraient être par proportion plus riches et en moindre nombre, que dans un autre royaume où les hommes seraient occupés à fabriquer des marchandises de main-d'œuvre.

Thus Quesnay's simple assumption is this, that value-added productivity per capita will, under free trade, be higher in agriculture than in manufacture, although he does not here clarify the reason (probably owing to so-called productivity of the net product (*produit net*) over cost in agriculture).

REFERENCES

Dobb, M. H. (1973), *Theories of Value and Distribution Since Adam Smith* (Cambridge: Cambridge University Press).

Hishiyama, Izumi (1954) 'Jûnôshugi' ('Physiocracy') in S. Kishimoto (ed.) *Keizaigakushi* (History of Economic Thought) (Tokyo: Seirin-shoin) pp. 78–189.

Hishiyama, Izumi (1960) 'The *Tableau Economique* of Quesnay – its analysis, reconstruction, and application', *Kyoto University Economic Review*, 30 (April), pp. 1–46; reprinted in Italian in G. Candela and M. Palazzi (eds). *Dibattito sulla Fisiocrazia* (Florence: La Nuova Italia, 1979) pp. 119–60.

Hishiyama, Izumi (1962) *Jûnôgakusetsu to Keizaihyô no Kenkyû* (The Study of Physiocratic Thought and *Tableau Economique*) (Tokyo: Yushindo).

Hishiyama, Izumi (1986) 'Quesnay's *Tableau Economique* and interindustry model', *Kyoto University Economic Review*, 56 (April), pp. 1–22.

Kubota, Akiteru (1942), *Kinsei-Keizaigaku no Seisei-Katei* (The Process of Formation of Modern Economic Thought) (Tokyo: Risosha).

Le Trosne, G. F. (1846), *De l'Intérêt Social, par rapport à la Valeur, à la Circulation, à l'Industrie et au Commerce intérieur et extérieur* (first published in 1777) in E. Daire and H. Dussard (eds), *Physiocrates, Collection des Principaux Economistes*, vol. 2 (Paris, 1846); reprinted, (Osnabrück: Otto Zeller, 1966) pp. 885–1023.

Marx, Karl (1963 a) *Theories of Surplus Value, Capital – A Critique of Political Economy*, vol. 4 (London: Lawrence and Wishart).

Marx, Karl (1963 b) *Das Kapital Kritik der politischen Ökonomie*, Zweiter Band Buch 2: Der Zirkulationsprozeß des Kapitals, (Herausgegeben von F. Engels), Institut für Marxismus-Leninismus beim ZK der SED, *Karl Marx F. Engels Werk*, Bd. 24 (Berlin: Dietz).

Marx, Karl (1965) *Theorien über den Mehrwert*, Institut für Marxismus-Leninismus beim ZK der SED, *Karl Marx F. Engels Werke*, Bd. 26–1 (Berlin: Dietz).

Marx, Karl (1967) *Capital. A Critique of Political Economy*, vol. 2 Book 2: *The Process of Circulation of Capital* (ed. F. Engels) (Moscow: Progress Publishers).

Meek, R. L. (1962) *The Economics of Physiocracy – Essays and Translation* (London: Allen and Unwin).

Oncken, August (1902), *Geschichte der Nationalökonomie* (Leipzig: C. L. Hirshfeld).

Pasinetti, L. L. (1965) 'A new theoretical approach to the problem of economic growth', *Pontificiae Academiae Scientiarum Scripta Varia*, 28 (Vatican City) pp. 571–696.

Pasinetti, L. L. (1977) *Lectures on the Theory of Production* (London: Macmillan).

Pasinetti, L. L. (1981) *Structural Change and Economic Growth. A Theoretical Essay on the Dynamics of the Wealth of Nations* (Cambridge: Cambridge University Press).

Pasinetti, L. L. (1986) 'Theory of value – a source of alternative paradigms in economic analysis', in M. Baranzini and R. Scazzieri (eds), *Foundation of Economics, Structures of Inquiry and Economic Theory* (Oxford: Basil Blackwell).

Quesnay, François (1888) *Œuvres Économiques et Philosophiques* (ed. August Oncken) (Francfort/Paris: Joseph Baer/Jules Peelman).

Quesnay, François (1958) *François Quesnay et La Physiocratie* (ed. Institut National d'Études Démographiques), vol. 2 (Paris: Institut National d'Études Démographiques).

Quesnay, François (1972) *Quesnay's Tableau Economique* with the *Extrait des Economies Royales de M.De Sully* and the *Explication de Tableau Economique* (ed. M. Kuczynski and R. L. Meek) (London: Macmillan).

Ricardo, David (1951–73) *Works and Correspondence* (ed. P. Sraffa with M. H. Dobb) (11 vols) (Cambridge: Cambridge University Press).

Schumpeter, J. A. (1954) *History of Economic Analysis* (London: Allen and Unwin).
Smith, Adam (1950) *An Inquiry into the Nature and Causes of the Wealth of Nations* (ed. E. Cannan) (2 vols), 6th edition (London: Methuen).
Sraffa, Piero (1960) *Production of Commodities by Means of Commodities. Prelude to a Critique of Economic Theory* (Cambridge: Cambridge University Press).
Turgot, A.-R. J. (1844, 1914), *Œuvres de Turgot* (eds E. Daire and H. Dussard), Vol. 3, 1844, Paris: and (ed. G. Schelle), Vol. 2, 1914 (Paris: Félix Alcan).
Vaggi, Gianni (1987), *The Economics of François Quesnay* (London: Macmillan).

3 The 'Standard commodity' and Ricardo's Search for an 'Invariable Measure of Value'*

Heinz D. Kurz and Neri Salvadori

'Who seeks to find eternal treasure must use no guile in weight or measure'
                        (epigram in the Manchester Cotton Exchange)

INTRODUCTION

Even three decades after the publication of Piero Sraffa's *Production of Commodities by Means of Commodities* (1960) and in spite of extended discussions on the matter there does not yet exist a commonly accepted view as to the meaning of the 'Standard commodity' and the rôle it plays in Sraffa's analysis. Moreover, it seems to be still unclear what is the relationship between this concept and Ricardo's search for an 'invariable measure of value'.[1]

The present paper attempts to contribute to a clarification of the questions involved. This makes it necessary, first, to reconstruct, albeit briefly, Ricardo's search for an 'invariable measure of value'; this is done in the second section. Emphasis is laid on Ricardo's concern with intertemporal and interspatial comparisons, on the one hand, and his concern with the impact of changes in distribution on relative prices, on the other. The third section deals with Sraffa's interpretation of Ricardo's analysis of value and distribution and the rôle the 'invariable measure of value' plays in it. The following section scrutinizes carefully the structure of Part I of Sraffa's book, with special regard to the elaboration of the concept of the Standard commodity. It is argued that Sraffa considers this device essentially an analytical tool capable of simplifying the study of price changes as income distribution changes. It is shown that a few sections in Part I would not be necessary for the general argument, but have been included to pay a tribute to Ricardo's search for an 'invariable measure of value': we know now when this problem is solvable and when it is not, and what is the solution when there is one. However, it is clear that Sraffa refers exclusively to the second aspect of Ricardo's problem mentioned. In the course of this argument many of the opinions found in the literature are shown to be difficult to sustain. The final section contains some concluding remarks.

RICARDO'S SEARCH FOR AN 'INVARIABLE MEASURE OF VALUE'

As has been pointed out by Sraffa in his Introduction to Ricardo's *Works*, the search for an invariable measure of value 'preoccupied Ricardo to the end of his life' (Sraffa, 1951, p. xl). However, in the course of time Ricardo's view as to the function such a standard would have to perform and the characteristic features it would have to exhibit underwent considerable change. Hence in order to be clear about which of Ricardo's conceptualizations of the 'invariable measure of value' may be related to Sraffa's Standard commodity, if any, it is necessary to recapitulate briefly Ricardo's changing views on the matter.

Intertemporal and Interspatial Comparisons

The first time we encounter in Ricardo's writings the problem of an invariable standard of value is in his contribution to the Bullion Controversy in 1810 (cf. Marcuzzo and Rosselli, 1986). There Ricardo opposed the popular view that the value of a currency should be measured in terms of its purchasing power over the 'mass of commodities' (*Works* III, p. 59); it should rather be measured by the purchasing power over the commodity which was used as the standard. The choice of a monetary regime would have to comply with the task of keeping the purchasing power of money over the standard fairly constant. Changes in money prices of commodities (other than the standard) could then be unambiguously traced back to 'real' causes. In *The High Price of Bullion* Ricardo argues.

> Strictly speaking, there can be no permanent measure of value. A measure of value should itself be invariable; but this is not the case

with either gold or silver, they being subject to fluctuations as well as other commodities. Experience has indeed taught us, that though the variations in the *value* of gold or silver may be considerable, on a comparison of distant periods, yet for short spaces of time their value is tolerably fixed. It is this property, among their other excellencies, which fits them better than any other commodity for the uses of money. Either gold or silver may therefore, in the point of view in which we are considering them, be called a measure of value. (*Works* III, p. 64 n.; Ricardo's emphasis)

Here Ricardo is concerned with a standard which would measure the value of commodities at different times and places, that is, he is interested in *intertemporal* and *interspatial comparisons*, a concern which is closely related to the time-honoured problem of distinguishing between 'value' and 'riches' (cf. *Works* I, ch. XX), which had already worried authors such as Petty and Smith: in this regard Ricardo's contribution is largely in accord with the discussion of his time. While no single commodity can be considered a perfect and thus 'permanent' measure, it is Ricardo's contention that gold and silver are least subject to fluctuations and hence, for comparisons of periods which are not too distant from one another, may reasonably be used as measures of value.

The problem of an invariable measure of value is dealt with in greater detail in Ricardo's *Principles*. In editions 1 and 2 he maintained that in order to be invariable in value a commodity should require 'at all times, and under all circumstances, precisely the same quantity of labour to obtain it' (*Works* I, p. 27 n.). Here again the criterion of invariability is defined in terms of the intertemporal and interspatial constancy of the total amount of labour needed to produce one unit of the respective commodity. If such a commodity could be found and were used as a standard of value, any variation in the value of other commodities expressed in terms of this standard would unequivocally point towards changes in the conditions of production of these commodities. Value measured in the invariable standard Ricardo called 'absolute value'. (In the third edition of his *Principles* he also used the term 'real value'.) Ricardo's early approach to the problem under consideration is neatly summarized in the following passage:

> If any one commodity could be found, which now and at all times required precisely the same quantity of labour to produce it, that

commodity would be of an unvarying value, and would be eminently useful as a standard by which the variations of other things might be measured.

The passage continues:

> Of such a commodity we have no knowledge, and consequently are unable to fix on any standard of value. It is, however, of considerable use towards attaining a correct theory, to ascertain what the essential qualities of a standard are, that we may know the causes of the variation in the relative value of commodities, and that we may be enabled to calculate the degree in which they are likely to operate. (*Works* I, p. 17 n.3)[2]

Basically the same opinion as to the 'essential qualities' of the invariable measure of value is expressed in several other places. For example, in his *Notes on Mr. Malthus' work*, completed in November 1820, Ricardo emphasized: (i) 'Length can only be measured by length, capacity by capacity, and value by value'; (ii) 'invariability is the essential quality of a measure of value'; and (iii) invariability means 'that precisely the same quantity of labour was required' at different times for the production of the standard (cf. *Works* II, pp. 29–33).

The Impact of Changes in Distribution

Although Ricardo in editions 1 and 2 was clearly aware of the modifications necessary to the labour embodied rule of relative value,[3] he apparently did not think that these modifications rendered obsolete his original definition of the invariable measure of value or his approach to the theory of profit. In edition 3, however, he conceded that the same difficulties encountered in determining relative prices also carried over to his attempt in defining the essential properties of a correct standard. He argued that even if

> the same quantity of labour [would] be always required to obtain the same quantity of gold, still gold would not be a perfect measure of value, by which we could accurately ascertain the variations in all other things, because it would not be produced with precisely the same combinations of fixed and circulating capital as all other

things; nor with fixed capital of the same durability; nor would it require precisely the same length of time, before it could be brought to market ... Neither gold then, nor any other commodity, can ever be a perfect measure of value for all things (*Works* I, pp. 44–5).

Whereas in his original approach to the problem of the standard of value Ricardo was exclusively concerned with intertemporal and interspatial comparisons, that is, measurement with respect to *different* technical environments, he is now in addition concerned with the different problem of measurement with respect to the *same* technical environment, but changing distributions of income.[4]

Indeed, Ricardo considered both the problem of interspatial and intertemporal comparisons and the problem of price changes due to changes in distribution as theoretical issues (ibid., p. 45). Yet it is a common feature of all approaches to the theory of value and distribution, including Ricardo's, that the socio-technical environment is taken as given. Therefore, the first aspect of Ricardo's concept of an 'invariable measure of value' simply cannot in general be treated within this context.[5]

A similar criticism was put forward by McCulloch in his letter to Ricardo of 11 August 1823:

There is a radical and essential difference between the circumstances which determine the exchangeable value of commodities, and a measure of that value, which I am afraid is not always kept sufficiently in view. If you are to measure value, you must measure it by the agency of some one commodity or other possessed of value . . .; and as the circumstances under which every commodity is produced must always be liable to vary none can be an invariable measure, though some are certainly much less variable than others and may, therefore, be used as approximations. It is evident, I think, that there neither is nor can be any real and invariable standard of value; and if so it must be very idle to seek for that which can never be found.

McCulloch continues:

The real inquiry is to ascertain what are the circumstances which determine the exchangeable value of commodities *at any given period*. (*Works* IX, p. 344; emphasis added)

And in his reply of 24 August to Ricardo's answer three days earlier McCulloch put his view on what he called 'the *vexata questio* of value' even more succinctly. He expressed anew his conviction that the problem of the invariable measure of value, as stated by Ricardo, 'is quite insoluble' and that he himself did not want to enter 'this transcendental part of Pol Economy':

> before I attempt to get a measure of the value of cloth and wine in the reign of Augustus and George IV, I must obtain a measure of their value in the same market. (*Works* IX, p. 369).

Ricardo in his answer to the first of the two letters insisted that despite their disagreement even McCulloch 'will still contend for the mathematical accuracy of the measure'. He continued:

> I do not see the great difference you mention between the circumstances which determine the exchangeable value of commodities, and the medium of that value . . . Is it not clear . . . that as soon as we are in possession of the knowledge of the circumstances which determine the value of commodities, we are enabled to say what is necessary to give us an invariable measure of value? (*Works* IX, p. 358).

A similar passage is to be found in his letter to Trower of 31 August 1823, in which his dispute with McCulloch is touched upon. Ricardo criticizes the latter for not seeing 'that if we were in possession of the knowledge of the law which regulates the exchangeable value of commodities, we should be only one step from the discovery of a measure of absolute value' (*Works* IX, p. 377). According to Sraffa 'this came close to identifying the problem of a measure with that of the law of value' (1951, p. xli).

'Absolute Value and Exchangeable Value'

As is well known, two most important documents of Ricardo's search for an invariable measure of value are a complete draft and an unfinished later version of his paper 'Absolute Value and Exchangeable Value', which must have been written shortly before Ricardo fell ill in early September 1823 (cf. Sraffa's Note in *Works* IV, pp. 359–60). In the two manuscripts Ricardo attempted to render precise his own concept of the standard of value and confront it with those advocated by Malthus, Torrens, Mill and McCulloch. Here a brief summary of Ricardo's argument must suffice.

To begin with, it is important to notice that Ricardo's main concern was still with intertemporal and interspatial comparisons. This is expressed in various passages, the most emphatic of which is perhaps the following:

> It is a great desideratum in Polit. Econ. to have a perfect measure of absolute value in order to be able to ascertain what relation commodities bear to each other at distant periods. Any thing having value is a good measure of the *comparative value* of all other commodities at the *same time and place*, but will be of no use in indicating the variations in their *absolute value at distant times and in distant places*, (*Works* IV, p. 396; emphasis added).

Next it deserves to be mentioned that Ricardo's own efforts were explicitly directed at establishing a straightforward analogy between measurement in natural sciences and in economics. In one place he writes:

> There can be no unerring measure either of length, of weight, of time or of value *unless there be some object in nature* to which the standard itself can be referred and by which we are enabled to ascertain whether it preserves its character of invariability. (*Works* IV, p. 401; emphasis added)

Referring implicitly to his earlier views on the subject he continues:

> It has been said that we are not without a *standard in nature* to which we may refer for the correction of errors and deviations in our measure of value, *in the same way as in the other measures which I have noticed*, and that such a standard is to be found in the *labour of men*. (ibid.; emphasis added)

However, this opinion has turned out to be erroneous, the reason being that commodities 'will not vary only on account of the greater or less quantity of labour necessary to produce them but also on account of the greater or less proportion of the finished commodity which may be paid to the workman . . . It must then be confessed that *there is no such thing in nature as a perfect measure of value*' (*Works* IV, p. 404; emphasis added).[6]

The study of the impact of distribution on relative prices is frequently couched in terms of intertemporal comparisons of situations before and after a change in the real wage rate.[7] However, the real point at issue is not what may cause real wages to rise or fall, but rather that there are *two* circumstances affecting relative value at any point in time, i.e., the technical conditions of production and the division of the product between wages and profits. The impact of the second factor on 'natural' prices is best studied by carrying out some thought experiments. This is what Ricardo does in a couple of simple numerical examples, where he hypothetically varies the wage rate, taking into account that with *given technical conditions of production* the rate of profits is bound to vary in the opposite direction, and then tries to ascertain the involved movement of relative prices (cf., for examples, *Works* IV, pp. 373–8).

After having disposed of the idea that there might exist such a thing as a perfect standard of value, fulfilling both criteria enunciated by him, Ricardo asks: 'But as it is desirable that we should have one measure of value . . ., to which shall we give the preference [?]' (*Works* IV, p. 389). On the premise that the criterion of technological invariability is met, what does invariability with respect to variations in income distribution mean? Since 'the value of all commodities resolves itself into wages and profits' (ibid., p. 392), the proximate answer to be given is: that commodity is invariable in value, in which the fall in the profit component is equal to the rise in the wage component (consequent upon a rise in the real wage rate and a corresponding fall in the general rate of profits). This is in fact the answer implicit in Ricardo's argument (cf., e.g., ibid., pp. 372–3, 404 and 407). The conclusion is close at hand that the commodity under consideration should 'require capital as well as labour to produce [it]' (ibid., p. 371): 'To me it appears most clear that we should chuse a measure produced by labour employed for a certain period, and which always supposes an advance of capital' (ibid., p. 405). Accordingly, the standard advocated by Ricardo is different from Malthus's:

> It is not like Mr. Malthus's measure one of the extremes it is not a commodity produced by labour alone which he proposes, nor a commodity whose value consists of profits alone, but one which may fairly be considered as the *medium between these two extremes*, and as agreeing more nearly with the circumstances under which the greater number of commodities are produced than any other which can be proposed. (*Works* IV, p. 372; emphasis added)

In another place Ricardo is more explicit about what he thinks the 'medium' actually is:

> That a commodity produced by labour employed for a year is a mean between the extremes of commodities produced on one side by labour and advances for much more than a year, and on the other by labour employed for a day only without any advances, and the mean will in most cases give a much less deviation from truth than if either of the extremes were used as a measure. (ibid., p. 405)

As can already be seen from the last few quotations, Ricardo was not content with the proximate answer referred to above. His concern was with rendering as precise as possible the causes which account for the dependence of relative prices on income distribution. Clearly, the major cause is 'the variety of circumstances under which commodities are actually produced' (*Works* IV, p. 368). This in conjunction with the fact that 'profits [are] increasing at a compound rate . . . makes a great part of the difficulty' (*Works*, IX, p. 387; similarly IV, p. 388). Hence an important part of Ricardo's efforts was directed at describing more carefully the 'variety of circumstances' under which commodities are produced.

This Ricardo tried to effectuate in various terms. We have already seen that one way of differentiating between these circumstances was in terms 'of the different proportions in which the whole result of labour is distributed, between master and workers' (*Works* IV, p. 385). However, since these proportions are themselves but a reflection of differences in the underlying conditions of production, it is desirable to conceive of these differences more directly. As we have seen in the above, the most general distinction of the circumstances under discussion given by Ricardo is in terms of different proportions of fixed and circulating capital, where circulating capital includes the wages of labour, different durabilities of fixed capital, and different durabilities of circulating capital (cf. also Sraffa, 1951, p. xlii).

In addition, Ricardo used more compact formulae to express these differences. For example, he talks of the 'proportions in which immediate labour and accumulated labour enter into different commodities' (*Works* IV, p. 379), or the proportions in which 'labour and capital' are employed in their production. Apparently, Ricardo was aware that since the means of production are heterogeneous the concept of 'capital' is an intricate one.[8]

Therefore it comes as no surprise that Ricardo was in search of a description of the differences under consideration which is less assailable. In his letter to McCulloch of 13 June 1820 he had already hinted at what appeared to him to be the most abstract denomination of the circumstances which account for the deviation of relative prices from relative quantities of labour embodied in the various commodities: 'All the exceptions to the general rule come under this one of time'; and 'there are such a variety of cases in which the time of completing a commodity may differ' (*Works* VIII, p. 193). This idea is taken up again in his essay 'Absolute Value and Exchangeable Value', in which he stresses: 'In this then consists the difficulty of the subject that the circumstances of time for which advances are made are so various' (*Works* IV, p. 370). Finally, it deserves mention that the reduction of all differences to one of time complies with Ricardo's preconception that the standard of value should ultimately be referred back to some 'object in nature'.

The 'Medium Between the Extremes' Standard

Let us now turn briefly to Ricardo's choice of a 'medium between the extremes'. According to Ricardo 'it is evident that by chusing a mean the variations in commodities on account of a rise or fall in wages would be much less than if we took either of the extremes' (*Works* IV, p. 373). The motivation for this choice comes out somewhat more clearly in the above quoted letter to McCulloch of 13 June 1820:

> The medium . . . is perhaps the best adapted to the general mass of commodities; those commodities on one side of this medium, would rise in comparative value with it, with a rise in the price of labour, and a fall in the rate of profits; and those on the other side might fall from the same cause. (*Works*, VIII, p. 193).

However Ricardo did not take the composite commodity 'social product', or, in his terms, the 'mass of commodities', as the standard of value. Ricardo considered this possibility, but rejected it on the grounds that '[i]f it be admitted that one commodity may alter in absolute value, it must be admitted that 2, 3, 100, a million may do so, and how shall I be able with certainty to say whether the one or the million had varied' (*Works* IV, p. 401).[9] The same opinion is expressed in another place. Ricardo there declines the proposed measure, which was taken into consideration in the context of a discussion of the impact of distribution on relative value, given the technical conditions of production, with the argument that it does not meet with the criterion of technological invariability: 'In our own times great improvements have been made in the mode of manufacturing cloth, linen and cotton goods, iron, steel, copper, stockings – great improvements have been made in husbandry, all which tend to lower the value of these goods and of the produce of the soil and yet these are made a part of the measure by which you would measure the value of other things' (ibid., p. 374).

The basic idea underlying the concept of the 'medium between the extremes' seems to be that the processes of production of the different commodities can somehow be expressed in terms of a single variable, that is, the time that elapses between an initial expenditure of labour and the completion of the product. In other words, Ricardo's approach appears to start from the supposition that commodities can somehow be distinguished in terms of the length of their production periods. With some circularity of production this idea necessarily breaks down, while with unidirectional processes of production it is applicable in very special cases only. There is ample evidence that Ricardo was aware of the fact that most commodities are produced by means of commodities. However, he did not succeed in grasping fully the implication of the interindustry relationships for his specification of the standard of value.

A further remark concerns the fact that even though Ricardo refrained from taking the aggregate of commodities as his measure of value, he nevertheless invoked 'the circumstances under which the greater number of commodities are produced' to rationalize his own choice. The measure is supposed to reflect to some extent the conditions of production of 'the generality of commodities which are the objects of the traffic of mankind', 'the greatest number of commodities which are the objects of exchange' (*Works* IV, pp. 389 and 405). Interestingly, whenever Ricardo gives examples of which particular commodities should by all means be taken into consideration in defining the properties of the standard, he always refers to necessaries (as opposed to luxuries). In one place he writes: 'The circumstance of this measure being produced in the same length of time as corn and most other vegetable food which forms by far the most valuable article of daily consumption would decide me in giving it a preference' (ibid., pp. 405–6).

SRAFFA'S INTERPRETATION OF RICARDO

In the above we frequently referred to Sraffa's Introduction to Vol. I of Ricardo's *Works* containing the *Principles*. Sraffa carefully delineates the development of Ricardo's approach to the theory of value and distribution. With regard to Ricardo's search for an invariable measure of value, Sraffa, as we have seen, arrives at the conclusion that the way in which the problem was formulated by Ricardo 'came close to identifying the problem of a measure with that of the law of value' (1951, p. xli). This remark might give rise to the impression that Ricardo's first and foremost concern was with the 'law of value'. However, this was not the case, as the previous section has demonstrated, nor is it implied in Sraffa's statement. What can be said about Sraffa's interpretation is that it emphasizes particularly those aspects of Ricardo's thoughts which point into the direction of the Standard commodity and its role as an analytic device to simplify the investigation of the mathematical properties of the system of production prices. This can best be seen by looking at Sraffa's treatment of Ricardo's successive attempts to simplify the problem of distribution, such that it can easily be solved (cf. Sraffa, 1951, pp. xxxi–xxxiii).

In Sraffa's interpretation, Ricardo's procedure may be divided into four steps. The *first* step consisted in eliminating the problem of rent: 'By getting rid of rent, which we may do on the corn produced with the capital last employed, and on all commodities produced by labour in manufactures, the distribution between capitalist and labourer becomes a much more simple consideration' (*Works* VIII, p. 194). The *second* step consisted in trying to get rid of the problem of value by assuming the 'corn model', in which the rate of profits can be ascertained directly as a ratio of quantities of corn without any need to have recourse to prices. Since Ricardo had to accept Malthus's criticism that there is no industry in which the product is exactly of the same kind as the capital advanced, in the *Principles* he presented (a *third* step) a fully-fledged theory of value, according to which the relative value of commodities is governed by the quantities of total labour needed in their production. Hence, as Sraffa concludes, 'the rate of profits was no longer determined by the ratio of the corn produced to the corn used up in production, but, instead, by the ratio of the total labour of the country to the labour required to produce the necessaries of that labour' (1951, p. xxxii). However, Ricardo soon realized that the labour theory of value cannot generally be sustained. According to Sraffa the search for an 'invariable measure of value' may be considered the *final* step in Ricardo's efforts to simplify the theory of value and distribution. In particular, the measure was designed to corroborate Ricardo's dictum that the laws of distribution 'are not essentially connected with the doctrine of value' (*Works*, VIII, p. 194). The parallel to Sraffa's ingenious concept of the Standard system is close at hand: in the latter '[t]he rate of profits . . . appears as a ratio between quantities of commodities irrespective of their prices' (Sraffa, 1960, p. 22). In this interpretation the purpose of the invariable measure of value was basically to render a system with heterogeneous commodities in regard of some of its features as simple and transparent as the corn economy.

Summarizing the argument, it can be said that in his Introduction Sraffa focused his attention on those aspects of Ricardo's search for an invariable measure of value which concerned the theory of value and distribution with a given technological environment, whereas the intertemporal and interspatial aspect of Ricardo's problem is neglected. As a matter of fact there is no *general* theoretical solution to the problem of intertemporal and interspatial comparisons. A solution to the problem of intertemporal comparisons can be found only in special cases of technological change.

SRAFFA'S STANDARD COMMODITY[10]

We now turn to a detailed analysis of Sraffa's *Production of Commodities* and the role of the Standard commodity in it. The basic premise Sraffa starts from is that commodities are produced by means of commodities. This then leads to the concept of surplus, to the distinction between basic and non-basic products, and to the assumption that there exists at least one basic commodity (Chs. I and II, §§ 1–12). Ch. III (§§ 13–22) is highly relevant for the issue at hand and will be scrutinized here section by section except for sections 17, 21, and 22 which will be put aside for the moment and analyzed later. We want to stress that the main aim of Ch. III is to provide a 'preliminary survey' (§ 20) of price movements consequent upon changes in distribution on the assumption that the methods of production remain unchanged, the complete analysis of these movements being presented, as is well known, in Ch. VI. Only sections 17, 21, and 22 serve a different aim.

A 'Preliminary Survey'

Section 13 states what will be done in the chapter, i.e., 'to give the wage (w) successive values' and 'to observe the effect of changes in the wage on the rate of profits and on the prices of individual commodities'. Section 14 is devoted to clarifying that if 'the whole national income goes to wages', prices of commodities are proportional to 'the quantity of labour which directly and indirectly has gone to produce them', and Sraffa adds: 'At no other wage-level do values follow a simple rule'.

When the wage rate w is decreased from its maximum level a rate of profits arises (§ 15). 'The key to the movement of relative prices consequent upon a change in the wage lies in the inequality of the proportions in which labour and means of production are employed in the various industries' (ibid.), whereas 'if the proportion were the same in all industries no price-changes could ensue' (ibid.). On the contrary, 'it is impossible for prices to remain unchanged when there is inequality of "proportions"' (§ 16). In order to clarify this Sraffa performs the intellectual experiment in which prices are unchanged and a profit rate arises: 'industries with a sufficiently low proportion of labour to means of production would have a deficit, while industries with a sufficiently high proportion would have a surplus, on their payments for wages and profits' (ibid.), and this would be so whatever is the wage-reduction and the corresponding rate of profits (ibid.). It is then clarified that 'with a wage reduction, price-changes would be called for to redress the balance in each of the "deficit" and each of the "surplus" industries' (§ 18).

But it is not possible to assert that 'the price of the product of an industry having a low proportion of labour to means of production . . . would necessarily rise, with a wage-reduction, relative to its own means of production', since 'the means of production of an industry are themselves the product of one or more industries which may in their turn employ a still lower proportion of labour to means of production' (§ 19). Finally, Sraffa can 'conclude this preliminary survey' (§ 20) by asserting that

> the relative price-movements of two products come to depend, not only on the 'proportions' of labour to means of production by which they are respectively produced, but also on the 'proportions' by which those means have themselves been produced, and also on the 'proportions' by which the means of production of those means

The 'Standard commodity' and Ricardo's 'Invariable Measure' 109

of productions have been produced, and so on. The result is that the relative price of two products may move ... in the opposite direction to what we might have expected on the basis of their respective 'proportions'; besides, the prices of their respective means of production may move in such a way as to reverse the order of the two products as to higher and lower proportions; *and further complications arise, which will be considered subsequently.* (ibid., emphasis added)

We now turn to the complete analysis of price movements in Ch. VI (§§ 45–9) and point out why the considerations contained in it were not to be found in the 'preliminary survey'.

The Complete Analysis

Section 45 states what will be done in the chapter, i.e., to consider prices 'from their cost-of-production aspect, and the way in which they 'resolve themselves' into wages and profits'. Sraffa's doubts on when to present this analysis are also made explicit jointly with the reason for the choice which has been made and the reference to previous 'allusions' to the subject. Section 46 introduces the reduction to dated quantities of labour. The concept of the *Maximum rate of profits*, R, is assumed to be known. In section 47 the pattern of the movement of the value of each of the labour terms of the reduction to dated quantities of labour is analyzed. This analysis is significantly simplified by the fact that the wage rate w is assumed to be a linear function of the profit rate, r:

$$w = \frac{R - r}{R} \quad (1)$$

This allows Sraffa to prove that these patterns can be divided into two groups: those that correspond to labour performed $\frac{1}{R}$ or less years ago, 'which begin at once to fall in value and fall steadily throughout; and those representing labour more remote in time, which at first rise and then, as each of them reaches its maximum value, turn and begin the downward movement', where 'the rate of profits at which any term of date n is at its maximum is

$$r = R - \frac{1 + R'}{n + 1} \text{ (ibid.).}$$

Section 48 enters into a discussion of the issue introduced in section 20 and presents the results announced there:

> The labour terms can be regarded as the constituent elements of the price of a commodity, the combination of which in various proportions may, with the variation of the rate of profits, give rise to complicated patterns of price-movement with several ups and downs.

As an example of these ups and downs Sraffa introduces the well-known example of the 'old wine' and the 'oak chest'. Once again the analysis is dramatically simplified by the assumption that the wage rate as a function of the profit rate has the form (1). Section 48 concludes with the famous paragraph on the 'impossibility of aggregating the "periods" belonging to the several quantities of labour into a single magnitude which could be regarded as representing the quantity of capital'.

In the last section of Ch. VI, section 49, it is clarified that there is 'a restriction to the movement of the price of any product: if as a result of a rise in the rate of profits the price falls, its rate of fall cannot exceed the rate of fall of the wage'. This is important since if it is possible to prove that the wage rate is a decreasing function of the profit rate for some choice of the numeraire (as in eq. (1)), then it is a decreasing function of the profit rate whichever is the numeraire.

To conclude, it should now be clear why the results presented in Ch. VI could not have been contained in the 'preliminary survey'. This is so because it was first necessary to show that

(i) the rate of profits, r, reaches a finite and unique maximum, R, when the wage rate, w, equals zero and the corresponding prices of basic commodities are positive (§§ 39–41);

(ii) R is the lowest positive real number such that the price equations are satisfied with w = 0 (§ 42);

(iii) for $0 \leq r \leq R$ the prices of basic commodities in general vary with r but remain positive and finite (§ 39);

(iv) in each system of production there exists a (composite) commodity such that if it is chosen as numeraire, then the wage rate w is a linear function of the profit rate with the form (1) (§ 43).

The Standard commodity: a Tool of Analysis

In order to demonstrate the above statements Sraffa introduces the *Standard commodity*, the *Standard system*, and the *Standard national income* (§ 26 and, in general terms, §§ 33–4). Then he shows that within the Standard system

$$r = R(1 - w) \qquad (2)$$

where R is the *Standard ratio*, which coincides with the Maximum rate of profits (§§ 27–30). This relation is then shown to be valid also in the 'actual economic system' if the Standard commodity is chosen as numeraire (§ 31).[11] Finally it is shown that non-basic products play no role in the construction of the Standard system (§ 35) and that there exists a Standard commodity on the assumption that there is at least one basic commodity (§ 37), and the former is unique (§ 41).

It deserves mention that these results can also be obtained by using the Perron-Frobenius Theorem. In fact, Sraffa's demonstration of the existence and uniqueness of the Standard commodity can be considered a (not fully complete) proof of this theorem. Yet Sraffa does even better, simultaneously providing an economic rationale of the analytical tools he uses. It should be clear now that for Sraffa the Standard commodity was first and foremost an analytical tool useful in the study of price changes as income distribution changes (see Kurz and Salvadori, 1987).

The Standard commodity: a Physical Analog?

Until now we left aside sections 17, 21–5, 32, 36 and 44. Section 36 states what is done in Ch. V. Sections 17 and 21–5 will be scrutinized in the next subsection; sections 32 and 44 will be analyzed here. In section 44 the practice, common to the classical economists and Marx, of treating the wage rate rather than the rate of profits as the 'given' distribution variable is reversed. Sraffa remarks that since wages, besides the ever-present element of subsistence, may include a share of the surplus, the real wage rate can no longer be considered given. Hence, *if* the wage rate were still to be given from outside the system of production, it would have to be 'in terms of a more or less abstract standard, and [would] not acquire a definite meaning until the prices of commodities are determined'. On the contrary, '[t]he rate of profits, as a ratio, has a significance which is independent of any prices, and can well be "given" before the prices are fixed'. Section 32 applies the results of section 31 to the example of section 25 (mentioned also in section 27). But it contains also an interesting caveat which it is better to quote in full.

> [I]f in the actual system (. . . with R = 20%) the wage is fixed in terms of the Standard net product, to w = $\frac{3}{4}$ there will correspond r = 5%. But while the share of wages will be equal in value to $\frac{3}{4}$ of the Standard national income, it does not follow that the share of profits will be equivalent to the remaining $\frac{1}{4}$ of the Standard income. The share of profits will consist of whatever is left of the *actual* national income after deducting from it the equivalent of $\frac{3}{4}$ of the *Standard* national income for wages. (Sraffa's emphases)

Therefore, the fact that '[t]he rate of profits *in the Standard system* . . . appears as a ratio between quantities of commodities irrespective of their prices' (§ 29, emphasis added) cannot be generalized to the actual system even if the Standard commodity is the numeraire. These remarks contained in sections 32 and 44 constitute also an *ante litteram* criticism to the interpretation of the Standard commodity as a *physical or corn analogue*.[12] In the 'corn model' corn is also the only commodity consumed by workers and the only basic commodity.[13] Therefore, to give the real wage rate in terms of corn from outside the system is quite natural, whereas to give the real wage rate in terms of the Standard commodity requires one to know the value of the commodities which constitute the real wage rate, as an aggregate, in terms of the Standard commodity. Moreover, even if the real net national income is given, as in the thought experiment performed by Sraffa, its value in terms of the Standard commodity is variable; therefore to determine the point on the linear wage-profit relationship corresponding to a given share of wages requires knowledge of the function relating the value of net national income in terms of the Standard commodity to the rate of profits.[14]

A Solution to Ricardo's Search for an 'Invariable Measure of Value'?

Sections 23–5 connect the Standard commodity to that part of Ricardo's problem of an 'invariable measure of value', which relates to the impact of (changes in) distribution on relative prices, taking the technical conditions of production as given and constant:

The 'Standard commodity' and Ricardo's 'Invariable Measure' 113

The necessity of having to express the price of one commodity in terms of another which is arbitrarily chosen as standard, complicates the study of the price-movements which accompany a change in distribution. It is impossible to tell of any particular price-fluctuation whether it arises from the peculiarities of the commodity which is being measured or from those of the measuring standard. (§ 23)

Sections 17 and 21–22 prepare the field for this tribute to Ricardo. There does not exist a commonly accepted interpretation of these sections: for instance, Schefold (1986) criticized his own previous interpretation (Schefold, 1976) in the course of criticizing an interpretation by Flaschel (1986). The one given here comes close to the last interpretation by Schefold (1986).

After having introduced 'deficit' and 'surplus' industries in section 16 (see above), Sraffa remarks:

There would be a 'critical proportion' of labour to means of production which marked the watershed between 'deficit' and 'surplus' industries. An industry which employed that particular 'proportion' would show an even balance – the proceeds of the wage-reduction would provide exactly what was required for the payment of profits at the general rate. (§ 17)

It is obvious, and can easily be calculated, that for a given wage-reduction this 'critical proportion' depends on the rate of profits, and, therefore, on the numeraire chosen.[15] But at the end of section 16 there is a parenthetical sentence stressing:

Nothing is assumed at the moment as to what rate of profits corresponds to what wage reduction; all that is required at this stage is that there should be a uniform wage and a uniform rate of profits throughout the system.

Moreover, after the previously quoted sentences of section 17 there is another sentence, in the same paragraph, just asserting that, whatever is the value of that 'critical proportion', if there exist 'two or more basic industries, the industry with the lowest proportion of labour to means of production would be a "deficit" industry and the one with the highest proportion would be a "surplus" industry'. Thus, it seems that such 'critical proportion' is not yet fixed and only its lower and upper bounds are determined: the way to fix it is postponed to a later section. The interpretation given here is also substantiated by section 2 of Appendix D, where Sraffa refers explicitly to section 17 in asserting that '[t]he conception of a standard measure of value as a medium between two extremes (§ 17 ff.) . . . belongs to Ricardo'.

Section 17 is incidental with respect to the 'preliminary survey' of price movements consequent upon changes in distribution which constitute the main theme of Ch. III. As soon as this survey is concluded, Sraffa reverts (§ 21) to the 'critical proportion' mentioned in section 17. He starts his reasoning by supposing not only that there is an industry employing labour and means of production in that proportion, but also that the means of production used by this industry, taken as an aggregate, are produced by labour and means of production in that proportion, and similarly for the aggregate means of production of those means of production, and so on. That is, the 'critical proportion' – still unknown – is supposed to recur in all the successive layers of the industry's aggregate means of production without limit. The commodity produced by such an industry would have two properties:

(i) it 'would be under no necessity, *arising from the conditions of production of the industry itself*, either to rise or to fall in value relative to any other commodity when wages rose or fell' (§ 21, emphasis added);
(ii) it 'would in any case be incapable of changing in value relative to the aggregate of its own means of production' (ibid.).

Therefore, when this commodity is compared with other commodities, the relative prices can go up and down, but these patterns will depend, not on the peculiarities of its production, but on the peculiarities of the production of the commodities it is compared with. However, when this commodity is compared with the aggregate of its own means of production the relative price is independent of distribution. Property (i) is the property required to solve that aspect of Ricardo's problem of an 'invariable measure of value' connected with the impact of changes in distribution within a given technical environment and in fact will be used for this purpose in section 23. Property (ii) is the property which is used to identify the 'critical proportion' (sometimes called also the 'balancing' proportion). When property (ii) holds, the ratio between the value of the product of the industry which exhibits the 'balancing' proportion to the value of its

The 'Standard commodity' and Ricardo's 'Invariable Measure' 115

means of production is independent of distribution, but then such a ratio cannot differ from the Maximum rate of profits since, '[w]hen we make the wage equal to zero and the whole of the net product goes to profits, in each industry the value-ratio of net product to means of production necessarily comes to coincide with the general rate of profits' (§ 22).

Thus, the only candidate for being the 'balancing' proportion is the proportion of an industry whose ratio between the value of the net product to the value of its means of production equals R, the Maximum rate of profits. After having replaced 'the hybrid "proportion" of the quantity of labour to the value of the means of production' with 'the value-ratio of net product to means of production', which is one of the two 'corresponding "pure" ratios between homogeneous quantities' (§ 22), Sraffa can assert:

> 'the only "value-ratio" which can be invariant to changes in the wage, and therefore is capable of being "recurrent" in the sense defined in § 21, is the one that is equal to the rate of profits which corresponds to zero wage. And *that* is the "balancing" ratio' (§ 22, Sraffa's emphasis).

Hence, if we could discover a commodity exhibiting a 'balanced' proportion between labour and means of production in all its 'layers', we would be 'in possession of a standard capable of isolating the price-movements of any other product so that they could be observed *as in a vacuum*' (§ 23; emphasis added).[16]

Such a commodity is not likely to be found among the individual commodities, yet it can be constructed from among them. In section 24 Sraffa argues that it can be obtained from the basic system by hypothetically reproportioning the industries in it in such a way that the product of the resulting artificial economy consists of the same commodities in the same proportions as does the aggregate of its own means of production. (Section 25 provides a three-industry example of construction of such a composite commodity.) This is Sraffa's solution to Ricardo's search for a commodity produced under 'average' conditions of production, which, as we have seen, forms only a part of Ricardo's search for an 'invariable measure of value'.

Additional Evidence

Next it is worthwhile to have a closer look at Sraffa's careful wording in his discussion of the problem of the measure of value. In the table of contents (cf. Sraffa, 1960, p. ix) section 23 is announced under the heading '"An invariable measure of value"'.[17] Note that Sraffa put the term in inverted commas. Clearly, this is meant to refer back to the title of section VI of Ch. I of Ricardo's *Principles*: 'On an invariable measure of value'. In the text of section 23 the term 'invariable measure of value' does not recur.

According to the index to Sraffa's book there are two other places in which the notion of an '[i]nvariable standard of value' makes an appearance. The first is in section 43; the second is in section 2 of the Appendix D. Sraffa's introductory remark to section 43, entitled 'Standard product replaced by equivalent quantity of labour', reads: 'The Standard system is a *purely auxiliary construction*. It should therefore be possible to present the essential elements of the mechanism under consideration without having recourse to it' (emphasis added). Sraffa then proceeds in two steps. First, he argues that if it is assumed that the wage rate is linearly related to the rate of profits, 'the wage and commodity-prices are then *ipso facto* expressed in Standard net product, without need of defining its composition' (ibid.). In other words, if we use formula (2) we actually *do* reckon in terms of the Standard commodity, and 'it is curious that we should thus be enabled to use a standard without knowing what it consists of' (ibid.). In the second step Sraffa then shows that there 'is available however a more tangible measure for prices of commodities which makes it possible to displace the Standard net product even from this attenuated function. This measure . . . is "the quantity of labour that can be purchased by the Standard net product"' (ibid.). Sraffa concludes: 'Thus all the properties of "an invariable standard of value", *as described in § 23*, are found in a variable quantity of labour, which, however, varies according to a simple rule which is independent of prices' (ibid.; emphasis added). With the annual labour of the system taken as unit, the quantity of 'labour commanded' referred to is given by

$$\frac{1}{w} = \frac{R}{R-r}.$$

Any doubts the reader of Sraffa's book may still have, despite the unequivocal statements quoted in the above, whether Sraffa was, or was not, concerned with solving 'the' Ricardian enigma, are finally cleared away in the Appendix D to the book, entitled 'References to the literature'. There Sraffa explicitly refers only to that aspect of

Ricardo's search for an invariable measure, which relates to the impact of distribution on relative value, and which prompted Ricardo to advocate '[t]he conception of a standard measure of value as a medium between two extremes' (ibid., p. 94; see also the last sub-section of section 2 above). The other aspect of Ricardo's search does not, and indeed cannot, play any role whatsoever in Sraffa's attempt to lay bare the connection of his work with the theories of the old classical economists.

CONCLUDING REMARKS

It has been shown that (i) the Standard commodity is a useful, although not a necessary, tool of analysis; (ii) Sraffa relates the Standard commodity to Ricardo's search for an 'invariable measure of value'; (iii) this is done only with regard to that aspect of Ricardo's search which is concerned with the impact of changes in distribution on relative prices within a given technique; (iv) whenever the notion of 'invariable measure of value' is utilized by Sraffa (1960) this is to refer to Ricardo's own wording (the sense in which the Standard commodity is an 'invariable measure of value' being that it is 'a standard capable of isolating the price-movements of any other product so that they [can] be observed as in a vacuum', Sraffa, 1960, § 23).

Finally, can we say that Sraffa's Standard commodity has fulfilled Ricardo's dream of an 'invariable measure of value' at least with respect to the impact of changes in distribution? Even this would be an overstatement unless by 'a given technical environment' we mean 'a given technique'. What Sraffa has provided is a tool which allows us to say both when this part of the Ricardian problem is solvable (and when it is not), and to construct the solution whenever it exists.

In special cases of technological change the Standard commodity may even be used for intertemporal comparisons. A condition for the applicability of the Standard commodity to this problem would of course be that it is not affected by technological change. This holds good, for example, in the following cases: (i) technological change affects only non-basic commodities; (ii) and (iii) technological change is 'neutral' in the sense of Harrod or in the sense of Hicks as formulated in a linear multisectoral model by Steedman (1985); (iv) technological change transforms technique $(A, 1)$ in technique $(\lambda A, \mu 1)$, with $0 < \lambda < 1$ and $0 < \mu < 1)$. It would of course be possible to redefine as 'neutral' all forms of technological change which leave unaltered a given Standard commodity. However, even if this sort of neutrality would include Harrodian neutrality and Hicksian neutrality, next to nothing would be gained by it since the class of cases captured by such a concept of neutrality would be rather insignificant.

Sraffa, for perfectly good reasons it seems, saw only a single analytical purpose of the Standard commodity, i.e. to simplify the analysis of the effects of changes in the division of the product between profits and wages on prices.

NOTES

* We thank without implicating Christian Bidard, Antonio D'Agata, Pierangelo Garegnani, Peter Flaschel, Geoff Harcourt, Bruno Jossa, Carlo Panico, Alessandro Roncaglia, Bertram Schefold, and Ian Steedman for helpful comments and discussions. Neri Salvadori thanks the MPI (the Italian Ministry for Public Education) for financial support.

1. There is a third aspect discussed in the literature which is highly controversial and which concerns the relationship between the Standard commodity and Marx's labour value-based approach to the theory of value and distribution. This aspect will be entirely set aside in the present paper and will rather be dealt with in a separate study by us; for a discussion of some of the questions involved in this connection, see Kurz and Salvadori (1987).
2. To a similar passage in Chap. XX he added: 'still it [i.e. the correct standard of value] would not be a standard of riches, for riches do not depend on value' (*Works* I, p. 275).
3. Interestingly, even in editions 1 and 2 Ricardo did not advocate a pure labour theory of value, according to which prices are proportional to quantities of labour embodied in the different commodities. In edition 1 we read: 'Besides the alteration in the relative value of commodities, occasioned by more or less labour being required to produce them, they are also subject to fluctuations from a rise of wages, and consequent fall of profits, if the fixed capitals employed be either of unequal value, or of unequal duration' (*Works* I, p. 53). And in another passage Ricardo stressed that 'different proportions of fixed and circulating capital' in different trades and 'different degrees of durability' of fixed capital introduce 'a considerable modification to the rule, which is of universal application in the early stages of society' (*Works* I, p. 66). Hence relative prices are seen to depend on two circumstances instead of on only one: (i) the conditions of production of the various commodities and (ii) the division of the product between wages and profits, that is, the real wage

rate. It deserves to be mentioned, however, that Ricardo did not think that this finding undermined his explanation of the rate of profits in terms of the quantities of labour embodied in the surplus product (net of rent) and capital advanced, respectively (see, for example, *Works* I, pp. 49 and 64).
4. Ong (1983) connects the first of these two aspects of Ricardo's search for an invariable measure of value to the measure of the 'difficulty of production'. He contends that the first aspect

> is central to Ricardo's argument regarding how income distribution is determined over the long-term course of capital accumulation by the deteriorating marginal conditions of production of a constant real-wage basket, while the second [aspect] is important chiefly in buttressing one side of his theory of short-run equilibrium movements in the labor market under constant conditions of production. (p. 208)

This opinion cannot be sustained. There is ample evidence that Ricardo did not assume the real-wage basket to be constant in the long run. Changes in the real wage rate therefore cannot be limited to the short run. Hence long run changes in (relative) prices are the combined results of changes in technical conditions of production and changes in the real wage rate. Ricardo was well aware of this. Indeed, his disenchantment with a measure of value which would be always produced under the same conditions of production resulted precisely from his clear understanding that such a measure would not at the same time be, and forever remain, a measure which is also invariant with respect to changes in distribution.
5. It could be treated only in a theory of technical change; we will come back to this in the concluding remarks.
6. Similarly, in his letter to McCulloch of 21 August 1823 Ricardo stressed: 'When we measure the length of a piece of linen we measure length only, . . . but value is compounded of two elements wages and profit mixed up in all imaginable proportions' (*Works*, IX, p. 361).
7. For example, in several places he assumes that 'an epidemic disorder carried off a vast number of the people', with a consequent rise in real wages (*Works* IV, p. 362); or that a 'vast number of people come into this country from Ireland and by their competition sink the price of labour' (ibid., p. 408). (In this connection it is worth pointing out that the notion of 'substitution' between 'factors of production' and thus the explanation of distribution and employment in terms of opposing forces of supply and demand are absent in Ricardo. Hence there is no presumption that a fall in real wages will lead to full employment of labour. See on this Garegnani, 1984.)
8. Commenting on a proposition by Torrens he asks what the latter means by 'equal capitals':

> If he answer I mean what I have often mentioned equal quantities of loaves and suits of cloathing for the support of labourers I understand him, but I again ask him to compare the capital of the cloathier consisting of buildings steam engines, raw material & c^a., with the

120 *Ricardo and Classical Political Economy*

> capital of the sugar baker consisting of a very different set of commodities, and then to tell me what he means by equal capitals – he must answer that by *equal capitals* he means *capitals of equal value*. (ibid., p. 393, emphasis added)

In this argument it is implicitly acknowledged that to describe different technical conditions of production with reference to the 'capitals' applied is problematic, since it implies that the problem (of value) has already been solved, to the solution of which that very description was meant to provide a first step.

9. The reader will recall that the 'mass of commodities' as a standard had already been taken into consideration by Ricardo and then rejected in his contribution to monetary theory.
10. In what follows we shall concentrate on the simple case of single-product industries.
11. Clearly, the role of the Standard commodity is that of a special numeraire. The numeraire is chosen by the theorist; it neither depends on 'observed facts' nor can it alter their 'mathematical properties'. This simple fact does not seem to have been always understood properly. For example, Blaug in an entry to *The New Palgrave* contends:

> It is obvious . . . that an exogenous change in wages unconnected with a change in productive techniques alters the rate of profit but has no effect on relative prices measured in terms of the Standard commodity for the simple reason that the change alters the measuring rod in the same way as it alters the pattern of prices being measured. (Blaug, 1987, p. 436; similarly Blaug, 1985, p. 140)

If this were true, by mere choice of numeraire prices could be made independent of distribution and therefore the choice of numeraire would affect relative prices! P. A. Samuelson in another entry showed full awareness that the choice of the numeraire cannot affect relative prices, but insinuated that Sraffa was not so aware:

> Sraffa, for reasons not easy to understand, thought that $[(w = 1 - (r/R)]$'s truth somehow provided Ricardo with a defence for his labour theory of value. (Samuelson, 1987, p. 456)

There is no evidence whatsoever in support of this interpretation. On the contrary, Sraffa quite explicitly emphasized that the Standard commodity 'is a purely auxiliary construction' (p. 31) and 'cannot alter its [the system's] mathematical properties' (p. 23). For an opinion similar to Samuelson's, see Burmeister (1980a, 1980b, 1984). For a more detailed criticism of the view under consideration, see Kurz and Salvadori (1987).

12. See, for instance, Medio (1972), Eatwell (1975), Broome (1977), Bacha, Carneiro, and Taylor (1977). For a position which is similar to ours, see Roncaglia (1978).
13. In Appendix D to his book Sraffa points out: 'It should perhaps be stated that it was only when the Standard *system* and the distinction between

basics and non-basics had emerged in the course of the present investigation that the [corn model] interpretation of Ricardo's theory suggested itself as a natural consequence' (Sraffa, 1960, p. 93; emphasis added). This must certainly not taken to support the physical analogue interpretation of the Standard *commodity*. In fact, in the paragraph preceding the one just quoted, Sraffa stresses that 'in the terms adopted [in Sraffa (1960)] . . . corn is the sole "basic product" in the economy' (ibid.) considered by Ricardo in the *Essay on Profits*.

14. Flaschel (1984) has made this clear in terms of a nice numerical example. However, he used this example to argue that the analysis of income distribution is 'obscured if the Standard [c]ommodity is used for *numeraire*' (p. 129). Clearly this 'obscurity' derives from the fact that the Standard commodity is used for a purpose it was not designed for. Flaschel (1984) is interested in determining the wage share in an economy with one technique and given produced quantities: in this case the most useful numeraire is perhaps the actual real net national income so that its value is constant with respect to changes in distribution. It can be remarked, however, that if the thought experiment is different (for instance, to determine the wage share in an economy with one technique, constant returns to scale, a positive uniform growth rate and/or different consumption bundles for workers and capitalists), then 'actual real net national income' cannot be determined independently of distribution and a distribution numeraire is to be used.

15. This fact has been 'discovered' several times. Recently Woods (1987) has presented a simple proof to show that the Standard commodity satisfies the 'critical proportion' at any possible wage rate if and only if it itself is utilized as numeraire. Flaschel (1986) uses this fact to argue that there are flaws in the construction of the Standard commodity and that it cannot be an 'invariable measure of value' unless the actual system is a Standard system from the beginning. The whole criticism by Flaschel (1986) is based on the elementary misconception that an 'invariable measure of value' is a commodity whose price is constant in terms of the 'national income' (see, for instance, pp. 597 and 600). On the basis of this misunderstanding it comes as no surprise that the Standard commodity 'is devoid of economic content' (ibid., p. 600).

16. This possibility of telling of any particular price-fluctuation that it arises from the peculiarities of the commodity which is being measured and not from those of the measuring standard may perhaps be further clarified by the following argument. Let the pair $(A, 1)$ denote a technique, where A is the material inputs matrix and 1 is the labour input vector, the output matrix being set equal to the identity matrix I by appropriate choice of physical units. (Let (A, y) be a fictitious technique where the vector 1 has been replaced by vector y which is the eigenvector of matrix A corresponding to the eigenvalue of maximum modulus normalized in an appropriate way. Techniques $(A, 1)$ and (A, y) have the same Maximum rate of profits, and at this rate of profits they have the same prices. In the fictitious technique (A, y) relative prices do not change as distribution changes: the conditions of production of each commodity do not necessitate a price-change with respect to any other commodity. If any

commodity produced under the conditions of the fictitious technique (A, y) should stay side by side with the commodities produced under the conditions of the actual technique (A, l) it would be a commodity whose conditions of production do not enforce for a price-change with respect to any other commodity and, therefore, any actual price-change would be enforced by the conditions of production of the other commodities. *But* techniques (A, l) and (A, y) have the same Standard commodity. Hence the Standard commodity of technique (A, l) *is* produced under the conditions of the fictitious technique (A, y) and stays side by side with all the commodities produced under the conditions of the actual technique (A, l).

17. Notice that Sraffa uses the indefinite article. This can perhaps be considered an indirect evidence that he was aware of the fact that the Standard commodity does not need to be the only numeraire that yields a linear relationship between the wage rate and the rate of profits (a complete analysis of this issue has been provided by Miyao, 1977). The following paragraph (§ 24) introduces the idea that both the input and the output of the standard might consist of quantities of the same commodity bundle and thus prepares the ground for the construction of the Standard system. Interestingly, now the definite article is used in the heading, which reads 'The perfect composite commodity'.

REFERENCES

Bacha, Edmar, Carneiro, Dionisio, and Taylor, Lance (1977) 'Sraffa and Classical Economics: Fundamental Equilibrium Relationships', *Metroeconomica*, 29, pp. 39–53.

Blaug, Mark (1985) *Economic Theory in Retrospect*, fourth edition (Cambridge: Cambridge University Press).

Blaug, Mark (1987) 'Classical Economics', in *The New Palgrave: A Dictionary of Economics*, ed. John L. Eatwell, Murray Milgate and Peter K. Newman (London: Macmillan) vol. I, p. 434–45.

Broome, John (1977) 'Sraffa's Standard commodity', *Australian Economic Papers*, 16, pp. 231–6.

Burmeister, Edwin (1980a) *Capital Theory and Dynamics* (New York: Cambridge University Press).

Burmeister, Edwin (1980b) 'Critical Observations on the Labor Theory of Value and Sraffa's Standard Commodity', in *Quantitative Economics and Development: Essays in Memory of Ta-Chung Lin*, ed. by Lawrence R. Klein, Marc Nerlove, and Sho Chieh Tsiang (New York: Academic Press) 81–103.

Burmeister, Edwin (1984) 'Sraffa, Labor Theories of Value, and the Economics of Real Wage Rate Determination', *Journal of Political Economy*, 92, pp. 508–26.

Eatwell, John (1975) 'Mr. Sraffa's Standard commodity and the Rate of

Exploitation', *The Quarterly Journal of Economics*, 89, pp. 543–55.
Flaschel, Peter (1984) 'The Standard commodity and the Theory of Income Distribution – A Critical Note', *Australian Economic Papers*, 23, pp. 123–9.
Flaschel, Peter (1986) 'Sraffa's Standard commodity: No Fulfillment of Ricardo's Dream of an "Invariable Measure of Value"', *Journal of Institutional and Theoretical Economics*, 142, pp. 588–602.
Garegnani, P. (1984) 'Value and Distribution in the Classical Economists and Marx', *Oxford Economic Papers*, 36, pp. 291–325.
Kurz, H. D. and Salvadori, N. (1987) 'Burmeister on Sraffa and the Labor Theory of Value: A Comment', *Journal of Political Economy*, 95, pp. 870–81.
Lutz, F. A. and Hague, D. C. (eds) (1961) *The Theory of Capital* (London: Macmillan).
Marcuzzo, M. C. and Rosselli, A. (1986) *The Theory of the Gold Standard and Ricardo's Standard commodity*, Discussion Paper No. 13, Dipartimento di Economia Politica, Università degli Studi di Modena (Italy).
Medio, Alfredo (1972) 'Profits and Surplus-Value: Appearance and Reality in Capitalist Production' in E. K. Hunt and J. G. Schwartz (eds), *A Critique of Economic Theory: Selected Readings* (Harmondsworth: Penguin) pp. 312–46.
Miyao, T. (1977) 'A Generalization of Sraffa's Standard commodity and its Complete Characterization', *International Economic Review*, 18, pp. 151–62.
Ong, Nai-Pew (1983) 'Ricardo's Invariable Measure of Value and Sraffa's "Standard commodity"', *History of Political Economy*, 15, pp. 207–27.
Ricardo, D. (1951 ssq.) *The Works and Correspondence of David Ricardo*, 11 volumes, ed. by P. Sraffa with the collaboration of M. H. Dobb (Cambridge: Cambridge University Press).
Roncaglia, Alessandro (1978) *Sraffa and the Theory of Prices*, translated by J. A. Kregel (London: Wiley).
Samuelson, Paul Anthony (1987) 'Sraffian Economics', in Eatwell, Milgate and Newman (eds) op. cit., IV, p. 452–61.
Schefold, Bertram (1976) 'Nachworte', in Schefold, Bertram (ed.) *Warenproduktion mittels Warren*, German translation of Sraffa (1960) (Frankfurt: Suhrkamp).
Schefold, Bertram (1986) 'The Standard commodity as a Tool of Economic Analysis: A Comment on Flaschel', *Journal of Institutional and Theoretical Economics*, 142, pp. 603–22.
Sraffa, P. (1951) 'Introduction', in Ricardo (1951 ssq.), I, pp. xiii–lxii.
Sraffa, P. (1960) *Production of Commodities by Means of Commodities* (Cambridge: Cambridge University Press).
Steedman, Ian (1985) 'On the "Impossibility" of Hicks' – Neutral Technical Change', *Economic Journal*, 95, pp. 746–58.
Woods, John E. (1987) 'Sraffa's Critical Proportion and the Standard commodity', *Economic Notes*, 16, p. 60–6.

4 Ricardian Comparative Advantage and the Perils of the Stationary State
Andrea Maneschi

INTRODUCTION

Professor Luigi Pasinetti's 'A Mathematical Formulation of the Ricardian System' has justly earned him a lasting reputation among scholars of Ricardian economics, and remains one of the contributions for which he is best known to the profession at large (Pasinetti, 1960). It inspired many of the subsequent attempts to capture the essential features of the system of thought of Ricardo and other classical economists in mathematical form. Pasinetti's model is couched in explicitly dynamic form and establishes the existence, uniqueness and stability of the stationary-state equilibrium solution obtained. As Professor Pasinetti acknowledges in his paper, his two-sector model can be reduced to the one-sector one in terms of corn developed by Nicholas Kaldor a few years before (Kaldor, 1955–6). However, in contrast to Kaldor's primarily graphical exposition, Pasinetti's model is not only presented with full mathematical rigour, but has the advantage of being cast in terms of two sectors, with a further generalization to many nonwage goods.

The two-sector formulation makes Pasinetti's closed economy model amenable to being adapted to a two-commodity international trade setting, which allows it to reflect the impact of international trade on the economy's trajectory over time, as well as the principle of comparative advantage with which Ricardo's name is widely associated. This open-economy version of the Ricardian system helps to place Chapter VII of Ricardo's *Principles of Political Economy and Taxation* (Ricardo, 1951) in its proper perspective, in view of the frequent allusions contained in it (and elsewhere in the *Principles*) to the dynamic benefits, in terms of higher growth and profit rates, which can accrue to an economy which allows the importation of wage goods from cheaper foreign suppliers.

Pasinetti's model provides an elegant demonstration that a closed Ricardian economy tends, in the absence of technological progress, towards a stationary state in which the rate of profits is reduced to zero (or to the minimum rate acceptable to capitalists before they cease to invest), and the workers' wage rate has sunk to its 'natural' level 'which is necessary to enable the laborers, one with another, to subsist and to perpetuate their race, without either increase or diminution' (Ricardo, 1951, p. 93). Because the margin of cultivation has been extended as much as possible, given the size of the natural wage rate, landlords' rental income is maximized. Throughout the economy's path towards the stationary state (which, as Pasinetti rigorously proves, defines a unique and stable equilibrium), the rate of profits is set by the margin of cultivation in the agricultural (corn) sector, as is the associated rate of capital accumulation. The other (gold) sector merely reflects these changes and serves primarily as the ('unproductive') destination of the landlord's consumption. The corn sector is a 'basic' sector in the sense of Sraffa (1960), in that corn is the sole wage good and any changes in the margin of cultivation due to the growth of population have an immediate impact on the money (gold) wage, and hence on the rates of profits and accumulation. By contrast, the 'nonbasic' gold sector produces a luxury good whose conditions of production do not affect the rate of profits or the economy's growth rate (Pasinetti, 1960, p. 85).

Following Ricardo's own exposition, Pasinetti distinguishes between labour's market wage rate and its natural wage rate. An excess of the former over the latter results in

> a growth of population [which] again brings back the real wage-rate to its *natural* level. It is very impressive to notice how strongly Ricardo is convinced of the operation of this mechanism. To be precise, he always speaks of a process which will operate 'ultimately' but the emphasis on it is so strong that his analysis is always carried on *as if* the response were almost immediate. . . . In other words, he concentrates on describing the changing characteristics of his system in terms of *natural* behavior of the variables in a process of capital accumulation. (Pasinetti, 1960, pp. 81 and 87–8; emphasis in the original)

Subsequent contributions to the interpretation of the Ricardian system have challenged this assumption, and there has emerged a so-called 'New View' which proposes that the market wage can not only deviate from its natural level along the economy's trajectory, but can actually rise for a considerable length of time before eventually sinking towards the natural wage rate as the stationary state approaches. The proponents of the New View have provided extensive textual support for their position.[1] Responding to it in 'A Comment on the "New View" of the Ricardian Theory', Professor Pasinetti (1982) notes that this contrast between what he calls the 'Pasinetti-Sraffa version of the Ricardian system' and the Hicks-Hollander-Casarosa view is more apparent than real: the former fully allows for distinct market and natural wage rates, and is in no sense a 'fix-wage' system. Indeed, it is the very difference between these wage rates which acts as a stimulus for the growth of population, and 'it follows – as a strict logical consequence – that, in an economy with population growth and constant technology, as it is considered by Casarosa, the actual wage rate will normally be *above* its "natural" level, which in turn will itself normally be above the subsistence level' (op. cit., p. 241). At the same time, Pasinetti sees some dangers in 'Casarosa's type of analysis, if not appropriately understood':

> by concentrating all emphasis on the Ricardian notion of *market* wage rate, Casarosa's approach is open to the danger of neglecting – or reducing to irrelevance – the much more fundamental notion of a *natural* wage rate. This is in fact the trap into which – it seems to me – Hicks and Hollander (1977) have fallen. In their analysis, the 'natural' wage rate plays no role. To begin with, they confuse it with the 'subsistence' wage; and second, they relegate the latter to play the external role of a boundary 'floor'. All their attention is concentrated on the *market* wage rate. (ibid.)

To my mind, a careful reading of the Casarosa and Hicks-Hollander papers does not support this last contention. In both their models there is a clear tendency for the economy ultimately to attain the stationary state, in which the market wage is reduced to the level of the natural wage. Although Pasinetti's formalization of the Ricardian system does distinguish between market and natural wage rates, Caravale and Tosato (1980) correctly point out that his analysis is not a fully dynamic one in the sense that much of it is in fact conducted – as he himself states – *as if* the wage rate were at its natural level, which would then make it impossible for capital accumulation to lead to a rise in population.[2]

Comparative Advantage and the Stationary State

THE OPEN RICARDIAN SYSTEM

Rather than dwell further on these controversies, I wish to explore here the open-economy implications of the dynamic Ricardian model. I have previously (Maneschi, 1983) modified the Hicks-Hollander-Casarosa version of this model in order to allow for international trade, and to highlight the dynamic nature of the gains from trade which accrue to a Ricardian economy and can radically modify its path over time. Ricardo masterfully expounded the nature of both static and dynamic gains from trade in Chapter VII of his *Principles*. The static gains are the ones celebrated by all textbooks on international economics. In Ricardo's words, trade 'will very powerfully contribute to increase the mass of commodities, and therefore the sum of enjoyments' (Ricardo, 1951, p. 128). The dynamic gains have instead been neglected in most accounts of the open Ricardian system. Ricardo expected such gains to accrue to a country like England if it were to abolish the Corn Laws and thus permit the free importation of a wage good like corn when this can be produced more cheaply abroad. The consequent decrease in the money wage in terms of gold would entail a corresponding rise in the rate of profits and hence (given the classical accumulation function) in the economy's growth rate.[3]

After briefly reviewing in this section of the paper the mathematical structure of the closed and open Ricardian systems, and the nature of the gains from trade enjoyed by two open Ricardian economies, I plan to analyze in the next section the types of adjustment which two such economies must undergo as they approach the stationary state, and to examine in detail the impact of trade on the equilibrium they attain when the latter is reached. The two-sector closed Ricardian system, based on Pasinetti (1960) and Casarosa (1978), is given by equations (1) – (6) below. The economy consists of an agricultural ('corn') and an industrial ('gold') sector. Let N_i = labour force employed in sector i (i = 1, 2), N = total labour force (synonymous with population), X_i = output of sector i, w = market wage rate, w_n = natural wage rate (both wage rates being expressed in terms of corn), r = rate of profits, K (= wN) = corn capital stock, or wage fund. The corn sector (sector 1) produces corn subject to the production function $X_1 = f(N_1)$, assumed to be such that $f(0) = 0$, $f'(N_1) > 0$, $f'(0) > w_n$, $f'(\infty) < w_n$ and $f''(N_1) < 0$. Sector 2 produces a manufactured good ('gold') using labour alone subject to constant returns, so that $X_2 = aN_2$, where a is a constant.

Wages are advanced at the beginning of the period of production, which is the same in both sectors. Workers spend their entire wage on corn, landlords their entire rent income on gold, and capitalists invest a fraction s of their profits in addition to the corn wage fund, while spending the rest on the consumption of gold. The output of the corn sector is identically equal to the replacement of the wage fund plus any net change in it, or

$$f(N_1) = wN(1 + \hat{K}), \qquad (1)$$

where $\hat{}$ denotes a proportional growth rate, so that $\hat{K} = (dK/dt)/K$. The economy's profit rate, r, is determined in the agricultural sector, and is equal to non-rent income in that sector net of the wage fund, divided by the wage fund:

$$r = [f'(N_1)/w] - 1. \qquad (2)$$

The growth rate of the wage fund is given by the classical savings function

$$\hat{K} = sr, \qquad (3)$$

where $0 < s \leq 1$, and the growth rate of population is a positive function of the difference between the market and natural wage rates:

$$\hat{N} = h(w - w_n), \qquad (4)$$

where $h(0) = 0$ and $h'(w - w_n) > 0$.[4]

Differentiation of the identity $K \equiv wN$ results in

$$\hat{w} \equiv \hat{K} - \hat{N} \qquad (5)$$

The economy's price ratio p, defined as the relative price of gold in terms of corn, P_2/P_1, is obtained by equating the profit rate in agriculture, given by (2), to that in the gold sector, $(pa/w) - 1$, which yields

$$p = f'(N_1)/a. \qquad (6)$$

The model consisting of equations (1) – (6) can be solved for the endogenous variables N_1, r, $\hat{K}$, $\hat{N}$, $\hat{w}$ and p in terms of the instantaneously given exogenous variables K and N (and hence $w = K/N$),

Comparative Advantage and the Stationary State 129

and the parameters s, w_n and a. The values of K and N thus help to determine their growth rates and hence the trajectory of the economy over time.

The open version of the Ricardian system allows for an economy's export of one of the two goods, matched in value by the import of the other good. Equations (3), (4) and (5) defining its equilibrium over time are the same as before, but (1), (2) and (6) may differ, depending on whether the economy becomes fully specialized in one of the commodities, or remains diversified. If (a) denotes a diversified economy, (b) complete specialization in corn and (c) complete specialization in gold, the equations corresponding to these three cases, denoted by (1a), (1b), etc., are

$f(N_1) - E_1 = wN(1 + \hat{K})$ (1a) $f(N) - E_1 = wN(1 + \hat{K})$ (1b)

$r = f'(N_1)/w - 1$ (2a) $r = f'(N)/w - 1$ (2b)

$p = f'(N_1)/a$ (6a) $p \leq f'(N_1)/a$ (6b)

$-E_1 = wN(1 + \hat{K})$ (1c)

$r = pa/w - 1$ (2c)

$p \geq f'(0)/a$ (6c)

where E_1 = exports (if positive) or imports (if negative) of corn.[5] If the economy specializes in corn, $N_1 = N$ and p must be smaller than (or in the limit equal to) the marginal product of the last (or N^{th}) unit of labour in the corn sector divided by a. If it specializes in gold, the productivity of labour in the gold sector expressed in terms of corn, pa, must exceed the marginal product $f'(0)$ of the first unit of labour hypothetically employed in the corn sector, as stipulated by equation (6c).

The opening of trade between two hitherto closed Ricardian economies can have a dramatic impact on their trajectories. Trade 'rejuvenates' (to use Burgstaller's (1986) apt term) the corn-importing economy since its profit and growth rates suddenly increase. It is even possible that its market wage rate, which had been declining towards the natural level, starts rising over time. The corn-exporting economy suffers a corresponding senescence in that its profit and growth rates fall, hastening its approach towards the stationary state.[6]

The pattern of specialization between two open Ricardian economies depends on their terms of trade. The two economies are assumed to be governed by one of the three alternative equation systems specified above, and the terms of trade, p^i, are found by stipulating that one country's corn imports equal the other's exports. The terms of trade can be obtained graphically by the intersection of the two countries' offer curves, which can result in neither economy being specialized, or in one or both of them being specialized.[7]

To explore further the trajectories followed by two free-trading Ricardian economies, consider first the case where neither of them is specialized. The 'Foreign' country's variables and parameters are distinguished from the 'Home' country's by having asterisks attached to them. Without loss of generality, assume that $a^* = 1$, so that $p^* = f^{*\prime}(N_1^*)$. Since trade equalizes relative prices in the two countries, the terms of trade are given by

$$p^i = f'(N_1)/a = f^{*\prime}(N_1^*). \qquad (7)$$

Substituting (1a), (2a) and (3) into the international equilibrium condition

$$E_1 + E_1^* = 0, \qquad (8)$$

we obtain

$$f(N_1) - wN(1 + sf'(N_1)/w-s) + f^*(N_1^*) \\ - w^*N^*(1 + s^*f^{*\prime}(N_1^*)/w^*-s^*) = 0. \qquad (9)$$

Omitting functional arguments, differentiation of (7) and (9) results in

$$dN_1^*/dN_1 = f''/af^{*\prime\prime} > 0 \qquad (10)$$

and

$$dN_1^*/dN_1 = -(f' - sNf'')/(f^{*\prime} - s^*N^*f^{*\prime\prime}) < 0. \qquad (11)$$

For given values of N, N^*, w and w^*, (7) and (9) define two implicit functions $\phi(N_1, N_1^*) = 0$ and $\psi(N_1, N_1^*) = 0$ whose slopes are given by (10) and (11). These functions are depicted graphically in the right-hand panel of Figure 4.1, where the axes measure the agricultural labour forces of the Home and Foreign countries. The function $\phi(N_1,$

Comparative Advantage and the Stationary State

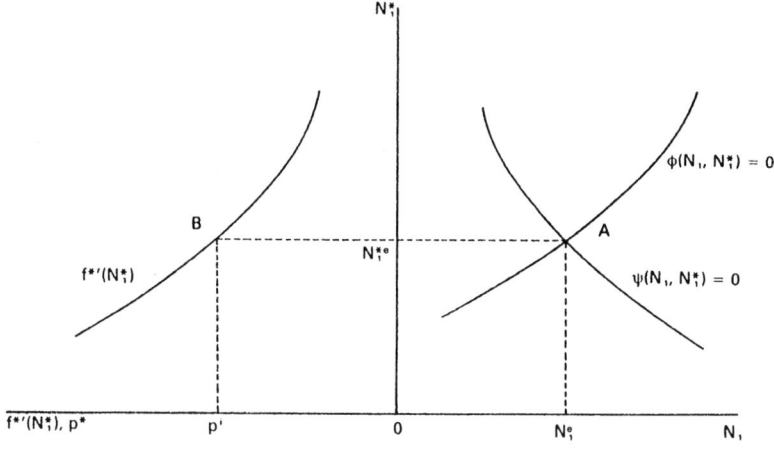

FIGURE 4.1

$N_1^*) = 0$ slopes upward since, given that both economies produce corn, the condition that their price ratios be the same requires that their marginal corn products of labour should move in the same direction over time, so that N_1 and N_1^* vary positively with each other. On the other hand, $\psi(N_1, N_1^*) = 0$ slopes downward since, for given values of all the other variables, a larger value of N_1 implies that the Home country's net exports of corn are larger and hence, because of (8), that the Foreign country's net exports of corn should be smaller, which in turn requires N_1^* to be smaller. The intersection A of $\phi = 0$ and $\psi = 0$ yields the temporary equilibrium values of N_1 and N_1^*, N_1^e and N_1^{*e}. The left-hand panel plots the marginal product of the Foreign country's agricultural labour force (measured leftwards from the origin 0) and hence, by (6a), the Foreign country's price ratio against N_1^*. Because of (7), the equilibrium terms of trade p^i are given by the value of p^* at point B corresponding to N_1^{*e}. The profit rates and all other variables of interest in the two countries follow immediately from these values.

Over time, barring technological changes, the function $\phi(N_1, N_1^*) = 0$ remains stationary while $\psi(N_1, N_1^*) = 0$ shifts up as K, N and w change according to (3), (4) and (5) in the Home country, and K*, N* and w* change according to the analogous equations for the Foreign country. The shift in ψ causes both N_1 and N_1^* to rise over time, while (from the left-hand panel of Figure 4.1) p^i falls over time, so that the terms of trade deteriorate for the gold-exporting country. It is possible for one or both countries to become fully specialized, in which case its behavior would be governed by the equation system (b) or (c) above with its implied changes for the functions θ and ψ. Moreover, it is conceivable that on the way towards the stationary state, one or more reversals of comparative advantage can occur.[8]

Although the 'gains from trade' in each economy can be separated into static and dynamic ones, as argued above, the intra-country distributional implications of the static 'gains' should be noted. In the corn-importing country, the share of national income accruing to landlords is lower than it would be if the economy were suddenly to revert to autarky, and the absolute level of their real income is also lower, both because their rent in terms of corn is lower, and because the higher price of gold causes the purchasing power of this rent in terms of gold to be even lower. In the corn-exporting country, the opposite phenomena are observed, with a higher corn rental accruing to landlords than under autarky, and an even higher purchasing power of this rent in terms of gold. In each country, the interests of the other two social classes are opposed to those of landlords. Because of the distributional changes wrought by trade, the expression 'gains from trade', as has been repeatedly emphasized by trade theorists (e.g., Samuelson, 1962), must therefore be carefully qualified. The 'static' gains which an economy can attain by consuming at a point located beyond its transformation curve are only potential, and can be realized without harm to any social class only by the implementation of a suitable tax-transfer mechanism such that the losers are compensated by the gainers. However, in the absence of international transfers, it is not possible to compensate the corn-exporting country for the dynamic losses which trade inflicts upon it.

TRADE IN THE STATIONARY STATE

Rather than delve further into the dynamic analysis of two free-trading Ricardian economies, I now wish to examine the implications of the pattern of trade which emerges between them in the stationary state, and the 'gains from trade' associated with it. I believe that this concern with the 'ultimate' implications of the open Ricardian system is consistent with Professor Pasinetti's emphasis on the importance in Ricardo's framework of thought of the natural levels towards which the main variables of interest, such as the wage and profits rates, tend over time.[9] One such interesting implication concerns the size of the population in the two countries in the cum-trade as opposed to the autarkic stationary state, which is a consequence of the patterns of specialization entailed by their long-run comparative advantage. A country's possible loss of population can be expected to be a cause of concern for its policymakers, impelling them to interfere with the free trade policy which leads to this outcome.

If the Home country were to attain the stationary state as a closed economy, its price ratio would equal $f'(N_1)/a = w_n/a$. If the Foreign country were in the same position, its price ratio would equal $w_n^*/a^* = w_n^*$. If the two countries had attained stationariness as closed economies and were now opened to trade, it is clear that the adjustment required of both of them would imply the end of their stationary states. Since w_n/a can equal w_n^* only by a fluke, it is moreover impossible that, after whatever dynamic adjustment processes their economies underwent as a result of their opening to trade, they would revert to their original stationary states. The latter would imply inequality in their price ratios, which is ruled out by the assumptions of free trade and zero transport costs. In order to analyze the possible open-economy stationary-state equilibria, consider Table 4.1, where the subscripts c, n and g attached to the two countries, H and F, refer to their being specialized in corn, non-specialized, and specialized in gold.

TABLE 4.1 *Possible stationary-state patterns of specialization*

		Foreign country		
		c	n	g
	c	–	H_cF_n	–
Home country	n	H_nF_c	–	–
	g	–	–	–

The patterns of specialization implied by the main diagonal of this table are ruled out either because of what was stated in the previous paragraph regarding the H_nF_n possibility, or because both countries would be specializing in the same commodity. A possible H_nF_g (or H_gF_n) equilibrium is ruled out since the implied price ratios would again be w_n/a and w_n^*, which are in general unequal. The possibility that one country specializes in gold and the other in corn is also ruled out. In the case H_gF_c, for example, the Home country's specialization

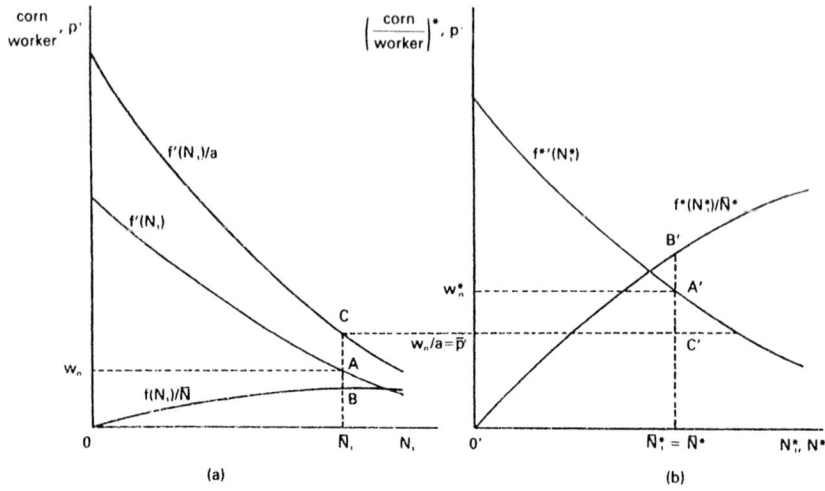

FIGURE 4.2

in gold implies that its stationary-state terms of trade, w_n/a, must exceed $f'(0)/a$, i.e., that $w_n > f'(0)$. But this contradicts one of the assumptions on which Pasinetti's Ricardian model is based, namely that $f'(0) > w_n$.[10] The only remaining possible equilibria are therefore the two shown in the table, of which we need only consider one, H_nF_c, since the other is symmetrical to it with the two countries interchanged.

The stationary equilibrium achieved in the case H_nF_c is illustrated in Figures 4.2 and 4.3. Figure 4.2 illustrates the Home country's (panel (a)) and Foreign country's (panel (b)) equilibria in the stationary state. The marginal products of labour in the corn sector, $f'(N_1)$ and $f^{*\prime}(N_1^*)$, are plotted as functions of their respective agricultural labour forces. Panel (a) also shows the curve $f'(N_1)/a$, which yields the price ratio in the Home country as a function of N_1. Denoting stationary-state values by a bar over a variable, point A corresponds to the value of N_1, $\bar{N}_1$, such that $f'(N_1)$ equals the natural wage rate w_n. This implies that the Home country has reached the stationary state where $w = w_n$ and, by (2a), (3), (4) and (5), $r = \hat{K} = \hat{N} = \hat{w} = 0$. The corresponding price ratio, w_n/a, is given by point C on the curve $f'(N_1)/a$ where $N_1 = \bar{N}_1$, and is carried over to panel (b) by means of the horizontal line CC'. The curve OB plots corn output per capita, $f(N_1)/\bar{N}$, corresponding to the stationary-state population $\bar{N}$. By (1a), the Home country's imports per capita are $-\bar{E}_1/\bar{N} = w_n - f(\bar{N}_1)/\bar{N}$, shown by the distance AB between the horizontal line $w_n A$, whose height is w_n, and the curve $f(N_1)/\bar{N}$ at the point where $N_1 = \bar{N}_1$.

In panel (b), the terms of trade $\bar{p}^i = w_n/a$ are assumed to be lower than w_n^*, the Foreign country's closed-economy stationary-state price ratio, which by (6b) implies that it specializes in the production of corn. Point A' is analogous to point A and represents the stationary-state equilibrium in the Foreign corn sector given by $f^{*\prime}(\bar{N}^*) = w_n^*$, corresponding to $r^* = \hat{K}^* = \hat{N}^* = \hat{w}^* = 0$. The Foreign country's corn exports per capita, which by (1b) are $\bar{E}_1^*/N^* = f^*(\bar{N}^*)/\bar{N}^* - w_n^*$, are shown by the distance B'A' between the curves $f^*(N_1^*)/\bar{N}^*$ and the horizontal line $w_n^* A'$ at $\bar{N}_1^* = \bar{N}^*$.

With the Foreign country's stationary-state population determined in panel (b) by the abscissa of point A', that of the Home country can be found from the balance of trade condition (8), $\bar{E}_1 + \bar{E}_1^* = 0$, which yields[11]

$$\bar{N} = [f(\bar{N}_1) + f^*(\bar{N}^*) - w_n^* \bar{N}^*]/w_n$$
$$= [f(\bar{N}_1) - w_n \bar{N}_1 + w_n \bar{N}_1 + f^*(\bar{N}^*) - w_n^* \bar{N}^*]/w_n$$
$$= \bar{N}_1 + (\bar{R} + \bar{R}^*)/w_n = \bar{N}_1 + \bar{N}_2 \qquad (12)$$

where $\bar{R}$ (or $\bar{R}^*$) is the annual rent in terms of corn accruing to landlords in the Home (or Foreign) country in the stationary state. As expected, the labour force employed in the gold sector in the Home (nonspecialized) country is equal to the sum of corn rents in the two countries divided by the Home country's natural wage rate. The Foreign country's exports of good 1, $\bar{R}^*$, equal the rent share of its output of that good and, given the terms of trade $\bar{p}^i = w_n/a$, are matched by imports in the amount aR^*/w_n of good 2. The two countries' trade triangles, and their production and consumption equilibria in both the autarkic and the free trade stationary states, are shown in Figure 4.3.

For the Home country, shown in panel (a), Q_a represents the production (and consumption) point in the autarkic stationary state. It is located on the transformation curve $T_a T_a$ at the point where its slope with respect to the vertical axis is equal to w_n/a. Q_t and C_t are its production and consumption points in the cum-trade stationary state, with Q_t located on the transformation curve $T_t T_t$ where its slope is again equal to w_n/a. Note that Q_t is vertically above Q_a since $T_t T_t$ differs from $T_a T_a$ by the Home country having a larger labour force.[12] The Home country's trade triangle is $Q_t Q_a C_t$, whose sides $Q_t Q_a$

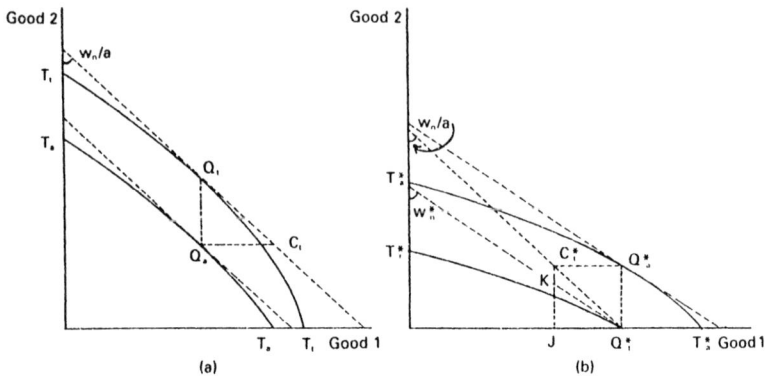

FIGURE 4.3

$= a\bar{R}^*/w_n$ and $Q_a C_t = \bar{R}^*$ measure its exports and imports. The Foreign country's corresponding equilibrium is shown in panel (b), where the cum-trade transformation curve $T_t^* Q_t^*$ now lies below the autarkic one $T_a^* T_a^*$. The slopes of these transformation curves at Q_a^* and Q_t^* are equal to the Foreign country's autarkic stationary-state price ratio w_n^*, which by assumption exceeds the terms of trade w_n/a. The trade triangle $C_t^* Q_a^* Q_t^*$ is of course identical to the Home country's, with $C_t^* Q_a^* = Q_a C_t$ and $Q_a^* Q_t^* = Q_t Q_a$.

The labour forces of the two countries and their allocation between the two sectors, in the autarkic and cum-trade stationary states, are depicted in Figure 4.4, where the vertical axis measures the labour force of the Home country and the horizontal one that of the Foreign country. The coordinates of points A, $(\bar{N}_a^*, \bar{N}_a)$, and T, $(\bar{N}_t^*, \bar{N}_t)$, measure the autarkic and cum-trade total labour force in each country, and those of point B, $(\bar{N}_{1a}^*, \bar{N}_{1a})$ or $(\bar{N}_{1t}^*, \bar{N}_{1t})$, show both the autarkic and cum-trade size of their agricultural labour forces, where $\bar{N}_{1t}^* = \bar{N}_t^*$. The two countries' labour forces in sector 2 are given by the difference $\overrightarrow{BA}$ between the vectors $\overrightarrow{OA}$ and $\overrightarrow{OB}$ in the autarkic stationary state, and by $\overrightarrow{BT} = \overrightarrow{OT} - \overrightarrow{OB}$ in the cum-trade stationary state. Trade causes the Foreign country's population to shrink by the size of its autarkic labour force in the gold sector, so that B is vertically below T.

The world's total labour force in the autarkic and cum-trade stationary states can be compared by evaluating the slope of the line

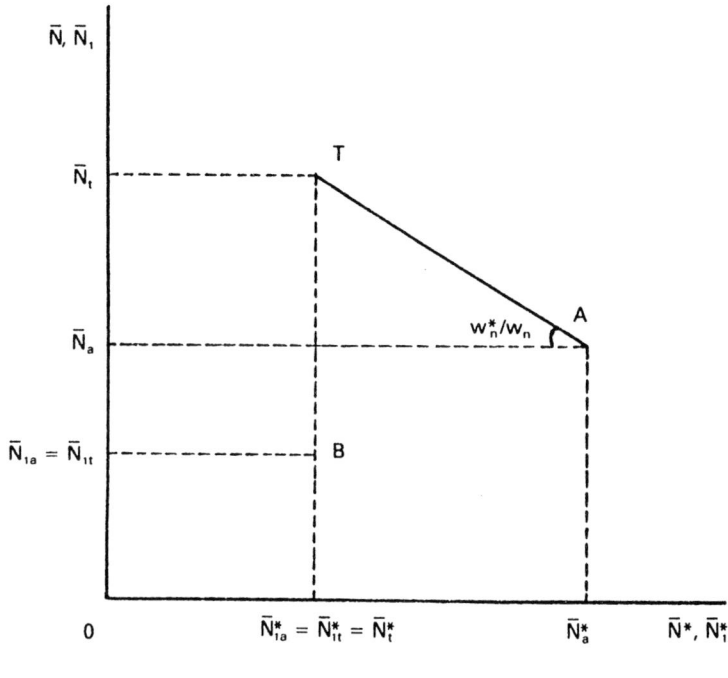

FIGURE 4.4

TA. From (12), given $\bar{N}_a = f(\bar{N}_1)/w_n$, $\bar{N}_a^* = f^*(\bar{N}_1^*)/w_n^*$, $\bar{N}_{1a} = \bar{N}_{1t}$ and $\bar{N}_{1a}^* = \bar{N}_{1t}^* = \bar{N}_t^*$, we obtain

$$\bar{N}_t - \bar{N}_a = w_n^*(\bar{N}_a^* - \bar{N}_t^*)/w_n.$$

Hence the slope of TA, $(\bar{N}_t - \bar{N}_a)/(\bar{N}_a^* - \bar{N}_t^*)$, is equal to w_n^*/w_n. We conclude that $\bar{N}_t + \bar{N}_t^* \gtreqless \bar{N}_a + \bar{N}_a^*$ according as $w_n^* \gtreqless w_n^*$. If the natural wage rates of the two countries were by chance equal, trade would leave the world's total labour force unchanged, with the elimination of one country's gold-sector labour force matched by an equal increase in the other country's. If $w_n^* > w_n/a$ and the Foreign country's natural wage were to exceed (or fall short of) the Home country's, the cum-trade stationary state would be characterized by a larger (or smaller) world labour force than the autarkic one.

It is instructive to examine more closely the reasons for the different values of the two countries' labour force in the cum-trade and the autarkic stationary states. As discussed above, comparative advantage in the long run is determined by whether $w_n/a \gtreqless w_n^*$, i.e., by comparing the ratio of the Home country's stationary-state marginal labour coefficients in gold and corn to the Foreign country's. If this ratio is smaller in the Home country than in the Foreign country, as assumed above, the Home country has a long-run comparative advantage in gold and remains therefore nonspecialized in the cum-trade stationary state, whereas the Foreign country's comparative advantage in corn forces it to become specialized in this commodity, with a corresponding shrinkage of its labour force compared to the autarkic steady state.

To understand the mechanism which causes this shrinkage to occur, imagine both countries to be in their autarkic long-run equilibria when suddenly they become open to trade. Since the price of gold is initially higher in the Foreign country, it starts to import this commodity from the Home country in exchange for corn. But this implies extending the margin of cultivation in the Foreign country, which causes the marginal product of labour in agriculture to sink below the natural wage rate. The profit rate, and hence the growth rate of the corn wage fund, become negative, causing the population and labour force to contract. This continues until the Foreign country becomes fully specialized in corn. This corner solution for its equilibrium output vector allows its marginal rate of transformation, equal to its autarkic stationary-state price ratio, to be different from (larger than) the terms of trade given by the Home country's stationary-state price ratio, as illustrated in panel (b) of Figure 4.3.

Figure 4.3 thus illustrates another dimension of the gains or losses from trade in open Ricardian economies, which is the implication of trade for the size of a country's population in the stationary state. This is itself, of course, a direct result of the trajectory followed by its economy on the way towards the stationary state, as modified by the trading possibilities open to it, and should therefore be viewed in the light of the dynamic gains or losses from trade associated with this trajectory. In comparison with the autarkic stationary state, the (Home) country with the long-run comparative advantage in gold remains diversified in production and gains population at the expense of the other (Foreign) country, which becomes fully specialized in corn. In the Home country, landlords are equally well off in the autarkic and cum-trade stationary states, since agricultural output and relative prices are identical in the two cases. In the Foreign country, however, though agricultural output is also the same, the relative price of gold is lower, so that landlords' consumption is higher. This is illustrated in panel (b) of Figure 4.3, where JQ_t^* ($= C_t^* Q_a^*$) represents rent in terms of good 1; JK is landlords' gold consumption in the autarkic stationary state, given the price ratio w_n^*; and JC_t^* is their gold consumption in the cum-trade stationary state. Capitalists' share is of course zero in either type of stationary state, since profits are zero. Though the size and composition of the labour force differ in each country in the two types of stationary state, the real wage of its workers is of course identical in both cases, being equal to its subsistence wage.[13]

The policy implications of these findings are troubling for the corn-exporting country, assuming this remains the same country over time because of the absence of any reversal in comparative advantage, or of any technological change, along its trajectory towards the stationary state. Not only does the Foreign country advance its own approach to the stationary state by extending the margin of cultivation in order to export corn, thus lowering its profit and growth rates, while allowing its trading partner a corresponding postponement of its own approach to the stationary state. Because of this change in its trajectory with respect to the autarkic one, the Foreign country may eventually become fully specialized in corn, with a resulting sizable loss in population. Its landlord class is the sole beneficiary of this specialization. Just as the capitalist and worker classes can be expected to press for free trade in the Home country in opposition to the landlord class, landlords will be advocates of free trade in the Foreign country in opposition to workers and capitalists whose interests are directly threatened by it.

CONCLUSIONS

Ricardo's scant comments on the stationary state, 'from which I trust we are yet far distant' (Ricardo, 1951, p. 109), suggest that he was not very concerned about the long-run implications of the open-economy model discussed above, if indeed he even foresaw them. Alternatively, if his primary concern was with England's own welfare, both the short- and long-run implications of this model favoured the abolition of the Corn Laws.

If the Home and Foreign countries were to become stationary as free-trading economies, trade between them would be governed by the same principle of comparative advantage expounded by Ricardo in Chapter VII of his *Principles*. Thus, even if $w_n > w_n^*$, so that the Home country's agricultural labour is more productive than the Foreign country's in the stationary state, the Home country will nevertheless export gold if its labour productivity in the gold sector is sufficiently higher than the Foreign country's, i.e., if $a > w_n/w_n^*$. The importance of comparative advantage in the determination of the direction of trade is thus fully vindicated.

The fact that the Home country remains nonspecialized and that its autarkic stationary-state price ratio sets the international terms of trade bears some analogy to the textbook 'Ricardian' model according to which, if one of two constant-cost trading economies remains non-specialized after the opening of trade, the terms of trade coincide with its autarkic price ratio. Note, however, that according to this model *all* the gains from trade then accrue to the Foreign, fully specialized economy. In our stationary-state model, instead, all the dynamic gains from trade prior to the stationary-state equilibrium have been enjoyed by the Home country, which has also gained in population at the expense of the Foreign one. Paradoxically, the Home country reaps these dynamic gains in spite of a continuous deterioration in its terms of trade. In the Foreign country, only the landlord class can be said to profit from the economy's full specialization in its export commodity.

The welfare implications of a Ricardian economy's trade thus appear to be more complex than had previously been imagined. To the traditional static gains from trade must be added the more important dynamic gains as its trajectory towards the stationary state is either accelerated or slowed down. The gold-exporting, corn-importing country (assuming it remains the same country over time, with no reversal of comparative advantage) not only benefits from higher rates of profits and growth, and possibly from a higher corn wage rate, along its modified trajectory. If it maintains a long-run comparative advantage in gold as it approaches the stationary state, its economy remains diversified and gains population at the expense of the other country, which becomes fully specialized in corn.

The Heckscher-Ohlin model is in a sense stood on its head: instead of factor endowments determining trade, trade determines long-run factor endowments.[14] This adds a third dimension to the gains or losses from trade experienced by open Ricardian economies: a long-run endowment-cum-diversification gain or loss. If policymakers are indifferent about the size of their country's population and the prospect of its becoming specialized in a single commodity, this would not be counted as a 'loss' from trade, matched by a 'gain' for its trading partner in terms of an increased population and a diversified economy. But even if a country's policymakers were to abjure all mercantilist tendencies, it is hard to imagine that they would countenance such cataclysmic events with indifference. These additional gains or losses from trade therefore deserve to be noted alongside the traditional ones with which Ricardo's name is associated.

NOTES

1. See Hicks and Hollander (1977), Casarosa (1978, 1982) and Hollander (1979). The contrast between the traditional ('Sraffian') and the New views has been ably drawn and analyzed by Rutherford (1986). The Samuelson (1957) version of the Ricardian system, like Findlay's (1974), assumes that the wage rate is always at the natural level.
2. It is true that in the Appendix to his paper, Pasinetti (1960, pp. 95–8) presents '[a] more rigorous proof of stability' where he shows by means of Taylor series expansions that the stationary state equilibrium is locally stable. But Caravale and Tosato are correct in claiming that his model does not fully reflect the interaction between the two dynamic mechanisms – population adjustment and capital accumulation – except with regard to the properties of the stationary state. 'This aim can be attained solely through the use of a truly dynamic model, incorporating as integral parts the two dynamic mechanisms and their interaction . . .' (Caravale and Tosato, 1980, p. 95). They themselves (pp. 113–14) define the natural wage rate as 'the one at which the labour force expands at exactly the same rate as capital, i.e., the wages fund', a definition which they claim accords with Ricardo's *Essay on Profits*, even though it is inconsistent with that given in the *Principles*. This is an interesting assumption, which is further elaborated in Caravale (1985) but cannot be discussed here in detail (see Maneschi and Thweatt, 1983). Suffice it to say that the Caravale-Tosato analysis is marred by the additional assumption that the natural wage remains constant over time, even as the economy approaches the stationary state. Moreover, in their disequilibrium models, positive population growth can occur even if the market wage is considerably below the natural wage, which seems inconsistent with the Malthusian population hypothesis.
3. The preeminence of this dynamic gain from trade in Ricardo's framework of analysis, as opposed to the traditional static gain, has also been stressed by Robinson (1974), Findlay (1974), Thweatt (1976), Kregel (1977), Walsh (1979) and Burgstaller (1986). Both types of gain are mentioned by Ricardo when he states that

> it is quite as important to the happiness of mankind that our enjoyments should be increased by the better distribution of labour, by each

country producing those commodities for which by its situation, its climate, and its other natural or artificial advantages, it is adapted, and by their exchanging them for the commodities of other countries, as that they should be augmented by a rise in the rate of profits. (Ricardo, 1951, p. 132)

4. Eq. (4) is equivalent to Pasinetti's eq. (17) (Pasinetti, 1960, p. 86) and eq. (3) is the same as Casarosa's eq. (V) (Casarosa, 1978, p. 45). As Pasinetti (op. cit., p. 87, footnote 1) points out, the capital accumulation function can be readily modified so as to require a minimum profit rate to induce a positive rate of accumulation.
5. See Maneschi (1983), p. 73.
6. See Maneschi (1983) and Burgstaller (1986). A possible offset to these tendencies would follow from Casarosa's (1978) assumption that the propensity to accumulate of capitalists is inversely related to the price of gold, which makes the effects of trade in the corn-importing economy less favourable, and those in the other economy less unfavourable, than otherwise. Note that the possibility that the real wage rate rises over a certain period of time before eventually falling can also occur in the case of the closed Ricardian system, as pointed out by Hicks and Hollander (1977), who quote (p. 365) Ricardo's assertion that 'notwithstanding the tendency of wages to conform to their natural rate, their market rate may, in an improving society, for an indefinite period be constantly above it'. Moreover,

> it has been calculated, that under favourable circumstances population may be doubled in twenty-five years; but under the same favourable circumstances, the whole capital of a country might possibly be doubled in a shorter period. In that case, wages during the whole period would have a tendency to rise, because the demand for labor would increase still faster than the supply. (Ricardo, 1951, pp. 94–5 and 98)

Although not explicitly mentioned by Ricardo, the possibility of importing cheap corn could be the cause of such a 'doubling' of capital in a short span of time.
7. See Maneschi (1983). No problem of terms of trade indeterminacy arises in this Ricardian model, as opposed to Ricardo's original numerical example designed to illustrate the workings of comparative advantage in Chapter VII of the *Principles*. The reason is that, with each social class consuming a single commodity, their demand patterns are well specified. See also Burgstaller (1986, p. 477).
8. As I pointed out in my 1983 paper, comparative advantage is affected by a number of variables and parameters pertaining to the two countries, such as their market wages, land-labour ratios, technological advantages (comparative and/or absolute) in either corn or gold production, and capitalists' propensities to consume out of profits. The first two variables depend of course on the trajectories followed by the two economies up to a given point in time, which are in turn conditioned by their labour growth and capital accumulation functions.

Burgstaller (1986, fn. 17, p. 480) takes me to task for failing to distinguish in that paper between the role of structure and the role of time in causing trade. 'Structure' refers to parameters such as those underlying the technology and the consumption propensities of the three social classes. It is indeed true that two 'structurally' identical economies have the incentive to trade if they differ in such respects as the time elapsed since the same parameter change occurred in them. For example, Burgstaller (p. 474) shows that if two such economies experience the same shift in landlord consumption towards manufactures at different points in time, the 'more mature' country (i.e., that where this shift occurred first) ends up exporting manufactures to the other until the stationary state is reached. However, the possibility of two Ricardian economies being structurally identical seems so remote that it may be legitimately neglected.

9. On the role and practical relevance of the stationary state for the classical economists and Ricardo in particular, see Schumpeter (1954, pp. 562–4), who distinguishes between the stationary state as 'an actual condition of the economic process which they expected to materialize sometime in the future' and 'a conceptual construct or tool of analysis that serves to isolate, for the purposes of a preliminary study, the group of economic phenomena that would be observable in an unchanging economic process' (p. 562). He adds that J. S. Mill was the first to use the concept in the latter sense. However, 'Mill also, like Ricardo, expected the economic process to settle down, at some future time, into a stationary state of a special kind that will not be an analytic device for facilitating the study of a nonstationary reality but will itself be a reality' (p. 563). In discussing the classical economists' theories of economic development, Schumpeter later argues that the theory 'associated with the names of Malthus, West, Ricardo, and James Mill, fully justifies their being labeled "pessimists"' (p. 570), and that this vision was in fact unwarranted by the actual economic developments of their time. *Per contra*, Hollander (1979, ch. 11) downplays the importance of the stationary state in Ricardo's economics and asserts (p. 600) that

> Ricardo did not envisage the 'pessimistic' predictions which apparently flow from the theoretical model to be of great practical relevance, and this because of the allowances he made for technological progress not only in agriculture but, significantly, also in manufacturing. Ricardo had great faith in British prospects despite agricultural protection.

I prefer to adhere to the traditional view of the development process according to the classics, even though the model presented in this section may be regarded by some as a latter-day example of the 'Ricardian Vice' of which Schumpeter was so critical.

10. At least when the economic system begins to operate and workers are employed on the most fertile piece of land, they must produce more than what is strictly necessary for their support, otherwise the whole economic system would never come into existence. (Pasinetti, 1960, p. 82; this comment refers to his equation (1b).)

11. The balance of trade condition implies in Figure 4.2 that the area of the rectangle $w_n^* A'C'\bar{p}^i$ in panel (b) should equal that of a rectangle (not shown) in panel (a) with height AB and base given by $\bar{N}$.
12. As Findlay (1974, p. 5) has pointed out, 'this is a special case of the theorem of Rybczynski (1955), in which the labour-intensive good uses no land at all and hence does not require a contraction of the land-intensive good for its expansion at constant relative factor prices'. In other words, if the labour force increases and prices remain constant, the gold sector expands without causing any change in the output of corn. This can also be seen from the fact that the slope of the transformation curve is $dX_1/dX_2 = f'(N_1)dN_1/(adN_2) = -f'(N_1)/a$ since $dN_1 = -dN_2$ along the transformation curve, and this slope is independent of N_2.
13. In his interesting attempt to 'unify' Ricardo's theories of growth and comparative advantage, Burgstaller (1986) makes a number of assumptions, and obtains some results, which bear comment. Among his assumptions, he rejects the 'New View' of a flexible market wage rate in favor of a rather un-Ricardian fixwage assumption. Secondly, the labour force adjusts instantaneously to equal the wage fund divided by the fixwage, thus abstracting from the Hicks-Hollander-Casarosa population adjustment mechanism where the wage rate, rather than the labour force, is endogenous to the system at a given point in time. Thirdly, Burgstaller assumes that both commodities (which he calls food and manufactures) are subject to standard neoclassical production functions having both land and labour as arguments. The properties of the resulting model depend, as in the Heckscher-Ohlin theory, on whether food or manufactures is the land- (or labour-) intensive commodity. The apparent reason for taking manufactures to be a function of both labour and land, instead of making the standard Ricardian assumption that they are produced by labour alone according to constant costs, is that Burgstaller is thereby enabled towards the end of his paper to obtain linear production-possibility frontiers (PPFs) by making the further assumption that land and labour are used in the same proportions in both sectors. These linear PPFs resemble those in the textbook version of the Ricardian trade model, and thus serve Burgstaller's intent to unify Ricardo's growth theory with the comparative advantage theory expounded in Chapter VII of the *Principles*.

This last assumption, convenient as it may appear, entails to my mind too high a cost, since it is inconsistent with the basic Ricardian view that in a closed economy additional food can be obtained only at increasing costs in terms of manufactured goods. Burgstaller (pp. 477–9) obtains for his stationary-state equilibrium of two open Ricardian economies with linear PPFs the standard textbook result that one or both economies become fully specialized. He notes that if the assumption of a uniform factor intensity in both sectors were dropped, 'the primary goods exporter may actually suffer a long-run contraction' and 'since [country] B's employment gains could fail to outweigh [country] A's losses, the stock of productively employed world resources, though more efficiently allocated than before trade, may end up lower after trade than under autarky' (p. 479). These results are similar to those which Burgstaller

(1985, 1987) has obtained in the context of North-South trade models. My findings, while in broad agreement with these, are based on a rather different model. Note, however, that Burgstaller (1986, p. 479) allows for the possibility that both countries may in the long run be completely specialized – which is at variance with the results I obtained above. Maneschi (1983, p. 79) is also mistaken in assuming that, in the stationary state, the terms of trade must lie between two countries' autarkic stationary-state price ratios.

14. See also Burgstaller (1986, pp. 475–6).

REFERENCES

Burgstaller, A. (1985) 'North-South trade and capital flows in a Ricardian model of accumulation', *Journal of International Economics*, 18, pp. 241–60.
Burgstaller, A. (1986) 'Unifying Ricardo's theories of growth and comparative advantage', *Economica*, 53, pp. 467–81.
Burgstaller, A. (1987) 'Europe's industrialization and colonial underdevelopment in the light of Ricardo's corn model', *Journal of International Economics*, 22, pp. 157–69.
Caravale, G. A. (1985) 'Diminishing returns and accumulation in Ricardo', in Caravale, G. A. (ed.), *The Legacy of Ricardo* (Oxford: Blackwell).
Caravale, G. A. and Tosato, D. A. (1980) *Ricardo and the Theory of Value, Distribution and Growth* (London: Routledge and Kegan Paul).
Casarosa, C. (1978) 'A new formulation of the Ricardian system', *Oxford Economic Papers*, 30, pp. 38–63.
Casarosa, C. (1982) 'A new view of the Ricardian theory of distribution and economic growth', in Baranzini, M. (ed.), *Advances in Economic Theory* (Oxford: Blackwell).
Findlay, R. (1974) 'Relative prices, growth and trade in a simple Ricardian system', *Economica*, 41, pp. 1–13.
Hicks, J. and Hollander, S. (1977) 'Mr. Ricardo and the moderns', *Quarterly Journal of Economics*, 91, pp. 351–69.
Hollander, S. (1979) *The Economics of David Ricardo* (Toronto: University of Toronto Press).
Kaldor, N. (1955–56) 'Alternative theories of distribution', *Review of Economic Studies*, 23, pp. 83–100.
Kregel, J. A. (1977) 'Ricardo, trade and factor mobility', *Economia Internazionale*, 30, pp. 215–25.
Maneschi, A. (1983) 'Dynamic aspects of Ricardo's international trade theory', *Oxford Economic Papers*, 35, pp. 67–80.
Maneschi, A. and Thweatt, W. O. (1983), review of G. A. Caravale and D. A. Tosato, *Ricardo and the Theory of Value, Distribution and Growth*, in *History of Political Economy*, 15, pp. 139–41.
Pasinetti, L. L. (1960) 'A mathematical formulation of the Ricardian system', *Review of Economic Studies*, 27, pp. 78–98.

Pasinetti, L. L. (1982) 'A comment on the "New View" of the Ricardian theory', in Baranzini, M. (ed.), *Advances in Economic Theory* (Oxford: Blackwell).

Ricardo, D. (1951) *On the Principles of Political Economy and Taxation*, in *The Works and Correspondence of David Ricardo* (P. Sraffa, ed.), vol. I (Cambridge: Cambridge University Press).

Robinson, J. (1974) *Reflections on the Theory of International Trade* (Manchester: Manchester University Press).

Rutherford, R. P. (1986) 'Ricardo's mantle', *Australian Economic Papers*, 25, pp. 206-21.

Rybczynski, T. M. (1955) 'Factor endowment and relative commodity prices', *Economica*, 22, pp. 336-41.

Samuelson, P. A. (1959) 'A modern treatment of the Ricardian economy', I and II, *Quarterly Journal of Economics*, 73, pp. 1-35 and 217-31.

Samuelson, P. A. (1962) 'The gains from international trade once again', *Economic Journal*, 72, pp. 820-9.

Schumpeter, J. A. (1954) *History of Economic Analysis* (New York: Oxford University Press).

Sraffa, P. (1960) *Production of Commodities by Means of Commodities* (Cambridge: Cambridge University Press).

Thweatt, W. O. (1976) 'James Mill and the early development of comparative advantage', *History of Political Economy*, 8, pp. 207-34.

Walsh, V. C. (1979) 'Ricardian foreign trade theory in the light of the classical revival', *Eastern Economic Journal*, 5, pp. 421-7.

Part II
On Capital Theory

5 Samuelson and the 93% Scarcity Theory of Value

Avi J. Cohen*

INTRODUCTION

In 'Ricardo and the 93% Labor Theory of Value', Stigler (1958) demonstrates that Ricardo's labour theory of value cannot be defended as an analytical proposition but can be defended as an empirical proposition. Here, Stigler's criteria for analytical and empirical value theories are used to evaluate the Cambridge capital theory controversies, particularly Samuelson's contribution. The evaluation demonstrates that the neoclassical scarcity theory of value – the conception of price as an index of resource scarcity relative to consumption demand – cannot be defended analytically but can be defended empirically. The analytical deficiencies in both theories of value stem from capital-related problems. For neoclassical theory, which is the focus of this paper, these problems are not eliminated at the general equilibrium level. Instead, the problems are sidestepped by abandoning the scarcity theory of value as an analytical proposition.

The first section outlines the role of value theory in economic analysis. The second section summarizes Stigler's evaluation of Ricardo's theory. In the third and fourth sections, Stigler's criteria are used to evaluate the scarcity theory in, respectively, aggregate production function models and disaggregated general equilibrium models. The fifth section discusses the analytical implications while the final section discusses the empirical implications and argues that only a hybrid analytical-empirical value theory has a future role in economic analysis.

VALUE THEORY

All economic theories attempt to explain how the complex interdependence of market economies is coordinated through the price mechanism. While classical and neoclassical theories may focus on different aspects of that interdependence (Dobb, 1973; Walsh and Gram, 1980) – classicals on the allocation of surplus output to ensure the reproduction and growth of the economy, neoclassicals on the optimal allocation of scarce resources – both theories provide a detailed elaboration of the factors affecting relative prices. For a given output, classical 'prices of production' depend on the technical conditions of production and the real wage. Neoclassical prices depend on preferences, endowments and the technology. Price theory captures, using a set of simultaneous equations, the way in which the complex interdependence of such elements determines relative prices for each theoretical approach.

In contrast to price theory, value theory attempts to go beyond the interdependence of such factors to identify a price-independent parameter which is the source of price (Lowe, 1981, p. 803). According to Meek (1977, p. 151), value theory involves 'the postulation of some kind of (relatively) independent "determining constant" from which one proceeds to the final conclusion by means of a simple one-directional *catena* of causes'. Value theory recognizes the simultaneous determination of price theory but attempts to expose an underlying or ultimate determinant of price.

The two major value theories in the history of economic thought use either labour or utility as the ultimate determinant of price. For the classical labour theory of value, the relative price of a commodity reflects its difficulty of production, which is determined by its price-independent quantity of embodied labour. All increases (decreases) in relative price are ultimately caused by increases (decreases) in the quantity of embodied labour. For the neoclassical scarcity theory of value, the relative price of a commodity reflects its relative scarcity, which is determined by its utility and its quantity, both of which are price independent. All increases (decreases) in relative price are ultimately caused by increases (decreases) in utility or scarcity. These simple one-directional *catenae* of causes are at the heart of Stigler's criteria for evaluating Ricardo's labour theory of value.

RICARDO'S LABOUR THEORY OF VALUE

The key proposition of Ricardo's labour theory of value appears in the heading of Chapter 1 of the *Principles*:

The value of a commodity, or the quantity of any other commodity for which it will exchange, depends on the relative quantity of labour which is necessary for its production, and not on the greater or less compensation which is paid for that labour (I, p. 11).

Ricardo illustrates this proposition in a sequence of models.

The first model is of Adam Smith's 'early and rude state of society, which precedes both the accumulation of stock and the appropriation of land'. Ricardo endorses Smith's labour theory of value in this model[1] and concludes:

If the quantity of labour realized in commodities, regulate their exchangeable value, every increase of the quantity of labour must augment the value of the commodity on which it is exercised, as every diminution must lower it (I, p. 13).

Changes in embodied labour cause determinate and corresponding changes in relative prices, while changes in wages – which affect all commodities equally – leave relative prices unchanged.

Ricardo's second model assumes the accumulation of capital so that relative prices now reflect both the labour embodied directly in a commodity and indirectly through fixed capital inputs (I, p. 24). The key proposition of the labour theory of value is retained by assuming 'that the ratio of fixed capital to labor is the same in every industry' and 'the capitals have equal durability' (Stigler, p. 360). Although absolute prices now include a rate of profits (equalized across industries) on inputs, relative prices are still proportional to embodied labour and are invariant to changes in wages and profits. Changes in relative prices result only from corresponding changes in embodied labour.

When Ricardo relates the assumptions of equal factor proportions and equal durability of capital in his third model, the labour theory of value is 'considerably modified' (I, p. 30).

This difference in the degree of durability of fixed capital, and this variety in the proportions in which the two sorts of capital [fixed and circulating] may be combined, introduce another cause, besides the greater or less quantity of labour necessary to produce commodities, for the variations in their relative values – this cause is the rise or fall in the value of labour [wages] (I, p. 30).

With the allowance for different time structures of production,[2] changes in the relative prices of commodities can now result from changes in quantities of embodied labour *and* changes in wages and profits.

While Ricardo freely admits that the quantity of embodied labour is not the sole determinant of relative price,[3] he believes 'that the changes brought about in the relative values of commodities by fluctuations in wages and profits were very small relative to those brought about by fluctuations in the quantity of labor . . .' (Stigler, p. 361).

> The reader, however, should remark, that this cause of the variation of commodities is comparatively slight in its effects. . . . The greatest effects which could be produced on the relative prices of these goods from a rise of wages could not exceed 6 or 7 percent . . . (I, p. 36).

Ricardo's estimation in the above passage of the empirical insignificance of the effect on relative prices produced by a change in wages and profits forms the inspiration for the title of Stigler's article.[4] That empirical estimation also leads Ricardo to the following conclusion:

> In estimating, then, the causes of the variation in the value of commodities, although it would be wrong wholly to omit the consideration of the effect produced by a rise or fall of labour [wages], it would be equally incorrect to attach much importance to it; and consequently . . . though I shall occasionally refer to this cause of variation, I shall consider all the great variations which take place in the relative value of commodities to be produced by the greater or less quantity of labour which may be required from time to time to produce them (I, pp. 36–7).

On the basis of these assessments by Ricardo of his own theory of value, Stigler argues that Ricardo did not hold an *analytical* labour theory of value but rather held an *empirical* labour theory of value. According to Stigler (1958, p. 366):

> An analytical statement concerns functional relationships; an empirical statement takes account of the quantitative significance of the relationships. When Marshall viewed the demand for a commodity as a function of its price, the prices of closely related

goods, and of income, he was criticized by members of the Walrasian school for failing to recognize that all prizes [sic] in principle influence the demand for any commodity. This is a characteristic instance of the distinction in question: No Marshallian ever denied the existence of the formal relationships that were omitted; no Walrasian ever presented an empirical example of important errors resulting from their neglect.

For Stigler, the two criteria for an analytical theory of value are the complete specification of: (i) the factors that determine fully price and (ii) the functional relationships in which changes in parameters have determinate and unambiguously signed effects on price. Stigler's analytical criteria are consistent with the notion that value theory provides a price-independent parameter as the basis of a simple one-directional *catena* of causes. An analytical labour theory of value would specify the quantity of embodied labour as the exclusive determinant of relative price *and* would account for all changes in relative price in terms of corresponding changes in embodied labour. Ricardo clearly did not hold this view:

> On the other hand, there is no doubt that he held what may be called an *empirical* labor theory of value, this is, a theory that the relative quantities of labor required in production are the dominant determinants of relative values. Such an empirical proposition cannot be interpreted as an analytical theory . . . (Stigler, p. 361).

THE SCARCITY THEORY OF VALUE AND AGGREGATE PRODUCTION FUNCTION MODELS

The scarcity theory of value is associated with the optimal allocation of scarce resources. The simplest conception of allocation is in a model of pure exchange where preferences and resource endowments (goods) are given exogenously. Price functions as a quantitative index of resource scarcity relative to consumption demand. The allocation resulting from the coordination of the price mechanism is optimal because prices channel scarce resources to their most valuable uses.[5]

Malinvaud (1985, ch. 5) presents a typical pure exchange model exhibiting the key propositions of the scarcity theory of value: (i) As a good becomes scarcer, its price increases; (ii) If the utility of a good increases, its price increases. The model has an analytical (in Stigler's sense) theory of value in that prices are completely determined by preferences and endowments and a change in either of these exogenous parameters has a determinate and unambiguously signed effect on prices.[6]

Although this value theory is most often referred to as the utility theory of value, the term 'scarcity theory' is equally appropriate and provides a sharper focus on the production/supply issues which were the subject of debate in the Cambridge controversies. In what follows, utility/demand conditions are assumed not to change, focusing attention on Malinvaud's proposition (i).

Starting with Böhm-Bawerk, many attempts have been made to extend proposition (i) of the scarcity theory of value to models including capital and production. As Solow (1963, p. 14) notes, 'the theory of capital is after all just part of the fundamentally microeconomic theory of the allocation of resources, necessary to allow for the fact that commodities can be transformed into other commodities over time'. With diminishing marginal productivity, the scarcity theory can be extended to obtain a positive relation between relative factor scarcity and factor price. In particular, capital services are treated as a factor of production the price of which – the rate of interest – is determined by the relative scarcity of capital. With this extension, the distribution of income to factors of production becomes merely a subset of general price determination.[7]

Issues of capital, production and distribution have been explored largely in aggregate production function versions of marginal productivity theory. Following in the tradition of J. B. Clark (1891, 1899), Ramsey (1928) and Hicks (1932), Samuelson's surrogate production function attempts to treat aggregate capital as a resource whose price is determined by its relative scarcity. His model assumes a variety of physically distinct capital goods, each of which, when combined with labour, can be used to produce either more of the capital good or a consumption good. A critical further assumption is 'that the same proportion of inputs is used in the consumption-goods and [capital]-goods industries . . .' (Samuelson, 1962, pp. 196–7).

As a result of the assumption of equal factor proportions, the production function is well-behaved. In competitive equilibrium the price of labour services (the wage rate) is determined by the relative scarcity and marginal productivity of labour. Analogously, the price of capital services (the interest rate) is determined by the relative scarcity and marginal productivity of aggregate capital. There is a unique inverse relationship between factor intensity and relative

Samuelson and the Scarcity Theory of Value

factor price. The scarcer a factor is, the higher its price. These results constitute the neoclassical parable in which the scarcity theory of value obtains even with the existence of capital and production.

When Samuelson relaxes the assumption of equal factor proportions the possibilities of reswitching and capital reversing arise so that the scarcity theory of value 'cannot be universally valid' (Samuelson, 1966b, p. 568). Reswitching – where the same technique is preferred at two or more rates of interest while other techniques are preferred at intermediate rates – violates the uniqueness of the relation between capital intensity and the rate of interest. More importantly, the inverse nature of that relation is violated by capital reversing – a positive relation between capital intensity and the rate of interest.

With capital reversing, a 'lower capital/labour ratio' is associated with a lower interest rate. In comparing two equilibrium positions it is as though capital services have a *lower* price in the position where capital is 'more scarce'. The conception of price as a quantitative scarcity index is violated (Garegnani, 1966, 1970; Pasinetti, 1969, 1970).

Since 1966, Samuelson and others have freely admitted the logical possibilities of reswitching and capital reversing and their implication – that the price of capital services may be an exception to the scarcity theory of value.[8] For Samuelson however, the significance of the exceptions is an empirical issue.

> The science of political economy has not yet the empirical knowledge to decide whether the real world is nearer to the idealized polar cases represented by (a) the neoclassical parable or (b) the simple reswitching paradigm (Samuelson, 1980, p. 576).[9]

Others have echoed the sentiment that the significance of the exceptions to the scarcity theory of value is not an analytical or theoretical issue but rather an empirical issue.[10] According to Solow (1975, pp. 277–8):

> It turns out that it is in general impossible to give rigorous meaning to such assertions [that more 'capital' will be found always to be associated with lower rates of interest]. The mainstream replies that this is only a crude simplification made for the purpose of applying the theory to real numbers, and so it has to be judged pragmatically and not by the standards of rigorous analysis.

Ferguson (1969) is even more explicit:

> The crucial point to emphasize is that the validity of neoclassical theory is an *empirical*, not a *theoretical*, question (p. 258, emphasis in the original).
>
> The question that confronts us is not whether the Cambridge Criticism is theoretically valid. It is. Rather, the question is an empirical or an econometric one: is there sufficient substitutability within the system to establish the neoclassical results? (pp. 265-6).

Ricardo's and Samuelson's respective theories of value are both analytically defensible when equal factor proportions are assumed. When that assumption is relaxed, there are obvious parallels between Ricardo's assessment of the empirical insignificance of the exceptions that arise to the labour theory of value, and the neoclassical assessment of the empirical insignificance of exceptions to the scarcity theory of value. Stigler's and Ricardo's assessments (p. 152 above) are easily paraphrased to apply to the neoclassical case.

> Fluctuations in the relative prices of commodities are generally positively related to fluctuations in the scarcity of those commodities (Malinvaud's proposition (i) above). Inverse relations are possible but unlikely.
>
> In estimating, then, the causes of the variations in the price of commodities, although it would be wrong wholly to omit the consideration of the possibilities of reswitching and capital reversing, it would be equally incorrect to attach much importance to them; and consequently . . . though neoclassical theory will occasionally refer to these possibilities, the neoclassical parable will consider all the great variations which take place in the relative prices of commodities to be positively related to variations in the scarcity of the commodities.[11]

Applying Stigler's criteria to the neoclassical assessments of neoclassical value theory leads to the conclusion that the scarcity theory of value is not an analytical theory but is rather an empirical theory.

A generalized analytical scarcity theory of value would have properties similar to those of Malinvaud's pure exchange model. Prices would be completely determined by preferences and endowments (and technology in a generalized model with production), and a change in any one of the exogenous parameters would have a determinate and unambiguously signed effect on price. A problem exposed by the Cambridge controversies is the ambiguous relationship in aggregate production function models between changes in the scarcity of capital and the price of capital services. This ambiguity violates Stigler's second criteria for the functional relationships necessary for an analytical theory. What remains is an empirical theory in which relative scarcities can be argued to be the *dominant* determinants of relative prices.[12]

Of course, the significance of these results depends critically on the relationship between aggregate production function models and neoclassical analysis in general. Neo-Ricardians continue to claim that these results vitiate totally both the general conception of price as an index of resource scarcity relative to consumption demand and the specific neoclassical theory of distribution.[13] The standard neoclassical counter-claim is that the logical inconsistencies revealed by the Cambridge controversies are limited to aggregate production function versions of neoclassical analysis. Disaggregated general equilibrium versions are logically consistent and are unscathed by the controversies.[14]

By applying Stigler's criteria for analytical and empirical theories to neoclassical general equilibrium models, new insights emerge about these now standard claims.

THE SCARCITY THEORY OF VALUE AND GENERAL EQUILIBRIUM MODELS

General equilibrium models meet Stigler's first criterion for an analytical theory – the complete specification of the factors that fully determine price – and avoid the analytical inconsistencies of aggregate production function models. Prices are fully determined by preferences, endowments and the technology. Individual (disaggregated) factors of production are paid their marginal products. Prices are also consistent with both a competitive equilibrium outcome and a Pareto-efficient disposition of output. Hahn (1982, p. 373) correctly asserts that 'These results are theorems and they are not at risk. They are not based on any aggregation hypothesis'. As in the pure exchange model, prices support an optimal allocation of resources so there is a parallel to the pure exchange conception of price as a scarcity index.

The parallel fails for Stigler's second criteria. The sign of the effect on prices of a given change in the parameters of a general equilibrium model is, with few exceptions, indeterminate.[15] This general indeterminacy has long been recognized as the product of the complex interdependencies and the paucity of restrictions on the excess demand functions within general equilibrium models (Archibald, 1965). Arrow and Hahn (1971, p. 245), after investigating 'the power of general equilibrium models in giving unambiguous predictions of how the equilibrium of an economy will be affected by a given parameter change', find that even with the strong assumptions necessary to guarantee the uniqueness of an equilibrium, 'the kind of parameter changes for which predictions become possible is pretty limited'. Because of this general indeterminacy, the conception of price as a scarcity index, in the sense of Malinvaud's propositions – (i) as a good becomes scarcer its price increases; and (ii) if the utility of a good increase, its price increases – are not universally sustained in general equilibrium models.

Not surprisingly, investigations of capital theory within general equilibrium models yield similar ambiguous results. Bliss, for example, considers the price effects of a change in the quantity of capital[16] available in an economy. Using intertemporal general equilibrium models to generate comparative static results, he demonstrates that the economy with 'more capital' does not necessarily have a lower interest rate or price of capital services.[17]

> Even people who have made no study of economic theory are familiar with the idea that when something is more plentiful its price will be lower, and introductory courses on economic theory reinforce this common presumption with various examples. However, there is no support from the theory of general equilibrium for the proposition that an input to production will be cheaper in an economy where more of it is available (Bliss, 1975, p. 85).[18]

Thus, comparative static results from disaggregated general equilibrium models do not meet Stigler's second criterion for an analytical theory – unambiguously signed functional relationships between exogenous parameters and prices. What does exist, though, is the possibility of an empirical theory. In evaluating the (lack of) comparative static results, Arrow and Hahn (1971, pp. vii–viii) state that:

our conclusion is that the postulates [of general equilibrium models] are too weak to allow one to make much headway. This can be taken as evidence of the deficiency of the theory. It can also be taken to show its strength, however, for it suggests that sufficient degrees of freedom have been left for empirical information to make a difference to prediction; it is not a totally *a priori* construction.

The issue of strength or weakness aside, there could be no clearer statement that, for general equilibrium analysis, the scarcity theory of value is not a fully analytical (*'a priori'*) theory but can be defended on empirical grounds.

ANALYTICAL IMPLICATIONS

For both aggregate production function versions and disaggregated general equilibrium versions of neoclassical theory, the scarcity theory of value – the conception of price as an index of resource scarcity relative to consumption demand – cannot be considered an analytical theory of value. The theory can, however, be defended as an empirical theory of value in that relative scarcities can be argued to be the dominant determinant of relative price.[19]

What do these results imply for the conflicting neo-Ricardian and neoclassical claims about the analytical significance of the Cambridge controversies?

As the neo-Ricardians claim, reswitching and capital reversal do vitiate the scarcity theory of value as an analytical proposition. Samuelson's surrogate production function was an attempt to provide one-directional causal explanations in the value theory tradition. His attempt 'to provide *some* rationalization for the validity of the simple J. B. Clark parables' (Samuelson, 1962, p. 194), can be linked to Clark's (1891, p. 312) straightforward causal explanations: 'as capital increases, while other things remained unchanged, interest falls and as the labor force increases, if other things remain the same, wages fall.' Changes in relative factor prices are explained by corresponding changes in the underlying factor scarcities.[20] The demise of the aggregate production function version of the analytical scarcity theory of value prompted a neoclassical 'retreat' to general equilibrium models, which have no logical problems. But the switch to general equilibrium, rather than saving the analytical scarcity theory of value, abandoned it.

The significance of the vitiation of the analytical scarcity theory of value has not been emphasized sufficiently. Given the general indeterminacy of comparative static results in general equilibrium models, aggregate production function models had provided the only economy-wide or macroeconomic context where the scarcity theory of value (it was thought) could be extended beyond pure exchange to encompass production and distribution. When this extension was shown to be impossible, the move to general equilibrium marked the final abandonment of the scarcity theory.[21] The Cambridge controversies demonstrated that – outside of one-commodity models, which all sides recognize as too restrictive and where, in any case, the labour theory of value is equally valid – there is no neoclassical model where the analytical scarcity theory of value can explain the set of all relative prices, including factor prices. Neoclassical theory, as Hahn (1981, p. 128) puts it, 'is not committed to a relative scarcity theory of distribution'.

Thus, *on a purely analytical level* aggregate production function models (and general equilibrium models) fail to meet the criteria for a 'useful' theory that Samuelson (1947, p. 257) himself put forward:

> It is the task of comparative statics to show the determination of the equilibrium values of given variables (unknowns) under postulated conditions (functional relationships) with various data (parameters) being specified. Thus, in the simplest case of a partial-equilibrium market for a single commodity, the two independent relations of supply and demand, each drawn up with other prices and institutional data being taken as given, determine by their intersection the equilibrium quantities of the unknown price and quantity sold. If no more than this could be said, the economist would be truly vulnerable to the gibe that he is only a parrot taught to say 'supply and demand'. Simply to know that there are efficacious 'laws' determining equilibrium tells us nothing of the character of these laws. In order for the analysis to be useful it must provide information concerning the way in which our equilibrium quantities will change as a result of changes in the parameters taken as independent data.

With the causal claims abandoned, what remains of neoclassical distribution theory are, using Samuelson's terms, 'parrot'-like specifications of simultaneous equation systems, and (correct) statements about how factor returns are *equal to* or *measured by* disaggregated marginal productivities (Blaug, 1974, p. 7; Bliss, 1975, p. 110; Hahn, 1972, pp. 2–4). Gone are the 'useful' claims about unambiguously signed changes in the interest rate resulting from changes in the quantity of capital.

The value theory perspective also provides insight into the fruitless interchanges during the Cambridge controversies about simultaneous equations.[22] Neoclassicals often complained that Cambridge UK economists did not understand that the equilibrium solution to a set of simultaneous equations does not entail causal relationships. Von Weizsacker (quoted in Harcourt, 1982, p. 249) provides a typical example:[23]

> I really fear that Joan Robinson . . . has not really understood the basic principle of a system of simultaneously solvable equations and therefore worries about the derivation of the rate of interest from the capital stock, while the definition of the capital stock presumes the knowledge of the interest rate. Where does the puzzle come in all this if one has really understood what a system of interdependent variables is all about?

While this characterization of simultaneous equations is correct, it ignores the fact that the neoclassical parable was an attempt to go beyond simultaneous interdependence and provide one-directional causal explanations. When that attempt failed conclusively (outside the one-commodity model), neoclassicals retreated to a defense of simultaneous equations and general equilibrium. The Cambridge UK critics continued to press the causal point that had been at issue in the neoclassical parable, but the neoclassicals had sidestepped the point by abandoning the analytical scarcity theory of value.

The analytical problems that vitiate the scarcity theory of value, as well as the labour theory of value, are due, in part, to the existence of capital. Capital violates the price-independence of the exogenous parameters that are essential to the one-directional causal explanations of value theory.[24]

The analytical scarcity theory of value works in Malinvaud's pure exchange model because endowments are given exogenously and can be measured in price-independent units. As a good becomes scarcer, there is no interdependence between the higher price of the good and the physical measure of its scarcity (i.e., its quantity). In models with heterogeneous capital goods, capital must be measured in price terms which include a rate of interest. As capital becomes physically scarcer, the rate of interest changes which, in turn, affects the measure of the capital goods. The price dependence of the measure of capital transforms what were exogenous parameters in the pure exchange model into endogenous variables in models with production. This endogeneity is the source of reswitching and capital reversal problems and the resulting simultaneous determination eliminates any simple one-directional *catena* of causes.

The analytical labour theory of value works in models with equal factor proportions because the difficulty of production can be measured in price-independent quantities of inputs. As a good becomes more difficult to produce (while maintaining factor proportions) there is no interdependence between the higher price of the good and the physical measure of its difficulty of production (i.e., its quantity of embodied labour inputs). In classical models with unequal factor proportions, prices are no longer proportional to embodied labour inputs, so the difficulty of production must be measured in price terms. An increase in the difficulty of production of a good affects relative prices, including the prices of capital inputs. The price dependence of the measure of inputs transforms what were exogenous parameters into endogenous variables and eliminates any simple one-directional *catena* of causes.

The endogeneity caused by capital, referred to in the earlier von Weizsacker quote, is irrelevant from the simultaneous equations perspective of price theory. But it is fatal for the one-directional causal explanations of both analytical value theories which are based on exogenous price-independent parameters.

EMPIRICAL IMPLICATIONS AND THE FUTURE OF VALUE THEORY

Over 200 years of intensive economic theorizing have failed to produce any comprehensive theory of value that is determinate at the purely analytical level. It is time to abandon the notion that such determinacy exists. This does not imply, however, that we should abandon the *objective* of value theory – to provide simple one-directional causal explanations. Beginning with Marshall, Cambridge UK economists have always stressed the importance of such explanations. Marshall (1920, p. 776) said that we 'should strive to select the true causes of each event and assign to each its proper weight; and above all to detect the remoter causes of change'. Pasinetti (1974, p. 44) endorses almost verbatim the value theory objective:

> One of the tasks of the economic theorist [is] to specify which variables are sufficiently interdependent as to be best represented by simultaneous relations, and which variables exhibit such an overwhelming dependence in one direction (and such a small dependence in the opposite direction) as to be best represented by one-way-direction relations.

Cambridge USA economists share this objective. After recognizing the limitations of purely analytical theories. Solow (1985, p. 23) says:

> There is enough for us to do without pretending to a degree of completeness and precision which we cannot deliver. To my way of thinking, the true functions of analytical economics are best described informally: to organize our necessarily incomplete perceptions about the economy, to see connections that the untutored eye would miss, to tell plausible – sometimes even convincing – *causal stories* [emphasis added] with the help of a few central principles and to make rough quantitative judgements about the consequences of economic policy and other exogenous events. In this scheme of things, the end-product of economic analysis is likely to be a collection of models contingent on society's circumstances – on the historical context, you might say – and not a single monolithic model for all seasons.

All of Samuelson's work, from his criteria in *Foundations* for a 'useful' theory to the objective of his surrogate production function, makes clear his commitment to causal explanation.[25]

The implication of the abandonment of analytical value theory should not be to de-emphasize the role of value theory but instead to emphasize the necessity of empirical and historical information for an adequate analytical-empirical value theory. All economic theories are in the same analytical boat that sinks in a sea of causal indeterminacy unless the holes are plugged by empirical work. As Lowe (1981, p. 815) puts it, we must recognize that 'there is no ultimate determinant of . . . prices without abandoning the realm of pure analysis for that of history'.

Just as Stigler defended Ricardo by differentiating him from proponents of an analytical labour theory of value, the neoclassical approach can be defended by separating it from an analytical scarcity theory of value. By shifting from the purely analytical level to a hybrid analytical-empirical level, the neoclassical approach can be defended as 'useful' for providing causal explanations of economic phenomena. If empirical information is used to overcome the causal indeterminacy of general equilibrium models, then, as Arrow and Hahn suggest, the deficiency of the models may become their strength. The resulting analytical-empirical approach can be defended as a powerful and flexible set of tools for economic analysis.

No judgements will be passed here about which value theory – the neoclassical scarcity theory or the neo-Ricardian descendants of the labour theory – should be pursued. Since both theories have analytical (in Stigler's sense) deficiencies outside of one-commodity models (Cohen, 1989), any choice between them will depend on how well each incorporates empirical information to provide convincing causal explanations. And to the extent that the theories attempt to answer different questions, choice between them may not be a pressing issue.

Regardless of any choices, the obvious implication for all economic analysis, neoclassical or other, is the importance of supplementing theory by empirical work. The importance of such work – whether it takes the form of data gathering, inductive generalizations, historical studies, institutional description or econometric estimation – must be re-emphasized. 'The facts' must not be viewed as just a data base for testing theories but rather as a necessary part of *theory construction*. Samuelson (1966b, p. 583) concludes his 'Summing Up' of the Cambridge controversies by saying that

> If all this causes headaches for those nostalgic for the old-time parables of neoclassical writing, we must remind ourselves that scholars are not born to live an easy existence. We must respect, and appraise, the facts of life.

This means not only recognizing the lack of a 100% analytical theory of value, but paying more attention to the empirical facts of economic life.

NOTES

* For suggestions and encouragements, thanks to Ian Kerr, Jon Cohen, Neil de Marchi, Amitava Dutt, Harald Hagemann, Wade Hands, Geoff Harcourt, Tony Lawson, Gary Mongiovi, Robert Solow, and George Stigler.

1. Quoting (I, p. 13) Smith's statement that 'the proportion between the quantities of labour necessary for acquiring different objects seems to be the only circumstance which can afford any rule for exchanging them for one another'.
2. Ricardo allows for 'variations in (1) the ratio of fixed capital to labor (I, 34), (2) the durability of fixed capital (I, 31, 40), and (3) the rate of turnover of circulating capital (I, 37)' (Stigler, p. 360).
3. 'Mr. Malthus shows that in fact the exchangeable value of commodities is not *exactly* proportional to the labour which has been employed on them, which I not only admit now, but have never denied' (II, p. 66).
4. Ricardo elsewhere makes similar estimates of magnitudes of importance. In a letter to James Mill (VII, p. 377) Ricardo argues 'that exchangeable value varies . . . owing only to two causes: one the more or less quantity of labour required, the other the greater or less durability of capital: – that the former is never superseded by the latter, but is only modified by it'. In responding to Malthus, Ricardo writes (VIII, pp. 278–80):

> You say that my proposition 'that with few exceptions the quantity of labour employed on commodities determines the rate at which they will exchange for each other, is not well founded' [.] I acknowledge that it is not rigidly true, but I say that it is the nearest approximation to truth, as a rule for measuring relative value, of any I have ever heard.

5. In describing the neoclassical pure exchange model, Pasinetti (1986, p. 419) says 'The set of prices associated with the equilibrium (optimum) solution has a very evident economic meaning – it provides an index of relative scarcities'.
6. Modern neoclassicals, interested in price theory only, would not subscribe to these strong claims about value theory. Malinvaud's model makes the strong assumption that all goods are gross substitutes. In models with less restrictive assumptions, they would claim only that prices *depend* on preferences and endowments (and technology in models with production). No claims would be made about unambiguously signed effects of parameter changes. Nonetheless, there are two reasons why it is legitimate to posit these strong claims about neoclassical *value* theory. First, the originators of the neoclassical approach made such claims. Consider, for example, Walras's (1954, p. 148) claims about his pure exchange model:

> Given two commodities in a market in a state of equilibrium, if, all other things being equal, the utility of one of these two commodities increases or decreases for one or more parties, the value of this

commodity in relation to the value of the other commodity, i.e. its price, will increase or decrease. If, all other things being equal, the quantity of one of the two commodities in the hands of one or more holders increases or decreases, the price of this commodity will decrease or increase.

Second, the scarcity theory of value is part of the Schumpeterian vision underlying the neoclassical approach (Cohen and Cohen, 1983; Cohen, 1989), even though such strong claims do not appear in neoclassical price theory.

7. Böhm-Bawerk (1959, vol. II, p. 347) makes the earliest explicit statement of this principle: 'The exchange . . . which constitutes the source of the phenomenon of interest, is merely one special case under the rubric of the exchange of goods in general. And so it follows as a matter of course that determination of price in this field cannot proceed under any laws other than those which govern determination of price in all economic exchange.' And the general laws which determine price or exchange value stem from the fact that goods 'are *useful* and . . . they are *scarce*' (Böhm-Bawerk, 1959, vol. I, p. 91).

8. For example, Ferguson (1969, p. 365) writes 'the Cambridge Criticism is a valid one. . . . [With] heterogeneous capital goods, one cannot legitimately postulate *a priori* a unique relation between capital intensity and the factor-price ratio, either within a sector or in the aggregate'. In Hahn's (1972, p. 8) words,

> it has often been the case that a neo-classical theory has been attempted in terms of aggregate production functions and aggregates like capital. Except under absurdly unrealistic assumptions such an aggregate theory cannot be shown to follow from proper theory and in general is therefore open to severe logical objections. For instance it is not in general possible to argue that the steady state with a lower interest rate must on some index of capital always have more capital per man that [sic] the steady state with a higher interest rate.

9. See also Samuelson (1966b, p. 582).
10. The list includes Blaug (1975; 1980, ch. 10), Brown (1969), Eltis (1973, ch. 5), Ferguson and Allen (1970), Hicks (1965, p. 154; 1973, p. 44), Sen (1974, pp. 330–31) and Stiglitz (1973, p. 118; 1974, p. 896).
11. Samuelson's (1966a, pp. 444–5) own words match almost exactly my paraphrase above of Ricardo:

> Until factors cease to have their rewards determined by bidding in quasi-competitive markets, I shall adhere to (generalized) neoclassical approximations in which relative factor supplies are important in explaining their market remunerations. . . . a many-sectored neoclassical model with heterogeneous capital goods and somewhat limited factor substitutions can fail to have some of the simple properties of the idealized J. B. Clark neoclassical models. Recognizing these com-

plications does not justify nihilism or refuge in theories that neglect short-term microeconomic pricing.

Continuing in a footnote, Samuelson adds 'In my model . . . I do confine myself to well-behaved properties in which . . . the relative share of factors does depend on relative factor supplies.'

12. Stigler's elaboration of the distinction between analytical and empirical statements (1958, p. 366, above pp. 152-3) can also be paraphrased to apply to the Cambridge controversies:

> When Samuelson's parable viewed all prices, including the price of capital, as positively related to resource scarcity, he was criticized by members of the Cambridge (UK) school for failure to recognize the possibilities of reswitching and capital reversing. This is a characteristic instance of the distinction in question. No informed neoclassical (after 1966) ever denied the existence of the possibilities of reswitching and capital reversing; no Cambridge (UK) critic ever presented an empirical example of an important error resulting from their neglect.

13. The strongest statement of this claim appears in Garegnani (1966, p. 565):

> Up to now, however, the tendency has been to dismiss such instances [reswitching and capital reversing] as 'exceptions'; as if the traditional principle [the scarcity theory of value] they contradict resulted from observed empirical regularities liable to exception, and was not purely a deduction from postulates generally recognized as invalid. What these instances really show, is that the traditional principle – drawn from incorrect premises – is itself incorrect.
>
> The consequences of admitting this, however, are far-reaching, because on that principle has been erected the dominant theory of distribution. From the rise of the proportion of capital to labor in the economy as interest falls, there have been deduced 'demand functions' for 'capital' (i.e., 'saving') and for labor; and with them, the idea of distribution as governed by a tendency to the equality between demand and supply for these 'factors of production'. Hence, in particular, the explanation of interest (profits) by the scarcity of 'capital' and as the reward for 'waiting'. It is hard to see how this elaborate structure can stand, when its premise is found wanting.

14. [T]he neoclassical parable claim that of two economies in Sraffian equilibrium, the one with the higher rate of interest (profit) will have the lower 'capital' labour ratio [is invalid]. . . . All of this is simply a reiteration of the proposition that there is no valid aggregation of wheat and barley into something called capital. But unless one wishes to claim that aggregation is essential if a theory is to be called neoclassical, none of this has any bearing on the main issue . . . Sraffa performed a service in showing how neoclassical arguments can be

used to show neoclassical aggregation parables to be in logical difficulties. But that cannot help with a critique of [the general equilibrium version of] marginal theory. (Hahn, 1982, p. 373)

Ferguson (1972, p. 164) makes the same point:

> The neoclassical paradigm envisages a world in which Walrasian general equilibrium prevails. Technology, commodity and factor prices and commodity and factor markets are linked together through the independent maximizing behavior of individual economic agents. Marshall's theory of marginal productivity factor pricing emerges; and if one wishes to aggregate . . . a theory of aggregate distribution and relative factor shares emerges as well. To be sure, these are by-products of the general equilibrium system; and it should be emphasized that neoclassical economic theory does not stand or fall on the basis of [aggregate] marginal productivity theory.

15. The most important exceptions take the form of gross substitute systems, which include the case of 'binary changes' that affect only two goods. Such a restricted change can be used to show that if there is an exogenous increase in the amount of a factor ('capital') available, 'the equilibrium with more capital, other things constant, must also have a lower rental of capital' (Arrow and Hahn, 1971, p. 247). This result, however, will not generalize for non-binary changes.

> Without further restricting the model that we use in comparing equilibria it does not seem possible to obtain any further results for general parameter changes. This is neither surprising nor a cause for despondency. The analysis of binary changes does in a general equilibrium context what Marshallian partial analysis achieves in a much more restricted setting; for general changes we must expect to have fairly precise quantitative information as to the relationship between goods before being able to make the kind of statement that was possible for binary changes. (Arrow and Hahn, p. 254)

16. See Bliss (1975) for the assumptions necessary for his comparison of pairs of economies along different semi-stationary growth paths.
17. Malinvaud (1985, p. 303) stresses the indeterminacy of sign in general equilibrium models

> between the rate of interest and the 'scarcity' of capital, or between interest and 'capital-intensity'. In a given state of technique, that is, for given production functions of sets, the price-system varies *a priori* as a function of (i) the resources available to the economy, (ii) consumer preferences and (iii) the distribution of property rights. The description of such variations may be very complex. However, are they not compatible with the existence of a simple relation between the rate of interest and certain physical characteristics of the programmes under consideration? Most economists who have approached this question

have believed it possible to give a positive answer, at least so long as the investigation is confined only to stationary regimes. However, we must now recognise that there is no simple universal relation between the rate of interest and capital intensity. Certainly a tendency exists, but it is often contradicted by examples which are not particularly abnormal.

See also Malinvaud (1966, pp. 237–8).

18. These results are not only due to the general indeterminacy of general equilibrium models. In comparing stationary states without net production, Bliss demonstrates that the economy with more capital will necessarily have a lower interest rate and price of capital services. It is the introduction of net production that yields indeterminacy, a point that will be taken up on pp. 161–2.
19. This argument is, in an important respect, overly generous to the neoclassical position. In estimating the impact on relative prices of a change in parameters, the labour theory of value yields a close approximation to prices of production if differences in capital intensities are sufficiently small. In contrast, the scarcity theory of value does not posit any separate 'scarcity values' which are approximations to the prices determined by the given preferences, endowments and technology.
20. All participants in the debate tried to be careful in their use of language and to make statements like 'more capital *will be associated with* a lower rate of interest', rather than 'an increase in capital will *cause* a fall in the rate of interest'. Samuelson (1975, p. 45) writes 'that when a mathematician says, "y rises as x falls", he is implying nothing about temporal sequences or anything different from "when x is low, y is high"'. He uses this careful language not because of a lack of belief in causal explanations, but to avoid Joan Robinson's criticism about deducing causation from comparisons of equilibrium states. See Cohen (1984) on the role of Robinson's methodological criticism in the Cambridge controversies.
21. Just as the move to general equilibrium marked the neoclassical abandonment of the concept of long-period equilibrium (Garegnani, 1976; Milgate, 1979).
22. This argument is taken largely from Harcourt (1982, pp. 249–51). For an alternative argument using Schumpeter's concept of vision to distinguish between simultaneous equations and causal explanations in general equilibrium theories see Cohen and Cohen (1983).
23. See also Bliss (1975, ch. 5), Hahn (1975, p. 362) and Stiglitz (1974, p. 894).
24. See Cohen (1989) for a more detailed exposition of this argument.
25. Even after acknowledging Joan Robinson's criticism about the illegitimacy of deducing causation from comparisons of equilibrium positions, Samuelson (1975, p. 46) maintains his belief that a causal relationship exists between relative factor scarcity and factor returns: 'So even after the logical issues have been put in their proper uncontroversial place, the arguments can go on as to whether the distribution of income does or does not depend significantly in real life on the *relative supplies of labor and of diverse capital goods.*'

REFERENCES

Archibald, G. Christopher (1965) 'The Qualitative Content of Maximizing Models', *Journal of Political Economy*, 73 (February), pp. 27–36.
Arrow, Kenneth J. and Hahn, Frank H. (1971) *General Competitive Analysis* (San Francisco: Holden-Day).
Blaug, Mark (1975) *The Cambridge Revolution: Success or Failure?*, revised edition (London: Institute of Economic Affairs).
Blaug, Mark (1980) *The Methodology of Economics* (Cambridge: Cambridge University Press).
Bliss, Christopher J. (1975) *Capital Theory and the Distribution of Income* (Amsterdam: North-Holland).
Böhm-Bawerk, Eugen von (1959) *Capital and Interest, Vols. I – III*, translated by George D. Huncke (South Holland, Ill.: Libertarian Press).
Brown, Murray (1969) 'Substitution – Composition Effects, Capital Intensity, Uniqueness and Growth', *Economic Journal*, 79 (June) pp. 334–47.
Clark, John Bates (1891) 'Distribution as Determined by a Law of Rent', *Quarterly Journal of Economics*, 5 (April) pp. 289–318.
Clark, John Bates (1899) *The Distribution of Wealth* (New York: Macmillan).
Cohen, Avi J. (1984) 'The Methodological Resolution of the Cambridge Controversies', *Journal of Post Keynesian Economics*, 6 (Summer) pp. 614–29.
Cohen, Avi J. (1989) 'Prices Capital and the One-Commodity Model in Neoclassical and Classical "Theories"', *History of Political Economy*, 21 (Summer) pp. 231–51.
Cohen, Avi J. and Cohen, Jon S. (1983) 'Classical and Neoclassical Theories of General Equilibrium', *Australian Economic Papers*, 22 (June) pp. 180–200.
Dobb, Maurice (1973) *Theories of Value and Distribution Since Adam Smith* (Cambridge: Cambridge University Press).
Eltis, Walter A. (1973) *Growth and Distribution* (London: Macmillan).
Ferguson, Charles E. (1969) *The Neoclassical Theory of Production and Distribution* (Cambridge: Cambridge University Press).
Ferguson, Charles E. (1972) 'The Current State of Capital Theory. A Tale of Two Paradigms', *Southern Economic Journal*, 39 (October) pp. 160–76.
Ferguson, Charles E. and Allen, Robert F. (1970) 'Factor Prices, Commodity Prices, and Switches of Technique', *Western Economic Journal*, 8 (June) pp. 95–109.
Garegnani, Pierangelo (1966) 'Switching of Techniques', *Quarterly Journal of Economics*, 80 (November) pp. 554–67.
Garegnani, Pierangelo (1970) 'Heterogeneous Capital, the Production Function and the Theory of Distribution', *Review of Economic Studies*, 37 (July) pp. 407–36.
Garegnani, Pierangelo (1976) 'On a Change in the Notion of Equilibrium in Recent Work on Value and Distribution', in *Essays in Modern Capital Theory*, edited by Murray Brown, Kazuo Sato and Paul Zarembka (Amsterdam: North-Holland) pp. 25–45.

Hahn, Frank H. (1972) *The Share of Wages in the National Income* (London: Weidenfeld and Nicholson).
Hahn, Frank H. (1975) 'Revival of Political Economy: The Wrong Issues and the Wrong Argument', *Economic Record*, 51 (September) pp. 360–4.
Hahn, Frank H. (1981) 'General Equilibrium Theory', in *The Crisis in Economic Theory*, edited by Daniel Bell and Irving Kristol, pp. 123–38 (New York: Basic Books).
Hahn, Frank H. (1982) 'The Neo-Ricardians', *Cambridge Journal of Economics*, 6 (December) pp. 353–74.
Harcourt, Geoffrey C. (1982) 'The Cambridge Controversies: Old Ways and New Horizons – Or Dead End?', in *The Social Science Imperialists*, edited by Prue Kerr, pp. 239–78 (London: Routledge & Kegan Paul).
Hicks, John R. (1932) *The Theory of Wages* (London: Macmillan).
Hicks, John R. (1965) *Capital and Growth* (Oxford: Oxford University Press).
Hicks, John R. (1973) *Capital and Time* (Oxford: Oxford University Press).
Lowe, Adolph (1981) 'Is Economic Value Still A Problem?', *Social Research*, 48 (Winter) pp. 786–815.
Malinvaud, Edmond (1966) 'Interest Rates in the Allocation of Resources', in *The Theory of Interest Rates*, edited by Frank H. Hahn and Frank Brechling, pp. 209–41 (New York: St. Martin's Press).
Malinvaud, Edmond (1985) *Lectures on Microeconomic Theory*, revised edition (Amsterdam: North-Holland).
Marshall, Alfred (1920) *Principles of Economics*, 8th edition (London: Macmillan).
Meek, Ronald L. (1977) 'Value in the History of Economic Thought', in *Smith, Marx & After*, pp. 149–64 (London: Chapman and Hall).
Milgate, Murray (1979) 'On the Origin of the Notion of "Intertemporal Equilibrium"', *Economica*, 46 (February) pp. 1–10.
Pasinetti, Luigi (1969) 'Switches of Technique and the "Rate of Return" in Capital Theory', *Economic Journal*, 79 (September) pp. 508–31.
Pasinetti, Luigi (1970) 'Again on Capital Theory and Solow's "Rate of Return"', *Economic Journal*, 80 (June) pp. 428–31.
Pasinetti, Luigi (1974) *Growth and Income Distribution* (Cambridge: Cambridge University Press).
Pasinetti, Luigi (1986) 'Theory of Value – A Source of Alternative Paradigms in Economic Analysis', in *Foundation of Economics*, edited by Mauro Baranzini and Roberto Scazzieri, pp. 409–31. (Oxford: Basil Blackwell).
Ramsey, Frank P. (1928) 'A Mathematical Theory of Saving', *Economic Journal*, 38 (December) pp. 543–59.
Ricardo, David (1951–73) *Works and Correspondence* (I–X), edited by Piero Sraffa (Cambridge: Cambridge University Press).
Samuelson, Paul A. (1947) *Foundations of Economic Analysis* (Cambridge, Mass.: Harvard University Press).
Samuelson, Paul A. (1962) 'Parable and Realism in Capital Theory: The Surrogate Production Function', *Review of Economic Studies*, 29 (June) pp. 193–206.
Samuelson, Paul A. (1966a) 'Rejoinder: Agreements, Disagreements,

Doubts and the Case of Induced Harrod-Neutral Technical Change', *Review of Economics and Statistics*, 48 (November) pp. 444–8.

Samuelson, Paul A. (1966b) 'A Summing Up', *Quarterly Journal of Economics*, 80 (November) pp. 568–83.

Samuelson, Paul A. (1975) 'Steady-State and Transient Relations: A Reply on Reswitching', *Quarterly Journal of Economics*, 89 (February) pp. 40–7.

Samuelson, Paul A. (1980) *Economics*, 11th edition (New York: McGraw-Hill).

Sen, Amartya (1974) 'On Some Debates in Capital Theory', *Economica*, 41 (August) pp. 328–33.

Solow, Robert M. (1963) *Capital Theory and the Rate of Return* (Amsterdam: North-Holland).

Solow, Robert M. (1975) 'Cambridge and the Real World', *Times Literary Supplement* (14 March) pp. 277–8.

Solow, Robert M. (1985) 'Economics: Is Something Missing?', in *Economic History and the Modern Economist*, edited by William N. Parker, pp. 21–9 (Oxford: Basil Blackwell).

Stigler, George J. (1958) 'Ricardo and the 93% Labor Theory of Value', *American Economic Review*, 48 (June) pp. 356–67.

Stiglitz, Joseph E. (1973) 'The Badly Behaved Economy with the Well-Behaved Production Function', in *Models of Economic Growth*, edited by James A. Mirrlees and Nicholas H. Stern, pp. 117–37 (New York: Wiley).

Stiglitz, Joseph E. (1974) 'The Cambridge-Cambridge Controversy in the Theory of Capital: A View From New Haven: A Review Article', *Journal of Political Economy*, 82 (July/August) pp. 893–903.

Walras, Léon (1954) *Elements of Pure Economics*, translated by William Jaffe (Homewood, Ill.: Richard D. Irwin).

Walsh, Vivian and Gram, Harvey (1980) *Classical and Neoclassical Theories of General Equilibrium* (Oxford: Oxford University Press).

Part III

Post-Keynesian Income Distribution and Growth Theory

6 The Method of the Pure Ratio in Economic Analysis
Amit Bhaduri

INTRODUCTION: THE METHOD OF THE PURE RATIO IN CLASSICAL ECONOMICS

The method dates back to Ricardo's seminal *Essay on Profits* in 1815.[1] According to Sraffa's interpretation in his celebrated *Introduction*, the rate of profit in agriculture can be defined as a pure ratio independent of relative prices, if 'corn' is both the output and also the only input in the form of capital advanced. With corn as the sole basic product required both for its own production and for the production of all other commodities, Ricardo's conclusion follows that 'it is the profits of the farmer that regulate the profits of all other trades'.[2]

The method of the pure ratio devised by Ricardo could work only under the artificially restrictive assumption that the same commodity 'corn' appears both as output as well as the sole input or means of production. Consequently, in search of a more general approach, Ricardo took recourse to the labour theory of value in his later work, where 'labour' instead of 'corn' served to determine the overall rate of profits as a pure ratio.[3] Thus, the method of the pure ratio got entangled with the labour theory of value and profits as surplus came to be defined through labour value rather than as a surplus of physical products.

That Ricardo's argument regarding the rate of profit of the corn growers as a pure ratio was generalizable was not realized until Sraffa (1960) constructed his 'Standard commodity'. The Standard commodity is in the image of Ricardian corn in so far as each individual commodity in that composite basket in physical terms has the same ratio of output to its deployment as means of production or input.[4] Consequently, the physical surplus emerges as a uniform pure ratio on the stock of each commodity advanced as working capital in the composite basket of the Standard commodity, irrespective of changes in relative prices.

THE METHOD OF THE PURE RATIO IN POST-KEYNESIAN ECONOMICS

Although devised in the context of the classical theory of value and distribution to show the emergence of profits as surplus, this method of the pure ratio can be generalized to yield powerful results in other areas of economic theory. One of the most striking results in post-war growth theory is Pasinetti's demonstration that the workers' saving propensity (s_w) is irrelevant in determining the equilibrium rate of profits in steady state growth (Pasinetti, 1962; 1974). In essence, this apparently intriguing result can be seen to follow from an application of the method of the pure ratio. So long as the capitalists receive their income *entirely* from properly income or profits (P_c), the rate of growth in the value of their capital (K_c) is governed strictly by their saving propensity (s_c) and the (uniform) rate of profits (r) on their capital. That is to say,

$$g_c = \Delta K_c/K_c = S_c/K_c = s_c \, P_c/K_c = s_c \, r \qquad (1)$$

In the Pasinetti steady state, the value of capital owned by the workers (K_w) also grow at the same rate,[5] i.e.

$$g_c = g_w = \Delta K_w/K_w = S_w/K_w = s_c r, \text{ from (1)} \qquad (2)$$

Hence, the flow of saving by the workers (S_w) must satisfy the relation,

$$S_w = s_c r K_w = s_c P_w \qquad (3)$$

where, P_w = workers' profits on the capital they own (K_w).

Pasinetti's paradoxical result follows immediately from (2) because the rate of saving by the workers is governed exclusively by the capitalists' saving propensity! And, the solution to the paradox lies in the fact that the growth rate of the capital owned by the capitalists is defined *independently* as a pure ratio (in equation (1)) to which the growth rate of the workers' capital must adjust (equation (2)). As a result, the saving rate of the workers is governed entirely by the capitalists' but not their own saving propensity (equation (3)). As Pasinetti noted in his original article, the workers' saving propensity is rendered irrelevant in the steady state because, from their mixed bag of wage (W) and non-wage (P_w) income, the additional saving generated by wage income is exactly compensated for by the extra amount that the workers consume compared to the capitalists out of their profit (P_w). In other words, (3) can be rewritten as

$$s_w W = (s_c - s_w)P_w = (1 - s_w)P_w - (1 - s_c)P_w \qquad (4)$$

Analogous to the rate of profits in the Ricardian corn sector, in Pasinetti's model, the rate of growth of the capitalists' capital is independently determined by equation (1) and it regulates the rate of growth of the workers' capital in the steady state by equation (2). Therefore, even if the rate of profits is *not* uniform, similar results would obtain so long as (1) and (2) hold. Assume workers receive a rate of interest (i) on the capital they own (K_w) which is lower than the rate of profits (r) that the capitalists receive on their capital (K_c). With equations (1) and (2) still valid, equation (3) is now modified as,

$$S_w = s_w W + s_w i K_w = s_c r K_w, \quad r > i \text{ or instead of (4)}$$

$$s_w W = (s_c r - s_w i) K_w = [\{r - (1 - s_c)r\} - \{i - (1 - s_w)i\}] K_w \qquad (5)$$

Each unit value of capital transferred from the workers to the capitalists would result in additional saving, ($s_c r - s_w i$) because the capitalists not only have a higher propensity to save ($s_c > s_w$) but they also receive a higher rate of return ($r > i$) per unit of capital transferred to them. Thus, the extreme right hand side of equation (5) has a similar interpretation to (4), i.e. the extra saving out of wages is exactly compensated for by the extra consumption of the workers due to their ownership of property, K_w.

The above argument suggests that, whenever in an economic model an independently defined pure ratio describes the relevant property of a (basic) sector, it regulates the *equilibrium* properties of all the other sectors as well. It was this insight of the Ricardian corn model which Sraffa exploited to restate the classical theory of value and distribution and Pasinetti exploited it in the context of growth theory. The method can be applied also to describe the equilibrium property of other important growth or planning models.

THE EQUILIBRIUM PROPERTY OF THE MODEL

Consider, for example, the well-known Feldman-Mahalanobis two sector model of non-shiftable capital (Mahalanobis, 1953; Domar,

1957, essay 8). The rate of growth of the investment or the capital goods sector in this model is independently defined as a pure ratio which depends only on the proportion of investment devoted to that sector (λ) and on the incremental capital output ratio of that sector (v_i). Consequently, the rate of growth of the investment sector is given by the ratio,[6]

$$g_i = \Delta I/I = \lambda/v_i \qquad (6)$$

Similarly, the additional capacity creation in the consumption sector is given as

$$\Delta C = (1 - \lambda)I/v_c$$

where v_c = incremental capital output ratio of the consumption sector.

Hence the growth rate of the consumption sector is

$$g_c = \Delta C/C = (1 - \lambda)I/v_c C \qquad (7)$$

In steady-state growth, both the sectors grow at the same rate, i.e.:

$$g_c = g_i \text{ implying, } I/C = [\lambda v_c]/[(1 - \lambda)v_i] \qquad (8)$$

But in the steady state, the rate of return on investment must be equal in both sectors so that there is no incentive to alter the sectoral allocation of investment, λ. If h_i and h_c stand for the (average as well as marginal) share of profit per unit of value added in the investment and in the consumption sector respectively, then the assumption of a uniform rate of return in both the sectors entails,

$$h_i/v_i = h_c/v_c \text{ implying, } v_c/v_i = h_c/h_i \qquad (9)$$

and consequently, (8) becomes,

$$I/C = [\lambda h_c]/[(1 - \lambda) h_i] \qquad (10)$$

In order to keep the algebra simple, assume that there is no saving by the workers (i.e. $s_w = 0$) and the entire profit goes to the capitalists, who save a constant fraction s_p. The equality between investment and saving in the economy requires,

The Pure Ratio in Economic Analysis 179

$$I = S = s_p (h_i.I + h_c C)$$

or,
$$I/C = s_p h_c/(1 - s_p h_i) \qquad (11)$$

In the steady state in which both the investment and the consumption sector grow at the same rate (equation (8)), with an equal rate of return on investment in both sectors (equation (9)) and without any excess demand or supply of consumption goods (equation 11), the equilibrium proportion of investment λ^* devoted to the investment sector is given by equating (10) and (11) to yield,

$$\lambda^* = s_p h_i \qquad (12)$$

The interesting point about the equilibrium value of $\lambda = \lambda^*$ in (12) is that it is defined irrespective of the value of the profit share h_c in the consumption sector. This resembles Pasinetti's result; just as the workers' saving propensity did not enter in his case in determining the equilibrium rate of profits; in equation (12) the profit share of the consumption sector does not enter in determining the equilibrium allocation of investment between the two sectors. The resemblance derives analytically from the method of the pure ratio which Professor Pasinetti had applied so imaginatively in his work on growth theory.

NOTES

1. David Ricardo (1815): *Essay on the Influence of a Low Price of Corn on the Profits of Stock* in *The Works and Correspondence of David Ricardo* (1951–73), ed. P. Sraffa with collaboration of M. Dobb, pp. IV, 1–42. (Hereinafter, *Works and Correspondence*).
2. See *Works and Correspondence*, I, Editorial Introduction pp. xxxi–xxxii. Also, P. Sraffa (1960) Appendix D, p. 93. (Hereinafter, *Production of Commodities*).
3. *Works and Correspondence*, vol. 1, Introduction p. xxxxii.
4. *Production of Commodities*, pp. 19–20: for a similar interpretation of the Standard commodity, see Broome (1977).
5. We ignore the economically uninteresting 'anti-Pasinetti' steady state in which the proportion of the total capital owned by the capitalists tends to zero.
6. It is assumed that there is always enough demand for investment goods so that the capacity of the investment sector is fully utilized. The investment

saving equality (later equation (11)) then ensures no excess demand or supply of consumption goods either; see Bhaduri, 1986, Chapter 7, for elaboration.
7. With full capacity utilization, the rate of return on investment in either sector is defined at full capacity; see preceding footnote.

REFERENCES

Bhaduri, A. (1986) *Macroeconomics: the Dynamics of Commodity Production* (Macmillan: London) Ch. 7.
Broome, J. (1977) 'Sraffa's Standard commodity', *Australian Economic Papers*, 16, pp. 231–6.
Domar, E. (1957) *Essays in the Theory of Economic Growth* (Oxford University Press, New York) essay 8: 'A Soviet model of growth'.
Mahalanobis, P. (1953) 'Some observations on the process of growth of national income', *Sankhya*, September.
Pasinetti, L. (1962) 'Rate of profit and income distribution in relation to the rate of economic growth', *Review of Economic Studies*, 29, pp. 267–79.
Pasinetti, L. (1974) *Growth and Income Distribution: Essays in Economic Theory* (Cambridge University Press: Cambridge).
Ricardo, D. (1951–73) *The Works and Correspondence of David Ricardo*, I–X ed. P. Sraffa with collaboration of M. H. Dobb (Cambridge University Press: Cambridge) especially vols I and IV.
Sraffa, P. (1951–73) Editorial Introduction to *The Works and Correspondence of David Ricardo* (Cambridge University Press, Cambridge), vol. I.
Sraffa, P. (1960) *Production of Commodities by Means of Commodities* (Cambridge University Press: Cambridge).

7 A Post-Keynesian Theory of Growth, Interest and Money*

Amitava K. Dutt and Edward J. Amadeo

INTRODUCTION

While firmly based in the classical tradition, the work of Luigi Pasinetti, together with that of Joan Robinson and Nicholas Kaldor, has laid the foundations of a Post-Keynesian approach to the theory of growth, interest and money. The approach is 'Post-Keynesian' in the sense that it combines elements of Keynes's (1936) ideas in the *General Theory*, as well as the extension of those ideas as developed in the last three decades by economists following the Cambridge tradition in Keynesian economics.[1] The purpose of this paper is to attempt to synthesize the Post-Keynesian contributions by providing a critical discussion of the conceptual elements of the approach, and by developing a formal model of growth in which monetary aspects are explicitly taken into consideration.

In our conceptual discussion (in the next section), we shall emphasize the central elements of the Post-Keynesian approach, namely the roles of income distribution, uncertainty, money and interest in explaining the macroeconomic performance of capitalist economies, and the appropriateness of the notion of equilibrium as an instrument for analyzing these economies. Then, in the remaining sections, we shall develop a model of the determinants of accumulation, inflation and the distribution of income and wealth, to examine the impact of a change in monetary policy through its influence on the rate of interest. The examination of these effects in the short period is a part of the Keynesian literature, but the extension of the analysis to the long period still lacks a deeper discussion.

ELEMENTS OF THE POST-KEYNESIAN APPROACH

In this section we discuss some central elements of the Post-Keynesian approach. While it is beyond the scope of this paper to discuss the many different aspects of Post-Keynesian analysis, we comment on a few important issues which are of particular relevance to the long-period analysis of growth, money and interest. We discuss, in turn, the Post-Keynesian attitudes towards the importance of class distinctions, uncertainty, and money and interest.

The Post-Keynesians have followed the classical approach in emphasizing the distinction between classes, especially between profit-receivers and wage-earners. One aspect of this distinction is the so-called Cambridge savings assumption. Kaldor (1955–6) assumed that the propensity to save out of wages was lower than the propensity to save out of profits. Pasinetti (1962) went more directly to the distinction between the two classes, assuming that wage-earners had a lower propensity to save than did profit-receivers. This assumption implies that income distribution became closely connected with the rate of capital accumulation and growth in the economy, and this idea has become a standard feature of Post-Keynesian analysis. A second aspect of this distinction leads to the explanation of income distribution and inflation in terms of the conflict between classes. With its roots in Marx, this approach has been developed in a variety of Marxist, structuralist and Post-Keynesian contributions: the attempts by different classes to garner a larger share of income results in inflation, and the relative strength of the different classes determines income distribution.[2] The focus on these distinctions and the analysis in terms of class behaviour is diametrically opposed to the methodological individualism of neoclassical economics.

Uncertainty plays a crucial role in the writings of the Post-Keynesians, particularly those who stress that economic behaviour takes place in historical time which flows from an irreversible past to an unknown future. Unlike in neoclassical economics, in which uncertainty is treated as actuarily calculable risk, the Post-Keynesians emphasize that important economic decisions are made on the basis of expectations about the future based on extremely flimsy foundations. Both the persistence of unemployment and macroeconomic instability can be seen to be the result of uncertainty.[3] In the face of great uncertainty, and therefore difficulty in anticipating the probable profitability of investment, firms prefer to hold their wealth in liquid form; likewise, economic decision-makers in general tend to turn to liquid assets (money in the limit), and postpone their expenditure in goods. This reduces the demand for labour, and results in unemployment. Fluctuations in the rate of employment, prices and other economic variables may also reflect the effect of uncertainty as economic decision-makers change their plans due to changes in their degree of confidence in their beliefs regarding the future.

In recognizing the importance of uncertainty, we can be led to one of two views on the relevance of modelling using equilibrium analysis. One is to see uncertainty as continuously altering the values of the parameters affecting the behaviour of decision-makers, thus rendering attempts at modelling completely futile. The other is to take the view that in the face of uncertainty economic decision-makers resort to the use of conventions and rules of thumb, which make the behavioural parameters relative stable, thereby making economic behaviour particularly amenable to mathematical modelling.

According to the former view, which is subscribed to by several Post-Keynesians, the economic system is in permanent flux, and models employing the notion of equilibrium are inappropriate instruments for the analysis of actual economic processes. In other words, equilibrium is inconsistent with the analysis of capitalist economies in which there is no tendency towards a tranquil state.[4] While it is an important insight that the economy is always in a state of flux and never in a tranquil state, so that economic decision-makers are always subject to uncertainty, it does not necessarily follow, however, that models employing equilibrium analysis are flawed. Equilibrium models are not supposed to describe the path of the system over calendar time, but are organizing instruments which highlight the interrelation between the relevant variables at each point in time, under the (admittedly unrealistic) assumption that the parameters are unchanged. Since the parameters can change in a manner unknown to economic decision-makers, they do not find themselves in a tranquil state. Equilibrium analyses are of special interest if the models are able to trace the path of the system over a series of partial or short-period equilibrium situations, using dynamic analysis. It is even possible that the economy may tend to a position of long-period equilibrium in some sense, but in any event the analysis cannot be faulted in ignoring history and in failing to take into account short-period features of the economy, including the influence of uncertainty. According to the latter view modelling becomes no more than an exercise in understanding the interactions between economic variables based on the notion that there is a certain degree of stability and regularity in the decision-makers' behaviour. The behaviour most discussed in Post-Keynesian theory are firms' pricing and output behaviour, and investment behaviour.

In modelling the firms' pricing and output decision, one alternative is to assume that firms maximize profits at an expected price, given the nominal price of its inputs.[5] While some Post-Keynesians have followed this approach in their expositions of Keynes's *General Theory* analysis, the more popular approach is to follow Kalecki (1971) in assuming that firms set the price as a fixed mark-up over variable costs, and adjust to unexpected changes in demand through changes in the levels of output. In Kalecki's formulation, the mark-up depends on the degree of monopoly of the industry and the bargaining power of labour in fixing the money-wage, and recent attempts to model the determination of the mark-up take into account the distributive conflict between the firms' desired mark-up and the wage-earners' desired real wage.[6]

Firms also form expectations in order to decide the level of investment. In an advanced capitalist economy, firms have access to credit, and the decision to invest is relatively independent of the level of current saving. Indeed, the independence of investment in relation to saving is at the root of the explanation of fluctuations of output, employment and prices. In the Post-Keynesian tradition firms are assumed to follow the rule of thumb of making their investment depend on the rate of profit, the cost of 'finance' (the rate of interest), and the rate of capacity utilization.[7]

Finally, we turn to money and interest. As noted already, money (and quasi-monies) play a central part in the way decision-makers protect their wealth against uncertainty, and in the explanation of unemployment and instability. According to the Post-Keynesian view, when the decision-makers' preference to maintain wealth in liquid form increases, the banking system will supply the additional demand for liquidity. The Post-Keynesian notion of an 'endogenous money supply' is based on the fact that the banking sector, with the Central Bank in its role as lender of last resort behind it, will supply any amount of credit desired by the economy at a given level of the interest rate.[8] If the Central Bank chooses to limit the growth of liquidity it can do so by increasing the interest rate by moving upwards its discount rate. Hence, the rate of interest is seen as a central parameter in the Post-Keynesian approach.

The interest rate can be seen to be closely related to several of the other issues with which Post-Keynesians are concerned. First, it is related to the distinction between classes. We have commented already on the theory of conflict in which inflation is the result of the conflicts between the different classes. A third group can be introduced into the analysis of this distributive conflict, namely, the banking system: given the money-wage rate, firms and banks would battle over the surplus, and if firms wish to fix the level of the net profit margin (above interest charges), an increase in the interest rate will imply an increase in the price level. The change in the price level, as well as the change in the rate of interest which caused it, will redistribute incomes between different groups and this, due to the differences in saving propensities discussed above, would have an impact on the level of economic activity and hence, on the rate of capital accumulation. This effect will depend in part on the nature of class ownership of different assets. While Pasinetti (1962) initially assumed that both profit-receivers and wage-earners could hold capital which yielded the same return, later contributions have taken differences in the assets held by the two groups into account.[9] Second, it is related to the behavioural rules that firms follow in an uncertain environment. As just mentioned, firms may push up prices when the interest rate rises; moreover, they may reduce their rate of investment due to changes in the cost of credit.

The analysis of changes in the rate of interest or the supply of money is a commonplace in short-period models. They are not as common in long period models, and in recent contributions, Taylor (1985, 1988) and Skott (1988) are notable exceptions. In considering the effect of exogenous changes in the rate of interest, a central question is the extent to which we could refer to a theory of the long period rate of interest. Keynes was quite confident that the monetary authorities are capable of affecting the long period position of the economy.[10] In the contributions of Pivetti (1988) and Panico (1985, 1988) the notion that the monetary authority can fix the rate of interest is expanded and turned into an argument to substantiate Sraffa's (1960, p. 33) argument that the long period rate of profit is 'susceptible of being determined from outside the system of production, in particular by the level of the money rates of interests'.[11] Thus, according to this approach, the long period rate of interest depends on the structural factors determining the state of liquidity preference, the management of the public debt, the international rates of interest, and most importantly in a relatively closed financial system, the monetary policy of the Central Bank.

STRUCTURE OF THE MODEL

In this section we develop a model which seeks to bring together the central features of the Post-Keynesian analysis we have just discussed. We consider a closed economy producing one good with labour and capital (physically the same as the produced good) using a fixed-coefficients production function. For simplicity we abstract from government fiscal activity.

There are two classes in the economy – wage-earners and profit-receivers, and two types of institutions – firms and banks. Wage-earners derive their income primarily from wage income, but since they also save a fixed fraction of their income and hold deposits with banks, they also earn interest income. Profit-receivers do not work, and own the firms through their ownership of stocks; since they also hold deposits their income comes from both interest and returns to stock-ownership. Profit-receivers also save a constant fraction of their income, but have a higher propensity to save than do wage-earners. Firms hire wage-earners to produce output. They operate with excess capacity in an oligopolistic environment, set their price as a markup on labour costs *à la* Kalecki (1971), and produce according to demand. They also make investment decisions according to the size of excess capacity and the interest rate. Finally, banks borrow funds from depositors (wage-earners and profit-receivers) and lend to the firms. They are assumed usually to operate with excess reserves and supply credit according to the demand for it; if they ever run out of reserves they are assumed to have access to loans from the Central Bank at a fixed interest rate (determined by its monetary policy). For simplicity we assume that banking is costless, and the interest rate charged by the banks is equal to the rate at which they can borrow.

We may examine the structure of the model by describing in turn the asset market, the labour market and pricing side of the economy, and the goods market.

For the asset market, the asset balance sheets for the four groups is given by Table 7.1 where P is the price level, K is the physical stock of capital, P_e is the price of equities and E the volume of stocks. Note that all high-powered money is held as bank reserves, and that wage-earners hold their entire wealth as bank deposits (perhaps because the holding of stock is too risky for them).[12] Noting that $D = D_c + D_w$, these balance sheets imply that

$$H + PK = W_c + W_w \equiv W$$

A Theory of Growth, Interest and Money

TABLE 7.1

Banks		Firms	
H – reserves L – loans	D – deposits	PK – physical capital	L – loans P_eE – equity

Profit-receivers		Wage-earners	
D_c – deposits P_eE – equity	W_c – wealth	D_w – deposits	W_w – wealth

where W denotes total wealth. Assume that the profit-receivers choose to allocate a fraction σ of their wealth to deposits, and that this fraction depends (positively) on the interest rate, i (among other variables which are ignored for simplicity).[13] Assume that the stock of deposits of wage-earners is given, demand supply balance for deposits is given by

$$H/\mu = \sigma(i)(H + PK) + [1 - \sigma(i)]D_w$$

where μ is the reserve-deposit ratio of the banks. We assume that the interest rate is fixed and that this equation is satisfied through variations in μ (which is possible because banks operate with excess reserves) or through changes in H (as a result of bank borrowing from the Central Bank). These assumptions represent the Post-Keynesian analysis of endogenous money.

Turning next to the labour market and pricing, we assume that at a point in time the money-wage, w, and the price, p, are given, and given Kalecki's pricing equation

$$p = (1 + z)\, wa \qquad (1)$$

where a is the fixed labour-output ratio, so is the markup, z. This equation implies that the real wage is given as

$$v = 1/[(1 + z)a] \qquad (2)$$

We assume that wage-earners have a desired or targeted real wage given by v_w which depends on the state of class struggle, treated as a parameter in our model, and that they push up the money wage over time when their desired real wage exceeds the actual one. We formalize this with the assumption

$$\hat{w} = \theta [v_w - v] \tag{3}$$

with $1 > \theta > 0$ and where hats over variables denote time rates of change. We assume that firms have a desired or targeted markup, which by (2) implies a desired real wage v_f, and that they push up the price over time when their desired markup exceeds the actual one. We formalize this with

$$\hat{p} = \pi [v - v_f] \tag{4}$$

with $1 > \pi > 0$.[14] Following Kalecki, we may assume that v_f depends on the extent of industrial concentration. But because firms also have to make interest payments out of markup income we assume that a higher interest rate will induce firms to desire a higher markup and hence a lower real wage. We assume that

$$v_f = v_0 - v_1 i \tag{5}$$

to capture this effect.[15]

Finally, turning to the goods market, we assume that firms distribute all profits to profit-receivers.[16] This, given our assumptions about profit-receivers and wage-earners, implies that the demand-supply balance equation is

$$X = (1-s_c) [(1-va)X - i(D_w/p)] + (1-s_w) [vaX+i(D_w/p)] + I \tag{6}$$

where X denotes output, I the level of real investment, and s_c and s_w (with $s_c > s_w$) the saving propensities of profit-receivers and wage-earners, respectively. Dividing through by K and rearranging, we can obtain the saving-investment equality condition

$$s_c [(1 - va)u - i\delta] + s_w (vau + i\delta) = g^I \tag{7}$$

where $u = X/K$ is a measure of the degree of capacity utilization, $g^I = I/K$ is the rate of accumulation of capital, and $\delta = D_w/pK$ is the share of physical capital owned by wage-earners (through their holding of deposits).

Finally, we assume that firms have a desired accumulation function given by

$$g^I = \alpha + \beta u - \tau(i - \hat{p}) \qquad (8)$$

As suggested by Steindl (1952) a higher rate of capacity utilization makes firms want to invest at a higher rate; the higher rate of capacity utilization also increases the rate of profit and this also encourages more investment.[17] A higher real interest rate is also assumed to reduce the rate of accumulation; for simplicity we do not distinguish between expected and actual rates of inflation.[18]

The behaviour of this model can be examined for the short and long periods. In the short period, we assume given values of D_w, K, p, and w, which imply given v and δ. In short-period equilibrium, in which we assume that the goods market clears through variations in capacity utilization, the inflation rate can be determined from (4), and (7) and (8) then may be solved for u which is given by[19]

$$u = \{\alpha + [(s_c - s_w)\delta - \tau]i + \tau(v - v_f)\}/[s_c - (s_c - s_w)va - \beta] \qquad (9)$$

Over the long period D_w, K, p and w change over time. Changes in p and w are shown by (3) and (4). Physical capital, for simplicity, is assumed not to depreciate, so that the change in capital stock is given by the rate of investment

$$\hat{K} = g^I \qquad (10)$$

and since wage-earners only hold deposits, the increase in their deposits is given by their saving out of wage and interest income, so that

$$dD_w/dt = s_w (waX + iD_w)$$

which implies, upon division by D_w,

$$\hat{D}_w = s_w [(vau/\delta) + i] \qquad (11)$$

The long-period behaviour of the economy can be analyzed by examining dynamic equations for v and δ.[20] From their definitions, we have

$$\hat{v} = \hat{w} - \hat{p} \qquad (12)$$

and

$$\hat{\delta} = \hat{D}_w - \hat{p} - \hat{K} \tag{13}$$

Using equations (3) and (4), (12) can be written as

$$\hat{v} = \theta v_w + \pi v_f - (\theta + \pi) v \tag{14}$$

while using (4), (8), (10) and (11), (13) can be written as

$$\hat{\delta} = (s_w + \tau)i - \alpha + [(s_w va/\delta) - \beta]u - (1 + \tau)(v - v_f)\pi \tag{15}$$

where u is given by (9). In long-period equilibrium, $\hat{v} = \hat{\delta} = 0$. The long-period equilibrium value of v, obtained by setting $\hat{v} = 0$ in (14) is given by

$$v^* = [\theta/(\theta + \pi)]v_w + [\pi/(\theta + \pi)]v_f \tag{16}$$

which is a weighted average of the real wages desired by the wage-earners and the firms, the weights depending on the rates at which the wage-earners and firms are able to adjust the money-wage and price, respectively, when the actual real wage is different from their desired one. The model can then be used for analyzing the implications of a change in monetary policy.

Rather than examine this model in detail, we will seek to capture some of its important properties by examining two simple special cases in the next two sections.

CASE WHERE WAGE-EARNERS DO NOT SAVE

One special case is the one in which wage-earners do not save, so that $s_w=0$ and D=0.

In this case, in the short period, given v, K and p, variations in the utilization of capacity bring about short-period equilibrium at which the demand for goods is equal to output. The determination of this equilibrium is shown in Figure 7.1, where the g^i curve is the investment curve showing the relation between the investment-capital stock ratio and the capacity utilization rate which is given by equation (8) after substituting from (4), for given v, and where $g^s = s_c(1-va)u$, the left-hand side of (7) with $s_w = \delta = 0$, is the saving curve showing

A Theory of Growth, Interest and Money

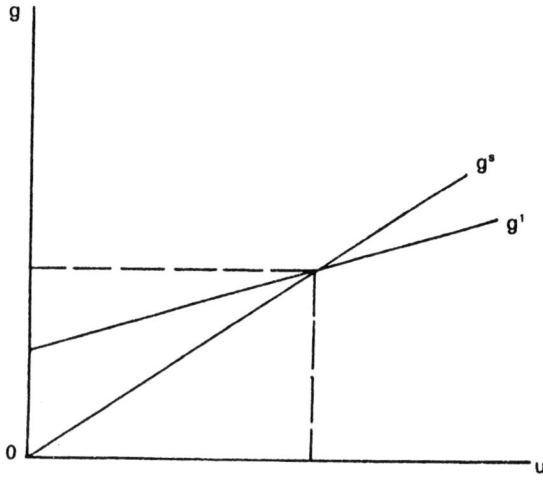

FIGURE 7.1

the relation between the saving-capital stock ratio and the capacity utilization rate. Given the short-period stability assumption, the g^s is steeper than g^I. The equilibrium value is, from equation (9) given by

$$u = \alpha - \tau i + \tau (v - v_f)/[(1 - va)s_c - \beta] \qquad (17)$$

A higher v pushes the g^s curve down by redistributing income towards wage-earners who do not save, while it pushes the g^I curve up by increasing the rate of inflation and thus reducing the real interest rate, as shown in equation (4). The result is a higher equilibrium u, as can also be verified from (17), and a higher rate of growth of capital. The positive relation between v and u is shown as curve IS in the upper part of Figure 7.2.

In the lower part of Figure 7.2 the $\hat{w}$ curve shows the inverse relation between the change in money-wage and the real wage given by the wage adjustment equation (3), and the $\hat{p}$ curve is the positive relation between the change in the price and the real wage given by the price-adjustment equation (4), given the rate of interest. Over the long period v moves according to equation (12). The figure shows this adjustment to be stable, and long-period equilibrium is achieved at $\hat{v} = 0$ when $\hat{w} = \hat{p}$, when, the long-period equilibrium value of v is seen to be given by (16). The long-period equilibrium value of u, u*, can then be seen from the upper part of the figure.

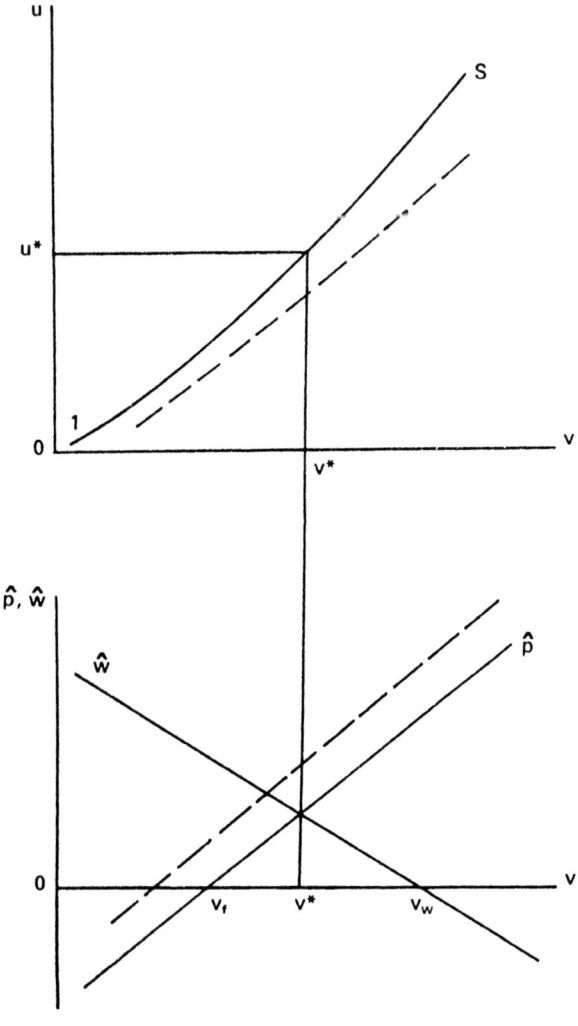

FIGURE 7.2

We may now examine the implications of a rise in i in the short period and the long period. In the short period, given v, the rise in i leaves the g^s curve unchanged in Figure 7.1, but it does shift the g^I curve. The effect depends on the effect on the real interest rate which, using (5), is seen to be

$$d(i - \hat{p})/di = 1 - \pi v_1$$

where the first term is the direct effect on the nominal rate and the second term is the effect on the rate of inflation due to downward pressure on the desired real wage of firms as they desire a higher markup to compensate for higher interest costs. Since $\pi < 1$, the condition that $v_1 < 1$ (or that the effect of the higher interest rate on the desired real wage of firms is small) is sufficient to make this expression positive, which we assume to be the case. Thus a rise in the nominal rate of interest increases the real rate as well (since inflation rises less than does the interest rate). The rise in the real interest rate therefore pushes the g^I curve down. The result is a fall in u and short-period equilibrium g. Note that since for any v the equilibrium u falls, the curve in the upper part of Figure 7.2 shifts downwards.

In the long period we have to take into account changes in v as well. The increase in i pushes the $\hat{p}$ curve in the lower part of Figure 7.2 upwards, as can be seen from equations (4) and (5). The long-period equilibrium value of v* therefore falls, while the long-period equilibrium rate of inflation rises compared to p*. The changes are given by

$$dv^*/di = -\pi v_1 / (\theta + \pi)$$

and

$$dp^*/di = \pi \theta v_1 / (\theta + \pi)$$

Since long-period equilibrium v falls and the IS curve shifts down, the long-period equilibrium value of u must also fall. It is also clear from the Figure 7.2 that the short-period impact on the inflation rate is higher than in the long period, while the short-period impact on the rate of capacity utilization is lower than in the long period. These results imply that the long-period negative effect on the rate of accumulation is greater than in the short period. The reason for this is that in the short period the real wage is fixed, so that the fall in aggregate demand is due only to the higher real interest rate; in the long period the real wage falls, reducing aggregate demand further by causing a redistribution of income from wage-earners to profit-receivers, and also by reducing the rate of inflation below (and hence the real interest rate above) the level it reached in the short period after the interest-rate increase because the actual real wage now comes closer to the real wage desired by the firms.

The effect of a fall in the interest rate may turn out to be different. This may in part be because v_f may be zero when i falls, or at least different from its value when i increased. Firms – as a group – may try to capture some of the benefits of a lower interest rate for themselves. But in major part, a fall in i need not stimulate investment if the fall is small and firms believe market prospects to be bleak: τ may this be small or zero when i falls. Post-Keynesians will probably want to take account of these types of ratchet effects.

The implications of our analysis for the effectiveness of increasing the interest rate for raising the rate of growth in the economy, claimed by traditional neoclassical analysis, are not favourable. The traditional case for increasing the interest rate, in any case, is made by arguing that a higher interest rate will induce savers to save more, and these types of substitutions have not been considered in our model since s_c has been taken to be fixed. However, if the higher interest rate induces profit-receivers to save more, so that s_c rises, the g^s curve of Figure 7.1 will be pushed up, so that short-period equilibrium u and g will fall more when i rises than when the saving effect was ignored, because the higher saving rate depresses aggregate demand further. The long-period depressive effects will also be greater. These results follow because in our model growth is demand-determined rather than determined by the supply of saving; only in the latter case could a higher rate of interest induce individuals to consume less and save more and increase the rate of growth of the economy.

WHEN WAGE-EARNERS SAVE AND EARN INTEREST

It may be argued that a higher interest rate may redistribute income from profit-receivers to wage-earners if the latter can save and earn interest on their wealth and profit-receivers earn interest as well as profit, as in the general model described on pp. 186–90. We now consider our second special case, in which we allow wage-earners to save, but assume that $v_1 = 0$, so that a rise in i has no effect on the real wage desired by the firms.

In this case the model is identical to the general one discussed on pp. 186–90 as long as the interest rate is assumed to be fixed. In the short period, for given values of w, p, K and D_w, which implies given v and δ, (9) solves for the short-period equilibrium value of u. The equilibrium can be depicted again as in Figure 7.1, although the g^s

A Theory of Growth, Interest and Money

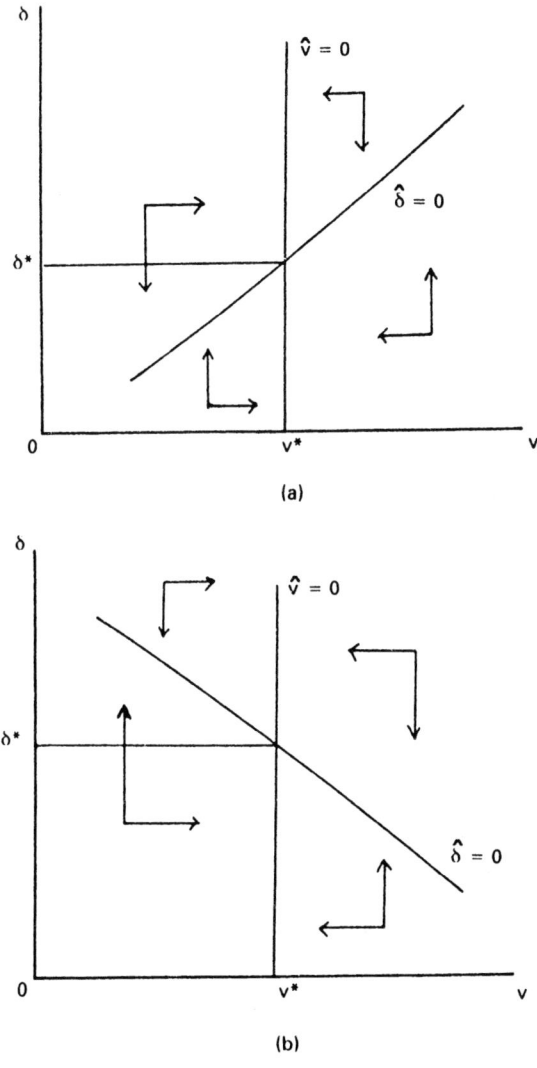

FIGURE 7.3

curve would now be given by the right-hand side of equation (7).

In the long period v and δ move over time according to equations (14) and (15). The dynamics of the system in the long period can be portrayed using the phase diagram in Figure 7.3.

The $\hat{v} = 0$ curve shows the value of v given by (16) which makes

$\hat{v} = 0$. Note that for $v < v^*$ $\hat{v} > 0$, and for $v > v^*$ $\hat{v} < 0$ from equation (14) so that the horizontal arrows are as shown.

The $\hat{\delta} = 0$ line shows combinations of v and δ which make $\hat{\delta} = 0$ in equation (15). To determine the slope of the line we examine the partials of $\hat{\delta}$ with respect to δ and v, respectively, holding $\hat{\delta} = 0$.

Differentiating $\hat{\delta}$ partially with respect to δ and rearranging implies

$$\partial\hat{\delta}/\partial\delta = -(s_w va/\delta^2)[\alpha - \tau i + \tau\pi(v - v_f)]/[s_c - (s_c - s_w)va - \beta]$$
$$- \beta(s_c - s_w)i/[s_c - (s_c - s_w)va - \beta] \quad (18)$$

where the denominators of both terms are positive. If we assume that $u > 0$ even for $\delta = 0$, we have $\alpha - \tau i + \tau\pi (v - v_f) > 0$ so that the entire expression is necessarily negative. A higher δ redistributes income from profit-receivers to wage-earners who have a higher propensity to consume, and by raising aggregate demand and capacity utilization this increases accumulation of physical capital by firms more than the saving of wage-earners increases due to their higher income, reducing $\hat{\delta}$.

Differentiation $\hat{\delta}$ now partially with respect to v and rearranging, we get

$$\partial\hat{\delta}/\partial v = s_w au/\delta - \pi(1 + \tau)$$
$$+ [(s_w va/\delta) - \beta][(s_c - s_w)au + \tau\pi]/[s_c - (s_c - s_w)va - \beta] \quad (19)$$

The first term captures the direct effect of an increase in the real wage for the wage-earners' saving for a given level of economic activity; it is positive. The second term captures the effects of the inflationary consequences of the higher real wage, both by direct erosion of wage-earners' wealth and by the acceleration the general rate of accumulation; it is negative. The last terms examines the consequences of a rise in the level of activity resulting from the redistribution of income towards wage-earners brought about by an increase in the real wage. Since this tends to increase wage-earners' saving as a result of their higher income and it increases the rate of accumulation, the effect on δ is ambiguous in general. If δ is small the proportionate effect on wage-earners' savings is greater and the term is positive, and conversely if δ is large. It appears, then that this derivative cannot be definitely signed, although for larger δ a positive sign seems likely.

If (19) is positive, the $\hat{\delta} = 0$ curve will have a positive slope as in

Figure 7.3 (a), while if it is negative the curve will be negatively sloped as in Figure 7.3 (b). The vertical arrows are as shown in these figures since the expression in (18) is negative for both cases. Thus in either case the long-period equilibrium will be a stable one, with the starred values showing the long-period equilibrium values of v and δ.

The parameters of the model will determine which types of long-period equilibrium the economy will have. This can be seen using an alternative graphical depiction which measures u and δ on the axes and fixing v at its long-period equilibrium level v* (which is determined only by (16)).

The short-period equilibrium level of u for v* and the associated level of inflation, $\hat{p}^*$ (obtained by substituting v* into (4)), is seen from (9) to be given by

$$u = [\alpha - \tau(i - \hat{p}^*) + (s_c - s_w)i\delta]/[s_c - (s_c - s_w)v^*a - \beta] \quad (19)$$

This shows that for a higher level of δ the goods-market clearing level of u is higher (since $s_c > s_w$). This relationship is shown as curves IS in Figure 7.4.

Long-period equilibrium also requires $\hat{\delta} = 0$. Setting $\hat{\delta} = 0$ in equation (15) we get

$$u = [\alpha + (1 + \tau)\hat{p}^* - (s_w + \tau)i]\delta/[s_w v^* a - \beta\delta] \quad (20)$$

Depending on whether the parameters of the model (specifically, α, τ, π, θ, v_f, v_w, s_w and i) make $[\alpha + (1 + \tau)\hat{p}^* - (s_w + \tau)i]$ positive or negative, the curve satisfying equation (20) will be as shown by the discontinuous $\hat{\delta} = 0$ curve of Figure 7.4 (a) or Figure 7.4 (b), with the discontinuity occurring at $\delta = s_w v^* a/\beta$. In the first case, equilibrium δ is 'small' and the second it is 'large'. As one would expect, if wage-earners have a higher propensity to save they will, in the long period, end up with a higher share of the physical capital both because they accumulate at a higher rate and the economy accumulates physical capital at a lower rate because of less favourable consumption conditions. Since we are assuming that $\alpha - \tau(i - \hat{p}^*) > 0$ (so that u > 0 even for $\delta = 0$), the positive case appears to be more likely, although if $s_w i > \hat{p}^*$, the negative case cannot be ruled out.

We may now examine the implications of a change in the interest rate; we only examine the effects of an increase and the opposite case can be analyzed allowing for ratchet effects of the type we discussed above.

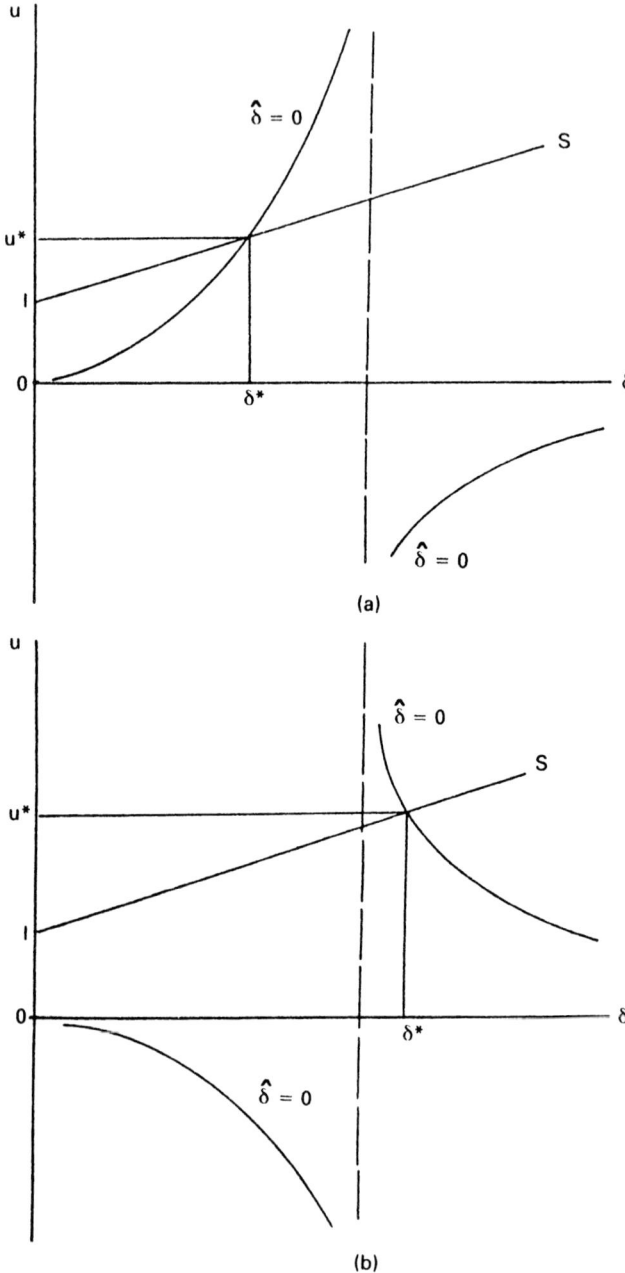

FIGURE 7.4

In the short period, equation (9) shows that

$$du/di = [(s_c - s_w) \delta - t]/[s_c - (s_c - s_w)va - \beta] \quad (21)$$

which can take either sign. The likelihood of a positive effect is increased the larger is $s_c - s_w$ and δ and the smaller is τ, that is, the larger is the expansionary consumption effect of a redistribution towards wage-earners brought about by a rise in the interest rate and the weaker the negative investment effect. The effect on the growth rate is given by

$$dg^1/di = \beta du/di - \tau$$

which may be negative even with $du/di > 0$ in (21), although with a small τ a positive growth effect is possible. The distribution between wage and non-wage income is fixed in the short period.

In the long period, the effects can be examined from Figure 7.4. If i is small enough so that we have the case of Figure 7.4 (a), a rise in i will shift down the $\hat{\delta}=0$ curve in the positive orthant (as is clear from equation (20)). The shift in the IS curve depends on the sign of the expression in (21). If it is positive so that the higher interest rate has a short-period expansionary impact, there will be a further expansionary effect in the long period and δ will be higher. This occurs because in the long period the wage-earners' share in capital (the relative size of their deposits) increases, further adding to consumption demand. Thus the expansionary effect of an interest rate increase cannot be ruled out. In the short-period contractionary case the effects on u^* and δ^* are in general not possible to determine from the figure. For the case in Figure 7.4 (b) the increase in i pushes the segment of the $\hat{\delta}=0$ curve in the positive orthant upwards, and thus the expansionary long-period effect again becomes a possibility, fuelled by a rise in δ over the long period.

We thus find that when wage-earners' saving is allowed for and wage-earners are allowed to earn interest income, a rise in the interest rate may expand utilization and even the rate of accumulation in the short and long periods, and shift the distribution of assets towards wage-earners. While this is a possibility, its likelihood diminishes if we take some further features of the economy into account.

First, in this section we have assumed that the interest rate does not have the effect of increasing v_f and therefore raising the inflation rate by equation (4). In the previous section we took this linkage into account and saw that an increase in the rate of interest reduced – in the long period – the real wage and therefore tended to reduce the rates of capacity utilization and accumulation. Incorporation of this effect will reduce the chances of an expansionary impact of a rise in the interest rate. Moreover, a higher rate of inflation in this model will have the effect of eroding the real value of wage-earners' deposits, and this will tend to reduce δ, further reducing the chances of any expansionary impact.

Second, throughout this paper we have assumed that the wage-earners' propensity to save out of interest income is lower than that of profit-receivers. It is likely, however, that wage-earners have a higher propensity to save out of interest income than out of wage income, especially if this saving is done for them institutionally by, say, pension funds. In this case the propensity to save out of interest income for wage-earners may exceed that of profit-receivers, so that redistributions from profit to wage-earners' interest income may have no positive consumption effects at all. This points out the importance of taking institutional factors into account more carefully before jumping to the conclusion that a higher interest rate may be expansionary.

CONCLUSION

In this paper we discussed what we believe are the central features of the Post-Keynesian approach concerning growth, distribution, interest and money, and attempted to incorporate them into a growth model in the Cambridge tradition – a tradition to which Pasinetti has made essential contributions. The model highlights an aspect of capitalist economies which has not adequately captured the attention of Post-Keynesians, namely, the short period and in particular, *long-period* effects of changes in the monetary policy, or more specifically, the rate of interest.

In the model, following Keynes and Kalecki, output is demand driven, and aggregate demand depends on the decision to invest of firms and the decision to consume out of income of profit-receivers and wage-earners. Firms invest more the greater the degree of capacity utilization, and the lower the real interest rate. In line with the formulations of Kaldor and Pasinetti, the propensity to save of profit-receivers is greater than that of wage-earners. Profit-receivers hold deposits and stocks whereas wage-earners only hold deposits which bear and interest which is fixed, perhaps by the Central Bank; the supply of money in endogenous at this fixed interest rate. Distribution and the rate of inflation are determined by distributional conflict between the different groups, and the rate of accumulation and growth is determined by the firms' investment behaviour, the saving parameters of the different groups, and the distribution of income.

The central implication of our model is that changes in the interest rate affect the level of investment and the distribution of income and wealth between profit-receivers and wage-earners, and thus the level of consumption. The effect of an increase in the rate of interest on the degree of utilization of capacity and the rate of growth in the long period is, in general, ambiguous. Keynesian short-period models, on the one hand, and neoclassical long-period models, on the other, predict unambiguous contractionary and expansionary effects, respectively. Our model suggests that depending on the propensity to save of wage-earners and profit-receivers, and the extent to which changes in the interest rate alters the distribution of wealth and income, the effect in the long period may be either contractionary or expansionary. Hence, the actual effect in different situations will depend on the specific behaviour of decision-makers and prevailing institutions.

NOTES

*The authors are grateful to Geoff Harcourt for his helpful comments on an earlier draft.
1. In addition to the names given in the text, other contributors to the literature include Davidson (1972), Minsky (1982), and Weintraub (1985). These names are given for illustrative purposes only: for an exhaustive survey of Post-Keynesian ideas see Hamouda and Harcourt (1988).
2. See Rowthorn (1977), Marglin (1984a, 1984b), Taylor (1983, 1985), Dutt (1987a, 1990a), and Amadeo and Camargo (1989).
3. For a discussion of the role of uncertainty see Shackle (1967), Carabelli (1988), Davidson (1988) and Lawson (1985, 1988).
4. See Robinson (1974, 1977) and Kaldor (1972, 1985).
5. This was essentially Keynes's procedure in the *General Theory*. For a detailed examination of Keynes's approach to the determination of the levels of output and employment, see Kregel (1976), Tarshis (1979), Chick (1983), Dutt (1987b), Amadeo (1987, 1989) and Asimakopulos (1988).

6. See especially Dutt (1987a, 1990a).
7. See Kalecki (1971), Steindl (1952), Robinson (1962), Dutt (1984), Asimakopulos (1988). Some Post-Keynesian contributions have emphasized the interaction between the pricing and investment decisions, which we have discussed independently here, by assuming that firms raise their markups to attempt to generate profits and hence financial resources, when they wish to invest at a higher rate. See Ball (1964), Wood (1975), Eichner (1976) and Harcourt and Kenyon (1976).
8. See Kaldor (1982), Moore (1979, 1988), Minsky (1982) and Rousseas (1986).
9. See, for example, Pasinetti (1983) and Fazi and Salvadori (1981, 1985).
10. Thus Keynes noted that 'there is no unique long-period position of equilibrium equally valid regardless of the character of the monetary authority. On the contrary there are a number of such positions corresponding to different policies' (Keynes, 1982, p. 55).
11. See also Pasinetti (1988).
12. As noted above, this departs from Pasinetti's (1962) assumption that wage-earners and profit-receivers receive the same rate of return from their assets, and follows Laing (1969), Balestra and Baranzini (1971) Pasinetti (1974a, 1983), Fazi and Salvadori (1981, 1985), in assuming that they hold different sets of assets. Unlike these contributions, however, we incorporate an explicit theory of interest and inflation rate determination into our analysis.
13. In particular we abstract from the influence of (expected) capital gains on equity, primarily to ignore issues relating to speculative bubbles.
14. The analysis so far follows Dutt (1987a, 1990a).
15. The implications will be the same as those of models which introduce interest effects by allowing for the financing of working capital. See, for example, Taylor (1983).
16. If firms happen to save, as long as we assume that they always save a constant fraction of profits and allocate their wealth in the same way as do profit-receivers, we would not need to modify our analysis: the firms would in effect be saving on behalf of the latter. Modifications in our analysis would, however, be required if firms, because of their concern for their valuation ratios, or other needs of investment financing, choose their saving rate. For example, if an increase in the desired rate of accumulation led firms to increase their retention rates, this would, *cateris paribus*, dampen the expansionary effect of the higher desired accumulation. A similar effect, paradoxically, would occur if they increase their desired markup-rates when their desired rates of accumulation increase along the lines mentioned earlier: the result could be to *reduce* their profits. These results, however, do not necessarily make these types of firm behaviour patterns irrational, because it is the joint behaviour of all the firms which reduces aggregate demand, as in the prisoners' dilemma problem.
17. See also Rowthorn (1981) and Dutt (1984) which assume that desired accumulation depends on both capacity utilization and the rate of profits. Here, for simplicity, we do not introduce the rate of profits as an additional variable.

18. There may also be a depressive effect of a higher inflation rate since this could cause greater uncertainty in the economy. We ignore this effect.
19. For the stability of short-period equilibrium, assuming that excess demand for goods leads to higher output, we assume $s_c - (s_c - s_w)$ va $> \beta$. This condition, which states that the responsiveness of saving to changes in the rate of capacity utilization is greater than the responsiveness of investment to changes in the same rate, is standard in macroeconomic models of the type we are concerned with; otherwise quantity adjustment would take the economy either to full capacity or zero output in the short period.
20. For similar models of the evolution of the distribution of assets, but which do not introduce inflation or the Post-Keynesian analysis of money and interest, see Darity (1981) and Dutt (1990b).

REFERENCES

Amadeo, E. (1987) 'Multiplier analysis', in J. Eatwell, M. Milgate and P. Newman (eds.), *The New Palgrave* (London: Macmillan).
Amadeo, E. (1989) *Keynes's Principle of Effective Demand* (Upleadon: Edward Elgar).
Amadeo, E. and Camargo, J. M. (1989) 'A Neo-structuralist Model of inflation and Stabilization', unpublished, WIDER/UNU; Discussion Paper # 212, Department of Economics, PUC/RJ.
Asimakopulos, A. (1988) *Investment, Employment and Income Distribution* (Cambridge: Polity Press).
Balestra, P. and Baranzini, M. (1971) 'Some optimal aspects in a two class model with a differentiated interest rate', *Kyklos*, 24 (2).
Ball, R. J. (1964) *Inflation and the Theory of Money* (London: Allen and Unwin).
Carabelli, A. (1988) *On Keynes's Method* (New York: St. Martin's Press).
Chick, V. (1983) *Macroeconomics After Keynes* (Cambridge: MIT Press).
Darity, W. A. (1981) 'The Simple Analytics of Neo-Ricardian Growth and Distribution', *American Economic Review*, December, 71, pp. 978–993.
Davidson, P. (1972) *Money and the Real World* (London: Macmillan).
Davidson, P. (1988) 'A Scientific Definition of Uncertainty and the Long Run Non-neutrality of Money', *Cambridge Journal of Economics*, 12 (3).
Dutt, A. K. (1984) 'Stagnation, income distribution and monopoly power', *Cambridge Journal of Economics*, 8 (1), March, pp. 25–40.
Dutt, A. K. (1987a) 'Alternative Closures Again: a Comment on Growth, Distribution and Inflation', *Cambridge Journal of Economics*, 11 (1), March, pp. 75–82.
Dutt, A. K. (1987b) 'Keynes with a Perfectly Competitive Goods Market', *Australian Economic Papers*, December.
Dutt, A. K. (1990a) *Growth, Distribution and Urban Development* (Cambridge: Cambridge University Press).
Dutt, A. K. (1990b) 'Growth, distribution and capital ownership: Kalecki and Pasinetti revisited', in B. Dutta, S. Gangopadhyay, D. Mookerjee and

D. Ray (eds), *Economic Theory and Policy: Essays in Honour of Dipak Banerjee* (Bombay: Oxford University Press).

Dutt, A. K. and Amadeo, E. J. (1990) *Keynes's Third Alternative? The Neo-Ricardian Keynesians and the Post Keynesians* (Upleadon: Edward Elgar).

Eichner, A. S. (1976) *The Megacorp and Oligopoly* (Cambridge: Cambridge University Press).

Fazi, E. and N. Salvadori (1981) 'The Existence of a Two-class Economy in the Kaldor Model of Growth and Distribution', *Kyklos*, 34, pp. 582–92.

Fazi, E. and N. Salvadori (1985) 'The Existence of a Two-class Economy in a General Cambridge Model of Growth and Distribution', *Cambridge Journal of Economics*, 9, pp. 155–64.

Hamouda, O. F. and G. C. Harcourt (1988) 'Post-Keynesianism: from Criticism to Coherence?' *Bulletin of Economic Research*, January.

Harcourt, G. C. and P. Kenyon (1976) 'Pricing and the Investment Decision', *Kyklos*, September.

Kaldor, N. (1955–6) 'Alternative Theories of Distribution', *The Review of Economic Studies*.

Kaldor, N. (1972) 'The Irrelevance of Equilibrium in Economics', *Economic Journal*, 82, pp. 1237–55.

Kalecki, M. (1971) *Selected Essays on the Dynamics of the Capitalist Economy* (Cambridge: Cambridge University Press).

Keynes, J. M. (1936) *General Theory of Employment, Interest and Money* (London: Macmillan).

Keynes, J. M. (1982) *The Collected Writings of John Maynard Keynes*, edited by D. Moggridge (London: Macmillan) vol. XXIX.

Kregel, J. (1976) 'Economic Methodology in the Face of Uncertainty', *Economic Journal*, 86.

Laing, N. F. (1969) 'Two Notes on Pasinetti's Theorem', *Economic Record*, 45 (3).

Lawson, T. (1985) 'Uncertainty and Economic Analysis', *Economic Journal*, 95, pp. 909–27.

Lawson, T. (1988) 'Probability and Uncertainty in Economic analysis', *Journal of Post Keynesian Economics*, 11 (1).

Marglin, S. A. (1984a) *Growth, Distribution and Prices* (Cambridge: Harvard University Press).

Marglin, S. A, (1984b) 'Growth, distribution and inflation: a centennial synthesis', *Cambridge Journal of Economics*, 8.

Minsky, H. (1982) *Can 'It' Happen Again?* (Armonk, NY: M. E. Sharpe).

Moore, B. J. (1979) 'The Endogenous Money Stock', *Journal of Post Keynesian Economics*.

Moore, B. J. (1988) *The Horizontalists and the Verticalists. The Macroeconomics of Credit Money* (Cambridge: Cambridge University Press).

Panico, C. (1985) 'Market Forces and the Relation between the Rates of Interest and Profit', *Contributions to Political Economy*, 4, pp. 37–40.

Panico, C. (1988) *Interest and Profits in the Theories of Value and Distribution* (London: Macmillan).

Pasinetti, L. (1962) 'The Rate of Profit and Income Distribution in Relation to the Rate of Economic Growth', *Review of Economic Studies*, October, pp. 267–79, repr. in Pasinetti (1974b).

Pasinetti, L. (1974a) 'The Rate of Profit in an Expanding Economy', in Pasinetti (1974b).
Pasinetti, L. (1974b) *Growth and Income Distribution* (Cambridge: Cambridge University Press).
Pasinetti, L. (1983) 'Condition of Existence of a Two Class Economy in the Kaldor and More General Models of Growth and Income Distribution', *Kyklos*, 36, pp. 91–102.
Pasinetti, L. (1988) 'Sraffa on Income Distribution', *Cambridge Journal of Economics*, 12 (1), March, pp. 135–8.
Pivetti, M. (1985) 'On the Monetary Explanation of Distribution', *Political Economy. Studies in the Surplus Approach*, 1, no. 2.
Robinson, J. (1962) *Essays in the Theory of Economic Growth* (London: Macmillan).
Robinson, J. (1974) 'History versus Equilibrium', *Thames Papers in Political Economy* (London: Thames Polytechnic).
Robinson, J. (1977) 'What are the Questions?', *Journal of Economic Literature*.
Rousseas, S. (1986) *Post Keynesian Monetary Economics* (Armonk, NY: Sharpe).
Rowthorn, B. (1977) 'Conflict, Inflation and Money', *Cambridge Journal of Economics*.
Rowthorn, B. (1981) 'Demand, Real Wages and Economic Growth', *Thames Papers in Political Economy*.
Shackle, G. L. S. (1967) *The Years of High Theory. Invention & Tradition in Economic Thought, 1926–1939* (Cambridge: Cambridge University Press).
Skott, P. (1988) 'Finance, Saving and Accumulation', *Cambridge Journal of Economics*, 12 (3).
Sraffa, P. (1960) *Production of Commodities by Means of Commodities* (Cambridge: Cambridge University Press).
Steindl, J. (1952) *Maturity and Stagnation in American Capitalism* (New York: Monthly Review Press).
Tarshis, L. (1979) 'The Aggregate Supply Function in Keynes's "General Theory"', in M. J. Boskin (ed.), *Economics and Human Welfare: Essays in Honour of Tibor Scitovsky* (London: Academic Press).
Taylor, L. (1983) *Structuralist Macroeconomics* (New York: Basic Books).
Taylor, L. (1985) 'A Stagnationist Model of Economic Growth', *Cambridge Journal of Economics*, 9, pp. 383–403.
Taylor, L. (1988) 'Real and Money Wages, Output, and Inflation in the Semi-Industrialized World', unpublished, Massachusetts Institute of Technology.
Weintraub, S. (1958) *An Approach to the Theory of Income Distribution* (Philadelphia: Chilton).
Wood, A. (1975) *A Theory of Profits* (Cambridge: Cambridge University Press).

Part IV

Structural Dynamics and Vertical Integration

8 Commodity Flows and Productive Subsystems: An Essay in the Analysis of Structural Change

Michael A. Landesmann and
Roberto Scazzieri

INTRODUCTION

The purpose of this paper is to consider alternative clustering criteria, based upon different analyses of commodity flows within the economic system. These may be used in order to group together productive activities that share a number of features distinguishing them from the remaining parts of the economic system.

In particular, we shall discuss the fundamental distinction between 'net product' subsystems and 'circular' subsystems, and we shall argue that all other analytical representations of productive subsystems (based on the consideration of commodity flows) may be reduced to these two fundamental types, or to a combination of them. We shall additionally explore whether the cross-fertilization of different approaches to the relationship between the specification of subsystems and the dynamics of economic systems (S_u-S dynamics) may illuminate features of economic dynamics that are not adequately examined when considering a single specification of subsystems.

The structure of the paper is as follows. The next section considers the utilization of non-overlapping net product subsystems (vertically integrated sectors) as a tool for the analysis of structural change. Here we especially focus on the relationship of the 'vertically integrated' view of the production system to the circular representation of productive activities on the one hand, and to the simplified picture of a 'pure labour' economy on the other hand. The third section considers an alternative way of constructing productive subsystems, which brings to the fore some fundamental features of interdependence among productive activities within the 'circular flow' of production and 'productive consumption'. Here we shall concentrate on recent contributions that have attempted to identify the analytical core of a circular economy by considering an artificial 'miniature' economy characterized by a uniform proportion among commodities entering the over-all product and the commodities making up the aggregate of the corresponding means of production (Standard system). In particular, the implications of the 'uniform proportion' assumption are assessed by considering its relationship to the analysis of the dynamic potential of any given economic system (von Neumann) and to the identification of distributional dynamics (Goodwin). The fourth section presents an overview of the utilization of productive subsystems as a tool for the analysis of structural economic change, and introduces three distinct approaches in which particular specifications of productive subsystems highlight features of a changing economic structure in the short- and medium-run. The three following sections consider three such approaches in greater detail.The fifth section discusses traverse analysis by means of temporally integrated and partially overlapping subsystems (the Hicksian approach). The sixth section considers the approach to traverse analysis based on fully interlinked 'circular' subsystems interrelated with one another by means of standard input-output flows. (In this case, at any point of time, the quantity of commodity j entering the means of production of commodity i may be delivered by a number of distinct processes using different techniques.) The seventh section discusses a third approach to the analysis of structural transformation, in which the productive system is first split into a number of non-overlapping subsystems of the circular type, then economic dynamics is examined on the assumption that such subsystems are related to one another by means of the accumulation of one subsystem's *net* product in order to expand the *gross* product of other subsystems. The latter device makes it possible to identify patterns of uneven dynamics in which the output level of specific commodities may expand at an increasing or decreasing rate depending on how 'close' the proportions between commodities used as means of production are in each pair of related subsystems. (A lower distance between input proportions makes it easier to use one subsystem's net product in order to expand another subsystem's gross product, and vice versa.)

The paper closes by discussing in which way the identification of relevant subsystems may be an important prerequisite for the analysis of specific patterns of structural transformation. In particular, it will be argued that structural change is generally a multi-dimensional process, and that a plurality of subsystem specifications may be necessary if the analysis of structural change has to capture the cluster of qualitative and quantitative transformations that characterize the historical dynamics of economic systems.

NET PRODUCT SUBSYSTEMS AND NON-PROPORTIONAL DYNAMICS

Much recent work by Luigi Pasinetti has been concerned with the formulation of a theoretical set-up suitable for the analysis of long-run patterns of structural change. In particular, Pasinetti has considered structural dynamics of a growing economic system that is experiencing non-proportional growth of sectoral productivities and where the growth in per capita incomes leads to changing demand patterns as a result of Engel's Law. The analytical device that allows Pasinetti to undertake this type of structural change analysis consists in the identification of 'net product' subsystems, that is, subsystems including all quantities of labour and intermediate products directly and indirectly required to produce the net output of particular commodities.

Pasinetti's subsystems may be considered a development and generalization of the concept of 'subsystem' introduced by Sraffa in Appendix A of *Production of Commodities by Means of Commodities* (Sraffa, 1960). There Sraffa had pointed out that

> [t]he commodities forming the gross product [. . .] can be unambiguously distinguished as those which go to replace the means of production and those which together form the net product of the system. Such a system can be subdivided into as many parts as there are commodities in its net product, in such a way that each part forms a smaller self-replacing system the net product of which consists of only one kind of commodity. These parts we shall call "subsystems". This involves subdividing each of the industries of the original system (namely, the means of production, the labour and the product of each) into parts of such size as will ensure self-replacement for each subsystem. (Sraffa, 1960, p. 89) (See also Harcourt and Massaro, 1964)

Building on Sraffa's formulation, Pasinetti has proposed a way of identifying net product subsystems that is compatible with the consideration of the structural dynamics of economic systems.[1]

Pasinetti's way of dealing with productive transformation reflects the special role of the capital structure in an economic system undergoing technical change. In particular, Pasinetti is able to identify a way of measuring the capital stock of any given economic system that allows him to keep track of the productive capacity of the economic system in spite of compositional changes of the stock of capital goods. This is obtained by means of a reclassification of the quantities of labour and intermediate products considered in standard input-output models leading to a vector representation of the stock of commodities used in each vertically integrated sector (see Pasinetti, 1973, sections 3 and 4).

The vertical integration of productive activities allows for intertemporal comparisons in purely physical terms across states of the economic system characterized by heterogeneous collections of capital goods. In particular, the influence of a changing composition of final demand upon the sectoral distribution of employment and the weights of different industries in gross domestic product may be examined independently of the transformation of the 'fund' of capital goods when the production system switches from one matrix of technical coefficients to another.

Pasinetti's analytical device is an essential step in the formulation of a theoretical framework which considers the long-run effect of basic dynamic forces, such as technical progress or population dynamics. As a matter of fact, the representation of the production system in terms of vertically integrated sectors makes it possible to identify a number of causal relationships that cut across the network of inter-industry linkages and highlight relationships among 'global factors', such as technological and demographic change, or technological change and environmental constraints, which are often concealed behind the mass of detailed transformations associated with changes of technical coefficients.

Pasinetti has shown how the method of vertical integration may be extended to the analysis of the investment behaviour of an economic system by considering growing subsystems or vertically hyper-integrated sectors (see Pasinetti, 1988). Here, each subsystem is characterized by a particular growth rate (the rate of growth of consumption for the corresponding final consumption good) and explicitly includes the quantities of intermediate products necessary to ensure the growth of productive capacity that is required to achieve a given growth in final consumption. Each growing subsystem is identified by a unit of vertically hyper-integrated productive capacity for commodity i and by a vertically hyper-integrated labour coefficient for the same commodity.

A remarkable feature of vertically hyper-integrated subsystems is that each unit of vertically hyper-integrated productive capacity is introduced 'without any specification of the composition of the unit concerned' (Pasinetti, 1988, p. 134). The relation between each unit of vertically hyper-integrated productive capacity and the physical commodities entering its composition may be changing under the influence of technical progress. However, such physical relations, which are essential for the analysis of the circular process at any given point of time, 'become irrelevant for all those dynamic analyses that concern the movements through time of the final consumption goods and of the corresponding physical quantities of labour, as well as for all those relations that follow therefrom', such as 'the analyses concerning the evolution of sectoral employment and income distribution' (Pasinetti, 1988, p. 134).

Pasinetti's contribution to the identification of vertically hyper-integrated sectors also has a remarkable implication in the field of the theory of value. Here, it emerges that it is possible to define 'a specific set of *natural prices* for each particular hyper-subsystem. In total, there will be m sets of natural prices, each one referring to the corresponding hyper-subsystem' (Pasinetti, 1988, p. 129). In particular, '[i]n all hyper-subsystems taken together, i.e. in the whole economic system, each good [. . .] has only one natural price as a consumption good, although it may have up to m different natural prices as a capital good' (Pasinetti, 1988, p. 129).

Pasinetti has shown that, by the method of vertical hyper-integration, it is possible to identify a set of hypothetical natural prices for each capital good within each vertically hyper-integrated sector on the assumption that such a capital good is produced as a consumption good (*not* as a capital good) within that sector (see Pasinetti, 1988, pp. 129–30). In this case, the price of each capital good would be equal to the corresponding quantity of labour directly and indirectly required to produce it as a consumption good within a particular growing subsystem.

The method of vertical integration (and hyper-integration) of productive subsystems has the remarkable property of showing a number of fundamental relationships that would be otherwise concealed behind the detailed framework of a circular and expanding economy. This can be seen by looking both at the relationships between physical quantities and at the natural prices which may be identified within a vertically integrated (and hyper-integrated) subsystem.

The quantity system brings to the fore a direct linkage between the use of labour in a productive system and the flow of consumption goods produced within that system. In particular, '[t]he complex circular (expanding) production process, which is in between, is taken for granted, as it is closed onto itself and merely fulfils an intermediate and ancillary function' (Pasinetti, 1988, p. 133). This approach may provide a conceptual apparatus useful in assessing some fundamental aspects of the dynamics of national wealth while the economy undergoes a sequence of structural changes.

The price system, on the other hand, highlights the possibility of identifying a number of simple and fundamental value relationships, independently of the complications arising from the characteristics of the circular flow in an economy. In particular, the consideration of vertically hyper-integrated subsystems suggests that the pure labour theory of value may be useful in assessing the 'wealth producing' power of any given labour force, independently of the technical distinction between consumption goods and capital goods. (As Pasinetti points out, all produced commodities are on a par provided capital goods are considered as final commodities just as the consumption goods.) If the distinction between capital goods and consumption goods is dropped, natural prices may be expressed as unweighted quantities of labour, and pure labour values may provide an 'objective', even if hypothetical, measurement of the productive potential of any given economic system that is undergoing a process of structural change.

The consideration of net product subsystems makes it possible to analyse the long-run features of an expanding economic system that is undergoing structural change, without explicitly examining the influence of growth patterns upon the inter-industry structure of the economic system. As a matter of fact, structural analysis in terms of net product subsystems highlights the changing character of the relationship between productive funds (such as labour and vertically integrated productive capacity) on the one hand, and the final demand basket on the other hand. This relationship is affected by dynamic impulses operating on the demand side, and brings to the fore two necessary conditions for full employment equilibrium growth. They concern the process of capital accumulation and the level of total expenditure in an economy.[2]

The essential character of the two conditions above may already be shown by considering the case of a pure labour economy, in which 'all consumption goods are made by labour alone', so that 'labour is [. . .] the only "factor of production"' (Pasinetti, 1986, p. 421). In this case the output levels and the labour quantities are linked with each other by the following system of equations (see Pasinetti, 1986, p. 422):

$$\begin{bmatrix} 1 & & & & -c_1 \\ & \ddots & & & -c_2 \\ & & 1 & & \vdots \\ & & & \ddots & -c_m \\ -l_1 & -l_2 & \cdots & -l_m & 1 \end{bmatrix} \begin{bmatrix} X_1 \\ X_2 \\ \vdots \\ X_m \\ L \end{bmatrix} = \begin{bmatrix} 0 \\ 0 \\ \vdots \\ \\ 0 \end{bmatrix}$$

in which l_i (i=1, . . ., m) are the labour coefficients for the production of the m consumption goods, c_i (i=1, . . ., m) are the consumption coefficients relative to the same goods (that is, the quantities of per capita consumption of these goods), and X_i (i=1, . . .,m) are the physical quantities of the m consumption goods produced in the economic system. Non-trivial solutions of system (1) may be found on condition that the determination condition $\sum_{i=1}^{m} c_i l_i = 1$ is satisfied. The economic meaning of the latter condition is that the sum of the proportions of the total labour force employed in the various sectors must be equal to unity if full employment of the available labour force is to be achieved (see Pasinetti, 1981, p. 34).

It is worth noting that the above condition for full employment gets modified without changing its fundamental character if we switch to the consideration of an economic system in which 'capital goods are required only for the production of consumption goods, while capital goods can be produced from labour alone' (Pasinetti, 1981, p. 37). In this case, full employment may be maintained on condition that the sum of the proportions of the total labour force employed to produce (i) consumption goods, (ii) the capital goods needed in each vertically integrated sector, (iii) the capital goods needed to replace worn out productive capacity, be equal to unity (see Pasinetti, 1981, pp. 38–9 and 46–9). This condition may be generalized to the case in which capital goods are needed to produce not only the consumption goods but also the capital goods themselves (see Pasinetti, 1981, pp. 43–7).

In this case the full employment condition must take into account the fact that part of the available labour force is employed to replace worn-out capacity in each capital goods sector. Furthermore, 'each sectoral new investment, in physical terms, must be equal to the corresponding sectoral final demand multiplied by the rate of growth of population' (Pasinetti, 1981, p. 53).[3] Full employment and full capacity utilization requires the equality between potential gross national income and total expenditure, which must be achieved by means of 'a very definite division of total expenditure between new investments, replacements, and consumption' (Pasinetti, 1981, p. 54). In this connection, Pasinetti points out that the 'equilibrium proportion' among components of effective demand ultimately depends on 'three exogenous forces of the economic system: population growth, technology, and consumers' preferences' (Pasinetti, 1981, p. 54). As a result, after account is taken of the 'employment requirement' associated with the production and replacement of capital goods, full employment and full capacity utilization require that demand for consumption goods absorbs 'the whole remaining proportion of total labour' (Pasinetti, 1981, p. 54).

It is worth noting that the latter requirement brings to the fore a direct relationship between employment of labour and consumption of goods, and that the fractions of over-all employment necessary to produce capital goods appear as performing a kind of ancillary role. For, in each time period, equilibrium productive capacity must reflect the capital goods requirement necessary to deliver the quantities of consumption goods that satisfy individual demand as per capita income is rising. It follows that 'each sectoral new investment, in physical terms, must be equal to the corresponding sectoral final demand multiplied by the rate of growth of population' (Pasinetti, 1981, p. 53). As a result, the consideration of a capital-using economy does not alter the fundamental picture of the economic system that may be obtained by looking at the simplified case of a pure labour economy. In both instances, the economic system is represented as a set of 'one-way' relationships that link over-all employment with final consumption. By looking at a pure labour economy, such relationships may immediately be identified; on the other hand, the analytical device of vertical integration makes it possible to reduce any capital-using economy to the logical analogue of a pure labour economy. As a matter of fact, vertical integration, by breaking the circular linkages among industries, makes it possible to identify the technological characteristics of each vertically integrated sector in terms of a specific level of sectoral employment and of a precise pattern of distribution of such employment among direct labour, labour employed to replace worn-out capacity, and labour employed to produced new capital goods.

The decomposition of an economic system into vertically integrated subsystems presents a picture of

> a growing economic system [in which] consumption appears at one extreme of the production process and labour appears at the other extreme, and the two are immediately and directly put into relation with each other. The complex circular (expanding) production process, which is in between, is taken for granted, as it is closed onto itself and merely fulfills an immediate and ancillary function. (Pasinetti, 1988, p. 133)

EIGENSECTORS, NET OUTPUT DISTRIBUTION AND THE CIRCULAR FLOW

The consideration of non-overlapping net product subsystems (as in Pasinetti) allows for the analysis of structural change by means of a type of analytical simplification in which productive inputs are reduced to 'original funds' (labour and vertically integrated productive capacity). As a matter of fact, labour is considered as a non-produced input, while the capital stock in each vertically integrated sector is measured in terms of units of a composite commodity, which is the vertically integrated productive capacity of that particular sector.[4]

Such a decomposition of the economic system, while highlighting a number of essential features of processes of structural change, may conceal others which are more immediately associated with the network of interlinked production processes supplying produced inputs to one another. One important feature that distinguishes the approach in terms of vertically integrated sectors from the one in terms of 'circular flows' is the fact that, in the former case, each productive sector i is identified by re-classifying inter-industry transactions such that it includes all quantities of labour and intermediate products that are directly and indirectly necessary to produce the corresponding ith element of the net product vector (that is, the quantity of commodity i that is produced over and above the quantity of the same commodity used as a means of production in the various industries of the economic system). Here, the relationship between the production of any given commodity and its utilization as a means of production (not only of itself but of other commodities as well) is not in the foreground. This is due to the fact that the method of vertical integration splits the economic system into a number of logically independent subsystems, so that the capital stock in each sector may be considered, from an analytical point of view, as an 'original' productive fund, that is, as a productive fund which is produced and reproduced within the same sector in which it is used (on this particular issue, see also the view expressed in Ziber, 1871, pp. 35–41, which has been recalled in footnote 4).

A distinctly different approach is adopted in economic theories of the *circular type*, which emphasize not the relative independence of different net product subsystems (as in the 'vertical integration' approach) but the mutual dependence of interrelated processes within a single 'block' of economic activities. As a result, circular theory emphasizes the fact that any given produced commodity may be used as a means of production in a number of *different* industries, and the proportion between the net output of any given commodity and the total output of the same commodity comes to the fore.

It is worth stressing that the circular view entails a different approach to the analysis of a productive system than that associated with the vertical integration of productive activities. For in the former case what may be called 'material producibility' is emphasized, that is the fact that, for any commodity with a positive surplus, the economic system's requirement for that commodity as a means of production is lower than the total corresponding output of the same commodity. As a result, no economic system as a whole can produce a 'complete' net output vector (that is, a vector including positive net outputs for all produced commodities) unless, for any commodity i, the following inequality holds:

$$a_i\, q\, \rho_i = q_i; \qquad i = 1, \ldots, m \qquad (2)$$

in which a_i is the vector of input-output coefficients corresponding to the ith row of a standard technology matrix A, q is the vector of total outputs, q_i (a scalar) is the total output of commodity i, and ρ_i (another scalar) is the proportion by which the total output of commodity i exceeds the sum of the requirements for this commodity as a means of production in the different industries of the economic system.

Condition (2) above brings to the fore an analytical requirement for the existence of a positive sectoral net output that may easily be generalized to the whole economic system if we consider a situation in which all sectoral outputs exceed the *corresponding* input requirement by the same proportion, so that $\rho_1 = \rho_2, \ldots = \rho_m = \rho^*$. In the latter case, the equivalent of condition (2) for the over-all economic system may be written as follows:

$$A\,q\,\rho^* = q, \qquad (3)$$

in which ρ^* is the uniform net output rate of the economic system.

The above approach to the analysis of economic interdependence shows an important feature of net product formation: If we consider a fully interlinked economic system, the formation of net product in industry i is not independent of the formation of net product in industry j. In particular, it may be shown that an increasing net output of commodity i is associated with a decreasing net output of commodity j, and vice versa.[5]

The above feature of a circular economy makes it interesting to consider the particular case of a uniform proportion between the sectoral outputs and the quantities of each commodity that are required as means of production in the over-all economy. For a uniform rate of net output permits us to identify in an unambigous way the degree to which any given economic system is capable of expanding from one time period to another. However, in any real economic system, there will normally be a range of different net output rates ρ_i, and it is likely that the commodity having the lower net output rate will set a lower bound to the expansion of the whole economy. This is not so if we consider a 'uniform net output rate' system, for in this case there are no bottlenecks due to inter-industry transactions and the dynamic potential of the economic system is fully described by the uniform proportion by which all sectoral outputs exceed the corresponding requirements as means of production.[6]

The assumption of a uniform rate of net output may seem to be an arbitrary one from the point of view of realism. However, it is possible to find a procedure by which the uniform rate of output economy may analytically be derived from an existing economic system by changing the proportions among the different industries that make up the real economy. This result may be achieved by constructing the 'Standard system' (in Sraffa's sense) that is embedded in the real economic system, that is by selecting 'from the actual economic system such fractions of the individual basic industries as will together form a complete miniature system endowed with the property that the various commodities are represented among its aggregate means of production *in the same proportions* as they are among its products' (Sraffa, 1960, p. 19).

The analytical procedure that identifies the Standard system implies that such a system is also a 'uniform net output rate economy'. As a matter of fact, as Sraffa points out, 'in the Standard system the various commodities are produced in the same proportions as they enter the aggregate means of production' (Sraffa, 1960, p. 20). As a result, 'the rate by which the quantity produced exceeds the quantity used in production is the same [for each commodity]' (Sraffa, 1960, p. 20).

By taking advantage of the latter property, it may be shown that under certain conditions on the matrix A of input-output coefficients,[7] it is possible to identify an *m*-dimensional vector of multipliers (*m* being the dimension of the A matrix) such that the gross output levels of the different industries may be weighted so as to obtain a 'miniature system' in which the same commodities enter, with the same proportions, the gross and net output of the whole economic system, as well as the vector of intermediate input requirements (produced means of production).

The above set of multipliers may be obtained by solving a particular system of equations that express the relationship between the gross output of each commodity and the quantities of such a commodity required as means of production in the different industries of the economic system (see Sraffa, 1960, pp. 23-4). Such a system of equations may be written as follows:[8]

$$\left[A - \frac{1}{1+R} I \right] \hat{q} \mu = 0, \qquad (4)$$

where R is the uniform net output rate, $\hat{q}$ the diagonal matrix of gross output levels, and μ the vector of unknown multipliers to be used as weights for the gross output system.

It is worth noting that, as the above procedure makes clear, the Standard system is obtained by assuming a uniform net output rate R in all industries and considering the maximum positive eigenvalue $1/(1+R)$ of technology matrix A (see Gossling, 1972, p. 185; and Pasinetti, 1975).

The Standard system is constructed from the real economic system by using gross output multipliers that reflect the basic idea of 'material producibility', that is, the fact that, in any given economic system with a positive surplus, there are commodities whose gross output exceeds the physical quantity of each which is required as a means of production in the different industries. The essential features of net product formation within a circular economy are related to the physical interdependence among production processes, and may be highlighted by considering a 'uniform net output rate economy', in which the differences among sectoral net output rates have been eliminated, and a clear linkage is established between material producibility and the maximum feasible expansion rate of the over-all economy. (Sectoral *physical* net output rates of steel, corn, etc. may not be unambiguously associated with the expansion potential of the economic system; on the other hand, the 'uniform net output rate economy' that may be associated with a certain technology in use makes it possible, by von Neumann's theorem, to identify the maximum feasible growth rate compatible with any given set of interdependent production processes.)

The system of equations (4) permits us to identify a set of multipliers that allows for the transformation of the real economy into a 'uniform net output rate economy'. From an analytical point of view, the latter transformation is obtained by taking the maximum positive eigenvalue of technology matrix A, that is $\lambda_{max} = 1/(1+R)$, as a 'proportionality parameter' between the gross output of each commodity and the quantity of the same commodity that enters the aggregate means of production.

A closer look at system of equations (4) shows that alternative transformations are possible by considering any positive eigenvalue λ_i of technology matrix A. In other words, the system of equations (4) may be written in a more general way as follows:

$$[A - \lambda_i I] \hat{q} \mu = 0, \tag{5}$$

where each λ_i is a distinct eigenvalue associated with A. (If A is of degree m, there are at most m distinct eigenvalues associated with it.)

The above argument implies that there can be as many different transformations of the real quantity system into a 'uniform proportion' system as there are distinct eigenvalues associated with technology matrix A.

This underlies the attempt by Richard Goodwin to use the concept of a 'uniform proportion' system in order to analyze issues that lie outside the original formulations of such an approach in von

Neumann and Sraffa. The economic interpretation of the multiple transformations compatible with relation (5) which could be suggested is that, if $\lambda_i = \lambda_{max} = 1/(1+R)$, the whole net output goes to profits and the share of surplus wages is null. This implies that any 'uniform proportion' system obtained by setting $\lambda_i \neq \lambda_{max}$ is associated with a distribution of net output in which the share of surplus wages is positive.

A remarkable feature of the above approach is that each pattern of net output distribution between wages and profits is associated with a different positive eigenvalue λ_i, and thus with a different 'uniform proportion' transformation. It follows that each transformation identifies a distinct composite commodity, which consists of a 'technologically determined, unchanging bundle of goods' (Goodwin, 1983, p. 131; 1st edn 1976). (In Goodwin's own terminology, each such composite commodity, or *eigengood*, is produced within an *eigensector*.) If all the physical quantities of an economic system are expressed in terms of eigengoods, we may again take advantage of the analytical simplification that was originally associated with the Standard system (although we are now considering a more general set-up): 'each good is produced entirely out of inputs of its own product; wages in each sector are paid out of its own product; any surplus or profit consists of each good itself' (Goodwin, 1983, p. 131; first edn 1976).

In the above case, the range of alternative net output distributions between profits and wages may be examined by considering, for each distributive pattern, an *ad hoc* artificial economy that embodies the most distinctive feature of a Ricardian corn economy, that is, the fact that '[t]he *i*th corn is produced by the *i*th corn, by labour that is paid in the *i*th corn, which leaves a profit in *i*th corn' (Goodwin, 1983, pp. 131–2; first edn 1976).

An important implication of the above approach is that 'the conflicting interests of workers and capitalists are not confused by complex value reactions; the greater the unit profit, the less the unit wage cost, and vice versa' (Goodwin, 1983, p. 135; first edn 1976).

More generally, the 'uniform proportion' approach shows that a number of important features of economic systems (such as their dynamic potential or the relationship between distributive shares) may be analyzed by concentrating upon what may be called the 'primitive' circular structure of the economic system (this is a circular structure that shows the material producibility features of the economic system by making use of the 'composite commodity' device and

Commodity Flows and Production Subsystems

thus allowing for the separation between the physical and value aspects of economic relationships).

PRODUCTIVE SUBSYSTEMS AND ECONOMIC TRANSFORMATIONS

In the two previous sections we have considered the essential features of the 'vertical' and 'circular' approaches to the analysis of economic structure. In particular, we have stressed that a number of important economic relationships may only be identified if one is looking either at the 'one-way' linkage between productive funds and final consumption goods or at the circular interdependence among productive processes delivering produced inputs to each other.

In the former case, a type of analytical short cut is obtained that brings to the fore a direct relationship between the level and composition of final consumption and the structure of the productive potential of any given economic system. The productive potential refers to the 'funds' (segments of the labour force and stocks of capacities) allocated to each vertically integrated sector.

In the latter case, we have seen that the circular network of input-output relationships may be examined from a number of different perspectives, and that important features of the 'physiology' of economic systems may be detected on condition that a simplified circular 'anatomy' is considered. In particular, the expansion potential of any given economic system (its maximum feasible growth rate) may immediately be identified if we consider the 'uniform proportion' system associated with the maximum positive eigenvalue of the matrix of technical coefficients. In this case, the real economic system is substituted by an artificial circular economy in which 'dynamic inefficiencies' are excluded; in other words, the pattern of co-ordination among interrelated productive activities and the pattern of net output utilization are such that the dynamic potential of technology in use is fully exploited.

The above analysis shows that there is a close relationship between structural specification and the type of dynamic investigation that may be undertaken. (See also Landesmann and Scazzieri, 1990, particularly pp. 101–2).

More specifically, the focus upon vertical linkages between productive funds and final consumption goods is generally associated with greater emphasis upon the 'malleability' of the productive structure, in the sense that any given collection of heterogeneous capital goods may be expressed in terms of units of vertically integrated productive capacity, thus allowing for the comparison between states of the economy characterized by qualitatively different stocks of capital goods (see Pasinetti, 1973).

On the other hand, the consideration of a pure circular economy of the 'uniform proportion' type shows another important feature of economic processes. This is the fact that any given network of fully interlinked productive activities makes such activities so completely interdependent that it may be useful, for certain purposes, to consider each bunch of interrelated processes as a single, fully integrated process delivering a particular composite commodity. If this perspective is adopted, it may be convenient to drop unnecessary complications due to the varying proportions in which the different processes are combined, and to concentrate on the special case of the 'uniform proportion' economy, in which the reproduction mechanism associated with technology in use can be analyzed in its pure form.[9]

The distinct features of the 'vertical' and 'circular' approaches to economic structure have remarkable implications for the analysis of structural change (see also Baranzini and Scazzieri, 1990). As a matter of fact, the vertical view calls attention to processes of transformation in which the pattern of utilization of existing productive funds is gradually transformed, and the actual course of economic transformation is constrained by the over-all availability of resources available in the economy as a whole (such as labour or capital funds) at any point of time. On the other hand, the circular view involves a concentration of attention on processes of transformation in which blocks of interdependent activities are substituted for each other. In this case, the pace and character of economic transformation are checked by internal constraints, such as the degree to which different circular blocks may be compatible with one another. (In general, a higher degree of compatibility is associated with a smoother and speedier transitional path than in the opposite case.)

The analysis of structural change requires the consideration of *compositional changes*. For this reason, the adoption of a particular subsystem specification is often the most critical step in order to select one specific dynamic rather than another. In the three following sections, we shall consider the essential features of three distinct types of subsystem specifications, and we shall examine in which way they impinge upon the pattern of structural transformation one is led to analyze.

VERTICAL INTEGRATION AND THE TIME STRUCTURE OF PRODUCTION: THE ANALYSIS OF THE TRAVERSE

In this section we shall consider a type of subsystem specification such that some degree of vertical integration is introduced, but the result is a set of partially overlapping subsystems, that is, subsystems that are not necessarily additive (this might happen, for example, in the case of joint utilization of a given input within two different subsystems).

An important application of the above approach is provided in Hicks's utilization of vertical integration in *Capital and Time* (Hicks, 1973). There Hicks refers to vertically integrated processes that are identified by the final output they are producing, but which might in their general form allow for the utilization of producible inputs that would in turn be obtained from other processes (see Hicks, 1973, pp. 5–6). This allows in principle for the integration of horizontal interdependencies and of vertical integration.[10] As a result, this system does not, in its general form, decompose into *separable subsystems* and is thus different from Pasinetti's system of vertically integrated sectors (see Pasinetti, 1973, 1988). Rather, the concept of 'vertically integrated process' is here just a means to follow a time sequence of productive operations (such as the construction and the utilization of equipment goods) even though in some phases of these processes horizontal interdependencies with other processes may occur, such as input-output links or the common utilization of fund inputs. In a sense, Hicks is using a vertical integration of a 'lower order' than does, for example, Pasinetti (1973, 1988) since a more extreme use of vertical integration could lead to the complete analytical separability of processes or sectors within the economic system.

Hicks's approach to vertical integration preserves a view of the time sequence of productive operations that is not explicit in Pasinetti's vertically integrated sectors or in Leontief-type systems in general. The preservation of such a time sequence is essential for traverse analysis, that is, for the analysis of 'change-over processes'. Such processes characterize the path that an economy follows when it switches from one technology to another, or when there is a change from one final commodity basket to another (see Hicks, 1973, pp. 144–5), or from one rate of growth to another (see Lowe, 1976). The essential feature of traverse analysis is the recognition that such changeover processes take place in historical time.

Hicks himself considered change-over processes that take place within single-process economies. However, it is also possible to use his type of vertical integration when a number of distinct vertically integrated processes are examined. In particular, it may be interesting to consider the implications of Hicks's distinction between the 'construction phase' and the 'utilization phase' in the production of durable instruments of production for the n-processes case. We may distinguish between two types of issues: One refers to changes in particular subsystems and to their effects upon other subsystems and thus upon the operation of the economic system as a whole. The other refers to changes in the over-all system dynamics and to their effects upon the dynamics of individual subsystems. In the former case, the following issues come to the fore:

(i) the shortening or lengthening of these two phases respectively in individual vertically integrated processes may be associated with interesting consequences at the level of the economic system as a whole. For instance, lengthening may result in temporary bottlenecks, while shortening may lead to additional storage requirements.
(ii) the switch to a new technique in one vertically integrated process may have an impact upon the arrangement of other processes, as well as upon the form of interdependence among processes. For instance, a new technique is often characterized by different flow input requirements over time, and also by different product types and output flows. It may also have different construction and utilization phases with respect to the old technique. As a result, the pattern of interrelatedness among individual processes will also be quite different from the previous one.
(iii) the speeding-up or slowing-down of changeover processes to new production techniques within different vertically integrated subsystems (Hicks's vertically integrated processes) may have an impact upon the dynamics of the over-all economic system.

In the case of changes in over-all system dynamics affecting the dynamics of individual subsystems, the following issues may emerge:

(i) Changes in the level of effective demand affect different types of vertically integrated processes differently. For example, vertically integrated processes with short construction and utilization phases might adjust much more easily to changes in levels of activity than would processes with long construction and utilization phases. (This is due to the fact that processes with long construction and utilization phases will have to be truncated before these phases have been completed from a purely technological point of view.) Similarly, processes that have a short construction phase but a (technologically) long utilization phase might be truncated before their technological life-time is over. In the latter case, production processes are likely to have started producing output and have thus recovered some of the initial outlays. The situation is much more severe for processes that are still in their construction phase and therefore have not recovered any of their initial outlays.

(ii) Changes in the composition of over-all demand in terms of consumption and investment expenditure may have a different impact upon different vertically integrated processes (subsystems).

An example may be the impact of a general shift of expenditure from consumption to investment, which may be considered as an attempt to have more processes in their construction phase rather than utilization phase. Such a shift in the composition of over-all expenditure may translate itself differently upon different vertically integrated subsystems for two reasons. One is the horizontal interdependence among vertically integrated processes of the Hicksian type. This requires that a larger number of certain processes have to be in their utilization phase in order to have a greater number of processes in their construction phase (since the latter require producible inputs from the former). The other reason has again to do with differences in the construction or utilization phases of different processes. For instance, if construction phases are very short for some processes and a distinct shift of expenditure from consumption to investment is foreseen, then there will be little incentive to invest into processes with short construction phases. Investment will go largely into processes with longer construction phases, that is into processes involving the utilization of more mechanized technical practices. Similarly, if there is an expectation of a short consumers' boom there will be an incentive to start processes with very short construction phases and – depending upon the length of the boom – longer or shorter utilization phases.

(iii) Changes in the product composition of final demand may have a differential impact upon different vertically integrated subsystems, due to the fact that some processes are completely rigid in the composition of the products they can produce, whereas other processes may change their production programme early on in the utilization phase, others even later in their utilization phase. Thus, a change in the over-all product composition of demand will have different effects on different processes depending upon the flexibility with which they may adjust their respective production programmes. However, because of horizontal interdependencies among vertically integrated processes, additional rigidities may arise due to the fact that new processes may require a different mix of producible inputs, and that there may be bottlenecks due to the limited capability of existing processes supplying them with the required inputs.

(iv) A change in over-all distributional variables (such as the interest rate or the wage rate) may have a different impact upon different vertically integrated subsystems, due to differences in the flexibility to adjust of the different processes. As a matter of fact, certain processes may require truncation, while others could adjust by changing the length of their construction or utilization phase as the input mix of such processes is changed. (See, for instance, Hicks, 1973, pp. 125–34, Bhaduri, 1975; and Nardini, 1990.)

ECONOMIC TRANSITION AND CIRCULAR INTERDEPENDENCE

In the traverse analysis of *Capital and Time* Hicks identifies each production technique by means of a given 'flow input-flow output' pattern; and the different techniques coexisting in a process of structural change are related with one another by the fact that all processes operated over a certain period make use of a common pool of resources, such as a given labour fund or a given amount of investible resources (goods in process). In this way, the processes of transition between techniques are constrained by the different time-profile of inputs utilization in each technique. At each point of time, the maximum level of operation of the new processes depends on the amount of resources that the 'death' of old processes makes available. As a result, we get a pattern of subsystem-system $(S_u - S)$ dynamics in which the speed of structural change associated with the substitution of one technique for another is constrained by the amount of resources that over-all dynamics makes available.

A different picture of (S_u-S) dynamics emerges if attention is focused upon the network of input-output interdependencies within a production system consisting of fully interlinked industries. (This is the case of the circular economy considered in section III above, in which all commodities appear both on the input and on the output side.) The problems associated with the analytical representation of a circular economy on the transitional path from one set of techniques to another have recently been considered by Quadrio-Curzio (1967, 1975, 1986, 1991a) and Baldone (1984, 1991).

Quadrio-Curzio has proposed what he calls a 'jointed techniques' approach (see Quadrio-Curzio, 1986, pp. 322–6), in which 'technology is represented so as to make it possible to describe in a *synthetic* way the physical system' (Quadrio-Curzio, 1986, pp. 322–3; our italics). In particular, given two 'primitive' matrices of technical coefficients A(I) and A(II), such that, within each matrix, there is a one-to-one correspondence between production processes and produced commodities, a jointed technique results from the combined utilization of processes belonging to A(I) and A(II) in order to deliver particular commodities either to final consumption or intermediate uses. In this case, the over-all technology of the economic system may be represented by means of a 'global technology' matrix such as $A_\alpha(I, II)$, in which the relative weights of technologies A(I) and A(II) are expressed by means of the 'splitting coefficients' α_{ij}, that is, by coefficients that may be used 'to "split", in proportions to be determined, the known technical coefficients' (Quadrio-Curzio, 1986, p. 324).

In the special case in which m commodities are produced by means of $m+1$ processes (and commodity 1 is simultaneously delivered by one process in matrix A(I) and another process in matrix A(II), the global technology $A_\alpha(I, II)$ may be represented as follows:

$$A_\alpha(I, II) = \begin{bmatrix} a_{11}^I & 0 & \alpha_{12}^I & \cdots & \alpha_{1,m+1}^I \\ 0 & a_{11}^{II} & \alpha_{12}^{II} & \cdots & \alpha_{1,m+1}^{II} \\ a_{21}^I & a_{21}^{II} & a_{22} & \cdots & a_{2,m+1} \\ \cdot & \cdot & \cdot & & \cdot \\ \cdot & \cdot & \cdot & & \\ \cdot & \cdot & \cdot & & \\ a_{m1}^I & a_{m1}^{II} & a_{m2} & \cdots & a_{m,m+1} \end{bmatrix} \quad (6)$$

subject to the condition that, for each commodity, the sum of splitting coefficients relative to its own intermediate uses be equal to the corresponding over-all technical coefficient, as derived from standard input-output tables (see also Quadrio-Curzio, 1967, pp. 99–100, and 1991a):

$$\overset{\text{I}}{\alpha_{1j}} + \overset{\text{II}}{\alpha_{1j}} = a_{1j} \qquad (7)$$

If the above representation of production technology is adopted, it is possible to follow the related dynamics of different subsystems, as the relative weights of each one go up or down depending on changes in the efficiency ranking of the different subsystems and on resource constraints. An instance may be the relationship between the 'high-grade land' subsystem and the 'low-grade land' subsystem on a dynamic path characterized by Ricardian diminishing returns. In this particular case, '[t]he increase of $\alpha_{1j}(II)$ with respect to $\alpha_{1j}(I)$, which correspondingly falls, [. . .] indicates that process $a_1(II)$ takes a greater relative weight in the economic system as it increasingly replaces process $a_1(I)$ in the supply of [the raw material commodity 1] to all the other processes in the economic system' (Quadrio-Curzio, 1991a, section 5).

Quadrio-Curzio's 'global technology' approach brings out the possibility of considering a network of 'mixed' input-output relationships without losing the analytical advantage due to the identification of primitive technologies. In particular, Quadrio-Curzio makes use of what may be called 'horizontal decomposition' of the changing mix of techniques characterizing any given economic system on a traverse path. Such an analytical device may be used not only if a Ricardian decreasing-returns path is considered, but also in order to analyze transitional paths on which the relative weight of any primitive technology at any point of time is independent of natural resource constraints and only reflects the internal dynamics (speed of reproduction) of each circular subsystem individually considered.

The latter approach has been followed by Baldone (1991), in a contribution that considers the transitional phase between the utilization of two different 'dominant' techniques as 'the emergence of a sequence of mixed techniques, one for each period, beginning from the moment at which the introduction of new activities begins until the moment at which there will be no more activities of the old kind functioning' (Baldone, 1991, section 4). In this case, the identification of circular subsystems is combined with a stage-structure picture of productive activities in order to obtain a sequence of temporally connected technology matrices. Such a sequence describes the historical process by which the advanced (expanding) subsystem displaces the obsolete (contracting) subsystem as the activities of the new type are gradually substituted for the old-type activities. In the course of this process, if technical change first affects the economic system at time t=0,

the input and output matrices at t=0, that is $\mathbf{A}(0)$ and $\mathbf{B}(0)$, will be different from those associated with the old technique only in the case of those activities [of the different industries] that are associated with the early phases [of each production process]. Such activities will be substituted by those corresponding to the new activities. In period 1, matrices $\mathbf{A}(1)$ and $\mathbf{B}(1)$ will also include the activities corresponding to the second stage of production processes relative to the new technique. At time t [of the transitional path] technique $\mathbf{A}(t)$, $\mathbf{B}(t)$, $\alpha_0(t)$ will consist of the first $t+1$ activities relative to the new activities and of the old-type activities corresponding to productive stages higher than t. After a number of periods T^* equal to the duration of the longest lasting old processes, only new type activities will be in operation, and [the new technique] will display its full range of activities after a number of periods T equal to the duration of the longest lasting new process (Baldone, 1991, section 4).

Horizontal decomposition of inter-industry flows makes it possible to describe any given production system on a transitional path as a linear combination of primitive technologies (each one identified by a one-to-one correspondence between commodities and production processes).

When considering a production system on a traverse path, the simplest possible state of technology is the one in which any commodity is produced by two different sets of technical coefficients. Thus, for example, on the traverse from the position characterized by primitive technology A to the one characterized by primitive technology B, the commodity 'steel' is produced either by the method characteristic of A or by the one characteristic of B. Steel will also be used on the traverse path as a means of production for machine-tools, cars, etc.

We may assume that the requirement of steel per unit of machine-tools, cars, etc. will be different depending on whether these commodities in turn are produced using a method belonging to technology A or B. However, it is interesting to look at the relationship between A and B by considering not only the different uses of steel as a means of production, but also the proportions in which steel produced by A and B respectively is used as an input in the production of machine-tools, cars, etc. In other words, it is interesting to keep track of the difference between A and B technologies in spite of the fact that the same commodities are produced at the same time by both technologies. Steel produced by means of A thus becomes separable from steel produced by means of B, even though the two types of steel are physically undistinguishable.

If the above decomposition is applied to all industries of the production system, the actual set of physical commodity flows on the traverse path may be decomposed into two distinct and non-overlapping subsystems by means of what may be called horizontal decomposition. For example, we could say that two thirds of the total amount of steel used in the production of machine tools are delivered by technique A and one third by technique B. A special feature of horizontal decomposition is that it allows for the study of sector-specific characteristics of the transition from one technology to another. For example, we could take into account transitional paths on which certain sectors make extensive use of A steel and negligible use of B steel.

Of course, horizontal decomposition of steel uses can be repeated from one 'layer' of means of production to another (note that, on the assumption of a fully interlinked set of productive sectors, steel is needed to produce machine tools and machine tools are needed to produce steel). At each layer two sets of equalities must hold to ensure that no commodity is either in excess supply or excess demand:

$$\sum_k \sum_j q_{ij}^k = q_i^k, \quad \begin{aligned} i &= i, \ldots, n \\ j &= 1, \ldots, m \\ k &= A, B \end{aligned} \qquad (8)$$

$$\sum_k \sum_j a_{ij}^k q_j = q_i^k, \quad \begin{aligned} i &= i, \ldots, n \\ j &= 1, \ldots, m \\ k &= A, B \end{aligned} \qquad (9)$$

where q_{ij}^k is the quantity of commodity i produced by technology k and delivered to sector j; and q_i is the total amount of i (say, steel) produced in the economic system at a given point of time. Of course, there is no reason to expect that the speed of substitution of A for B should allow for both sets of equalities to hold. For example, the scrapping of existing capacity might be too fast, so that the sum of the quantities of i required in the various sectors could be more than what is actually delivered by the various sources of supply. An opposite situation could arise if new capacities are installed before the old capacities are scrapped. In this case there might be temporary excess supply of certain commodities on the traverse path.

Horizontal decomposition allows us to keep track of the circular structure (input-output flows) of each primitive technology even if, on the traverse path, no primitive technology is ever observed in its pure state. By means of horizontal decomposition we can also determine whether, with certain levels and compositions of input uses, a particular primitive technology ceases to be viable, in the sense that another primitive technology must be operated jointly with it in order to avoid mismatching between input supply and input uses. For example, if too much steel produced by A is required from the group of steel-using sectors in A, it could happen that primitive technology A ceases to be capable of sustaining a self-replacing system.[11] In this particular case, the survival of the system depends on the existence of an adequate steel supply from the steel-producing sector of B.[12]

Horizontal decomposition makes it possible to analyze the speed of traverse in terms of the possibility for a given traverse to sustain itself at certain speeds of substitution of B for A but not at others (an early analysis of the speed of transitional paths is formulated in Lowe, 1976). For instance, if the supply of A steel declines too rapidly with respect to the rate of expansion of steel surplus produced in subsystem B (a surplus that can be delivered to the steel-using sectors of subsystem A), then subsystem A will stop operating at the given output levels and three possibilities arise: (i) A shrinks even more while B maintains the previous output levels; (ii) B is expanded and A maintains the previous output levels; (iii) there is both a contraction of A and an expansion of B. Technological substitution takes place in all three cases (B's output share is always declining relatively to A's) but the technological traverse takes on distinct features in each case. In particular, the system-wide activity level may either go up (case ii) or down (case i) and, as it turns out, the highest possible speed of transition (case iii) leaves both options open, depending on the relative speed of change in the over-all activity levels of subsystems A and B.

Horizontal decomposition makes it possible to analyze what may be called 'internal feasibility' of a technological traverse, so that feasibility of any given transitional path is assessed independently of the existence of resource constraints and by merely concentrating on the conditions for system-wide technological consistency that must be satisfied at any point on the traverse. This method is thus introducing a new important element in the analysis of production technology on transitional paths, for the consideration of static feasibility (as expressed in the Hawkins-Simon viability conditions) is now supplemented by the analysis of the *dynamic feasibility* of transitional paths, in which the mutual compatibility of given rates of expansion and contraction of different subsystems must be assessed. In this connection, it is possible to identify a number of necessary conditions that must be satisfied if we want to achieve the 'maximum speed of adjustment' on condition that 'malinvestment must be avoided' (Lowe, 1976, p. 124; see also Hagemann, 1990 and Hagemann and Gehrke, 1991).

CIRCULAR SUBSYSTEMS, NET PRODUCT ACCUMULATION AND ECONOMIC DYNAMICS

The above section has examined in which way the circular representation of production technology may highlight the relationship between expanding and contracting subsystems on the transitional path of an economic system. In particular, two features of transitional phases have emerged. One is the *complementarity* between contracting and expanding subsystems in delivering produced means of production to other processes of the economy (this feature may be analyzed in terms of changing splitting coefficients as the weights of component technologies are changing within each 'global technology'). The other feature is the *time connectedness* of productive activities that appear to be carried out side by side when a stationary state or an equilibrium expansionary path are being considered. (When considering a transitional path, the fictive simultaneity of the different activities breaks down, and asymmetric, sequential linkages among such activities come to the fore.) Both features have been identified by means of horizontal decomposition of inter-industry flows, that is, by splitting standard input-output flows and assigning particular means of production to their own specific sources of supply.

However, the relationship between productive subsystems on a transitional path is not always of this kind. For the global technology approach (or the splitting of individual processes into elementary stages supplied by different techniques) emphasize the linkages among individual processes that are supplying inputs to one another, rather than the connection between complete circular subsystems. On the other hand, there are interesting features of transitional paths that are better analyzed by maintaining the identity of the different circular subsystems that are linked to one another in the process of economic transformation. For instance, it may happen that a transitional path is 'sustained' by a set of separate subeconomies rather than by a fully integrated network of inter-industry flows. (A case in point may be the transformation path of a dual economy; see Mathur, 1965, pp. 310–11; and Chakravarty, 1987, pp. 16–18.)

A recent, explicit attempt to investigate the transformation path of an economic system whose dynamic is governed by the relationship among semi-independent subsystems is due to Quadrio-Curzio (1975, 1986, 1991a). In this case, the over-all economy is split into a number of self-contained subsystems A(h), such that the *self-replacement* of each subsystem is not dependent on the supply of means of production from other subsystems. However, the positive growth rate of the over-all economy implies that the different subsystems are 'connected in time, in that they rely upon the means of production of techniques [subsystems] already activated' (Quadrio-Curzio, 1986, p. 327). More specifically, it is assumed that, for reasons due to the limited availability of essential non-producible inputs, certain subsystems enter a stationary state, that is, continue to reproduce themselves without changing their scale of operation. Under such circumstances, each stationary subsystem 'generates net products, which cannot be accumulated within it' (Quadrio-Curzio, 1986, p. 328). In particular, the net products supplied by a stationary subsystem 'can be utilized as means of production to set in motion another technique [subsystem]' (Quadrio-Curzio, 1986, p. 328).

Each subsystem A(I), A(II), . . ., A(K) is characterized by a one-to-one correspondence between commodities and production processes and identifies a 'viable' technology, that is, it could provide the basis for an expanding economic system. We may determine the internal growth potential of each productive subsystem by considering the maximum von Neumann growth rate of each subsystem.

Let $g^*[A(I)]$, $g^*[A(II)]$ be the maximum growth rates of subsystems $A(I)$ and $A(II)$ respectively. If there are no other factors at work, the changes in splitting coefficients (α_{II}/α_I) from one period to another will become a function of the difference in the growth potentials of the two subsystems:

$$\Delta_t[\alpha_{II} / \alpha_I] = f[g^*(A_{II}) - g^*(A_I)] \qquad (10)$$

If both subsystems grow at rates equal to their growth potentials and these rates are unequal, then the changes in splitting coefficients will reflect differences in their 'internal rates of accumulation'. In other words, if the changes in the productive capacities that embody the two types of technologies are solely the result of the investment of the productive surpluses produced by the two subsystems, then the changes in splitting coefficients will exactly equal these.

Let the net outputs of subsystems $A(I)$ and $A(II)$ be

$$s^*(A_I), s^*(A_{II}),$$

and the stocks that embody the two technologies at the beginning of period 1 be S_I^1 and S_{II}^2.

The splitting coefficients will then simply reflect the ratios of productive capacities in which the different technologies are embodied. They will change as follows:

Productive stocks at the beginning of period 1	Productive stocks at the beginning of period 2	Splitting coefficients in period 1 and in period 2
S_I^1	$S_I^2 = S_I^1 + s^*(A_I)$	$\dfrac{\alpha_I^1}{\alpha_{II}^1} = \dfrac{S_I^1}{S_{II}^1} \rightarrow \dfrac{\alpha_I^2}{\alpha_{II}^2} = \dfrac{\Sigma_I^2}{S_{II}^2}$
S_{II}^1	$S_{II}^2 = S_{II}^1 + s^*(A_{II})$	

In any actual economic system, the expansion of the productive capacities that embody different technologies is not simply determined by the internal rates of accumulation of the two subsystems respectively. In fact, if there is a clear ranking of the two technology subsystems in terms of profitability, and no technological constraints, such as capacity or primary resource constraints, exist, then the productive surpluses produced by *both* technological subsystems will be used to expand the stocks of the more profitable subsystem.

For instance, if the profitability ranking is such that $\pi^*(A_{II}) > \pi^*(A_I)$ and no capacity or primary constraints exist, then

$$\Delta S_{II} = f[s^*(A_I)_t + s^*(A_{II})_t]. \tag{11}$$

The above would be an example of an extremely uneven expansion of the two subsystems, which might in turn be unrealistic for a number of reasons: For instance, in each period, the structure of production of producible inputs can only to a limited extent adjust to the changing input requirements that result from the unequal expansion of stocks. The limited adjustability of the output structure to the changing structure of input requirements may give rise to phenomena such as the emergence of residuals (stocks of produced commodities that may no longer be used as productive inputs) or blockages of the unequal expansion of different technology subsystems.

It is worth remembering that there is a continuous lag in the technology composition of the capacities that produce the outputs in one period and the technology composition that characterizes the capacities of the following production period. The continuous 'upgrading' in the technology mix of new capacities has to be facilitated by the production of inputs by capacities that always lag one step behind in their own technology mix. The inadequate adaptability of the output programme of given capacities to the requirement of new technology mixes gives rise to residuals and blockages.

A vector of residuals r may emerge because existing capacities deliver an output composition that is not strictly matching the input requirements for the construction and the utilization of new capacities.

$$r = q_{t-1} - \begin{bmatrix} \alpha_I & A_I & + \alpha_{II} & A_{II} \end{bmatrix} q_t. \tag{12}$$

Such residuals can take the form of either excess capacities or surplus production. In other words, surplus output is actually produced or some portions of existing capacities remain unutilized.[13]

Quadrio-Curzio (1986) has examined situations in which the above was the case *and* also the supply of different types of primary inputs could not be expanded at the rates required for a particular pattern of expansion of different subsystems. In fact, he studies an extreme case in which certain productive subsystems exclusively require particular types of primary inputs (the use of such inputs is amongst their distinguishing characteristics). In such a situation the expansion of a particular subsystem may be constrained by the expansion rate of the particular primary input that is required by that subsystem. If that expansion rate is $\bar{g}^*[A(I)]$, then we may have:

$$\bar{g}^*[A(I)] < g^*[A(I)].$$

An extreme case is where $\bar{g}^*[A(I)] = 0$, so that productive subsystem A(I) can expand no further. This is Ricardo's case of the limited availability of particular types of land

$$T_I, T_{II}, \ldots, T_K.$$

Such cases are a reason for the continued coexistence of different types of subsystems alongside each other for long periods of time.

However, at some point, a third type of technology A(III) may be invented that might overcome the primary input constraint holding back the relative expansion of productive subsystem A(II). In the latter situation, the expansion rate of the over-all economic system may be speeded up because methods that increase g^*_{ottn} have been found.

It is worth noting at this point that Quadrio–Curzio's 'disjointed techniques' or 'composite technologies' approach, which we are now considering, has the remarkable feature of allowing for the endogenous determination of the weighting of different subsystems within the over-all economic system. In particular, such weights are made to depend on the dynamics of the whole economic system. More specifically, they depend on scale constraints in the operation of particular subsystems and on the uneven (internal) expansion rates of each productive subsystem. As a result, the maximum expansion rate of any given composite technology may be a non-linear combination of the maximum expansion rates of its component subsystems, due to the possibility of higher or lower growth rates associated with the way in which different subsystems are combined and residuals created or utilized.[14]

Commodity Flows and Production Subsystems

As may be seen, the above approach allows for the consideration of the uneven dynamics of economic systems by focusing upon the change in the relationship between production subsystems as the over-all economy undergoes an acceleration or deceleration in its expansionary movement. A special feature of such an approach is that, by focusing upon the existence of relatively independent subsystems, it is possible to analyze the changing pattern of over-all dynamics in terms of the better or worse matching of distinct subsystems, which may be associated with different dynamic characteristics (such as different maximum growth rates).

The 'composite technology' approach, which we have been considering in the present section, lends itself to generalization in a number of different directions.

For example, the internal expansion rates of the various subsystems may themselves be variable, independently of resource constraints, because of learning phenomena or other technological improvements associated with Smithian division of labour. Or the dynamics of individual subsystems may be constrained by the existence of upper bounds upon the growth rates in the availability of primary resources, rather than by upper bounds upon their absolute levels.

In this case, the maximum potential growth rates of the different subsystems may become a function of the uneven rates at which the availability of the different primary inputs may be increased, which in turn may be variable with time.

CONCLUDING REMARKS

The analysis of structural change requires a combination of distinct conceptual frameworks and methods, which must be complemented with one another in order to get a sufficiently realistic picture of actual transformation processes and of the underlying causal mechanisms. In particular, the analysis of the over-all dynamics of the economic system, which may synthetically be described by macro-economic aggregates, must be complemented by an identification of relevant clusters of economic activities, of the way in which they relate to one another and of the implications of such an interactive pattern for the dynamics of the economy as a whole.

As has been pointed out, '[a] realistic causal analysis can result from a simultaneous use of both macro-economic concepts and concepts which are appropriate to the process of transformation, not by relying upon one or the other alone' (Dahmen, 1955, p. 295). One important instance is the formation of clusters of interrelated structural transformations, or 'development blocks' (see Dahmen, 1955, pp. 297–8).

In many uses, the existence of development blocks is due to technological interrelatedness. For example, as has been pointed out by considering Swedish industrial history in the period 1895–1914

> [s]ome inventions could not become innovations before complementary progress had been made in another phase in the production process. Innovations in the manufacture of steel could easily create difficulties in the coordination of production if complementary innovations were not made in the production of pig iron or in the manufacture of steel products, or if the distributive outlets were not adequately developed. (Dahmen, 1955, p. 297).

However, technological interrelatedness *per se* may either be an obstacle or a spur for structural transformation, depending on factors such as the degree of international integration, the saving and consumption behaviour, the institutional and financial set-up. In other words, the 'material bases' of any given economic system provide the structural framework within which actual dynamics take place; but the precise direction and course of such dynamics is, in general, determined by motive forces that are not purely technological in kind.

Against such a background, the organization of commodity flows according to a particular subsystem specification is a critical step in identifying the cluster of economic activities and the pattern of motive forces that are most relevant at any specific instance of transformation in the economic structure.

NOTES

1. It is worth noting that this is a major distinguishing feature of Pasinetti's subsystems with respect to those considered by Sraffa, whose starting point is provided by a 'system of industries (each producing a different commodity) which is in a self-replacing state' (Sraffa, 1960, p. 89).
2. In this connection, Pasinetti maintains that

two kinds of necessary conditions must be satisfied in order to keep equilibrium over time. First of all, there is a series of capital accumulation conditions [. . .], ensuring that each sector be endowed all the time with precisely that amount of additional productive capacity which is required by the expanding demand. These conditions state that the ratio of new investments to the level of production must be equal, in each sector, to the technologically determined capital/output ratio multiplied by the rate of population growth. Secondly, in order to ensure the full utilisation of the available productive capacity and the full employment of the available labour force, a further macroeconomic effective demand condition [. . .] must also be satisfied. This condition states that, given (by the first series of conditions and by replacement requirements) the total amount of equilibrium gross investment, total demand for consumption goods must be such as to absorb the whole remaining part of potential gross national income. (Pasinetti, 1981, pp. 54–5)

3. The above equalities identify a specific capital accumulation condition for each vertically integrated sector.
4. The representation of the productive system in terms of vertically integrated processes and productive funds that are either non produced or produced within the corresponding sector of utilization, may be traced back to certain formulations of classical economic theory. For instance, according to Hicks, a number of propositions of Ricardo's *Principles* may be associated with the view that '[t]hough horses were intermediate products in the production of corn, the production of horses could be regarded as a stage in corn production; the production of looms as a stage in the production of cotton goods; and so on' (Hicks, 1985, p. 309). This view was explicitly emphasized in Ziber's reformulation of classical economic theory: '[t]he *series of operations* performed on skin by the butcher, the tanner, the shoemaker, from the point of view of the social economy are nothing but a direct, *single operation of boot production*' (Ziber, 1971, p. 228). Ziber also maintains that 'it is entirely logical and correct to consider in the same category both the means of subsistence and the means of production of such means of subsistence' (see Ziber, 1871, pp. 196–7; see also Scazzieri, 1987, pp. 35–41).
5. This property may easily be identified by considering a two-good economy, in which commodities i and j are used as means of production both of themselves and of each other. In this case, a higher net output of i implies (for any given technology) a greater gross output of the same commodity. However, the gross output of i cannot increase unless there is greater utilization of both i and j as means of production in the ith industry. It follows that an increasing net output of i is associated with a smaller proportion of the outputs of commodities i and j going into the means of production of industry j. As a result, the gross and net output of j will be reduced.
6. This is also the economic rationale of the theorem, proved by von Neumann, according to which an economic system with constant technology that is expanding along a proportional growth path can also

achieve the maximum expansion compatible with the technology in use. (See von Neumann, 1945–6; see also Morishima, 1969, and Dore, Chakravarty and Goodwin, 1989.)
7. See Blakley and Gossling (1967) for a discussion of the properties of non-negative A matrices that allow for uniqueness and existence of the Standard system.
8. Here we follow the mathematical formulation by Gossling (1972, p. 111) with some change of notation.
9. See also Ando, Fisher and Simon (1963) and Ando and Fisher (1963) who analysed the decomposability of economies into subgroups of uniformly growing industries depending upon the degree of interdependence amongst these industries.
10. In his discussion of specific traverses, Hicks leaves out producible inputs and restricts himself to labour inputs; he thus abstracts from horizontal interdependencies within the production system. However, in his discussion of possible generalizations (see Hicks, 1973, Ch. 12, and Hicks, 1977, Ch. 9) he points to the extension of his analysis of traverses to include produced inputs.
11. Viable technology may or may not sustain a self-replacing system depending on actual proportions among sectoral output levels. (See, for example, Sraffa, 1960, ch. I.) But the ways in which the output levels delivered by the various technologies are expanded or contracted on a technological traverse do not normally follow the requirements for 'technological equilibrium' as expressed in conditions [8]–[9] above. It follows that the relationship among competing technologies on a traverse is not merely an antagonistic one. At any point of time technologies are part of a more general system, and the combined technologies characterizing a traverse could be capable of sustaining the production system in transition when no primitive technology would do it. This implies that structural change on a traverse cannot be taken for granted and that technical innovation might sometimes start an abortive substitution of A for B when the relative speeds of change of the outputs delivered by the various sources of supply are not in line with the system-wide requirements for the feasibility of the technological traverse.
12. From a historical perspective, a particularly important case of supply-constrained technological traverse is the substitution of a 'modern' for a 'traditional' productive subsystem on the development path of a dual economy. (See, for example, Mahalanobis, 1953; and Chakravarty, 1987.)
13. Quadrio-Curzio (1986, pp. 329–37) considers the possibility that residuals that may emerge in the course of a traverse can be used for the (continued) operation of even older technologies, such as A(0) or give rise to the invention of new technologies, such as A(III).
14. In a recent contribution, Quadrio-Curzio has specifically examined the way in which the dynamic efficiency of composite technologies (and their efficiency ranking in terms of maximum feasible expansion rates) may critically depend on the relationship between component technologies (subsystems) and residuals formation, or utilization, within the over-all economy (see Quadrio-Curzio, 1991b).

REFERENCES

Amendola, M. and Gaffard, J. L. (1988) *The Innovative Choice. An Economic Analysis of the Dynamics of Technology* (Oxford and New York: Basil Blackwell).

Ando, A. and Fisher, F. M. (1963) 'Near-Decomposability, Partition and Aggregation, and the Relevance of Stability Discussions', *International Economic Review*, 4, 1, pp. 53–67.

Ando, A., Fisher, F. M. and Simon, H. A. (1963) *Essays on the Structure of Social Science models*. (Cambridge, Mass.: MIT Press).

Baldone, S. (1984), 'Integrazione verticale, struttura temporale dei processi produttivi e transizione fra le tecniche', *Economia politica*, I, 1, April, pp. 79–105.

Baldone, S. (1991) 'Vertical Integration, the Temporal Structure of Production Processes, and Transition between Techniques', in M. Landesmann, R. Scazzieri et al., *Dynamics in Production Systems*, mimeo, Cambridge.

Baranzini, M. and Scazzieri, R. (1990), 'Economic Structure: Analytical Perspectives', in M. Baranzini and R. Scazzieri (eds), *The Economic Theory of Structure and Change* (Cambridge: Cambridge University Press) pp. 227–333.

Belloc, B. (1991), 'Traverse Analysis in a Neo-Austrian Framework', in M. Landesmann and R. Scazzieri, eds., *Production and Economic Dynamics*, mimeo, Cambridge.

Bhadhuri, A. (1975), 'On the Analogy between the Quantity-Traverse and The Price-Traverse', *Oxford Economic Papers*, n.s., XXVII, 3, pp. 455–61.

Blakley, G. R. and Gossling, W. F. (1967), 'The Existence, Uniqueness, and Stability of the Standard system', *The Review of Economic Studies*, XXXIV, 4, October, pp. 427–30.

Chakravarty, S. (1982) *Alternative Approaches to a Theory of Economic Growth: Marx, Marshall and Schumpeter* (Calcutta: Orient Longman).

Chakravarty, S. (1987) *Development Planning. The Indian Experience*, (Oxford: Clarendon Press).

Clark, J. B. (1899) *The Distribution of Wealth* (New York: Macmillan).

Dahmen, E. (1955) 'Technology, Innovations and International Industrial Transformation', in L. H. Dupriez (ed.), *Economic Progress. Papers and Proceedings of a Round Table held by the International Economic Association* (Louvain: Institut de Recherches Economiques et Sociales) pp. 293–306.

Dore, M., Chakravarty, S. and Goodwin, R. (1989) *John von Neumann and Modern Economics* (Oxford: Clarendon Press).

Goodwin, R. (1983) 'Use of Normalised General Co-ordinates in Linear Value and Distribution Theory' (first edn 1976), in R. M. Goodwin, *Essays in Linear Economic Structures* (London: Macmillan) pp. 130–52.

Gossling, W. F. (1972) *Productivity Trends in a Sectoral Macro-Economic Model. A Study of American Agriculture and supporting industries 1919–1964* (London: Input-Output).

Gossling, W. F. (1974) *Some Productive Consequences of Engel's Law*, Input-Output Research Association, Occasional Paper n. 2.

Hagemann, H. (1990) 'The structural theory of economic growth' in M. Baranzini and R. Scazzieri (eds), *The Economic Theory of Structure and Change* (Cambridge: Cambridge University Press) pp. 144–171.

Hagemann, H. and Gehrke, C. (1991) 'Efficient Traverses and Bottlenecks: a Structural Approach', in M. Landesmann, R. Scazzieri et al., *Production and Economics Dynamics*, mimeo, Cambridge.

Harcourt, G. C. and Massaro, V. G. (1964), 'A Note on Mr. Sraffa's Subsystems', *The Economic Journal*, LXXIV, pp. 715–22.

Hicks, J. (1953) *A Contribution to the Theory of the Trade Cycle* (Oxford: Clarendon Press).

Hicks, J. (1973) *Capital and Time. A Neo-Austrian Theory* (Oxford: Clarendon Press).

Hicks, J. (1977) *Economic Perspectives* (Oxford: Clarendon Press).

Hicks, J. (1985) 'Sraffa and Ricardo: a Critical View', in G. A. Caravale (ed.), *The Legacy of Ricardo* (Oxford and New York: Basil Blackwell) pp. 305–19.

Landesmann, M. A. and Scazzieri, R. (1990) 'Specification of Structure and Economic Dynamics', in M. Baranzini and R. Scazzieri (eds), *The Economic Theory of Structure and Change* (Cambridge: Cambridge University Press) pp. 95–121.

Leon, P. (1967) *Structural Change and Growth in Capitalism* (Baltimore: Johns Hopkins University Press).

Leontief, W. W. (1941), *The Structure of the American Economy, 1919–1929* (Cambridge, Mass.: Harvard University Press).

Lowe, A. (1976) *The Path of Economic Growth* (Cambridge: Cambridge University Press).

Magnan De Bornier, J. (1990) 'Vertical Integration, Growth and Sequential Change', in M. Baranzini and R. Scazzieri (eds), *The Economic Theory of Structure and Change* (Cambridge: Cambridge University Press) pp. 122–43.

Mahalanobis, P. C. (1953) 'Some Observations on the Process of Growth of National Income', *Sankhyā. The Indian Journal of Statistics*, XII, 4, pp. 307–12.

Mathur, G. (1965) *Planning For Steady Growth (Delhi: Oxford University Press)*.

Morishima, M. (1969) *Theory of Economic Growth* (Oxford: Clarendon Press).

Nardini, F. (1990) 'Cycle-Trend Dynamics in a Fixwage Neo-Austrian Model of Traverse', *Structural Change and Economic Dynamics*, I, 1, June, pp. 165–94.

von Neumann, J. (1945–6) 'A Model of General Equilibrium', *The Review of Economic Studies*, 13, pp. 1–9.

Nuti, D. M. (1970) 'Capitalism, Socialism and Steady Growth', *Economic Journal*, LXXX, March, pp. 32–57.

Pasinetti, L. L. (1973) 'The Notion of Vertical Integration in Economic Analysis', *Metroeconomica*, XXV, pp. 1–29; reprinted in *Essays on the Theory of Joint Production*, ed. L. L. Pasinetti (London and New York: Macmillan Columbia University Press).

Pasinetti, L. L. (1975) *Lectures on the Theory of Production* (London: Macmillan).
Pasinetti, L. L. (1981) *Structural Change and Economic Growth. A Theoretical Essay on the Dynamics of the Wealth of Nations* (Cambridge: Cambridge University Press).
Pasinetti, L. L. (1986) 'The Exchange-Production Duality and the Dynamics of Economic Knowledge', in M. Baranzini and R. Scazzieri (eds), *Foundations of Economics. Structures of Inquiry and Economic Theory* (Oxford and New York: Basil Blackwell) pp. 377–407.
Pasinetti, L. L. (1988) 'Growing Subsystems, Vertically Hyper-integrated Sectors and the Labour Theory of Value', *Cambridge Journal of Economics*, 12, pp. 125–34.
Quadrio-Curzio, A. (1967) *Rendita e distribuzione in un modello economico plurisettoriale* (Milano: Giuffrè).
Quadrio-Curzio A. (1975) *Rendita e accumulazione del capitale* (Bologna: Il Mulino).
Quadrio-Curzio, A. (1986) 'Technological Scarcity: an Essay on Production and Structural Change', in M. Baranzini and R. Scazzieri (eds), *Foundations of Economics. Structures of Inquiry and Economic Theory* (Oxford and New York: Basil Blackwell). pp. 311–38.
Quadrio-Curzio, A., Manara, C. F. and Faliva, M. (1991a) 'Production and Efficiency with Global Technologies', in M. Landesmann and R. Scazzieri eds., *Production and Economic Dynamics*, mimeo, Cambridge.
Quadrio-Curzio, A. and Pellizzari, F. (1991b) 'The Dynamic Order of Efficiency and the Choice of Technologies', mimeo, Milan.
Scazzieri, R. (1987) 'Ziber on Ricardo', *Contributions to Political Economy*, 6, March, pp. 25–44.
Smith, A. (1776) *An Inquiry into the Nature and Causes of the Wealth of Nations* (London: Strahan and Cadell).
Sraffa, P. (1960) *Production of Commodities by Means of Commodities. Prelude to a Critique of Economic Theory* (Cambridge: Cambridge University Press).
Stone, R. (1961) *Input-Output and National Accounts* (Paris: Organization for Economic Cooperation and Development).
Stone, J. and Brown, J. A. C. (1962) 'Output and Investment for Exponential Growth in Consumption', *Review of Economic Studies*, XXIX, 80, June.
Ziber, N. I. (1871) 'Teoriia Tsennosti i Kapitala D. Ricardo [. . .]' [Ricardo's theory of value and capital], *Universitetskiia Izviestiia* (Kiev), nn. 1–2 and 4–11.

9 On Economic Science, Its Tools and Economic Reality*

Alberto Quadrio-Curzio

INTRODUCTION

The relationship between economic science and mathematical tools for the analysis of economic reality is certainly one of the most important and fascinating topics of the current age, characterized by a great development of economic science and its connected mathematical methods.

Luigi Pasinetti dwelt upon such a subject during his opening lecture as Professor of Econometrics at the Università Cattolica of Milan in 1964. His lecture 'Causality and interdependence in econometric analysis and in economic theory'[1] has been an important methodological landmark for a wide group of Italian economists. Almost thirty years after that lecture my contribution, being part of the volume celebrating his sixtieth birthday, claims not to be off the point by carrying out a deliberation about topics which have shown Luigi Pasinetti's sensibility to the search for a proper conception of economic science, for which all his former students – including the writer who had him as intellectual guide with Siro Lombardini and Carlo Felice Manara – owe him much.

In this survey we will aim at simplicity, intending to make a contribution especially useful to social scientists who are different from economists.

OBJECT AND METHOD OF ECONOMICS

Economic science and *economic reality* move on together, in the sense that the first mainly aims at explaining the second, by interpreting its past, by interpreting and trying to rule its present, by anticipating and trying to rule its future. Economic science obviously aims at knowing economic reality in order to increase human control over it. That is why positive and normative aspects, being these latter rules and plans of action and control, are part of what economic science is about.

The most specific elements of economic reality (that is, in particular, production and exchange, which represent the archetypes of any economic reality) will be discussed later; for now, let us dwell upon the *method of economic science*, which development is characterized by continuity and progress. As a matter of fact such a method changes slowly, as the history of economic science shows, according to the alteration or to the specification of the object, so that the method has been greatly improved during the three or four centuries of growth of economic science, but has never altered its basic essence.

First of all, it is clear that economic science needs abstract systems which can capture the essence of economic phenomena and their relations of causality and interdependence, because only in this way can it aim at forecasting and controlling. Economic science breeds, and it must breed during its formulation, systems characterized by different degrees of generality: general theories, partial theories, models, theorems. Though, it should never limit itself to the mere description of facts, as they only represent reality but neither explain, anticipate, nor control it.

Then, what is the method of economic science? The question whether economic science is closer to the mathematical sciences, moral sciences or empirical ones has been discussed for a long time. This is not the place to start such an interesting discussion again, but let us just assert that economic science does have its own method, which borrows from other sciences other methods that better suit particular problems.

Indeed, *the method* of economic science includes at least *three elements simultaneously:*

(i) analytical-theoretical elements;
(ii) stylized elements of economic facts (factual-theoretical elements);
(iii) policy elements (normative-theoretical elements).

Then, if by economic science we mean a 'complete' system of cognitions, we can say that three partial, complementary and necessary elements contribute to such a construction: the analytical-theoretical ones; the factual-theoretical ones; the normative-theoretical ones.

The reference to the 'theoretical' attribute shows their generality, while the specification (empirical, analytical, normative) shows their non-completeness.

Economic science employs different tools: mathematical, econometric, historical, logical, analogical ones. In the latter sense, it *borrows* cognitions from many other sciences (from engineering to technological sciences, from demography to law, etc.). In both the first and the second case (tools and borrowing respectively) the whole thing must be part of a consistent system built according to the economic logic and method.

To exemplify: looking at the historical course of economic science, we can see that the great economists are those who have been able to merge the three elements pointed out before. Their greatness is recognized not only because of their ability to make theories, but because of the power of such theories to make real economic phenomena intelligible, to anticipate them, to control them.

Relations between these three mentioned elements and the tools have been quite complex, both during the historical course of economic science and in its current applications; but their explanation should never be given up, otherwise the inability to understand relations between economic science, mathematical methods, and economic reality would imply the inability to develop the potentialities of such knowledge.

These general lines explain why we talk of 'economic science' instead of 'economic sciences': it is important to stress that we face a unitary science, deeply aiming at the action and not only at defining a scientific area including different non-connected sciences.

It is true that, from both the academic and scientific viewpoints, different specializations have emerged: economics, mathematical economics, econometrics, economic history, economic policy; besides, other specializations have been developing around a more limited object (i.e. micro-economics, macro-economics, monetary, industrial, international economics, etc.). It is an important development, an indication of the growth of economic science.

Such a growth is consistent with the general lines defining economic science (or economics) as a set of theories, models, theorems where different methods (analytical-theoretical; factual-theoretical; normative-theoretical) and different tools (mathematical, econometric, historical, logical, analogic-acquisitive from other sciences, etc.) have contributed with variable roles to their specification and construction.

In what follows we will see the way the afore-mentioned elements and, in particular, the mathematical and econometric tools have helped in defining some of the most important general theories in economics. We are also going to show which problems nowadays need to be solved to avoid the fragmentation of such a unitary science; if such a fragmentation occurred, economics would fail in its purpose, which is to explain and try to rule reality.

THEORIES, THEOREMS, MODELS

It is simultaneously easy and difficult to say what the *corpus* of economic general and partial theories, models and theorems is, and how different elements and tools have helped their formulation.

It is easy when a good and a well-balanced handbook is considered. In such a manual, theories, models and theorems characterized by different degrees of generality and difficulty are proposed as a relatively homogeneous *corpus*. Looking at such a handbook, which is an important indicator of a science consolidation, we can say that economics has definitely achieved high and quite homogeneous levels, so that a wide and relatively homogeneous professional group of economists has emerged too.

However, the necessary search for homogeneity and consistency in handbooks should not hide the fact that there are many different ideas about which economic theories, models and theorems should still enjoy lasting validity.

This is connected to the history of economic thought which in our opinion is essential to economic science, since the latter is more akin – because of its way of looking back to its own history – to art and philosophy than to the natural sciences. Consequently, theories, models and theorems making up the *corpus* of economic science also specify the classic 'authors' or vice versa.

On this issue, at least three points of view among the many can be recalled.[2]

(i) The great Italian economist Maffeo Pantaleoni[3] defined 'classic' writers as those 'that in the past formulated theorems which today are still part of our knowledge'. From this, he concluded that the history of science changes as science changes, so that 'those that used to be the classics, or the orthodoxes, would not be considered as such in a different age . . .'.[4] In this way, through such an historical criterion, Pantaleoni concluded by saying that there are theories, models and theorems which are not part of our knowledge anymore; that is, propositions which are no longer scientific truths.

(ii) According to Alfred Marshall, one of the recognized masters, the distinction between true and false propositions in economics is not that strict. In his opinion, economic theory has not been progressing because of the replacement of the old truth (which is now falsehood) with the new truth, but through the formulation of more and more general theories, able to include the previous ones as special cases.[5]

(iii) In our opinion, the 'classics' of economic science, and the lasting theories, models and theorems, should be specified through a criterion different from those of Pantaleoni and Marshall. As a matter of fact, on the one hand it is still hard in economics to single out a straight progress (Pantaleoni); on the other hand, Marshall's idea runs the risk of ending up in theoretical eclecticism.

Indeed, it is necessary to recognize that different theories tend to different explanations for economic reality as a whole: still, it is often impossible to say that one is true and the other one is false (as Pantaleoni would do) or that one is a generalization of the other one (as Marshall would do).[6]

So we should accept a theory, a model, or a theorem according to its *correspondence to the methodological criteria* of economics mentioned beforehand and which will be now dealt with in depth.

Since economic theories cannot be verified in a laboratory and economic reality is changeable and multiform, then many theories may coexist as different interpretations of reality; their legitimation ('truth') must be based on a proper application of the mentioned methods and tools and on a continuous and repeated verification, as reality offers new elements and science improves methods and tools.

We are going to dwell upon such an issue, referring to some of the most important economic theories.

ANALYTICAL-THEORETICAL METHODS AND MATHEMATICAL TOOLS

Economic theories, models and theorems are today widely elaborated through mathematical tools which have made easier the construction of *pure theories*, i.e. a set of consistent propositions (or statements or axioms) which were acquired in the beginning from historical experience, from behaviour evidences and from introspective inspections, and from which one proceeds applying the rules of logical inference.

In economics a pure theory is a logical construction such that it is impossible to insert within its structure new elements without examining it again and sometimes even reconstructing it from the very beginning. Pure theory is supposed to try to understand most of the economic phenomena framing them into synthetic systems through abstraction.

It is clear that, for such purpose, mathematics has played and still plays a very important role. It is beyond doubt that, because of the nature of its object, among social sciences today's economics is the most advanced science as far as the use of mathematical tools is concerned.

From this point of view, and referring to the distinction between social sciences and natural sciences, it is necessary to recognize that *economics – among the social sciences – is the one which has been more formalized,* following in this way the evolution of natural sciences, where formalization has reached high levels, especially in physics.[7]

From the historical point of view, such a formalization of economic theory[8] has been characterized by a discontinuous trend up to the thirties in this century. More precisely, such a history can be divided into two stages: the stage of application of mathematics to economics (1838–1928); the stage of mathematical economics (starting about in 1930). The difference between the two stages is a qualitative but especially a quantitative one, since the second stage is characterized by a wider use of mathematics.

The first stage, concerning the use of mathematics in economics, probably starts from the contribution by A. A. Cournot, *Recherches sur les principes mathématiques de la théorie des richesses.*[9] Then it goes on with contributions by many economists among whom A. J. Dupuit,[10] M. E. L. Walras,[11] F. Y. Edgeworth,[12] A. Marshall,[13] and V. Pareto[14] stand out. These are just a few names but, since the second half of the nineteenth century, almost all great economists have shown familiarity with mathematical (and geometrical) methods in economics. It is meaningful in this regard to read the item 'Mathematical method in political economy' written by Edgeworth for the *Palgrave Dictionary of Political Economy,*[15] and the article by Pareto

'Economie mathématique' in *Encyclopédie des Sciences Mathématiques*.[16]

The second stage concerns mathematical economics and starts at the end of the Thirties, when real mathematicians entered the field of economics: F. P. Ramsey,[17] J. von Neumann[18] and A. Wald.[19] The mathematicians in question, especially the first two, are real geniuses of our century (Ramsey was a mathematician and a philosopher; von Neumann ranged in all mathematics and its application, up to computer engineering; Wald was an active member of the *Mathematische Wiener Kolloquium* too). On the one hand they imparted a great progress to some parts of the economic theory through a real scientific vision, on the other hand they were unique scientific characters. That is why the use of mathematics in economics is not enough to make someone a Ramsey or a von Neumann.

The following development of mathematical economics is really impressive. By using a questionable indicator (which can be considered acceptable only because recalled by the Nobel laureate G. Debreu), the number of pages about mathematical economics published in the five most important journals in the area, a yearly growth rate of 8.2 per cent in 1944–77 is revealed.[20] Moreover, excellent handbooks have come out, and in our opinion they constitute more important indicators, among which we recall in particular the internationally known one by K. Arrow and M. D. Intriligator[21] and the one by P. C. Nicola which is very famous in Italy.[22]

This shows that it is not possible to discuss all developments in mathematical economics briefly. That is why a choice becomes necessary, a choice that we will make by concentrating on two general theories, studying what in our opinion represents the two deepest phenomena of economic reality: *exchange* and *production* (that is to say prices and outputs, or 'market' and 'factory') which constitute the basis for the whole economic science. We will also consider a further general theory developing basic elements of the previous theories in dynamic terms.

Before speaking about these two general theories, it is useful to recall – through Debreu – that the 'benefit' for economics in using mathematics comes, as regards all the other social sciences, from the fact that two of its main variables of study, *prices* and *outputs* (goods), can be univocally measured and quantified:

> Thus for an economy with a finite number of commodities the action of an economic agent is described by listing his input, or his

output, of each commodity. Once a sign convention distinguishing inputs from outputs is made, the action of an agent is represented by a point in the commodity space, a finite-dimensional real vector space. Similarly the prices in the economy are represented by a point in the price space, the real vector space dual of the commodity space. (. . .) Finite dimensional commodity and price spaces can be, and usually are identified and treated as a euclidean space. The stage is thus set for geometric intuition to take a lead role in economic analysis.[23]

GENERAL THEORY OF EXCHANGE

General equilibrium is certainly one of the building-blocks of economic theory and one of the most important application fields for mathematics.

In our opinion the fundamental idea of exchange is already present in the studies about money and value that emerged between the sixteenth and seventeenth centuries; it was essential in the thought of the mercantilists who applied it to the analysis of commercial relations between states: the national wealth maximization principle is the first expression of such an idea. While early marginalists applied the fundamental idea of exchange to the individual behaviour to maximize utility, advanced marginalism applied it to the producer and consumer's behaviour to maximize profit and utility respectively. Then, the fundamental idea was applied to determine society's 'welfare'. Step by step, then, the fundamental idea of exchange was specified and it has been articulating through the concepts of 'scarcity' of resources as to 'efficiency' purposes relative to the employment of the given resources, of production 'unidirectionality' from the 'primary' productive factors to outputs. Such a fundamental idea is then summarized by the principle that any economic problem can be taken back to the mathematical one consisting in the maximization of an objective-function subject to scarcity constraints.[24]

Among theories inspired by the fundamental idea of exchange, Walras' general equilibrium theory[25] is certainly the most important one: it aims at the explanation of the way the co-ordination of actions by economic agents (firms and consumers) occurs, so that such actions are consistent and completely feasible in exchange processes. Consumers provide labour services to firms, receiving an income that will be used to purchase consumer goods produced by the firms. In their turn firms, after purchasing productive factors from consumers and other firms, transform them to sell them later to consumers and firms.

The co-ordination of actions by agents occurs through competitive markets where, by means of exchange, prices are determined; such prices are the unknowns of the general equilibrium problem, which can be formulated at different degrees of difficulty.

To introduce the problem, a basic model is the (Marshallian) partial equilibrium one, where all prices are supposed to be given, except for one which is free to vary, in this way determining variations in the demand and the supply of the corresponding commodity (neglecting demands and supplies for other commodities). In such a case, actions taken by agents usually turn out to be consistent at a certain price P_i only. At any other price the total demand is different from the total supply; thus, if the actual price is less than the equilibrium price, some consumers will not be able to carry out their decisions; on the contrary, when the actual price exceeds the equilibrium price, some firms will not be able to sell as much as they wish.

In reality, total demand and supply of each good depend on all prices, and each market equilibrium can only be determined simultaneously with the equilibrium on every other market through a system (of equalities between demand and supply) of non-linear equations for n unknowns. Then, it is a general equilibrium problem, and Walras[26] was the economist who first formulated such a theory. The existence of solutions in such case was proved by A. Wald[27] and, afterwards, by K. J. Arrow and G. Debreu,[28] by L. W. McKenzie,[29] D. M. Gale,[30] H. Nikaido,[31] using the fixed point theorem formulated by L. E. J. Brower[32] and generalized by J. von Neumann[33] and by S. Kakutani.[34] The great complexity of the problem is then revealed by the fact that it took eighty years to solve mathematically and in a complete way a problem initially set in mathematical economic terms by Walras in 1874.

This does not mean that the formulation[35] is difficult, being representable by 2n + 1 equations and disequations:

$$D_i(p_1, \ldots, p_n) \leq O_i(p_1, \ldots, p_n) \qquad i = 1, \ldots, n \qquad (1)$$

$$p_i(D_i - O_i) = 0 \qquad (2)$$

$$\sum p_i D_i(p_1, \ldots, p_n) = \sum p_i O_i(p_1, \ldots, p_n) \qquad (3)$$

where: $D_i (p_1, \ldots, p_n)$ is the total demand (that is, the sum of individual demands) of the i-th good as a price function; $O_i (p_1, \ldots, p_n)$ is the total supply of the i-th good (given by the sum of individual supplies). A general equilibrium solution for all markets is given by a price vector $P_i = (p_1, \ldots, p_n)$ such that:

(i) for each commodity the demand does not exceed the supply;
(ii) prices of goods for which the demand is less than the supply are equal to zero;
(iii) the Walras' law holds, so that it is always true that for each price vector the total demand value is equal to the total supply value since, by assumption, all consumers spend their whole income.

Such conditions and the existence of solutions occur when the demand and supply functions are continuous and homogeneous of degree zero in prices. Such a Walrasian general equilibrium formulation (and solution) is connected to the Pareto-efficiency criterion. This criterion states that, given the available resources and the other constraints, it is not possible to move away from a general equilibrium solution increasing at least one consumer's utility without making someone else worse off. Thus, a general equilibrium, defined by the equality of demand and supply for each good, determines the maximization of each consumer's utility.

Such a property fixes the maximum of social welfare and of individual utilities, given the initial distribution of income among consumers. When such a distribution is very uneven, the general equilibrium solutions will be unequal too.[36]

GENERAL THEORY OF PRODUCTION

The history of the emergence of such a theory is also quite complex. The fundamental idea of production first appeared in the works by British political arithmeticians (William Petty and others), by F. Quesnay and other physiocrats: these economists all considered the production (and reproduction) process within an economic system to be the main problem in economics. The concepts of 'circular models' of production, that is of production of goods by means of goods, of 'interdependence' between economic sectors, of 'net product', that is of excess of outputs over inputs, appeared at once. Such concepts were extended in different directions by many authors. The British and Scottish classical economists, A. Smith, T. R. Malthus and D. Ricardo, analyzed the relations between net product and accumulation; the problem concerning the distribution of output among social classes – wages, profits, rents; the 'effective demand' issue.

After a time of relative quiescence (although during this period important contributions about value theory and structural dynamics theory were introduced), the fundamental idea of production was considered again with different emphases by M. Kalecki, J. M. Keynes, J. von Neumann, W. Leontief, P. Sraffa, L. Pasinetti and others. In antithesis with the fundamental idea of exchange, the production one stresses the fact that the 'wealth' of an economic system depends either on its efficiency in producing net product and on its distribution among wages, profits and rents, and on the distribution between consumptions and investments: the growth of 'wealth' over time depends primarily on such investments.[37]

It is important now to concentrate on Leontief[38] and Sraffa's[39] theories, since they represent the prototype of many of the other ones.

Their basic structure is constituted by the technology of an economic system, expressed by n productive sectors; such sectors are connected to each other in the sense that each one of them is a seller or a (direct or indirect) buyer of commodities from every other sector. The matrix of technical coefficients becomes the basis for every other following analysis which assumes linear productive processes, so that technical coefficients do not vary as output and final demand vary.

Leontief's system basically analyzes relations among output, net product, inputs, employment levels. To exemplify: given a net products vector for consumption and investment, the system determines the necessary corresponding total output, necessary inputs, employment level in each economic sector.

Formally, the problem is quite simple, since it is specified by n linear equations connecting technology, inputs, output, net products, and by a relation about the workforce as follows:

$$AQ + N = Q$$

where A is the technology matrix, Q the output vector, AQ the input vector, N the net product vector:

$$L'Q \leq L$$

where L' is the direct labour technical coefficients vector and L is the labour force level in the economic system.

The system can be solved by assuming Q or N as given and consequently determining the other vector according to the labour force availability.

Starting from a similar production scheme, Sraffa concentrates on the dual system, that is, on the prices-income distribution system, pointing out basic properties about:

(i) pricing of goods when technology and wage or profit rates are given;
(ii) determining the maximum wage rate and the maximum profit rate within an economic system;
(iii) determining the maximum profit rate as correspondent to the net product uniform rate, being then independent from the price system;
(iv) determining relations between variations in the income distribution, prices and production technical choices.

Formally, Sraffa's general theory can be represented by a system of n linear equations and n + 2 unknowns.

$$A^T p(1 + \pi) + L w = P$$

where A^T is the transpose technological matrix, P the n prices vector, π the profit rate, w the wage rate; to find a solution it is necessary to choose a commodity as numéraire (with price equal to one) and a distribution variable (wage or profit) as exogenous.

Sraffa's theory has also given rise to a wide discussion where many aspects deal with criticism of other theories and with philologic strictness that we are not interested in. In addition to that we believe that it is misleading to associate an ideological bias with any quotation by Sraffa.

Leontief and Sraffa's most general conclusion about production, distribution and price theory is that such theory has allowed the specification of properties of an economic system that depends on technology (from the point of view of price determination on given production costs) and on income distribution between wages and profits.

Building on these conclusions, more complex descriptions of both the physical system and its dual prices-distribution system have been elaborated. They vary from the 'closed' model (where a net products vector does not exist), to the 'open' model, where the net products vector becomes fundamental for the analysis of consumers and firms' demands (for investments); from models characterized by circulating capitals only to models characterized by both fixed and circulating capitals; from models with neither natural resources nor raw materials, to models in which they are both taken into account; from models of single to models of joint production, where each sector produces more goods; from uniperiodal models to dynamic ones.

For such a theory, linear algebra, Perron-Frobenius' theorems and all their variants have been very important, since without such tools it would have been very difficult, maybe impossible, to obtain the extensions and the results of the theory. We believe we can assert that the solution to certain problems (such as the independence of wage-profit relations from prices when a proper numeraire is chosen), set first by David Ricardo in 1817 and analyzed by many other great economists, was given by Sraffa in 1960. We still do not know whether Sraffa, who inserted in his volume very few mathematical proofs, verified its formulation through mathematical reasoning or made it available to be verified; but we do know for sure that only the following applications of linear algebra have shown the robustness as well as the limits of the proposed solutions.

STRUCTURAL THEORY OF ECONOMIC DYNAMICS

In our opinion such theory is especially due to von Neumann and Pasinetti. Von Neumann's contribution is usually considered a turning-point either for general equilibrium theories and for production ones. For present purposes we are not interested in verifying whether this is true, but rather concentrate on the economic dynamics aspects of his theory.

Starting from the sort of technologies shown above and referring either to the case of single production and to the case of joint production (where each firm produces more than one good), the question concerns the productive methods and production configuration giving rise to the maximum rate of growth for the economic system, assuming the whole net product is invested. To find such a solution, von Neumann supposed that the output of all goods with positive prices (that is to say, goods in the economic sense) grows at a uniform rate. If the output of some goods grows at a higher rate (so that the supply will exceed the demand) the price of such goods will be equal to zero.

The problem concerns the choice of production technologies since we are interested in identifying those that relate to economic goods which give rise to the output highest uniform rate of growth.

By using a generalization of Brower's fixed point theorem, von Neumann proved that for a set of productive methods and of outputs corresponding to the economic system a maximum and uniform rate of growth always exists. The dual feature of such a solution relative to the physical quantity system shows that some of the prices relative to the profit rate are constant over time, and that the maximum rate of growth of physical quantities coincides with the minimum among the optimal profit rates, so that the basic relation between physical and prices-distribution systems (that we find again in Sraffa) is set.[40]

Another seminal work about structural economic dynamics came from Pasinetti.[41] His contribution consists of a theory of non-proportional growth and structural change – which is completely different from the proportional growth one – since this latter implies a necessary connection between per capita income increase and a change of proportions between industries in the economic system.

Pasinetti's theory is a masterful combination of those method criteria where theoretical and theoretical-historical analysis ('stylized facts') join together.

As a matter of fact his analysis is built on simultaneous consideration of facts and theory as the following points show:

(i) production processes in different sectors change according to their own specific rhythms, so that the growth rates of product per worker vary in each sector. Besides, the productive structure evolves as technical progress takes place; the latter does not consist of productivity increases only, but also implies the development of new sectors producing new goods;
(ii) the basic point of the analysis of demand dynamics is represented by the generalized Engel's law, according to which after a certain point the income share spent on purchasing goods decreases as income increases. This implies that, given a price structure, when we vary the income level, the proportion of income spent by the consumer for each good will vary according to the considered good.

Building on these two basic stylized facts and using rigorous formal tools, Pasinetti worked out a complex model, which gives rise to the following conclusions:

(i) productivity and income increases are two sides of the same coin. The first ones imply the second ones and vice versa, in the sense that the composition of the second determines the importance of the first. From this point of view, the importance of technical progress depends on potential demand;
(ii) the production of each good has a certain temporal trend, depending on the supply growth rate and on the per capita demand one, which varies differently from good to good, differing this way from the first rate. Since per capita demand varies over time, the productive structure keeps on changing too;
(iii) employment varies according to the population growth rate plus the demand rate for the considered good/sector, less the productivity growth rate. This means that even the employment structure, that is to say, total employment and sectorial distribution, changes continuously over time.

To sum up, Pasinetti's contribution, beyond specific results, is fundamental for the methodologies of structural economic dynamics because of his masterful application of formalized theory and stylized-historical theory.[42]

We have shown three general theories concerning three fundamental problems of economic reality: exchange and markets; production and productive structure; dynamics. We have also recognized in these cases the important role played by mathematics. This way we have privileged research paths in economics that will certainly last.

That is why we have preferred to dwell upon three general theories which, unquestionably and intelligibly, explain momentous economic phenomena and which have been attracting economists' consideration since the beginning of economics.

Such general theories stress one of the main features of economic reality (exchange or production), without leaving out the other one. There have been many attempts to show that general equilibrium implies Leontief and Sraffa's production theory.

From a mathematical point of view, previous orientations have certainly been legitimate and proper, but their utility for economics as a reflection of reality is doubtful. We have already underlined that economics needs general theories which should not be so general to miss those features that make economics able to explain different aspects of reality intelligibly.

Later we will deal with such specifications again; at this point, let us sum up what has been said about the use of mathematical tools in economic analytical-theoretical methods through an effective syntheses by C. F. Manara,[43] who points out four contributions mathematics has made to economics, claiming for mathematics the dignified role of carrying the structure of modern scientific thought:

(i) a language using artificial symbols and their syntactic laws, able to 'codify' reality;
(ii) its value for studying both measurable objects (often recurring in economics) and non-measurable ones (often recurring as well);
(iii) its value in making rigorous deductions;
(iv) the axiomatic method, according to which every scientific theory must be structured on a sure methodological basis, starting from primitive terms and propositions.

FACTUAL-THEORETICAL METHODS AND ECONOMETRICS

The fact that we reached positive conclusions about the mathematical tool in economics should not make us forget about the global method of economics and some caveats.

Recalling Manara's viewpoint, when dealing with mathematics it is necessary to assume the '*esprit de finesse*' Pascal in general longed for; besides, for economic applications, it is necessary to avoid attaching too much importance to mathematical theories and to pretend they breed 'certainties'. As a matter of fact these certainties are true within theoretical structures only, where real and conceptual operations, through which structures are adapted to reality, always admit approximation margins. Then, a good balance becomes necessary to choose the mathematical-theoretical sophistication level for a useful analysis and representation of economic phenomena. The problem concerns 'right' choices, in order to avoid too rudimentary mathematical models which therefore are not needed, or too refined ones, which reveal themselves as useless practices in high mathematics with no possible application.[44]

This is the rigorous and balanced position taken by a mathematician who leaves to the economists the duty of understanding how to avoid such useless exercises.

Let us now consider these 'correctives'.

The first corrective makes every *theoretical-analytical construction be 'open' with regard to its 'axioms'*. In particular, it is important that analytical principles are used not only for further deductive developments, but also to find out new facts and new relations through a direct application while studying reality.

Similarly, it was underlined that to theoretical construction processes '*a priori* no limit can be put, but a proper criticism should accompany the advancement of theories in this sense'.[45] A similar suggestion is offered to his students by Siro Lombardini: 'The observation – not only the one made through statistical methods but also the one implying historical research – offers elements to recognize theory, and theory offers suggestions to make a plan of empirical researches'.[46]

Then, while analytical-theoretical constructions bring economics closer to the mathematical sciences (either in the formulation of deductive systems and in the 'free' formulation of new conceptual schemes), the role of 'empirical criticism' is supposed to aim, within analytical-theoretical constructions, at telling the elements of actual knowledge from those assumptions which are merely a means for the acquisition of new cognitions.[47] In such a direction economics gets close to empirical sciences, because of the necessary aid brought by those factual-theoretical methods which on the one hand provide theories with starting points, and on the other hand criticize them empirically.[48]

That is why we will necessarily refer to two factual-theoretical methods in economics: stylized systems and econometrics. In economics there are a large number of stylized systems of economic facts, and many great economists made their main contributions through factual-theoretical methods. Since our current main interest concerns the application of mathematical tools, we will discuss factual-theoretical methods briefly.

First,[49] let us recall that stylization is not economic history, since the synthetic-systematic structure of the former misses the necessary descriptive acumen enjoyed by the latter. In our opinion, one of the most interesting cases of stylized systems is represented by the table of industrial interdependences, the basis for Leontief-Sraffa's production theory. It is a very synthetic 'description' of relations between economic sectors. Many relations in Keynes' theory are clear stylizations too: for instance, consider the consumption function connecting aggregate consumption to income. Finally, many theories of the business cycle or of growth proposed for instance by J. A. Schumpeter, by S. S. Kuznets and by G. Fuà are clear stylizations.

However, we are not interested in writing a list or analyzing cases; instead, we would like to mention what P. Sylos-Labini defined as the 'degree of historical content' of economic theories.[50] As a matter of fact, we do agree on the existence of an optimal degree of historical content or, on the contrary, of abstraction level for each economic theory. If we exceeded a certain level of historical content (being below a certain level of abstraction), we would leave economics and enter economic history. On the contrary, above a certain level of abstraction, we would leave economics to enter pure abstraction, with or without mathematics.

Such a formulation can be carried out in two different ways: on the one hand, stylization of facts can be the basis for theory; on the other hand the theory *a priori* formulated can look for verification and criticism through the stylization of facts it can offer.

From this point of view, dealing with mathematical tools, the contribution of *econometrics* must be considered; that is to say, according to Frish's formulation, from the applications of mathematical and statistical methods to the analysis of economic data, or better, the quantitative analysis of phenomena and observations correlated through proper inference methods.[51] The statute of the international Econometric Society states:

> The Econometric Society is an international society for the advancement of economic theory in its relation to statistics and mathematics.(. . .) Its main object shall be to promote studies that aim at a unification of the theoretical-quantitative and the empirical-quantitative approach to economic problems and that are penetrated by constructive and rigorous thinking similar to that which has come to dominate in the natural sciences. Any activity which promises ultimately to further such unification of theoretical and factual studies in economics shall be within the sphere of interest in the Society.[52]

Thus, econometrics aims at a unification in economics between measurement and theory, since the former without the latter has a limited ability to interpret economic phenomena, as well as the latter without the former.[53]

This new tool of economics has been developing over two stages. According to many economists, the first one began in the seventeenth century thanks to the studies by 'political arithmeticians', in particular by W. Petty, G. King and C. Davenant; it then evolved with the statistical elaboration of economic data and the search for correlation phenomena.

The second stage began with the development of modern statistics at the end of the nineteenth century, through correlation analysis and multiple regression models in economics. The great change came in the thirties, when an international society and two institutes were founded: the Econometric Society (counting A. K. Frish among its founders), the Cowles Commission in the USA, and the Department of Applied Economics at Cambridge (England). This was possible because of the concomitant development of econometrics' fundamental elements: economic theory, mathematical economics, statistical inference, systematic collection of statistical data and calculus techniques. When econometrics was born, two beliefs were dominant: on the one hand, there was the idea that economic theory was able to point out the basic relations of economic reality (almost as 'society's physics'); on the other hand, the idea that methods of statistical inference could be adequately used to give empirical content to economic theories.

Thus, it is clear that econometrics has developed a lot in about sixty years. Today, it is a homogeneous instrumentation for economists (and a discipline for others) as its handbooks, important indicators of the degree of professionality, reveal (we would like to recall those by E. C. Malinvaud,[54] H. Theil[55] and the latest by M. Faliva[56] which is quite famous in Italy). Nowadays we can state that the progress of economics has been the resultant of development of inferential methodologies tailored to non-experimental data; this occurs either as regards the estimation techniques of meaningful economic parameters and as regards the testing procedure of the model through which economic theory is formally represented.

The latest developments of such a discipline can be identified as follows:

(i) with multiple time series analysis, both in time and frequency domains;
(ii) with the analysis of the causal structure of econometric models through graph-theoretic and/or system-theoretic approaches;

(iii) with the development of control theory methods in econometric model analysis;
(iv) with the improving of model building and model selection techniques;
(v) with the advancements of estimation theory in non-linear and, more generally, in non-standard frameworks;
(vi) with the refining of model validation procedures, especially for what concerns explanatory ability, prediction accuracy and policy evaluation performances;
(vii) with the progresses of Bayesian inferential procedures for econometric estimation and prediction.

What conclusions can be drawn about what we called *factual-theoretical methods*?

About stylized empirical systems we can say that, in spite of their apparent lack of precision, they still play an important role. They emphasize the economist's 'vision' ability, his sensibility in understanding the complex set of economic relations, more than a 'safe' method to construct or verify an economic theory.

Such a method, sometimes described as that of the applied economist, through an inaccurate and probably limiting denomination, maintains its validity for the clear difficulties faced by econometrics as well.

As we drew our conclusions about merits and limits of mathematics in economics by recalling the opinion of a mathematician, we will do now for econometrics what we did for mathematics, recalling the point of view of an econometrician (Pesaran).[57]

Econometrics' limits are partly due to the nature of economic theories and partly to the nature of the econometric tool; this is because theory and/or tool:

(i) are based on the *coeteris paribus* clause, also concerning latent and non-observable variables and general functional forms;
(ii) have little to say about adjustment processes and about length of lags;
(iii) do not offer exact indications about variables to be included in econometric models. In general economic equilibrium, where variables are interdependent, it is difficult to leave out *a priori* some variable from equations;
(iv) do not give much room to institutional aspects and to accounting procedures which play an important role;

(v) refer to statistical data derived from non programmed experiments, so that some arbitrary elements might be implied, since they do not enjoy an experimental nature;
(vi) refer to statistical data which are often small samples, especially regarding time series;
(vii) do not solve aggregation problems over time for goods and individuals.

From all this we can conclude that economic theories cannot offer a complete specification of models, so that the verification of economic theories themselves and the evaluation of econometric models becomes complex.

Subject to such limitations and cautions, according to which to reject or to improve a theory thanks to econometrics might be impossible, we can assert that econometrics still offers important analysis, forecast and policy tools.

CONCLUSIONS

As we said before, we are not going to dwell upon *normative-theoretical methods* here, even if they are basically a set outcome for other methods that are supposed to measure, and also to anticipate in quantitative terms, the entity and the effects of economic policy decisions.

Still, the normative momentum is co-essential to economics: that is, economic policy is its final moment, connecting to its very initial moment, that is to those 'principles' representing a 'global' vision of the world and of the economic evolution that each economist is supposed to have. Such are the economic principles that could also confine with an ethical vision[58] of the 'society's welfare', of the 'civil economy', about which economic mathematics and econometrics can say little or nothing, as good scholars of such tools know very well.

When the 360 degrees of economics are finished, it is the time to recall the picture (as G. Becattini[59] recently reminded us) of the political economist that was so clearly given by John Maynard Keynes[60] in *Essays in Biography*:

> The master-economist must possess a rare *combination* of gifts. He must reach a high standard in several different directions and must combine talents not often found together. He must be mathema-

tician, historian, statesman, philosopher – in some degree. He must understand symbols and speak in words. He must contemplate the particular in terms of the general, and touch abstract and concrete in the same flight of thought. He must study the present in the light of the past for the purposes of the future. No part of man's nature or his institutions must lie entirely outside his regard. He must be purposeful and disinterested in a simultaneous mood; as aloof and incorruptible as an artist, yet sometimes as near the earth as a politician.

These words must be considered with understanding to realize that the economist is not supposed to be non-specific, but he must always show a wide sensibility that the mathematical tool itself does not guarantee. An example of such sensibility can be found in Pasinetti's work:

A combination of three factors – one factual and two theoretical – originally prompted this investigation. The factual element was provided by the extremely uneven development – from sector to sector, from region to region – of the environment in which I lived (post-war Europe) at the time I began my training in economics. The two theoretical factors are represented by the two types of theories – specifically the macro-dynamic models of economic growth and input-output analysis – that were offered to me when, as a research student, I came in contact with the economists of the University of Cambridge, England (1956–57 and 1958–59) and of Harvard University in the United States (1957–58).[61]

NOTES

* An early and partially different version of the present work appeared in *Scientia* and in a working paper IDSE/CNR, 1989, n.1.
1. Pasinetti, 1966.
2. Quadrio-Curzio and Scazzieri, 1985.
3. Pantaleoni, 1925, vol. I.
4. Ibid.
5. For this feature in Marshall, see Pigou (ed.), 1925.
6. Quadrio-Curzio and Scazzieri, 1985.
7. Nicola, 1983a.

8. See the brief treatments by Nicola (1983a) and Debreu (1987).
9. Cournot, 1838.
10. Dupuit, 1844.
11. Walras, 1874–7.
12. Edgeworth, 1881.
13. Marshall, 1890.
14. Pareto, 1909.
15. Edgeworth, 1894–9.
16. Pareto, 1911, vol. IV.
17. Ramsey, 1926, 1927, 1928.
18. von Neumann, 1928, 1944, 1945–6.
19. Wald, 1936.
20. Debreu, 1987.
21. Arrow and Intriligator, 1981–3.
22. Nicola, 1983.
23. Debreu, 1986.
24. Quadrio-Curzio and Scazzieri, 1985.
25. Walras, 1874–7.
26. Ibid.
27. Wald, 1936.
28. Arrow and Debreu, 1954.
29. McKenzie, 1954.
30. Gale, 1956.
31. Nikaido, 1956.
32. Brower, 1910.
33. von Neumann, 1941.
34. Kakutani, 1941.
35. See the brief treatment by Nicola (1966).
36. Nicola, 1983b, 1986.
37. Quadrio-Curzio and Scazzieri, 1985.
38. Leontief, 1941.
39. Sraffa, 1960.
40. See the brief treatment by Pasinetti (1975).
41. Pasinetti, 1981.
42. See the contribution by Scazzieri (1987).
43. Manara, 1986.
44. Ibid.
45. Enriques, 1985, p. 80.
46. Lombardini, 1960, p. 95.
47. For more about these general principles, see Enriques, 1985, p. 80.
48. Quadrio-Curzio and Scazzieri, 1988.
49. See Quadrio-Curzio and Scazzieri, 1985, 1988.
50. Sylos Labini, 1988.
51. Koopmans (ed.), 1954; Stone et al., 1954.
52. *Econometrica* (1) 1933, p. 106.
53. Pesaran, 1987; see also Pasinetti and Gambetta, 1988.
54. Malinvaud, 1964.
55. Theil, 1971.
56. Faliva, 1987.

57. Pesaran, 1987.
58. Quadrio-Curzio, 1985.
59. Becatini, 1988.
60. Keynes, 1972, vol. X, pp. 173-4.
61. Pasinetti, 1981, p. xi.

REFERENCES

Arrow, K. J., and Debreu, G. (1954) 'Existence of an equilibrium for a competitive economy', *Econometrica*, 22.
Arrow, K. J., and Intriligator, M. D. (eds) (1981-3) *Handbook of mathematical economics* (Amsterdam: North Holland) 3 vols.
Becattini, G. (1988) 'Per Napoleoni oltre Napoleoni', *Il Ponte*, 4-5.
Brower, L. E. J. (1910) 'Ueber eineindeutige, stetige Transformationen von Flachen in sich', *Mathematische Annalen*, 69.
Cournot, A. A. (1838) *Recherches sur les principes mathématiques de la théorie des richesses* (Paris: Hachette).
Debreu, G. (1987) 'Mathematical economics', in *The New Palgrave Dictionary of Economics* (London: Macmillan).
Dupuit, A. J. E. J. (1844) 'De la mesure de l'utilité des travaux publics', *Annales des ponts et chaussées*, 8.
Edgeworth, F. Y. (1881) *Mathematical physics* (London: Kegan Paul).
Edgeworth, F. Y. (1894-9) 'Mathematical method in political economy', in *Palgrave Dictionary of Political Economy* (London: Macmillan).
Enriques, F. (1985) *Problemi della scienza* (Bologna: Zanichelli).
Faliva, M. (1987) *Econometria: principi e metodi* (Torino: UTET).
Gale, D. M. (1956) 'The closed linear model of production', in H. W. Kuhn and A. W. Tucker (eds), *Linear inequalities and related systems* (Princeton, NJ: Princeton University Press).
Kakutani, S. (1941) 'A generalization of Brower's fixed point theorem', *Duke Mathematical Journal*, 8.
Keynes, J. M. (1972) 'Essays in biography', in *Collected Writings of John Maynard Keynes* (London: Macmillan), vol. X.
Koopmans, T. C. (ed.) (1954) *Studies in econometric method* (New Haven, Conn.: Yale University Press).
Leontief, W. (1941) *The structure of the American economy (1919-1932)* (Cambridge, Mass.: Harvard University Press).
Lombardini, Siro (1990) *Elementi di economia politica* (Torino: UTET).
McKenzie, L. W. (1954) 'Specialization and efficiency in world production', *Review of Economic Studies*, 3.
Malinvaud, E. C. (1964) *Méthodes statistiques de l'économétrie* (Paris: Dunod).
Manara, C. F. (1986) 'L'economia e il metodo matematico', *Economia politica*, 3.
Marshall, A. (1890) *Principles of economics* (London: Macmillan).
Nicola, P. C. (1983a) *Economia matematica* (Torino: UTET).

Nicola, P. C. (1983b) 'Teorie economiche e valori', *Rivista internazionale di scienze sociali*, 91.
Nicola, P. C. (1986) 'Modelli matematici in economia', *Synesis*, 3.
Nikaido, H. (1956) 'On the classical multilateral exchange problem', *Metroeconomica*, 8, pp. 135–45.
Pantaleoni, M. (1925) *Erotemi di economia* (Bari: Laterza) vol. I.
Pareto, V. (1909) *Manuel d'économie politique* (Paris: Giard et Brière).
Pareto, V. (1911) 'Economie mathématique' in *Encylopédie des sciences mathématiques* (Paris: Gauthier-Villars) 1, vol. IV.
Pasinetti, L. (1966) 'Causalità e interdipendenza nell'analisi economica e nella teoria economica', *Annuario dell'Università Cattolica del Sacro Cuore, 1964–5* (Milan: Vita e Pensiero).
Pasinetti, L. (1981) *Structural change and economic growth. A theoretical essay on the dynamics of the wealth of nations* (Cambridge: Cambridge University Press).
Pasinetti, L. L., and Gambetta, G. (1989) 'Econometria', in *Enciclopedia del Novecento*, Istituto della Enciclopedia Italiana, Vol. VIII, pp. 313–22.
Pesaran, M. H. (1987) 'Econometrics', in *The New Palgrave Dictionary of Economics* (London: Macmillan).
Pigou, A. C. (ed.) (1925) *Memorials of Alfred Marshall* (London: Macmillan).
Quadrio-Curzio, A. (1985) 'L'economista e i principi', *Economia politica*, 3.
Quadrio-Curzio, A., and Scazzieri, R. (1985) *Sui momenti costitutivi dell'economia politica* (Bologna: Il Mulino).
Quadrio-Curzio, A., and Scazzieri, R. (1988) 'La scienza economica e gli strumenti di analisi con applicazioni alla dinamica economica strutturale', *Società italiana degli economisti*, 29th annual reunion, 5.
Ramsey, F. P. (1926) 'Truth and probability', in R. B. Braithwaite (ed.), *The foundations of mathematics* (London: Routledge and Kegan Paul).
Ramsey, F. P. (1927) 'A contribution to the theory of taxation', *Economic Journal*, 37.
Ramsey, F. P. (1928) 'A mathematical theory of saving', *Economic Journal*, 38.
Scazzieri, R. (1987) 'Crescita non proporzionale e cambiamento strutturale', in M. Baranzini and R. Scazzieri, *Struttura e evoluzione delle economie industriali* (Lugano: Ed. Pantarei), pp. 98–104.
Sraffa, P. (1960) *Produzione di merci a mezzo di merci. Premesse a una critica della teoria economica* (Torino: Einaudi).
Stone, J. R. N. et al. (1954) *The measurement of consumers' expenditure and behaviour in the UK 1920–1938* (Cambridge: Cambridge University Press).
Sylos Labini, P. (1988) 'Le relazioni intime fra storia e teoria economica', in W. N. Parker (ed.) *Economia e storia* (Bari: Laterza).
Theil, H. (1971) *Principles of econometrics* (New York: Wiley; Amsterdam: North Holland).
von Neumann, J. (1928) 'Zur theorie des Gesellshaftsspiele', *Mathematische Annalen*, 100.
von Neumann, J. (1941) 'Distribution of the ratio of the mean square successive difference to the variance', *Annals of Mathematical Statistics*, 13.

von Neumann, J. (1945–6) 'A model of general equilibrium', *Review of Economic Studies*, 13 (first German ed. 1937).
von Neumann, J., and Morgenstern, O. (1944) *Theory of games and economic behaviour* (Princeton, NJ: Princeton University Press).
Wald, A. (1936) 'On the unique non-solvability of the new production equations', in K. Menger (ed.) *Ergebnisse eines mathematischen Kolloquiums*, 6 (1933–4); 7 (1934–5).
Walras, M. E. L. (1874–7) *Eléments d'économie politique pure, ou théorie de la richesse sociale* (Lausanne: Corbaz) 2 vols.

Part V

Development Economics and Models of Unstable Growth

10 Development Economics in Perspective*

Sukhamoy Chakravarty

INTRODUCTION

Development theorizing in economics is old but so-called 'development economics' is not. Economists from the middle of the eighteenth century onwards have been writing books on the subject even when the discipline of economics had not emerged as a distinct body of thought or as a self-contained mode of reasoning.

One needs only to recall names such as Sir James Steuart or Frederick List, to remind ourselves that they had a lot to say to the contemporary statesmen about tasks which needed to be done to speed up development.[1] It is of course, true that Steuart was eclipsed by Adam Smith, himself a development thinker of great insight, even though he believed that apart from providing elementary education and erecting lighthouses, the government would do well to stay away from issues of economic management, if a country were to prosper. It is interesting to note that during the nineteenth century there was hardly any mention of Steuart with any approbation by any serious economist, except Karl Marx, who praised him for his commanding historical vision.[2] One reason was that it was widely believed that Smith had completely 'confuted' his arguments without even once mentioning him by name. (Steuart himself was greatly disappointed with the reception of his book, as we know from Andrew Skinner's biographical introduction to the recent edition of Students' volume.[3])

Frederick List was, of course, in part a journalist, and was highly active in public life. He acquired both renown and notoriety. He had many admirers in the United States of America and Germany as well as in many 'backward countries', including India, where the greatest

---

* This paper is the first of two lectures which Professor Chakravarty delivered on 2 and 3 May 1989 as the 1988–9 Alfred Marshall Lectures in Economics at the University of Cambridge. The second, under the title 'Development Planning: A Reappraisal' was published in the *Cambridge Journal of Economics*, 15 March 1991, pp. 5–20.

among the first generation of Indian economists, M. G. Ranade, who was a judge of the High Court in Bombay, formulated an approach to the development of India along lines which had been enunciated by List in his *National System of Political Economy*.[4]

Marx, as we now know, wrote an uncomprehending review of List's book when he was still a student of Engels in economic questions.[5] Alfred Marshall, whose memory we are honouring today, was much better. He fully understood what List was driving at, as the following comment shows. In the concluding footnote of his Appendix 'A' to the *Principles*, he wrote, 'List worked out with much suggestiveness the notion that a backward nation must learn not from the contemporary conduct of forward nations, but from their conduct when they were in the same state in which it is now'. This is indeed a very perceptive comment. But Marshall goes on to write, 'but as Knies well shows (*Politische Œkonomie* II.5) the growth of trade and the improvement of the means of communications are making the developments of different nations tend to synchronize'.[6]

I believe that a very major impetus to the 'development' of development economics, which is the proper subject matter of my lecture today, came from the recognition by the profession of economics at large. Marshall may have strongly estimated the tendency towards synchronization that Karl Knies spoke about as well as the role that government policy can play in this respect.

Gunnar Myrdal was only partially right when he talked of the major impulse as coming from the fact of decolonization which strongly marked the first few years after 1945.[7] There is little doubt that political changes must have made the job seem very urgent and may have sometimes induced the profession to look at quick recipes, but there could have been other factors as well, such as the role of war-time controls and the experience of centrally-planned economies. On the intellectual level, there was a general sense of disenchantment with the operation of the market mechanism, born out of the experience of the 'Great Depression'. Moreover, long before Andre Gunder Frank had taught the growing band of radical economists to treat 'underdevelop' as a transitive verb, there were economists who worried as to whether the large differences in initial conditions from which developing countries were starting out around the middle of the twentieth century in their quest for a higher level of living, could indeed affect their characteristic laws of motion in ways which were significantly different from those which developed countries displayed.

This concern has by no means ceased even today after four decades of post-World War II development experience, even though a good deal has been learnt regarding the prospects and possibilities of growth in developing countries. It is precisely because of this concern and the fact that experience of development has been quite diverse that economists will continue to be attracted towards development economics. Its 'demise', put forward in some recent publications, has therefore been highly exaggerated. Gunnar Myrdal put forward the point of view that pre-war development thinking in relation to 'backward countries' was almost exclusively the preserve of social and cultural anthropologists and colonial administrators. Heinz Arndt in his history of development economics seems to support this view.[8] He could refer to only one 'lone attempt' by Ida Greaves in her London PhD dissertation to apply economic reasoning to problems of colonial countries. This is, indeed, very surprising considering that Arndt is a scholar who has specialized in the problems of Indonesia. While this is true of the work of Boeke,[9] who mentions and who was a strict believer in the inapplicability of Western economics to Eastern countries, Arndt does not even once mention the names of other Dutch scholars who had debated this issue of 'mono-economics' versus 'duo-economics', as Hirschman would put it, at considerable length during the inter-war period.

As one important example, I can only mention the case of Van Gelderen who has received some attention for his pioneering contribution to the 'long wave' literature.[10] In the Anglo-Saxon countries, Simon Kuznets and Wesley Mitchell were amongst the first to recognize the importance of his work. It is a pity that Van Gelderen has gone virtually unnoticed. The surprise is all the greater because Arndt does refer to Wertheim's collection of papers in which an English translation of an extensive part of Van Gelderen's lectures on tropical economies is included.[11] I may only briefly mention here Van Gelderen's conclusion. While recognizing the point made by Boeke about the lack of 'homogeneity' in terms of attitudes and institutions in colonial economies, he was nonetheless of the opinion that in the final analysis, the same methodological tools could be applied in analyzing economic problems of those societies if due regard were paid to some institutional specificities. 'Dualism' was accordingly described by Van Gelderen as a transitional phenomenon. His viewpoint is most succinctly stated in the following observation: 'the colonial system, in other words, is historically the political and economic form in which the . . . peoples of the tropics are led from the stage of a closed economy and of production only for their immediate surroundings to participation in an expanding world economy'.[12]

I mention Van Gelderen's work not merely because of a desire to point out his prescience in these matters, but also to stress that he was articulating a point of view which was shared by many economists in India, who were trained in the Western tradition, but were not oblivious to differences in objective situations.

Arndt's treatment of Indian economic thought seems to be even more deficient as even a quick look at the two important books written on the subject by the late Professor B. N. Ganguli of Delhi University and Professor B. Datta of the Presidency College, Calcutta would amply confirm.[13]

Among the British economists who were deeply interested in issues relating to economic development during the inter-war period, I would only like to mention the name of Vera Anstey. Although Anstey was not a theorist, as the term is understood these days, she had fully imbibed the spirit of Marshall's economic theory. Her book on the economic problems of India is generally regarded as a work of economic history and a dated one at that, but a close examination of this book provides, however, some understanding of the dominant perceptions of the inter-war period on development problems.[14] Anstey did not present any formal model of development in her book, but she gave certain insights about the economic and social constraints faced by countries like India in the process of their development. In particular, she highlighted the role of economic incentives as they were mediated through institutional arrangements, especially in agriculture and technical education, issues which are relevant even now for many parts of the developing world, including India after nearly half a century of independent development.

In the peripheral countries of Europe such as Rumania, there were economists whose contributions to development economics were significant. Mikail Manoilesco was the most well-known economist among them, but there were others. I may be permitted here to mention Michal Kalecki, who, coming from Poland, wrote a very perceptive review of Manoilesco's views,[15] which was in some ways a precursor to much theorizing later done by Nurkse and others. While I would like to stress the point that 'development economics' as emerged in the late forties and the early fifties had predecessors, and in some cases, important ones, there is no denying the fact that the intensity of the discourse and the emphasis changed significantly.

The single most important factor responsible for this change was probably the intellectual acceptance of Keynesian economics. Keynes had little to say directly on the problem of underdeveloped countries. He did deal with a simple type of growth model in his article, 'Economic Possibilities for our Grandchildren',[16] where we can find an early use of the concept of the 'capital-output ratio', but it would be hard to maintain that Keynes was addressing himself to problems of 'underdevelopment' as we understand it today. While writing *The General Theory*,[17] he developed the idea of a 'land trap' as a possible explanation of arrested development in certain phases of history for some countries. He held that the 'excessive preference for gold' historically described since the days of Pliny the Elder as one reason why Indians could not develop the productive potential of their country. The comments, pertinent as they are, do not affect the basic logical structure of his argument in any essential sense. What is, however, of great importance for our present purpose was the point that Keynes was making in regard to the inability of the market mechanism, irrespective of the nature of market imperfections, to achieve full utilization of the productive potential of an economy. Keynes was not propounding a simple theory of 'duo-economics', as is maintained by some economists; he was, of course, asserting that institutions do matter in determining final outcomes. As an example, we can cite the nature of the bargaining process in the labour market or money as a major social institution which equilibrium theory in its conventional formulation cannot adequately handle. But it was not his opinion that there were altogether different economic theories, one relevant for a 'fully employed economy', and another for an 'underemployed economy', some casual statements notwithstanding. A very important example of the point that Keynes' economics was not simple 'depression economics' is provided by his pamphlet, *How to pay for the War*.[18] Keynes influenced the formation of 'development economics' in three major ways: (i) by devising a methodology for dealing with economic aggregates, for which empirical correlates could be estimated; (ii) by questioning the alleged optimal characteristics of market economies; and (iii) by showing the necessity and effectiveness of public intervention in managing the economic system.

Finally, Keynes was pointing out the need for a 'new international economic order' by setting up or helping to set up institutions, which would lead to a more broad-based global development process, as he believed that a return to 'laissez-faire' would fail to cope with the great problems arising out of the war. Thus, in bringing about a

280 *Development Economics and Models of Unstable Growth*

changed climate of opinion, Keynes played a decisive role. Heterodoxies of yesterday which lived their own lives in the underworld of economics could be accommodated within the theoretical space opened up by Keynes. This helped also in the laying-down of rudiments of a 'development consensus' which writers whose outlook was moulded by him did much to promote. It is also true that in the process he may have also promoted an over-optimistic development outlook and short-circuited some critical questions. These will become apparent in the course of my subsequent discussion.

DIFFERENT PATTERNS OF GROWTH

It is not my purpose here to treat you for the nth time to a discourse on 'balanced' versus 'unbalanced growth' which seems to have occupied the attention of many practising development economists during the fifties and early sixties, following the pioneering contributions made by Rosenstein-Rodan, Kurt Martin (Mandelbaum), Ragnar Nurkse, Tibor Scitovsky and others.

I believe that much of this discussion on whether 'balance' was an essential desideratum for accelerating development in the so-called 'backward countries' was without any operational significance and may have sometimes deflected attention from the strategic issues involved.

First of all, let us be clear that the above writers did not all say the same thing. Despite the existence of certain common features, their formulations were not entirely homogeneous. Thus, I see Rosenstein-Rodan as more concerned with the problem of 'threshold effects' in investment planning, a point of view which was already present in his very first and highly influential contribution which was published in the *Economic Journal* in 1943,[19] but which became all-pervasive in his later writings. I want only to draw attention to his paper 'Notes on the theory of the "Big Push"',[20] which centred around indivisibilities. What Rosenstein-Rodan was trying to get at in his first attempt at conceptualizing the development problem was that a simple gradualist approach where each decision could be taken and justified on the margin would not do in this context. He was concerned with the problem of complementarities in production planning as much as he was concerned with complementarities in his earlier analytical work on 'consumption theory',[21] following the work done by his Austrian mentors, especially von Wieser. In his earlier work he highlighted the role of the hierarchial structure of wants which, if properly formalized, would lead to quite a few contemporary themes in the theory of choice and demand as well as to the concept of 'basic needs' which assumed some significance in the development literature during the mid-seventies. Rodan thought that the existence of 'surplus labour' for which he used the expression 'disguised unemployment', an expression which he borrowed from Joan Robinson, who had used it in a somewhat different context,[22] was a very helpful factor.

However, he did not think that unassisted labour could do very much, nor did he think that the Keynesian policy of stimulating monetary demand was applicable to less developed countries. In an article which he wrote in *International Affairs* (1944) which was basically a policy-oriented lecture that he had delivered at Chatham House, he stressed the need for much larger-scale capital transfer to countries like China and India.[23] He believed that with an injection of fresh capital of a sufficient magnitude, the surplus labour could be activized and a process of productive transformation of these economies would ensue. When asked in the course of discussion, which was reported in the same issue of the journal, whether this would not amount to exploitation of these countries, his answer was that such exploitation would be better than that not to be exploited at all, an idea that was later echoed by Joan Robinson in her *Economic Philosophy*.[24]

It was left to Nurkse to develop the 'saving implication' of 'disguised unemployment',[25] an idea which seems to me to have been foreshadowed in Kalecki's pre-war remarks which I quote here:

> For the assumption of a given supply of capital cannot, in my opinion, in itself be invariably accepted. It is, indeed, usually more realistic to assume that in an agricultural country there is some unemployment, manifest or disguised, and thus the supply of new savings is by no means fixed: it is equal to the investment undertaken (whose upper limit is that at which full employment is reached).[26]

It is no doubt true that both Rosenstein-Rodan and Nurkse had drawn attention to the problem of externalities in connection with the problem of the inducement to invest, but the kind of externalities which Rosenstein-Rodan had in mind was best exemplified by the training of labour. The heart of the problem as Rosenstein-Rodan saw it was that one could not take a mortgage on labour. Nurkse supported this view and believed that coordination of sectoral investment decisions would shift the investment demand schedule upwards.

It was left to Scitovsky to formalize these ideas in a neoclassical general equilibrium context where he stressed the nonexistence of a complete set of futures markets as the principal argument for investment planning.[27] While expressing 'the belief that there is need either for centralized investment planning or for some additional communication system to supplement the pricing system', he also mentions the formal point made by Kenneth Arrow that 'future markets and future prices could provide exactly such a signalling device'.[28]

While in a subsequent comment he seems to have clarified the point that he was not necessarily favouring centralized investment planning in all situations, and admitted that 'the case for the coordination of interrelated investment decisions is largely confined to the underdeveloped countries', he justified this position by reference to the greater role played by 'indivisibilities' and related scale economies in underdeveloped countries.[29] Such an argument does not express any specific preference for 'balanced growth', nor does it pay special attention to the existence of 'surplus labour' on which much of what Rosenstein-Rodan and Nurkse had to say rested.

I may also mention here the very important paper by Richard Kahn on 'The Pace of Development', which has not received the attention that it deserved.[30] Kahn pointed out that the existence of 'surplus labour' in a structural sense made it necessary to look at the problem of 'development' not merely as a distribution problem between generations, but also amongst contemporaries. He drew the inference that there existed modes of intervention which could accelerate the pace of growth provided current consumption could be more equitably distributed. He accordingly stressed that accumulation and consumption should not be treated as mutually exclusive categories.

I think that 'surplus labour' which is being maintained by the economic system in an overall sense is not a simple case of 'market-failure' in a simple sense, because it raises a whole range of questions regarding how social provisioning of goods and services is being carried out, even when markets do not exist. It has much less to do with the alleged 'zero-marginal productivity of labour', than with the fact that a sharing rule has to be defined and accepted by the community for 'surplus labour' to 'survive'. If one wishes to be formal, one could say that it has more to do with the 'nonexistence' of a competitive equilibrium than with the alleged lack of its Pareto-optimality.

Some Basic Issues   283

At this point, it is important to recall that it is the existence of massive surplus labour in rural areas which prompted Mikail Manoilesco to propose his special theory of a 'protectionist' model of industrialization, a model that was sharply criticized by Viner in the thirties,[31] favourably received by Hagen in the fifties,[32] and was dealt with as a form of domestic distortion by Bhagwati and Ramaswami in the sixties.[33] In fact, as Kurt Martin (Mandelbaum) cogently expressed it in his pioneering book, *The Industrialization of Backward Areas*: 'The economic case for the industrialization of densely populated backward countries rests upon this mass phenomenon of disguised rural unemployment'.[34] Mandelbaum's work has not been as frequently cited in recent years as much as it deserves to be. It is often described as a piece of proto-input-output form of reasoning which has been completely superseded by more sophisticated planning models which were first developed in the sixties and subsequently. This is obviously true in a technical sense but the analytical insights which his makeshift formal construction sought to concretize are not obsolete.

Furthermore, what is important is that the somewhat loose quantitative formulations allowed Mandelbaum to take into account many important qualitative considerations which are not present in many rigidly structured planning models. Mandelbaum's discussion was very down to earth. He proceeded to discuss the problem of development both from a demand angle as well as from the supply side. Moreover, he tried to integrate considerations based on 'internal linkages' with the classical argument of comparative advantage. In discussing the direction that industrialization may take, Mandelbaum said, 'The comparative cost doctrine would seem to provide the criterion once the problem of demand is solved',[35] obviously implying that slack exists in a 'labour surplus' situation. He also added,

> It is unavoidable that the theory of international division of labour lost much of its classical simplicity, once full allowance is made for the mutability of all but those cost factors which are natural in the narrowest sense. If prospective costs serve as a guide to policy, a wide range of possible aims and methods opens up.[36]

This formulation is not merely a great improvement on Marshall's use of 'Petty's rule', a rule which Marshall quotes several times in *Industry and Trade*,[37] but also on the static version of the Heckscher-Ohlin theorem. It points towards the dynamic theory of comparative advantage which Nurkse was trying to articulate towards the end of his life.[38]

Martin's analysis shows that there is no logical incompatibility between the case of planning principle and the principle of comparative advantage, a dichotomy which has often been drawn in the subsequent literature and misleadingly so. It also shows that the assumption of an 'export lag' was not an essential part of the structure of some of the very basic formulations which were developed in the forties, although possibly many would have agreed with D. H. Robertson's idea[39] that trade would cease to be a major engine to growth after the war. These cycles of optimism and pessimism in trade-led-growth are interesting facts in themselves but they ought to be treated separately.

In other words, the point that I am driving at is that it was not so much due to the alleged doctrine of 'markets failures' in the sense indicated by the fundamental theorems of welfare economics that policy makers in both developed and developing countries agreed to a theory of state directed policy of industrialization, but from a growth perspective furnished by data in regard to South and Eastern Europe on massive agrarian 'overpopulation'. Obviously the extension of this argument to deal with countries like India was done a little later, although it was present in a general way from the beginning. For this extension, I refer to the first report of the UN Expert Group that dealt with formulating means for the development of underdeveloped areas, which included among others, Arthur Lewis from the Caribbean, D. R. Gadgil from India and Theodore Schultz from the USA.[40] This report reflected the emergence of a 'development consensus' which lasted for nearly twenty-five years. This consensus broke down in the seventies and more prominently, in the eighties, based on criticisms which were first voiced from a resurgent neo-classicism on the one hand, and a 'radical critique' of the left on the other. As I shall try to indicate later, this implies not a demise of the sub-discipline of 'development economics' but the need to forge a new consensus. However, before we turn to these issues, it is necessary to notice the contributions of Arthur Lewis, which have been profoundly influential.

It is first of all important to take note of the fact that Arthur Lewis has written at least four major articles on the theme, of which only the first and probably the most important one dating back to the 1954 paper,[41] was very similar to an analytical construction which was developed around that time in my country by Professor A. K.

Dasgupta,[42] who presented it first at a seminar in Delhi. It was subsequently published in *Economic Weekly*. In some respects, it was similar to the Solow-Swan model, as Solow has also noted in his recent Nobel Lecture.[43] The 'Trade Part' of the model, which was subsequently developed by Lewis in his Wicksell Lecture, 'Aspects of Tropical Trade',[44] was at first not greatly discussed as attention was largely focused on the 'closed economy' version of the model. As became clear in the seventies, the 'open economy' version can easily be linked up with the Prebish-Singer doctrine of deteriorating terms of trade for tropical countries.[45] The Lewis model provides a very interesting explanation of the 'Deterioration Thesis', which was worked out by him in a three commodity-two country model, using the Ricardian version of the theory of comparative advantage.

What is important to note here is that the second Lewis article on the same theme, called 'Further Notes' (1958),[46] is an important elaboration of the first and widely cited 1954 article, for at least two reasons. First, in the latter article Lewis expounds at some length on the relationship between his earlier work and the classical point of view. This was the first major attempt to project very forcefully the continued relevance of the classical analytical perspective on development problems for contemporary developing societies. Secondly, the article also focuses attention on the relationship between 'industry and agriculture', an interpretation which was to later proliferate into a veritable literature called 'dualist development models'. Lewis seems to have kept away from this elaborate exercise which caused some confusion as to what he had meant. In a paper written in 1972,[47] he clarified his position relative to those taken by Dale Jorgenson, on the one hand, and to G. Ranis and J. C. Fey, on the other. In the silver jubilee article which he wrote in 1979 for *The Manchester School*,[48] he notes that his paper can be said to have explained more and less than he may have anticipated. More, because it has been applied to explaining the pattern of post-war growth of Western Europe by Kindleberger[49] and others; less because so many countries are still very far from the 'turning point' that he had presented.

In this article, Arthur Lewis avoids the use of the phrase 'surplus labour' which according to him 'causes emotional distress'. He then goes on to add that, 'as always, the idea intended to be conveyed is that of an infinitely elastic supply of labour to the modern sector at the current wage'. He next discusses why the 'law of one price' need not prevail in the labour market and refers to the co-existence of 'non-competing' groups which he noted, 'has been in our discipline ever since Alfred Marshall'. While Lewis was thinking of Marshall, if he had looked further back in time, he could have found earlier sources for this concept, notably in the work of John Elliott Cairns[50] and even in Longfield.[51] In my country, the late Professor B. N. Ganguli (to whom I have already made a reference) used this concept to explain the functioning of the Indian economy.[52] His was a highly suggestive piece of analysis which space prevents me from describing here in detail.

As far as Lewis is concerned, he uses this notion to explain in part why the predictions of his 1954 article have turned out to have had less predictive power in several countries, notably India, as I would stress myself. It may be recalled that the earlier Lewis model had a somewhat optimistic slant. If the terms of trade were constant between industry and agriculture, then the rate of profit need not decline with continued accumulation. If entrepreneurs are profit-maximising and also abstemious, a high rate of labour absorption into modern industry may be expected because capital accumulation will be labour-attracting as well. If labour absorption does not take place, it must be due to the relatively slow rate of growth of traditional agriculture or because capitalists are too fond of 'consumption'. In his two basic papers (1950 and 1958), Lewis did not specifically address himself to the factors limiting agricultural growth nor did he address himself to possibilities of biased technical change. In his growth model, he made the classical assumption that savings are automatically invested, thus obviating the need to look into issues of demand deficiency. While reviewing the issue of labour absorption in his 1979 paper, Lewis came to the conclusion that much would depend on whether there are significant economies of scale in industry or not. As he puts it:

> If there are no significant economies of scale, a vigorous class of small business will scour the cheap labour market for its best talents and will prevent the trade unions and the large capitalists from joining together to create restricted entry systems. If there are significant economies of scale, the large firms are not being pressured by the small. What they face is pressure from within, to create promotion ladders, training systems, pensions schemes and above all 'orderly' entry – all of which translate into a higher life-cycle income, financed from non-competing rents.[53]

I have quoted this paragraph from Lewis because it seems to me to throw an interesting light on the contrasting development experience of a country like India and the experience of the developing countries in East Asia. Obviously, the two different growth scenarios differ in many other respects as well. But it would appear that the choice of industries stressed early by the Indian planners were the ones where economies of scale were expected to be important. The Lewis explanation, which would seem to suggest that increasing returns to scale could lead to the slowdown of labour absorption into high wage sectors is only one aspect of what increasing returns to scale imply. If one were to look at it from a Kaldorian angle, increasing returns to scale appear in a somewhat different light.

Nicholas Kaldor was an exceedingly imaginative and fertile economic theorist. While his theory of economic development was an offshoot of his more basic work dealing with an extension of Keynesian economics to problems of long-run growth, it did not receive as much attention as it deserved as a somewhat novel way of looking at development problems. (He himself used to stress his great indebtedness to Allyn Young, who was his teacher at the London School of Economics.) Even in his last published work, *Economics without Equilibrium*,[54] after quoting profusely from Young as the progenitor of the theory of cumulative causation, Kaldor expressed his surprise as to why Young's work was largely ignored by the profession. However, Kaldor's own work is not a simple repetition of Young's article.

In particular, Kaldor stressed the great necessity for an agricultural surplus in the earlier stages of economic transformation of an industrially backward country.[55] The growth of this agricultural surplus affected employment opportunities in the non-agricultural sectors of the economy for two reasons: (i) through providing for the growing real wage bill in the non-agricultural sectors as well as (ii) by providing a growing market for industry. The growth of effective demand for industrial products provided by the growth of a marketed surplus of agriculture could turn into an upward cumulative process because of the prevalence of increasing returns in industry. He attached a strategic importance to the notion of increasing returns in industry which has not met with widespread acceptance, possibly because it subsumed several disparate items, such as static and dynamic externalities as well as the influence of indivisibility on the choice of the production process. It is well known that significant increasing returns to scale often create highly intractable problems for applying conventional equilibrium theoretic reasoning. Kaldor had rather strong views on the relevance of equilibrium economics. But even if we were to disregard his dismissal of equilibrium reasoning as an untenable method of theorizing about real life problems, it still does not follow that increasing returns to scale is not a pertinent explanation of the phenomena of widening disparities between nations in terms of relevant economic variables. (Kaldor's argument in this respect reminds me of some recent work on 'non-equilibrium thermodynamics' which alone could explain certain findings in the 'kineties of chemical reactions' which were earlier rejected as implausible because they did not fit into the equilibrium theoretic mould. I am, of course, referring to the work on 'ante-wave'.)[56] Thus it is well known that differences in growth rates between countries and/or differences in levels of per capita income are incompatible with the assumptions of thoroughgoing constant returns to scale unless ad hoc assumptions are made about the nature and extent at technological progress. Kaldor's formulation, therefore, deserves far more serious attention from development theorists than it has received so far.

While for early stages of developing economies, Kaldor considered an 'agricultural surplus' to be the triggering mechanism, for advanced economies he considered exports (or net exports) to be the principal propelling force. Kaldor also believed that while agriculture was generally supply-constrained, especially because land was often a limiting factor, industrial expansion was typically demand-constrained. Prevalence of increasing returns in industry implied that the typical industry cost curve had a large flat segment, so that industrial prices were generally cost determined with the markup varying with the nature and extent of competition, which is necessarily imperfect.

This required that for a cumulative process to turn into a structural transformation process, agriculture must be sufficiently responsive to outside forces, especially that the peasantry must be market-oriented in its behaviour. Land reform was an important factor in promoting agriculture as it would promote agricultural innovation.

Secondly, export to the rest of the world could help, provided judicious support were to be provided by the state in the form of suitable subsidies or protective tariffs. Kaldor believed that agricultural stagnation combined with an excessive degree of protection could stop the cumulative process from operating to the detriment of the country concerned. On the question of protection, Kaldor found much merit in List's ideas if they were applied to the question of

Some Basic Issues

deciding whether *industrial* protection needed to be applied 'in a less developed country against competition of manufacture produced in *more* [italics in the original] developed countries'.[57] He goes on to add, 'it [i.e. the Listian argument] provides no justification whatever for highly developed countries like countries of Europe, North America or Japan, to protect their *agriculture* [italics in original] against the competition of the less developed countries'.[58] That Kaldor was not a simple-minded protectionist is known to any who have cared to read him. He was, however, of the opinion that while Ricardo's original pamphlet, and the policy arguments based on it, were perfectly sound, Ricardo's later formulations of the doctrine of 'comparative' costs insinuated further assumptions into the argument with the unfortunate consequence that more was claimed for 'free trade' than was in fact justified.[59] He clarified the point further by his remarks that Ricardo's general conclusion was based on the postulate of the universality of linear homogenous production. Since Kaldor thought that there was enough evidence to suggest that the real world did not conform to such an assumption, the Ricardian conclusion was consequently not applicable as a universal rule. Kaldor's development perspective thus depends to a considerable extent on his understanding that economic development as a cumulative process rested largely on the combined operation of land-saving and labour-saving innovation in agriculture with increasing returns to scale in industry.

It is at this point important to note that while Kaldor, like Arthur Lewis, was trying to link up development economics with development theorizing in the grand classical tradition, they emphasized somewhat different strands of classical thought. It would be true to say that, on the one hand, Kaldor was trying to bring into contemporary attention the role of demand in determining the rate of economic expansion by a novel combination of Smith and Keynes. On the other hand, Lewis was providing a somewhat different perspective. Although it would be not correct to say that he was presenting Ricardo without diminishing returns, since he had a 'subsistence sector' where diminishing returns were presumably operative, he was not at all precise as to how the subsistence sector could also generate its own dynamic. We could get the impression that the main link between the 'modern' and the 'subsistence' sector were merely through labour transfer, a process which he did not analyze with any precision. There are some places where he did identify the sectors as 'industry' and 'agriculture', as noted already, but even there, his agriculture was not Ricardian agriculture, because in Ricardo a farmer is an agricultural capitalist which is not the case with Lewis.

As regards the Keynesian influence, Kaldor clearly recognized that while over the long run, Ricardo's reasoning was valid to the extent that manufacturers 'saved in order to invest' Keynes' ideas do have relevance in developing countries because of a 'fixed price situation', which in its turn was due to the existence of a 'fixed real wage giving a cost-determined supply price for industrial products'. In Kaldor's analysis, industrial output is governed by relationship OI = 1/m DA where OI = industrial output, DA = demand for industrial products coming from agriculture, m = share of expenditure on agricultural products in industrial increase. Kaldor described this as the analogue of the 'foreign trade' multiplier, which he considered to be the far more important concept in the long-run situation.

Kaldor's major writings on development date back to the mid-seventies, although he had been always interested in development issues as his work on India's tax policy[60] and his earlier contributions to the ECLA Bulletin[61] show. But it is only fair to say that he formulated his own distinctive ideas in the seventies as a part of his general critique of 'mainstream economics'. I consider that Kaldor's 'two-sector' model is an insightful conceptualization of the long-run dynamics of development. However, I believe that it underplays the role of certain forces of 'structural changes', on which a more disaggregated dynamic analysis can focus better. Two of Kaldor's conclusions can be retained while allowing for a far greater degree of disaggregation. In particular, it is possible to maintain the distinction between the 'fix-flex' price sectors, as well as the principle of the 'foreign trade multiplier', while allowing for certain essential distinctions within the industrial sector. As an example, we can mention the distinction drawn by Mahalanobis, Lowe and others between the 'machine building sectors' and the 'machine using sectors' for producing a whole variety of consumer goods. It is through the economies of scale which are a pronounced characteristic of 'machine building sectors' that we can bring in, in a simple, yet well specified, sense the role of knowledge, a factor otherwise emphasized by Kaldor but subsumed under increasing returns. If machines fall in cost over time, either from learning or through new knowledge, then in real terms, continued capital formation can be combined with increasing capital-labour ratios in the different sectors of the economy with a relatively unchanged capital-output ratio for the economy as a whole, one of the stylized facts of modern economic growth which Kaldor was so prone to underline.

It can be maintained, as I have tried to argue elsewhere, that the Indian development process could have been considerably speeded up if agricultural growth had been more rapid and economies of scale in the industrial sectors, especially in the machine-producing sectors as initially anticipated, had been fully realized, through maintaining a higher rate of real public investment and through greater sensitivity to technical changes taking place in the outside world, especially in the electronics sector. As it happened, demand constraints prevented economies of scale from being realized in practice, as large excess capacity emerged in the capital goods industries after the mid-sixties resulting in a high cost structure. Further, the lack of 'openness' to technological changes which were particularly important in sectors producing machines led to the emergence of a technological lag which is responsible for the failure of export substitution to materialize. Along with the emergence of non-competing groups in large industries, a point mentioned by Lewis, there was a prolongation and even an accentuation of the dualism which the planning process was supposed to eliminate.

Before I conclude this lecture, I would like to make some observations on the role of knowledge as a productive factor. In summing up his major quantitative studies (pertaining to several countries and stretching over nearly two centuries) Simon Kuznets came to the conclusion that in the final analysis, it was the growth of knowledge which was the most decisive characteristic of modern economic growth. Kuznets was not merely talking about practical knowledge in the sense of knowledge directly applied in transforming inputs into outputs, but also of the basic sciences which are increasingly having profound impacts on transformations in the sphere of production that are leading to changes in the international economy.

Marx very early on recognized the role of science as a directly productive force, as the relevant sections in the *Grundrisse* adequately demonstrate. In fact, it is interesting to note that in his *Theories of Surplus Value*, Marx quotes Hobbes as the progenitor of the idea that it is science, not operative labour, which is 'the mother of the arts'. In fact, the quotation from the *Leviathan* which Marx uses for this purpose, talks about 'science, namely, mathematics' which is even more interesting as a prescient observation.[62]

While quoting from Hobbes, Marx goes beyond Hobbes in noting a key characteristic of science which has been in the forefront of much contemporary discussion. I would like to quote the following passage of Marx as particularly relevant to my discussion here. He wrote,

'The product of mental labour – science – always stands far below its value, because labour-time needed to reproduce it has no relation at all to the labour-time required for its original production. For example, a school boy can learn the binominal theorem in an hour'.[63]

It is clear that Marx is implying that a systematic underinvestment in science is likely to be the result if the growth of science were to be left to competitive market forces. In contemporary works stemming from Arrow, Hurwitz and others,[64] we have become acutely conscious of the dilemma of 'knowledge'. The dilemma pertains to the lack of compatibility between institutions which lead to the widest possible diffusion and utilization of knowledge and those which are particularly relevant for its creation in the very first instance.

While the former may require direct public intervention, a process that is closely connected with the nature of the educational system and its links with industry, the issues posed by the latter are not yet fully understood. The experience of Japan is particularly relevant in this context. A frequently heard criticism of the Japanese educational system emphasizes the relative inability of the Japanese scientific and technological system to throw up new ideas, which contrasts very sharply with its ability to appropriate, assimilate and develop newly accruing scientific ideas for major product and process developments. We are here faced with one of the major issues in development theory which relates to the as yet unexplored territory of social learning. In her interesting work on South Korea, Alice Amsden has also emphasized the learning ability displayed by many newly industrializing countries of East Asia. She describe them as 'learning societies'.[65] However, in industrial learning relationships between a teacher and a student, we are aware that the advantage enjoyed by the teacher is generally a transient one. Unfortunately, this does not happen to be the case between countries, at least over fairly long periods of time. The 'quasi rents' enjoyed by the early starters, to use a Marshallian expression, tend to persist unless major institutional changes take place, the nature of which, I believe, require closer analysis. Development economists in the fifties and sixties hardly worried about this class of issues but these may well be the leading problems in the 1990s. I will return to these issues in my next lecture.

DISCONTINUITY BETWEEN DEVELOPMENT ECONOMICS AND DEVELOPMENT THEORIZING

In presenting my own understanding of how development economics has itself developed, I had to be extremely brief in presenting some of the debates which occupied hundreds of pages in leading journals and text books. In particular, I am of the opinion that much of the debate surrounding 'balanced vs unbalanced growth' was semantic in character, and, therefore, does not deserve the importance which text books accord to the subject. Similarly, I think that many of the purely mechanical extensions of the original Lewis model of development were exercises based on relatively elementary mathematical elaboration of the underlying relationships. This does not imply that the extensions have not brought in any additional insights, but they lie largely in the domain of taxonomy. Substantive additions can be possibly carried through in regard to the analysis of urban-rural migration. A great deal of work which lies in trying to reconstruct Lewis-type supply functions of labour which postulate positive real wages in the urban/industrial sectors along with significant un/underemployment, which implies that the rule of 'free goods' does not apply to the labour market, has more to do with the choice theoretic foundations of development economics, which differs in spirit from the historically illuminating parable that Lewis had employed. Kaldor's work, however, which differs in some substantive respects from Lewis and is explicitly cast is a disequilibrium mould, would appear to possess significant potential for further elaboration. The propositions which I have tried to render plausible can be briefly restated here.

First of all, I have tried to indicate that there was less of a discontinuity between 'development economics' and development theorizing of the earlier decades of this century than is normally thought. What happened in the forties and fifties was more in the nature of a change in intellectual *outlook*. In bringing about this change in outlook, the work of Keynes was of fundamental significance. It is not because that Keynes had something to say of direct significance to the development problem. It was firstly due to his successful redefinition of the agenda of the state, which was first stated very succinctly in his article, 'The end of Laissez Faire',[66] and carried to a successful completion in his *General Theory*.

Secondly, his rehabilitation of 'macro-economics' was responsible for a revival of interest in 'classical economics', even though he was himself highly critical of the influence exercised by some leading classical thinkers such as David Ricardo. The 'epistemological break', in so far as there was any, was represented by the Keynesian revolution.

Thirdly, understanding of the basic development problem, which earlier centred around the process of capital accumulation, has shifted to problems which are more closely connected with issues of technology and knowledge, which can be studied in complete disjunction from their embodiment in capital goods. There is great danger in mixing important problems if we treat technological change in the 'disembodied' or 'unembodied' sense. This is for one of two reasons, the first having to do with capital aggregation problems which Joan Robinson highlighted very strongly, which if ignored can be highly misleading. Technological changes in embodied form create disequilibria which are essential features of the development process.[67] There is little doubt that early optimism about the possibilities of technological borrowing irrespective of initial conditions has turned out to be very facile.

Fourthly, economists have become much more aware of the 'fallacy of misplaced concreteness' in connection with problems relating to capital formation, a point which was perceptively discussed a long time ago by Veblen, who distinguished between the different forms in which society may preserve its unlimited capital. It is clear that these comments do not question the legitimacy of 'development economics' in an analytical sense, for they suggest directions for further exploration which are clearly consistent with what the pioneers in the subject had to say. They also suggest that capital accumulation and capital decumulation are not symmetrical processes, an insight that business cycle theorists of an earlier generation understood, but has been altogether missing from much development literature. (It is interesting in this respect to read a recent and self-critical contribution by Theodore Schultz, where he writes that 'It took a lot of on the job shift experience' on (his) part to learn that the simplifying assumptions that capital is homogeneous is a disaster for capital theory.[68])

My presentation in this lecture has largely concentrated on some critical theoretical issues which have occupied development economists over the years. It is well known that development economics, in its initial formulation, was strongly interventionist, an important respect in which it differed from major development theories such as Marx and Schumpeter who, despite their differences, were mostly occupied with processes of long-term change. 'Development planning' was coterminous with 'development economics', but deals with a related, but somewhat different, class of issues. My next lecture[69] deals with certain basic issues in 'development planning', which hopefully will throw some light on the wider issues of 'plan' vs the 'market'.

NOTES

1. Steuart, 1966; List, 1965, 1966.
2. Marx, 1971, p. 399.
3. Steuart, 1966, p. lv.
4. Ranade, 1906.
5. Marx and Engels, 1975, vol. IV, p. 1265ff.
6. Marshall, 1961, vol. I, Appendix A, note p. 753.
7. Myrdal, 1957.
8. Arndt, 1987.
9. Boeke, 1961; also Boeke, 1953.
10. van Gelderen, 1961, pp. 111–64.
11. Ibid.
12. Ibid, p. 14.
13. Ganguli, 1961.
14. Anstey, 1952.
15. Manoilesco, 1931; see also Kalecki, 1938, pp. 708–11.
16. Keynes, 1933.
17. Keynes, 1954, p. 241.
18. Keynes, 1940.
19. Rosenstein-Rodan, 1943.
20. Rosenstein-Rodan, 1960a.
21. Rosenstein-Rodan, 1960b.
22. Robinson, 1947.
23. Rosenstein-Rodan, 1944.
24. Robinson, 1968, p. 45.
25. Nurkse, 1953.
26. Kalecki, 1938.
27. Scitovsky, 1964, p. 80.
28. Ibid, quoting Arrow, p. 80, n. 1.
29. Scitovsky, 1954.
30. Kahn, 1972.
31. Viner, 1953.
32. Hagen, 1958.
33. Bhagwati and Ramaswami, 1963.
34. Mandelbaum, 1955, p. 2.
35. Ibid, p. 12.
36. Ibid, p. 13.

37. Marshall, 1919.
38. Nurkse, 1959.
39. Robertson, 1953.
40. UN Group of Experts, 1951.
41. Lewis, 1954.
42. Dasgupta, 1965.
43. Solow, 1988.
44. Lewis, 1969.
45. Prebish, 1950; Singer, 1950, 1955.
46. Lewis, 1958.
47. Lewis, 1972.
48. Lewis, 1979.
49. Kindleberger, 1967.
50. Cairns, 1967.
51. Longfield, 1834.
52. Ganguli, 1956.
53. Lewis, 1979, p. 227.
54. Kaldor, 1985.
55. Kaldor, 1980.
56. Ibid.
57. Kaldor, 1974.
58. Ibid, p. 184.
59. Ibid, p. 238.
60. Kaldor, 1956, 1958.
61. Kaldor, 1985.
62. Marx, 1971, p. 353.
63. Ibid, p. 343.
64. Arrow, 1962, 1969; Hurwitz, 1987.
65. Amsden, 1989.
66. Keynes, 1926.
67. There has been a great deal of interesting work on structural change by Pasinetti and others and there is little doubt that development economics will be increasingly concerned with these issues.
68. Schultz, 1988, p. 344.
69. Chakravarty, 1991.

REFERENCES

Amsden, Alice (1989) *Asia's Next Giant: South Korea and Late Industrialisation* (Oxford: Oxford University Press).

Anstey, Vera (1952) *Economic Development of India* (London: Longman).

Arndt, H. W. (1987) *Economic Development: The History of an Idea* (Chicago: Chicago University Press).

Arrow, Kenneth J. (1962) 'Economics of Welfare and the Allocation of Resources for Invention', in National Bureau of Economic Research

Some Basic Issues 297

Publications in Reprint, *The Rate and Direction of Inventive Activity: Economic and Social Factors* (New York: Arno Press) pp. 609–26.

Arrow, Kenneth J. (1969) 'Classificatory Notes on the Production and Transmission of Knowledge', *American Economic Review*, March, pp. 23–35.

Bhagwati, J., and Ramaswami, V. K. (1963) 'Domestic Distortions, Tariffs and the Theory of Optimum Subsidy', *Journal of Political Economy*, 71, 1, pp. 44–50.

Boeke, J. H. (1953) *Economics and Economic Policy in Dual Societies* (New York: Institute of Pacific Relations).

Boeke, J. H. (1961) 'Dualist Economics', in W. F. Wertheim (ed.) *Indonesian Economics: The Concept of Dualism in Theory and Practice* (The Hague: van Hoeve).

Cairns, John Elliott (1967) *Some Leading Principles of Political Economy* (New York: Kelley) reprint; originally published 1874.

Chakravarty, Sukhamoy (1991) 'Development Planning: A Reappraisal', *Cambridge Journal of Economics*, 15 (1), pp. 5–200.

Ganguli, B. N. (1956) 'Rethinking on Indian Economics' (Presidential Address to the Indian Economic Association), *Indian Economic Journal*, 3, pp. 235–54.

Ganguli, B. N. (1961) 'Evolution of Economic Thinking in India', P. N. Banoji Memorial Lecture, 1961; reprinted in Babatosh Datta (ed.), *Indian Economic Thought* (New Delhi: Tata McGraw-Hill).

Hagen, E. (1958) 'An Economic Justification of Protectionism', *Quarterly Journal of Economics*, 72, 4, pp. 496–514.

Hurwitz, L. (1987) 'Economic Issues in the Utilisation of Knowledge', in P. R. Brahmananda et al. (eds), *Dimensions of Rural Development in India* (Bombay: Himalaya Publishing House) pp. 1–17.

Kahn, Richard (1972) 'The Pace of Development', in *Selected Essays on Employment and Growth* (London: Cambridge University Press) pp. 153–91.

Kaldor, Nicholas (1974) 'What is Wrong with Economic Theory', *Quarterly Journal of Economics*, reprinted in Kaldor, 1980, pp. 202–13.

Kaldor, Nicholas (1956) *Indian Tax Reform* (New Delhi: Government of India, Ministry of Finance, Department of Economic Affairs).

Kaldor, Nicholas (1958) 'Tax Reform in India', *Economic Weekly* (Annual Number); reprinted in Nicholas Kaldor, *Essays in Economic Policy* (London: Duckworth) vol. I.

Kaldor, Nicholas (1980) *Further Essays in Economic Theory* (London: Duckworth).

Kaldor, Nicholas (1985) *Economics without Equilibrium* (Cardiff: Cardiff University Press).

Kalecki, M. (1938) 'Review of M. Manoilesco', *Economic Journal*, 48, 192, pp. 708–11.

Keynes, J. M. (1926) 'The End of Laissez Faire', reprinted in Keynes, 1972, vol. IX, pp. 272–94.

Keynes, J. M. (1940) *How to Pay for the War* (London: Macmillan), reprinted in Keynes, 1972.

Keynes, J. M. (1933) 'Economic Possibilities for our Grandchildren', in

Essays in Persuasion (London: Macmillan), reprinted in Keynes, 1972.
Keynes, J. M. (1954) *The General Theory of Employment, Interest and Money* (London: Macmillan).
Keynes, J. M. (1972) *The Collected Writings of John Maynard Keynes*, ed. D. Moggridge (London: Macmillan for the Royal Economic Society).
Kindleberger, C. P. (1967) *Europe's Post-War Growth* (Cambridge, Mass.: Harvard University Press).
Lewis, W. Arthur (1954) 'Economic Development with Unlimited Supplies of Labour', *The Manchester School*, 22, 2, pp. 131–91.
Lewis, W. Arthur (1958) 'Unlimited Labour: Further Notes', *The Manchester School*, 26, 1, pp. 1–32.
Lewis, W. Arthur (1969) *Aspects of Tropical Trade, 1883–1965* (Stockholm: Almquist and Wiksell).
Lewis, W. Arthur (1972) 'Reflections on Unlimited Labour', in Luis Eugenic Di-Marco (ed.), *International and Development Essays in Honour of Raoul Prebish* (New York: Academic Press) pp. 75–96.
Lewis, W. Arthur (1979) 'The Dual Economy Revisited', *The Manchester School*, 47, 3, pp. 211–29.
List, Frederick (1966) *The National System of Political Economy* (New York: Kelley; also 1965 German ed.).
Longfield, M. (1833) *Lectures on Political Economy* (Dublin: Richard Milliken and Son; London: B. Fellowes).
Mandelbaum, K. (1955) *The Industrialisation of Backward Areas* (Oxford: Blackwell) revised 2nd ed.
Manoilesco, Mikail (1931) *The Theory of Protection and International Trade* (London: P. S. King and Son).
Marshall, Alfred (1919) *Industry and Trade* (London: Macmillan).
Marshall, Alfred (1961) *Collected Works*, vol. I (London: Macmillan for the Royal Economic Society) 9th ed.
Marx, Karl (1971) *Theories of Surplus Value*, Part III (Moscow: 1971).
Marx, Karl, and Engels, Frederick (1975) *Collected Works*, vol. IV (London: Lawrence and Wishart).
Myrdal, Gunnar (1957) *Economic Theory and Under-Developed Regions* (London: Duckworth).
Nurkse, Ragnar (1953) *Problems of Capital Formation in the Underdeveloped Countries* (Oxford: Blackwell).
Nurkse, Ragnar (1959) *Patterns of Trade and Development* (Stockholm: Almquist and Wiksell).
Prebish, Raoul (1950) *The Economic Development of Latin America and its Principal Problems* (New York: United Nations Economic Development for South America).
Ranade, M. G. (1906) *Essays in Indian Economics* (Madras: Natesan).
Robertson, D. H. (1953) 'The Future of International Trade', in H. S. Ellis and L. S. Metzler (eds), *Readings in the Theory of International Trade* (London: Allen and Unwin) pp. 497–513.
Robinson, Joan (1968) *Economic Philosophy* (Harmondsworth: Penguin).
Rosenstein-Rodan, P. N. (1943) 'Problems of Industrialization in Eastern and South-Eastern Europe', *Economic Journal* 53, 210 (June-September), pp. 202–11.

Rosenstein-Rodan, P. N. (1944) 'The International Development of Backward Areas', *International Affairs*, 20, pp. 157–66.
Rosenstein-Rodan, P. N. (1960a) 'Notes on the Theory of the "Big Push"', in H. S. Ellis (ed.) *Economic Problems of Latin America* (London: Macmillan) pp. 57–67.
Rosenstein-Rodan, P. N. (1960b) 'Marginal Utility', trans. by W. F. Stolper, *International Economic Papers*, 10 (London: Macmillan) pp. 71–106.
Schultz, Theodore W. (1988) 'On Investing in Specialised Human Capital to Attain Increasing Returns' in Gustav Ranis and T. Paul Schultz (eds), *The State of Development Economics: Progress and Perspectives* (Oxford: Basil Blackwell).
Scitovsky, T. (1954) 'Two concepts of external economies', *Journal of Political Economy*, 62, 1, pp. 143–51.
Scitovsky, T. (1964) *Papers on Welfare and Growth* (London: Allen and Unwin).
Singer, H. W. (1950) 'The Distribution of Gains Between Investing and Borrowing Countries', *American Economic Review*, 40, 2, pp. 473–85, reprinted in H. W. Singer, *The Strategy of Economic Development* (London: Macmillan, 1973).
Singer, H. W. (1955) 'Problems of Industrialisation of Underdeveloped Countries', in *Economic Progress: Papers and Proceedings of a Round Table Conference held by the International Economic Association* (Louvain: Institute of Economic and Social Research) pp. 171–92.
Steuart, Sir James (1966) *An Inquiry into the Principles of Political Oeconomy*, ed. with an introduction by A. S. Skinner (London: Oliver and Boyd) 2 vols.
van Gelderen, J. 'The Economics of the Tropical Colony', in W. F. Wertheim (ed.) *Indonesian Economics: The Concept of Dualism in Theory and Practice* (The Hague: van Hoeve).
UN Group of Experts (1951) *Measures for the Economic Development of Underdeveloped Countries* (New York: United Nations).
Viner, J. *International Trade and Economic Development* (Oxford: Clarendon Press).

11 The Economy as a Chaotic Growth Oscillator
Richard M. Goodwin

INTRODUCTION

Schumpeter was a pioneer in the analysis of the dynamics of the modern industrialized economies. When he said that the cycle is simply the form that growth takes, he made one of the most profound contributions to the understanding of the vicissitudes of contemporary societies. In perceiving the central importance of Kondratieff's detection of the existence of long waves of the order of fifty years, he posed a difficult but vital problem in the statistical and theoretical treatment of economics. He proposed three Kitchins to each Juglar and six Juglars to each Kondratieff cycle – a suggestive hypothesis but one far too simple; it is based on the too crude conception of the independently additive nature of the fluctuations of the economy. There is no possibility that each of the cycles could behave in independence of the other two. One cannot be severely critical of him about this since he was merely using the common conception of linear decomposition of economic time series in econometric analysis. Furthermore it is no easy task to formulate a single model which will explain the complex behaviour of economic time series.

GEORGE BIRKHOFF'S 'ERGODIC' THEORY

Frisch misled a whole generation of economic analysts with the brilliant half-truth that the economy must be asymptotically stable but kept in motion by exogenous shocks. By contrast, in my view, the economy is highly unstable but confined within a limit by such things as full capacity and full employment. Frisch's formulation had the great merit of explaining, by random shocks, the evident irregularity of economic time series. But we now know what neither he nor Schumpeter could know, that exogenous shocks, though sufficient, are not necessary to explain the erratic character of the statistics. It was not until the 1960s that an offshoot of the ergodic theory of George Birkhoff (1931) produced the theory of chaos, a term which I am using generically to cover a wide range from mild irregularity to unpredictable or totally formless behaviour. The fundamentally new concept of chaos is important because it shows that a completely endogenous, deterministic system can produce any degree of irregularity and unpredictability. It is not that one can deny that there are random exogenous shocks to the economy: rather it is that there are two, rather than only one, sources of the pervasive irregularity of economic time series.

RÖSSLER'S 'CHAOTIC ATTRACTOR'

It is surprising that Frisch proposed that random shocks were necessary to explain the persistence of wave-like behaviour in economics, since in one of the earliest issues of *Econometrica*, the French mathematician Philippe Le Corbeiller had called the attention of economists to the fact that van der Pol had developed a nonlinear theory of a persistent cycle as an equilibrium motion. In fact the theory goes back to H. Poincaré who developed the theory of the stable limit cycle. In that formulation the equilibrium is unstable, leading to expanding amplitude, but when a variable exceeds a given level, the system bifurcates to stability, so that there must be one or more closed curves in state space which separate the stable and unstable regions. In a sense, the theory of chaos is a straightforward generalization of this notion. A lucid and comprehensible formulation of chaos has been provided by the Tübingen mathematician Rössler (1977). In his version the bifurcation is provided, not by one of the behavioural variables, but rather by a variable control parameter. When one or more of the system variables exceeds a given limit, the control expands, and the more it expands the more it inhibits the system variables. It thus is a flexible dynamic control in sharp contrast to the rigid, static, upper limit control in the Poincaré-Bendixson type of theory. The consequences are astonishing: instead of one or more simple closed curves, one finds an outer boundary and an inner boundary in the state space, which define a limit region within which the motion can fluctuate in a seemingly more or less

302 Development Economics and Models of Unstable Growth

random fashion, although the motion is in fact completely deterministic. The equilibrium band may be large or small, but given the system structure, all motions, whether initially outside or inside, will in the limit be contained within the band. Such a system is therefore named a chaotic attractor.

THE DYNAMICS OF A CYCLICAL AND DYNAMICALLY UNSTABLE AGGREGATE SYSTEM

In economics we need an explanation of the major cycle, say eight to twelve years, and, at the same time, one of forty to sixty years. The shorter stocks cycle is well understood and is not involved in technical change, so that it may be left out of account. To analyze these two cycles we need to consider in particular innovational investment and the ensuing structural change. To isolate this aspect of the economy, it is helpful to formulate the model in terms of deviations from the equilibria determined by monetary and fiscal policy, foreign trade, and so on. The essential requirement is an economic model which will proceed in ever widening swings. To keep matters simple, consider a constant labour force; wage rates depend on the ratio, v, of employment to the labour force; v = 0 is the level which leaves unit labour cost, u, constant. Both v and u vary above and below zero by small quantities. The single real wage rate is w; a_1 is the input of labour per unit of output, the inverse of productivity; hence u = a_1w and measures the ratio of the real wage to productivity. If u increases, wages are rising faster than productivity; if it decreases, productivity is rising faster than the real wage. From this it follows that $\dot{u}$ (du/dt) is proportional to v, i.e. $\dot{u}$ = hv, h > 0. Also there are strong, realistic arguments for considering that the economy is unstable around equilibrium: therefore we may assume that $\dot{u}$ is proportional to u as well, giving $\dot{u}$ = hv + fu, f > 0. In this simple model, all wages (and salaries) are consumed and not profits, so that u is the share of wages and of consumption and 1 − u is the share of profits, of saving, and of investment. Assuming that output is dynamically adjusted to demand, the consequence is that its rate of change will be negatively proportional to u, i.e. $\dot{v}$ = −du, d > 0.

These two differential equations suffice to determine the dynamics of a linear, aggregative economic system which will be cyclical and dynamically unstable, as one sees by writing

The Economy as a Chaotic Growth Oscillator

$$\ddot{v} = -d(hv + fu) = -dhv + f\dot{v}. \qquad (1)$$

An example is given in Figure 11.1: this is the type of problem which the Rössler Band is designed to solve chaotically, by adding a third variable, which, by dynamic expansion and contraction, will generate an upper and lower bound to the amplitude of oscillation, thus providing a stable area of freely variable, aperiodic motion. Although every movement of the system is completely determined, these motions are not precisely predictable – how unpredictable depends upon the parameters. There is a whole range of behaviour types available, from only slight variation from a recurrent pattern, to totally wild variations of type and character of behaviour, limited only by the upper and lower bounds of the band. There is also the remarkable fact that initial conditions can produce quite different types of behaviour. In fact one way in which to gain an insight into such bizarre behaviour is to consider the fact that the position of the system at any point of time can be made the initial condition for subsequent motion: since these systems never repeat, they can be considered as giving an unending succession of different initial conditions.

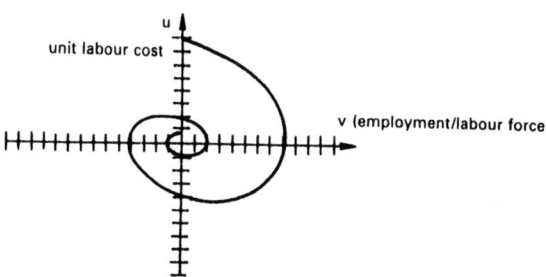

FIGURE 11.1

To make our economy perform in a circumscribed region of phase space we must therefore define a third variable, z, which will control the pair, u and v, so as to cancel their tendency to continuing expansion. To conform to the Rössler specification z must have a small constant growth rate plus one which is proportional to the difference between v and c; the constant c can be associated with an approach to full employment. The control variable must be bilateraly but asymmetrically coupled to the employment ratio, i.e. v must be negatively proportional to z, while $\dot{z}/z$ must be proportional to $v - c$. The chaotic system then becomes:

$$\dot{v} = -du - ez \qquad (2)$$

$$\dot{u} = hv + fu \qquad (3)$$

$$\dot{z} = b + gz(v - c). \qquad (4)$$

I take the unit of time to be one month, so that ten years is 120 units and fifty years is 600 units. This single system with only one non-linearity can perform the remarkable feat of producing over a fifty-year period a single Kondratieff in the form of four to five single cycles, each different from the other. In Figure 11.2 is given $v(t)$ resulting from a careful choice of parameters and initial conditions. In Figures 11.3 and 11.4 are given respectively $u(t)$ and $z(t)$. It is evident that such an economy is experiencing a succession of increasingly vigorous cyclical expansions, reaching a crescendo shortly after the twenty-fifth year and thereafter collapsing into relatively stagnant cycles. Only a chaotic attractor model could produce such a result, undisturbed by exogenous events. From Figure 11.4 one sees that weak cycles need only mild restraint to keep them from exploding, and one sees that over quite a long period a potentially unstable economy in fact never exceeds a determinate limit. In Figure 11.5 is given the phase portrait for u and v, where one sees that the motion consists of approximately three quite distinct cycles. Given initial values which lie outside of the stable region, the system will eventually arrive inside it, as is illustrated in Figure 11.6. The system is in this sense asymptotically stable to the Rössler Band and once inside will never leave it.

As one sees in Figures 11.2 and 11.3, neither $v(t)$ nor $u(t)$ are periodic nor do they repeat any single time shape, so that one would be justified in saying that this system exhibits a highly irregular behaviour. Indeed it would be difficult, if not impossible, with the traditional econometric methods to arrive at a correct estimate of the system's parameters. However, chaos is a generic term to cover a large range of types and degrees of irregularity. In the context of the whole gamut of chaotic attractors, this Long and Short Wave system exhibits a rather mildly erratic character. In spite of the irregular appearance of the temporal statistic, the phase portrait of the system over 600 months gives a distinct impression of something like a

The Economy as a Chaotic Growth Oscillator

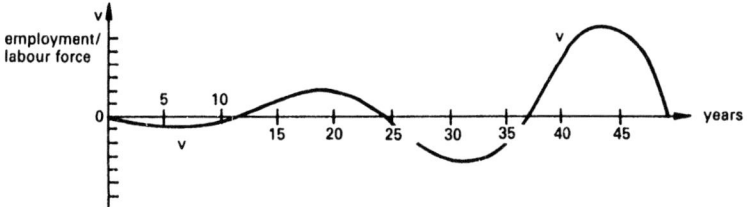

FIGURE 11.2

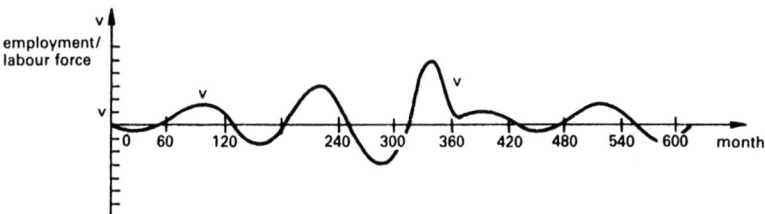

FIGURE 11.3(a)

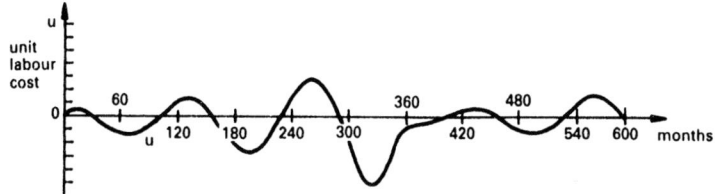

FIGURE 11.3(b)

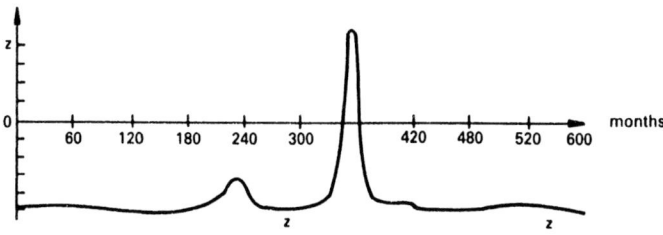

FIGURE 11.4

306 Development Economics and Models of Unstable Growth

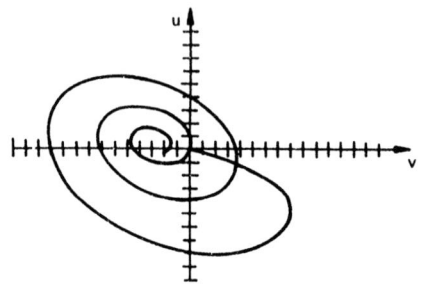

FIGURE 11.5

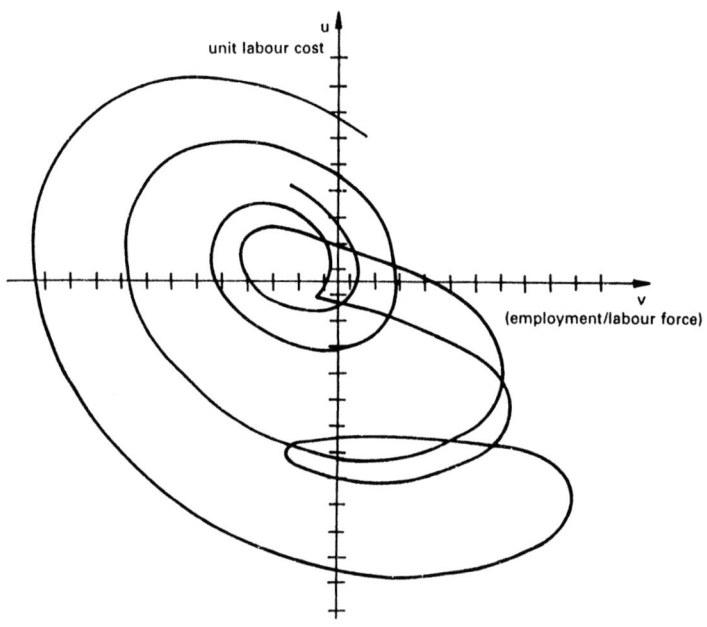

FIGURE 11.6

three-cycle mechanism. This superficial view is confirmed in Figure 11.7 where I have run a 2,400-month (200-year) simulation of the system, always with the same parameters and the same initial conditions. If undisturbed, the system will forever reproduce very nearly the same phase pattern. By contrast other parameters and other initial conditions can produce wildly irregular behaviour. Thus the simulation of Figure 11.8 over 1,200 months (100 years) was pro-

The Economy as a Chaotic Growth Oscillator 307

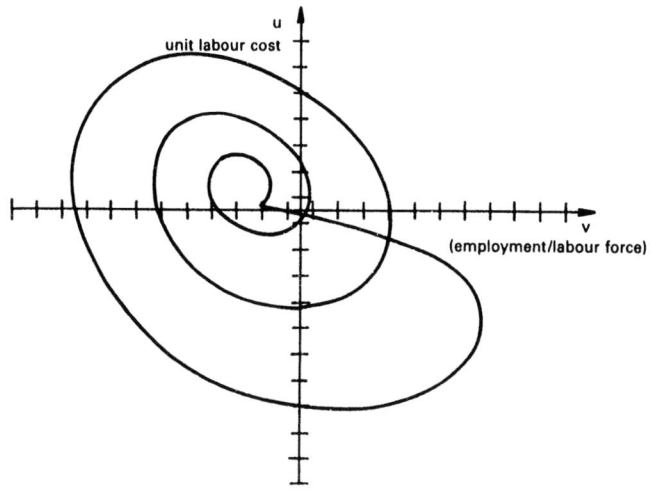

FIGURE 11.7

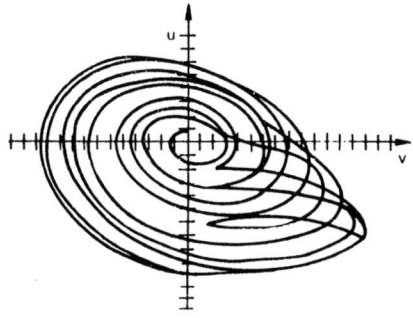

FIGURE 11.8

duced by the single perturbation of the control parameter c from 0.04 to 0.06; further variation could fill nearly the entire attractive basin with phase trajectories. While the simplicity of Figure 11.7 might encourage hope of an early solution to the problem of statistical estimation of such nonlinear chaotic models, Figure 11.8 must give some doubts. Social scientists are at a grave disadvantage compared to natural scientists, who have the possibility of using controlled experiments to determine parameters.

308 *Development Economics and Models of Unstable Growth*

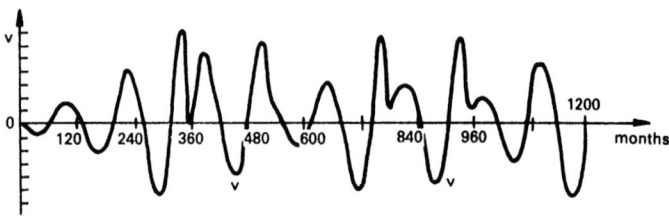

FIGURE 11.9

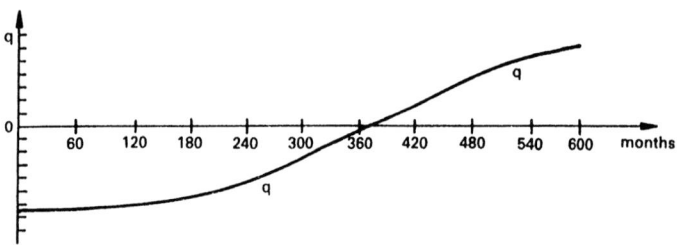

FIGURE 11.10(a)

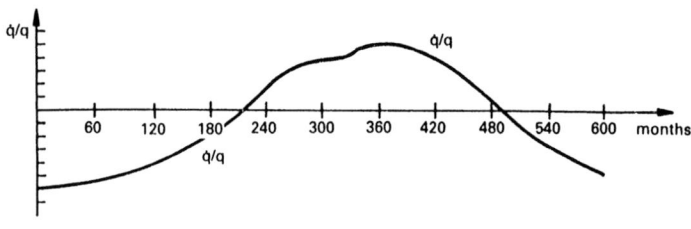

FIGURE 11.10(b)

INTRODUCING ECONOMIC GROWTH IN THE AGGREGATIVE ECONOMIC SYSTEM

The foregoing system has no growth, being constrained to a bounded region of state space. However, being formulated in terms of ratios, it is perfectly compatible with extension to include unbounded variables. To incorporate growth it suffices to introduce technical progress and/or growth of the labour force. Technology is the more important problem and I shall restrict the analysis to it.

There is widespread agreement that the Schumpeterian notion of 'swarms' of innovations can reasonably well be represented by logistic function, i.e.

$$\dot{k} = rk(1 - sk), \qquad (5)$$

where k is new innovational productive capacity. I assume that productivity growth is proportional to k, thus determining $\dot{a}_1/a_1$ and hence the growth of the real wage and u. The growth rate of output, $\dot{q}/q$, will be equal to the growth rate of employment, $\dot{v}/v$, plus the growth rate of productivity. A simulation of the growth of output over fifty years is given in Figure 11.9 and the modest irregularity of its growth rate in Figure 11.10.

REFERENCES

Birkhoff, G. D. (1931) 'Proof of the Ergodic Theorem', *Proceedings of the National Academy of Sciences of the USA*, 17, pp. 656–60.
Frisch, R. A. K. (1933) 'Propagation Problems and Impulse Problems in Dynamic Economics', in *Economic Essays in Honour of Gustav Cassel* (London: Allen and Unwin) pp. 171–205; reprinted in R. A. Gordon and L. R. Klein (eds), *Readings in Business Cycles* (London: Allen and Unwin, 1966).
Frisch, R. A. K. (1936) 'On the Notion of Equilibrium and Disequilibrium', *The Review of Economic Studies*, 3, pp. 100–5.
Goodwin, R. M. (1951) 'The Nonlinear Accelerator and the Persistence of Business Cycles', *Econometrica*, 19, pp. 1–17.
Goodwin, R. M. (1970) *Elementary Economics from a Higher Standpoint* (Cambridge: Cambridge University Press).
Goodwin, R. M. (1982) *Essays in Economic Dynamics* (London: Macmillan).
Goodwin, R. M. (1983) *Linear Economic Structures* (London: Macmillan).
Goodwin, R. M. (1989) *Essays in Non-Linear Dynamics* (Berne-Frankfurt-Las Vegas: Lange).
Goodwin, R. M., Krüger, M., and Vercelli, A. (eds) (1984) *Nonlinear Models of Fluctuating Growth* (New York: Springer).
Goodwin, R. M. and Punzo, L. F. (1987) *The Dynamics of a Capitalist Economy. A Multi-Sectoral Approach* (Cambridge, Polity Press: Oxford and New York, Basil Blackwell).
Le Corbeiller, Ph. (1933) 'Les systèmes autoentretenus et les oscillations de relaxation', *Econometrica*, I, pp. 328–32.
Kondratieff, N. D. (1925a) 'The Static and Dynamic View of Economics', *Quarterly Journal of Economics*, 39, pp. 575–83.

Kondratieff, N. D. (1925b) 'The Long Waves in Economic Life', *Review of Economics and Statistics*, 17, pp. 105–15.
Neumann, V. J. (1932) 'Proof of the Quasi-Ergodic Hypothesis', *Proceedings of the National Academy of Sciences of the USA*, 17, pp. 656–60.
Poincaré, H. (1881–6) 'Mémoire sur les courbes définies par une équation différentielle', *Journal de mathématiques pures et appliquées*.
Pol, van der, B. (1926) 'On Relaxation Oscillations', *Philosophical Magazine*, 2, pp. 978ff.
Rössler, O. E. (1976) 'Different Types of Chaos in Two Simple Differential Equations', *Zeitschrift für Naturforschung*, 31a, pp. 1664–70.
Rössler, O. E. (1977) 'Continuous Chaos', in H. Haken (ed.) *Synergetics: A Workshop* (Berlin: Springer Verlag).
Rössler, O. E. (1978) 'Chaos and Strange Attractors in Chemica Kinetics', in A. Pacault, and C. Vidal (eds) *Loin de l'équilibre* (Berlin: Springer Verlag).
Rössler, O. E. (1979) 'Continuous Chaos – Four Prototype Equations', *Annuals of the New York Academy of Sciences*, 316, pp. 376–92.
Rössler, O. E. (1983) 'The Chaotic Hierarchy', *Zeitschrift für Naturforschung*, 38a, pp. 788–801.
Schumpeter, J. A. (1934) *The Theory of Economic Development*, 46 in the Harvard Economic Studies Series (Cambridge, Mass.: Harvard University Press); reprinted by Oxford University Press, 1961.
Schumpeter, J. A. (1939) *Business Cycles* (New York: McGraw-Hill) 2 vols.
Schumpeter, J. A. (1954) *History of Economic Analysis* (London: Allen and Unwin).

12 Long-Run Changes in the Wage and Price Mechanisms and the Process of Growth*

Paolo Sylos-Labini

INTRODUCTION

If we compare the main characteristics of the growth process during the last century with our own we notice important differences, which must be taken into account in choosing the hypotheses on which to base our theoretical models. The differences between the wage and price mechanisms in the two periods are particularly interesting: it is to these mechanisms that I will devote my attention in this paper.

CHANGING TRENDS IN WAGES AND PRICES

It is worthwhile to reflect on the following data (Table 12.1) that refer to the United Kingdom and to the United States (see Appendix I for an explanation of the sources and data-gathering methods for this Table).

The contrast between the two centuries is spectacular: in the last century the long-run trend of all prices is decidedly downward, whereas in our century the trend is even more decidedly upward. During the last century there were, of course, short-run rises in prices or periods with relatively stable prices, but only in the early sixties was the three-year (1861–4) increase in prices considerable; an increase that is to be attributed mainly to a shock external to the economic system, that is, the American Civil War.

Whereas in the last century the rule was a fall in prices, and a rise the exception, in our century the opposite is true: the most important exception to the upward trend of prices is represented by the sharp fall during the first phase of the Great Depression, that is, the three

TABLE 12.1 Trends of prices and wages, 1800–1989

	Industrial prices (P_i)	Raw materials prices (P_{RM})	P_i/P_{RM}	Money wages	Cost of living	Real wages
United Kingdom						
1800	100	100	100	100	100	100
1861	30	62	48	110	88	125
1864	42	76	55	121	89	136
1897	22	37	59	165	66	250
1897	100	100	100	100	100	100
1913=1923	137	143	96	115	118	97
1929	115	123	98	116	109	106
1932	90	70	129	111	94	118
1938=1947	106	89	119	122	103	118
1989	1558	1195	130	3570	1706	209
United States						
1800	100			100	100	100
1861	69			160	53	302
1864	150			219	92	238
1897	53			190	49	388
1897	100	100	100	100	100	100
1913=1923	141	176	81	166	116	143
1929	137	176	77	180	117	154
1932	102	99	103	144	93	155
1938=1947	123	131	94	153	96	159
1989	530	418	127	1938	534	363

SOURCES
United Kingdom:
Mitchell, B. R. (1967) (in coll. with P. Deane), *Abstract of British Historical Statistics* (Cambridge: Cambridge University Press).
    Prices:
        1800–1913: Imlah, A. (1950) 'The Terms of Trade of the United Kingdom 1793–1913', *Journal of Economic History*, 2.
        1914–1965: Martin, K. and Thackeray, F. G. (1948) 'The Terms of Trade of Selected Countries, 1870–1938', *Bulletin of the Oxford Institute of Statistics*, November.
    Wages and cost of living:
        1800–1850 (estimates) and 1850–1860: Layton, W. T. and Crowther, G. (1935) *An Introduction to the Study of Prices* (London: Macmillan). Phelps Brown, E. H. and Hopkins, S. V. (1950) 'Wage-Rates in Five Countries. 1860–1939', *Oxford Economic Papers*, 2.

United States:
Historical Statistics of the United States. Colonial Times to 1957 (1960) (Washington DC: US Department of Commerce).

years 1929–32, a decline which, contrary to what occurred during almost all periods of falling prices in the last century, was accompanied in industry by a no less sharp fall in output (cf. Sylos-Labini, 1970, p. 96).

What are the reasons for the contrasting trends in prices? And why can the inversion of the trend be so precisely pinned down to 1897?

To explain the long-run fall in prices during the last century some economists have emphasized the role of gold, which in developed countries formed the basis of the monetary systems and which – if we except limited periods – turned out to be scarce with respect to the needs emerging from economic growth. While not fully rejecting this hypothesis,[1] I suggest that it is better to think of the process, described by Smith, consisting of an almost uninterrupted series of minor and major innovations, connected with a continuous interaction between innovations and the increase in the size of the market. In the Smithian process, the increase in productivity is accompanied by a slower increase in money wages, with the consequent fall of prices, precisely as happened in the last century. The Smithian process presupposes flexibility of both prices and wages and in both directions, upward and downward; thus it presupposes a situation not far from competition in the product and labour markets. The long-run upward trend of prices that emerged in our century is less easy to explain; even more difficult is the explanation of the inversion of the trend in 1897.

CONCENTRATION AND DIFFERENTIATION IN THE PRODUCT MARKETS AND THE GROWTH OF TRADE UNIONS

Let us start with the reasons for the inversion of trend. In the first place, 1897 is the lower turning point of a business cycle that took

---

Economic Report of the President, 1989 (1990) (Washington, DC: US Government).
The indices of money wages for the years 1800, 1861, 1864, 1897 and 1913 are estimates worked out on data not properly homogeneous by Dr Aviram Levy of the Research Bureau of the Bank of Italy, who has used the above-cited *Historical Statistics* of the United States. Dr Levy has also kindly supplied the most recent indices for the United Kingdom taken from the data bank of the Bank of Italy.

place when the large flow of agricultural products – grains and cattle products – entering the international markets from the New World had begun to shrink. In fact, that flow had been fed by the great innovations in means of transportation (railways and steamship) and had determined a sharp fall in agricultural prices since the early seventies; the slowing down of that flow was due primarily to the completion of the exploitation of the new lands rendered economically accessible thanks to those innovations. At the same time, the profound structural changes that were under way in both the product and the labour markets were probably surpassing a critical threshold and were becoming important enough to give rise to a new pattern in the price and wage mechanisms. Although the two mechanisms are strictly interrelated, we will discuss them separately, beginning with the product markets.

During the last century competition was the rule, not only in the markets of agricultural and mineral products, but also in those of industrial products. Presumably, it was not the rule in the service sector, where either imperfect competition or differentiated oligopoly were the prevailing market forms. But the service sector represented a relatively modest share of total employment. In the course of time both industry and services, but especially the latter, have gradually increased their relative weight. In industry as well as in certain services, like banking, during the last two decades of the last century and at the beginning of our own, a process of concentration took place and developed later on. With the increase in per-capita income a process of differentiation of needs and of goods occurred and continued to progress, especially after the twenties, owing to the spread of the mass media and of advertising. Both processes – concentration and differentiation – have given rise to forms of concentrated, differentiated and mixed oligopoly. In the markets of agricultural products and of many mineral products competitive forms are still the rule, although the behaviour of prices in such markets has been conditioned by public interventions and international agreements, adopted precisely to counterbalance the increasing market power of the firms of the other sectors. Such interventions, however, have slowed down but not overturned the trend, unfavourable to agriculture, of the ratio between industrial and agricultural prices; yet it is to be noticed that such a trend has stimulated the increase of productivity in agriculture.

Now, in competition price tends to be regulated by the cost of production, but in the long, not in the short run, during which it

Long-Run Changes in Wage and Price Mechanisms 315

depends on the variations of demand and supply. In oligopoly, instead, prices depend on costs even in the short run and not only in the long run; more precisely, in oligopoly the changes in the level of prices in the short run are given by the movements of direct costs, in the long run by total cost per unit.

Let us consider the question in more detail. In competition, if a firm succeeds in reducing the cost of production, it enjoys an extraordinary profit. But in competition there are no significant barriers to the entry of new firms, or to the expansion of existing firms. As a consequence, the extra profit is short-lived: the increase in output following the entry of the new firms or the expansion of the existing ones will bring the price down to the new, lower level of cost. Such a process implies that in the short run price depends on the interplay of the variations of demand and supply; in the long run the adjustment of price on the level of cost takes place through fluctuations. If price falls below the level of cost, then, a number of firms will reduce their output or certain firms will disappear from the market, so that price receives an upward push.

Things are different in oligopoly, where each firm has got market power, however limited. Each firm tends to regulate price on the basis of cost variations, provided that cost variations are common to all firms, in order not to lose its market share. As a rule, demand does not affect price simply because firms tend to regulate supply in such a way as to adapt it to demand variations – which is possible not only when output is to be reduced, but also when it is to be increased, since as a rule capacity is not fully utilized; thus demand and supply vary together and price is not affected by their variations. Price, then, is modified only if cost, particularly direct cost, varies. The main component of direct cost, that is, the cost of labour per unit of output, given by the ratio of wage rate to productivity, either remains stable or increases: only exceptionally does it decline, when productivity rises more rapidly than the wage rate. As for raw materials, if their prices go down, this decline can well be shifted onto prices, since this element of cost is common to all firms of a given industry. However, a fall in the price of a certain raw material seldom determines a fall in the price of the finished product, because it represents a relatively small share of direct cost and the cost of labour, which nowadays has a systematic tendency to rise, often fills up the space left by the fall in the cost of raw materials. In such circumstances the prices of the finished goods either remain stable or increase: only exceptionally do they diminish and, if so, only to a limited extent.

Under these circumstances, then, the long-run behaviour of prices of finished products depends mainly of the behaviour of the cost of labour. Now, hand-in-hand with the increase in the market power of firms in product markets, an increase has occurred in the market power of the workers and, in particular, of the trade unions.

THE SPREAD OF COLLECTIVE BARGAINING

The radical change in the price and wage mechanisms – more specifically getting over that critical threshold referred to above – occurred after collective bargaining had become the rule in the labour markets; and this, according to Hicks, in the United Kingdom took place in the nineties of the last century (Hicks, 1932, ch. VIII). The important point is that, with the spread of collective bargaining, wage cuts became more difficult and wage increases more frequent. In fact, in such circumstances wage increases tended to be common to all employers and this, as Hicks had pointed out, induced them not to resist too strongly the claims for those increases, since it was not too difficult to shift them onto prices, when they were higher than the increases in productivity – the situation was different when the bargaining was not collective but was left to individual firms and to scattered groups of workers.

The spread of collective bargaining had its origin in a long-running process of change. In particular, in the United Kingdom, where the trade union movement asserted itself earlier than elsewhere, in the last two or three decades of the last century real wages had increased rather rapidly, compared with the previous period (cf. Table 12.1); such an increase fostered the accumulation of funds in the hands of the trade unions, enabling them to finance relatively long strikes, not limited to individual firms but embracing whole industrial sectors. As for the employers, their bargaining power was strong as long as the unions did not exist or were small and economically weak. With the rise and the increasing market power of the unions, the balance became less unfavourable to workers in the labour markets, who were more and more often in a position to resist wage cuts, although for a relatively long period they were less capable of enforcing wage rises unless the cost of living was rising too. To counteract the trade unions in wage bargaining the employers also began to organize unions – mass production methods and large size of the firms in certain important industries have favoured the rise of both trade unions and of employers' associations. On the other hand, the increasing differentiation in the product markets, to be related with the rise in per capita income, has brought about an increasing differentiation in the skills of the workers and in the labour markets. As a consequence, the market power of workers has become higher, even independently of trade unions.

In conclusion, the fundamental change in the price and wage mechanisms is to be attributed, first, to the spread of collective bargaining – connected, to some extent, to the process of concentration in certain industries and, subsequently, to the spread of differentiation in the product and labour markets. To be precise, we have to distinguish between short-run and long-run variations of prices and wages. During the last century, in the short run prices were flexible both in the upward and in the downward direction, whereas in the long run the trend was downward. Money wages were also flexible, in the short run, in both directions but – as appears from the yearly data that can be found in the sources quoted in Appendix 1 – the flexibility was greater in the upward than in the downward direction, particularly in the second half of the century; in the long run money wages were either stable or rising, although less than productivity. In our century prices are flexible in the upward, not in the downward direction; and this is true in the short and in the long run: only rarely and in any case to a very limited extent do they show downward flexibility, in the short run: the Great Depression represents a special case, on which I will devote a few comments below (pp. 321–4). As for money wages, they are flexible only in the upwards direction. The long-run trend of both prices and wages is decidedly rising, but less so in the case of prices, due to the increase in productivity.

The turning point in the trend of prices that occurred at the end of the last century is to be attributed primarily to the fact that those changes in the wage and price mechanisms that I have mentioned above were surpassing a critical threshold – the system of collective bargaining, as I said, was rapidly spreading precisely in that period. At the end of the last century, however, as well as at the beginning of this one, important changes were also taking place in the financial sector, accelerated by the strains put on the credit markets by the increasing needs of the state – the South African War, for instance, took place just at this time (see Clapham, 1958, pp. 40 and 374–6). The said strains were originating, at least for a period, a demand pressure that contributed, directly or indirectly, to modify the wage and price trends – presumably that pressure reinforced the market power of the trade unions.

Two remarks are in order at this point. First, to explain the changes in the long-run trends of wages and prices: I attribute primary importance in the structural changes in the functioning of the two mechanisms, which can be included among the 'real' factors; but I accept the suggestion of Paolo Savona, according to whom the 'financial' factors that I have just mentioned and to which he has drawn my attention, have also played a relevant role. In my view, the two kinds of factors interact with each other and are to be considered together. In other words, the two explanatory hypotheses concerning the 'real' and the 'financial' factors are not alternative, but complementary.

Secondly, in order to explain the precise timing of the change in the trend of wages and prices in the nineties we have to consider not only the spread of collective bargaining but also the behaviour of raw material prices, that show an upward trend starting from 1898, owing, probably, to the slowing-down in the development of railways and steamship, which in the second half of the last century had made the products of lands and mines of the new world economically accessible to the international markets, even those from areas very far from the sea.

After the Second World War the trend of prices has become much steeper than before. The inflationary pressure, fundamentally due to the behaviour of the labour cost, has been intensified by the crisis in the international monetary system. In fact, the abandonment, in 1971, of the system instituted by the Bretton Woods agreements and of fixed exchange parities has made speculation both in foreign exchange markets and raw material markets much stronger, with the consequence that the variability of raw material prices has increased several times with respect to the previous period (Sylos Labini, 1984, ch. 6). Now, when the prices of finished goods rise as a result of a rise in the prices of raw materials, money wages increase; but wages do not diminish – on the contrary, as a rule they continue to increase – when the prices of raw materials fall, so that such a fall seldom affects the prices of finished goods. This is why the higher variability of raw material prices, originated by the crisis in the international monetary system, has imparted an additional upward push to prices in all countries.

The wage and price mechanisms working in the past and originally described by Adam Smith were characterized by a relative stability, in the long run, of money wages and by a downward trend of prices, whereas the new mechanisms, that fully asserted themselves only after the Second World War, are characterized by relatively stable prices and by rising money wages or by money wages rising more than prices – the divergence depending on the rise in productivity.

INDUSTRIAL PRICES AND PRICES OF RAW MATERIALS

In our century, in contrast with what was taking place in the last one, the behaviour of industrial prices is radically different from that of agricultural and mineral raw materials both in the short and in the long run. To fix the ideas we can say that in the last century the behaviour of both categories of prices could be formalized with the following two equations, the former for the short run, the latter for the long run (I trust that the two equations are consistent with the views summarized by Ricardo in Chapter XXX of his *Principles* – 'On the Influence of Demand and Supply on Prices'):

$$\text{short run } \hat{P}_s = a_s + b_s\hat{D} - c_s\hat{S} \qquad (1)$$

$$\text{long run } \hat{P}_l = a_l + b_l\hat{C} \qquad (2)$$

where P is the price index in a given country, D is an index of demand, S an index of supply, C is an index of total cost per unit, the cap over the variables indicates a rate of change in the unit of time. For the short run it is fitting to use yearly data; for the long run three-years moving averages.

In our century the above equations remain valid for raw materials (where an appropriate index of demand is given by the index of world industrial output); for the prices of industrial goods, instead, the following two equations apply:

$$\text{short run: } \hat{P}_s = a_s + b_s W/\pi + c_s\hat{RM} + d_s\hat{P}_{int-s} \qquad (3)$$

$$\text{long run: } \hat{P}_l = a + b\hat{C} + c\hat{P}_{int-l} \qquad (4)$$

where W is the wage rate, π the output per man-hour, RM the index of raw material prices, P_{int} is the price index, corrected for the exchange rate, of the same category of goods in the international markets and

$$C = \alpha W/\pi + \beta RM + \varphi OC$$

is the index of total cost per unit (OC is the index of overhead cost per unit, given by salaries of white collars and by costs related to fixed capital). (Equation (3) implies that the price leaders follow, for changing prices, one type or another of a *mark up* over variable costs.)

In equations (1) and (2), which in the last century were valid for all sorts of markets, the variable P_{int} did not appear. In fact, the markets of industrial goods were those of advanced countries and those of raw materials were largely controlled by the British financial institutions. In that time the gold standard was ensuring a monetary unit common to all the advanced countries and the exchange rates were fluctuating within very narrow limits. In such circumstances there was no need of introducing the above mentioned index (P_{int}) among the explanatory variables of the price index of a given country. Today for the international markets of raw materials, equation (1) is to be completed by introducing the weighted average of the quotations of the dollar in the main financial markets (Sylos Labini, 1984, p. 149).

Equations (3) and (4) apply to industrial markets in which today oligopolistic conditions prevail; in such markets the fact that price depends on cost not only in the long but also in the short run affects also its long-run behaviour, since, when in the short run a fall in demand takes place, this fall does not affect the price; and when, again in the short run, the raw material prices fall, the upward pressure of wages – as I have already remarked – often fills, at least in part, that space and thus puts an obstacle to the diminution in the prices of finished goods that would take place owing to the fall in raw material prices. Moreover, the prices of raw materials as a rule fall when industrial output declines and in such circumstances labour productivity slows down: this contributes to the increase in labour cost per unit.

The long-run trend of both categories of prices – industrial goods and raw materials – is upwards due to the behaviour of wages and of overhead costs and, in the case of raw materials, also of the behaviour of the means of production originating in industry. However, since the market power of the firms as a rule is greater in industry than in the primary sector, where a situation approaching competition often obtains, the upward trend of prices tend to be somewhat steeper in the industrial sector, so that the terms of trade tend to vary in favour of industrial goods – just the opposite of the trend

Long-Run Chances in Wage and Price Mechanisms

observable in the last century (see Table 12.1). The upward trend of the terms of trade is even pronounced when we consider only the prices of raw materials produced in underdeveloped countries, since in such countries the market power of workers is very limited and wages tend to increase more slowly than in advanced countries, or not to increase at all. Thus, in the two centuries the behaviour of the two categories of prices is decidedly different both in the long and in the short run. In the former case the difference appears in the behaviour of the terms of trade (see Table 12.1); in the latter, in the greater variability of raw material prices, due mainly to the influence of demand, a variability that has become even greater after the 1971 crisis of the international monetary system (see Figures 12.6 and 12.7).

Referring to Table 12.1, I call the reader's attention to the behaviour of industrial prices in the years preceding the Second World War: there is a pronounced decline during the first stage of the Great Depression, from 1929 to 1932 (-22 per cent in the U.K. and -25 per cent in the USA); the decline appears less pronounced but still remarkable if we consider the period 1929–38 (-8 per cent and -10 per cent respectively). This behaviour fully corresponds to the 'new' price mechanism operating in our century, since it is strongly affected by the much sharper fall in the prices of raw materials, which represent a sizable share of the variable cost of industrial goods.

THE INTERWAR PERIOD AND THE GREAT DEPRESSION: COMPARISON BETWEEN THE UNITED KINGDOM AND THE UNITED STATES

The violent and irregular oscillations of wages and prices during the two wars are clearly to be related to the economic and social upheavals following the First World War (including, in the United Kingdom, the attempts at revaluating the pound) and, then, the Great Depression and its aftermaths. The disciplining power of unemployment on wage movements, which forms the essence of the famous Phillips curve, seems to be lower after the First World War than in the fifty years preceding it. It is true that Phillips (1958) purports to show that his curve generally applies even in the period 1913–48 and 1948–57. But in the first of these two periods the deviations from his curve are numerous and relevant. As for the second period (1948–57), the points relating wage changes and unemployment follow a very steep line – almost vertical.[2] After the Second World War unemployment again attains statistical significance in the wage equation when we also consider the cost of living, as Lipsey has done (1960). In particular periods, in addition to unemployment and the cost of living, we also have to introduce dummies to take into account above-normal strike activity as measured by the number of day lost for strikes. However, in certain periods unemployment does not come out as significant even if considered together with the cost of living. In fact, it seems that the disciplining power of unemployment has been reduced not only by the market power of unions but also, and even more, by the influence of the political parties in some way connected with labour movements: thus, even in our time unemployment becomes significant in the wage equation when the said influences become weaker. As for the cost of living, it was significant but not important before the First World War (see Appendix III); afterwards it has become more and more relevant, as a consequence of the increasing market power of the unions, but who have been able to obtain adjustments of wages to the movements in the cost of living even in the short run. (This was not the case at the times of the classical economists: in that time the changes in the cost of living did affect wages but, as a rule, not in the short run.)

Let us consider the interwar period more carefully. If we put aside the years 1919–22, seriously disturbed by post-war adjustments, and compare the behaviour of wages in the United Kingdom and in the United States, we notice that the most violent oscillations occurred in the United States (see Figures 12.2 and 12.3): the variations of wages and prices are very limited in the United Kingdom. This, in my view, is further evidence of the role played by the trade union movement and by the use of collective bargaining: until 1932–3 this role was much more important in the United Kingdom than in the United States, where only under Roosevelt, after 1932, did the trade union movement gain real strength. In fact, from 1922 and until 1929 – a period of relatively favourable economic conditions, characterized by a particularly rapid increase of productivity in the United States – money wages increased very little (on the average, only 1 per cent per year). Considering the sustained increase of productivity and the restrictions to immigration from Europe introduced after the First World War, money wages should have increased more and not less than in the past. This did not happen because the market power of the unions was very weak, owing to the limitations put on the activity of the most radical leaders, especially after the outbreak of the Bolshevik revolution in Russia. One can presume that even the

Long-Run Chances in Wage and Price Mechanisms 323

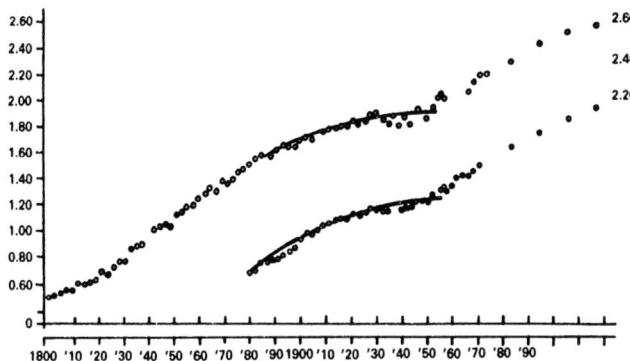

Industrial production (above); national income (below)
(semilogarithmic scale)

FIGURE 12.1   *United Kingdom: industrial production and national income*

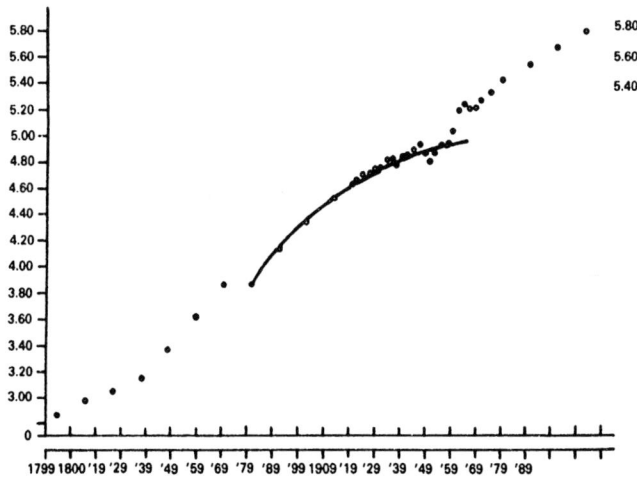

FIGURE 12.2   *United States national income*
(semilogarithmic scale)

SOURCES   For the data of both countries ending in 1950: P. Sylos Labini, 1954. For the more recent data: United Kingdom: *Relazione annuale, Appendice,* Banca d'Italia, various years; United States, *Economic Report of the President,* 1988, Washington, 1989.

restrictions to immigration from Europe – which, strictly speaking, were against the economic interest of the industrialists – were introduced mainly out of fear that a good number of the immigrating workers would be permeated by left-wing ideologies. Elsewere I have maintained that relatively stationary wages coupled with rapidly increasing productivity were a source of an extraordinary increase in the share of profits in the national income, and that such an increase was determining an important precondition of the Great Depression (Sylos Labini, 1984, chs. 8 and 9). Then, during the Great Depression, quite differently from the United Kingdom, in the United States money wages were severely cut: by 6 per cent in 1931 and by 14 per cent in 1932. It is true that prices fell in the United States more than in the United Kingdom; but, as is well known, wages and prices are strictly connected, so that to some extent a diminution of the latter can be attributed to a reduction of the former. From Figure 12.3 it appears that money wages increased considerably in 1934 – more than 14 per cent; but this is clearly the effect of the abolition in labour contracts of the clause forbidding the workers to strike or even to join a union: this clause was declared illegal by section 7A of the National Industrial Recovery Act of 1933 (see Fearon, 1987, p. 64; my colleague Ester Fano called my attention to these developments).

After 1934 money wages did not fall any more, both because of the relatively improved economic conditions and for further legal measures, in particular the Wagner Act of 1935, that decidedly increased the market power of the unions.

In short, wages have become more and more rigid downward and more and more flexible upward in all industrialized countries, particularly after the end of the Second World War, so much so that in the last forty years I do not know of any instance of a fall in money wages in industrialized countries. For a long time, managers have taken the downward rigidity of wages and their upward flexibility for granted: being assured by collective bargaining that no competitor could obtain an advantage through a wage cut and, to the contrary, being pressed by claims of wage increases, firms could generally decide not to reduce prices of finished goods or decide (within limitations) to reduce them only when substantial diminutions of raw material prices occur or when wages increase less than productivity. As a result, the downward rigidity of wages has been accompanied by an increasing downward rigidity of prices of finished products – this process being favoured by the increasing spread of non-competitive market forms outside agriculture and mining.

AGGREGATE DEMAND AND THE PROCESS OF GROWTH

Technical and organizational progress gives rise to a systematic increase in productivity and in production; in turn, the increase in production stimulates inventions and innovations and the increase of productivity engenders the almost uninterrupted interaction process that characterizes modern capitalism. The increase in productivity leads to an increase in real incomes; in the last century this was occurring via declining prices, money wages remaining stable or rising less rapidly than productivity; in our century this is caused by increasing money incomes, prices remaining stable, or via money incomes increasing more rapidly than prices.

Elsewhere I have tried to analyze the two mechanisms systematically, in which the variations of relative prices and of relative incomes play a fundamental role (Sylos Labini, 1969, chs. VI–VII). Here I intend to point out, in extremely concise terms, the role of demand in the two mechanisms.

If prices fall as a consequence of productivity increases, real demand rises automatically. Considering a given commodity and assuming an elasticity of demand equal to unity, a fall of 10 per cent of the price due to the increase of productivity automatically determines an increase by a similar proportion of the quantity absorbed by the market. If initially the price is 10 and output is equal to 100 units, the aggregate demand is equal to 1000 units; if price falls from 10 to 9 the quantity absorbed by the market – real demand – rises from 100 to 111 and aggregate money demand remains equal to 1000. But if price does not fall when productivity increases, real demand remains steady and the increase in productivity will determine a decline in employment. Real demand will rise if, assuming no price changes, money demand increases in proportion to productivity. If, then, the price rises due to a cost push, real demand will increase on condition that money demand increases more than price. But money demand – this is the point – does not increase automatically: it increases if money incomes increase. It is not enough, however, that labour incomes increase since, as a source of demand, they do not represent more than 70 per cent of total income. On the other hand, labour incomes as a rule are driven upward, at least in part, by an increase in the wage rate; if this rate rises more than productivity, however, in an open economy the consequence is a profit squeeze. All incomes should increase together with productivity, including labour incomes. This can take place through investment carried out in the expectation of profits created by innovations; alternatively, the rise in aggregate demand can originate in public expenditure. Both kinds of expenditures – private investment and public expenditure – can feed the growth of aggregate money demand. However, whereas it is possible to regulate the flow of public expenditure, it is not possible to regulate the flow of private investment; this means that, in conditions in which the growth of aggregate money demand has acquired an essential role in the growth process, public expenditure is certain to play an important role in the dynamic support of aggregate demand.

Whatever the source of additional demand, the new mechanism by which the fruits of technical progress are distributed – increasing money incomes and stable prices – tends to worsen the inequalities in income distribution; in fact, falling prices affect all income receivers, whereas this is not the case with increasing money incomes: even the distribution of labour incomes can become more unequal, since in 'privileged' industries not only profits but also wages and salaries tend, at least in certain periods, to increase more than in other industries (see Sylos Labini, 1969, ch. VI). Even more serious is the fact that the latter mechanism tends to slow down the process of growth, because – among other things – only the cost reduction originated by technical progress remains in operation: the cost reduction induced by the fall in the prices of the means of production tends to disappear.

Increasing inequalities, slowing down in the process of growth: are there empirical indications of these tendencies?

It is hard to find such indications for the former tendency (see, however, Sylos Labini, 1984, pp. 221 and 240; World Bank, 1981, Table 25; 1988, Table 30). It is less difficult to detect indications of a tendency toward stagnation. In my view, such a tendency becomes more and more evident from the end of the last century onward in the most important capitalist countries of the time, that is, the United Kingdom and the United States: the Great Depression that started in 1929 occurred when such a tendency had already asserted itself – of course, through the ups and downs of the business cycles. My thesis is that such a tendency was broken by a gigantic dose of a Keynesian-type recipe imposed by the Second World War and then by a new economic policy, adopted in a changed institutional and organizational pattern.

INSTITUTIONAL CHANGES AND THE MONETARY AND FISCAL POLICIES

In the new situation that emerged after a long series of changes, public intervention in the economy has become more and more important. Among the structural changes I can mention the reorganization of the banking system; the expansion or the creation of institutions for social welfare; the regulation or the nationalization of large-scale public utilities; the control or the promotion, carried out by the State, of certain productive activities which have a strategic role in economic growth. In certain countries like Italy, where the economic system was particularly weak, during the Great Depression the state had to rescue large banks and large industrial firms that were near bankruptcy, which would have had disastrous effects on the level of employment. (In Italy the state holding company IRI was created during this period.) It is well to point out that the monetary system based on the gold standard, which presupposed full flexibility of wages and prices and implied a sort of automatic control over money circulation, entered into an irreversible crisis: the inconvertible bank note became the basic money unit and money was managed at the discretion of the central bank; this – as has been correctly said – amounted to the nationalization of money. After the Second World War the methods and means of money management were greatly improved and money was used more and more systematically by the central authority to try and reduce the amplitude of the business cycles and to support the growth of aggregate demand. Money management, then, is relevant mainly in the short run, whereas fiscal policy is important in the long run. Money management, however, can follow different strategic lines depending on the monetary regime – convertible or inconvertible bank notes and, in the latter case, fixed or flexible exchange rate – and in this way it becomes relevant also in the long run. On the other hand, since the Second World War money management has become more and more connected with fiscal policy via public bonds which, due to the large and increasing share of public expenditure in national income, have acquired an important role: the main link is given by open market operations with public bonds.

The aim of systematically supporting the growth of aggregate demand in order to sustain growth has been pursued mainly through the expansion of public expenditure, fed by a combination of civilian and military expenses. If we consider the whole period following the Second World War in all Western countries, including the United

States, civilian expenses have increased more – as a rule, much more – than military expenses; and civilian expenses have consisted principally in transfer payments for social welfare, which tend to reduce inequalities in income distribution. In fact, with the increase of average per capita income it became possible to devote more resources to social welfare; at the same time, the influence was increasing of ideologies and theories – like the Keynesian theory – favourable to a process of democratization and of reduction in the inequalities in income distribution was increasing. This influence was backed by the trade unions, the power of which was increasing, at least until recently, and by political parties connected with trade unions. Such movements have been very pronounced in certain countries (like the United Kingdom and the Scandinavian countries), less pronounced in others like the United States and Japan, where the role of dynamic demand-support carried out elsewere by public expenditure has been largely played by foreign demand.

Let us consider Figures 12.1 and 12.2 and Table 12.2. The data of Figures 12.1 and 12.2 seem to show in both countries since the beginning of our century a tendency to stagnation, that is, a progressive slowing down of the rate of increase of total output, a tendency interrupted at the outbreak of the Second World War and even earlier in the United Kingdom.

To be sure, the data do not allow a univocal interpretation; particularly doubtful is the slowing down of growth in the United States before the First World War. Yet there can be no doubt that the twenty-one years between the two World Wars were a prevailingly depressed period: it was precisely in this time that the tendency to stagnation, already considered as a possibility by the classical economists, became a theoretical problem for several modern scholars. In any case the said data – which have to be considered together with the study of economic history – are consistent with the hypothesis that the tendency to stagnation was emerging even before the outbreak of the First World War. In my interpretation, this tendency is to be related to the structural transformations in the wage and price mechanisms; that tendency – again, in my interpretation – was broken owing to the swift rise in public expenditure which, after the world war, was occurring in a rapidly changing institutional framework. In the United States the increase in the ratio of public expenditure to gross national product since the beginning of this century has been impressive indeed (Table 12.2); the acceleration of this increase began at the outbreak of the Great Depression and

TABLE 12.2 Public expenditure in the United States 1903-87

	Public expenditure % of GNP		GNP	Civilian expenditure	Military expenditure
1903	7.4	1949	100	100	100
1913	7.7	1980	1050	1589	1100
1929	10.5				
1939	18.5				
1949	23.1	1980	100	100	100
1980	32.6	1987	166	171	206
1987	34.8	1949-87	1743	2717	2266

intensified after the Second World War. From 1949 until 1987 civilian public expenditure has increased more rapidly than national product. Although from 1949 to 1980 military expenses increased less rapidly than civilian expenses but more rapidly than national product, after 1980 those expenses outstripped both civilian expenses and national product. It is also to be noted that, between 1980 and 1987, in spite of the efforts made by the Reagan administration, not only military but also civilian expenses increased more than income, though by a small margin. As for military expenses, because of the current international *détente* they tend to increase more slowly than in the past or even to decrease, a tendency that can emerge in all countries, though not immediately. This, coupled with the process of liberalization in Eastern Europe, could open up great possibilities of development for the world economy.

THE KEYNESIAN THEORY

In the years following the end of the First World War it appeared clearly that wage and price flexibility, when needed, was much more difficult to achieve than in the past; at that time, discussions on the consequences of wage and price rigidity were numerous, without, however, enquiring into the reasons why that rigidity had increased. Keynes was fully aware that the downward flexibility of wages and prices could not be taken for granted, and in 1925 he criticized policy tending to restore the pre-war gold standard (Keynes, 1925) – a policy that required a sharp reduction of both wages and prices. Moreover, when unemployment had become a problem, he criticized the view that a wage cut would have been a proper remedy and advocated an active monetary and fiscal policy. He maintained that only a *general* wage reduction could have had a significantly positive effect on employment (Patinkin, 1987); but he recognized – without ever going into the reasons for this state of affairs – that this was impractical, except in 'authoritarian' societies (Keynes, 1936, p. 269). Keynes had criticized the proposal of a wage cut and advocated an active policy well before 1936; but only in the *General Theory* did he develop a systematic theoretical analysis for supporting his contentions. In fact, the structural changes occurring in the first two decades of this century and accelerated by the First World War had made the automatic re-equilibrating mechanism unworkable and made an active monetary and, even more, an active fiscal policy necessary to stimulate the increase of effective demand – these policies being the alternative to all-round downward wage and price flexibility. This was vigorously recognized by Keynes in his *General Theory*, in spite of the fact that he was thinking essentially with reference to the short run. It would be wrong, however, to believe that without Keynes the need for a policy in support of the aggregate demand would not have been perceived. It is enough to reflect on the experience of Nazi Germany to realize that this is not so: Hjalmar Schacht had understood the essence of the Keynesian theory a few years before the publication of the *General Theory*. On an abstract plane – and from a completely different political standpoint – the same statement can be made in reference to Michal Kalecki (Kalecki, 1971, ch. 1, orig. Polish ed. 1933) and to the so-called Stockholm School of the early thirties (Ohlin, 1937). After the Second World War the Keynesian ideas influenced more or less strongly a large number of economists and of politicians in Western countries for at least three decades; the emphasis was on fiscal policy and the expansion of public expenditure was often justified by referring to those ideas.

A matter of reflection. Keynes did not show a particular interest in historical changes, in sharp contrast with Schumpeter; yet, paradoxically, it now appears that Keynes interpreted the structural changes under way much better than Schumpeter.

In the new conditions the role of the state has considerably increased, first of all via public expenditure. It has been social expenses which have had the most rapid increase; Keynes himself (Keynes, 1980b, vol. XI) had contributed during the war to the preparation of that line of social policy that soon after the war had in the famous 'Beveridge Plan' its principal point of reference (Beveridge, 1946). With the systematic increase of the national product, fiscal receipts can increase at a similar or at an even higher rate, due to the progressive character of income taxes and, in certain periods, also to the fiscal drag caused by inflation. It is possible to finance a steady expansion of the so-called welfare state, of which medical care and pensions are the main pillars. Thus, the ratio of public expenditure to gross national product tends to increase: up to a point such an increase can be favourable to the growth process. However, it seems that when the ratio has reached a critical threshold – say 40–50 per cent – it can keep its favourable effects only if it ceases to increase; if, on the contrary, it continues to rise more rapidly than national product, then owing to the progressive character of taxation, public expenditure creates serious difficulties for the growth process, since it reduces for an increasing number of individuals or firms the incentive to make greater efforts to increase their earnings. If, to avoid such an outcome, the government accepts an increasing public deficit, then the need to sell a growing number of public bonds pushes up the interest rates. The ensuing heavy burden due to interest payments limits the range of choices of the government and hinders investment for firms.

The root of the problem lies in the fact that social expenditure, once decided on the basis of certain laws, tends to increase at a rather stable rate. It is also possible to say that social expenditure tends to follow the pattern established during the period of 'fat cows' and even, for a time, to increase more quickly than national product – in years of 'lean cows' expenses for subsidies of various kinds tend to grow. The situation is worsened by the fact that a non-negligible share of social welfare expenses, particularly those for medical care, consists mainly of services, whose prices tend to rise at a rate similar to that of wages and, thus, much more rapidly than the prices of commodities;[3] also for this reason, the rate of increase of social expenses, given the legislation, tends to be higher than the rate of increase of national product, which includes both commodities and services; this means that to keep social services stable in terms of purchasing power, social expenses have to increase more than GNP.

In several countries the increase of fiscal receipts has not kept pace with the rapid increase of expenses. The ensuing fiscal crisis has especially hit those countries in which the welfare state had made the most marked progress; such a crisis has been faced both by trying to raise tax receipts and to reduce public expenses: it appears that the latter line of action is no less difficult and is even more impracticable than the former. In any case, a moment arrives in which the rate of expansion of public expenditure in one way or another should be made equal or, at least for a number of years, should be pushed below the rate of increase of national product. This implies a quasi-stability of social welfare expenses in terms of purchasing power and a radical change in the institutions of the welfare state to improve the quality of the services and to concentrate the services financed by the government on the lower-bracket income receivers, leaving certain basic needs of persons belonging to the other brackets to be met by mechanisms of a private nature, such as insurance.

The fiscal crisis of the state, inducing governments to sell increasing amounts of bonds, has pushed up interest rates to levels never seen before in the economic history of advanced countries. In the United States the rise in interest rates was also prompted by a public deficit which in this case was due primarily to an increase in military expenditure coupled with a decision not to resort to an increase in fiscal pressure, which, in the United States, would have been perfectly possible. Given the relevance of that country in the international economy, the rise in interest rates very soon pushed up the rates of interest all over the world, with particularly disastrous effects on Third World countries. (The problem of external debt of these countries has become very serious mainly due to the great increase in their burden represented by interest payments.)

Going back to the fiscal crisis of the state, Table 12.3 can illustrate the main features of such a crisis; this table refers to Italy, but I believe that in the other industrialized countries – with the possible exception of Japan – the variables examined follow a similar pattern. (Let us remember that in the last ten to fifteen years economic growth has slowed down in all these countries.)

The divergence between the rate of increase of national product and that of public expenditure is quite relevant in the years of 'fat cows' (1963–73); it becomes acute in 1973–83; in the last period we observe a decline in the rate of increase of both public expenditure and receipts, but more in the former than in the latter. In spite of this the public deficit is still critical. I observe that the proportion of public expenditure to gross national product, which in the United States is 35 per cent, hovers around 50 per cent in Italy; in Sweden it is as high as 56 per cent: considering this figure, it is not surprising that the Swedish welfare state is in the midst of a serious crisis.

TABLE 12.3 Italy: economic growth, public expenditure and fiscal receipts (yearly rates of change of the variables expressed in real terms)

	1963–73	1973–83	1983–9
Gross national product	5.1	1.8	3.0
Public expenditure	6.1	6.6	2.9
Fiscal receipts	5.2	5.4	4.7

CONCLUDING REMARKS

In this paper I have concentrated my attention on the changes undergone by wage and price mechanisms in the last two centuries. Empirically, the consequences of these changes can be seen by examining the behaviour of wages and prices in the last century and in our own. If we reflect on such behaviour as shown from the few data reported in Table 12.1 and from the many data that can be found in the statistical sources cited in Appendix I, it is quite unbelievable that a great number of economists still assume, as a natural thing to do, full flexibility of wages and prices both in the downward and upward direction and both in the short and long run.

The change in wage and price mechanisms is only one aspect of a process of transformations that has affected all of economic life. The transformations have been so radical as to make legitimate the question of whether there is much in common between the laissez-faire capitalism of the last century and the present-day system. The truth is 'the end of laissez-faire' was prepared long before Keynes published the pamphlet with that title (Keynes, 1926). In the new system, which has been the result, not of a predetermined design, but of a long structural and cultural evolution, government intervention in economic life has acquired great importance. We might say that the optimum combination between the market and the state has shifted toward the state. In several countries, however, such a shift seems to have gone too far and we are now witnessing a reaction in favour of the market. This reaction is likely to bring to a halt the expansion of the public area and to modify the role of the state in several respects, so as to render it more consistent with the functioning of the market. But it seems unlikely that such a reaction can reduce in absolute or even in relative terms the weight of the state in the economy.

From the point of view of economic theory, the foregoing analysis shows that it is utterly unrealistic to assume full and bi-directional flexibility of wages and prices. We can assume such a flexibility only for prices of raw materials, whereas in the case of the prices of finished goods and of wages of all sort we have to assume flexibility only in the upward direction. Otherwise, our models will be deprived of any interpretative power and we will be wasting our time in purely intellectual games. But before making the said assumptions, we have to explain why and how wages and prices behave in that way, what are the impulses behind those movements and what are the consequences for the process of growth. In this respect modern theory seems to be very defective.

A general remark. Most economists, implicitly or explicitly, are in the habit of regarding trade unions as an obstacle in the way of the efficient working of the economic system; and many economists, at least in these days, consider government, with few exceptions, as a brake, not as a stimulus, on economic growth. Now, the market power of the unions has been systematically increasing since the last hundred years (it seems that the market power of the unions has been declining in the last two decades, but the market power of an increasing number of groups of workers has been increasing, due to the increasing differentiation in the supply of labour). During the same period government intervention, too, has been systematically increasing – the recent reaction against such intervention has only slowed down, not inverted, this trend. It is worth noting that the two trends have been accompanied, not by a reduction, but, on the average and over the long period, by an increase in the speed of growth and, after the end of the Second World War, by the transformation of most recessions into simple decelerations of the process of growth. To be sure this is surprising if one adheres to the idea that there is an equilibrium position of the economic system that represents an optimum – an equilibrium which presupposes perfect competition, perfect mobility of both capital and labour and full flexibility of wages and prices; in such a conception every departure from the equilibrium position represents a departure from the optimum, i.e. an inferior level of efficiency. But if one recognizes that the factors conditioning a position of static equilibrium are different from those determining growth and the rate of increase, not the level, of efficiency is what matters, then the outlook changes radically. In particular, if one accepts the view briefly presented in this paper, then it is not surprising that the performance of the economy has been better than in the past in a time in which an increasing number of sectors were becoming more and more distant from perfect competition, and trade unions and public intervention were becoming more and more important. Indeed, the downward rigidity of wages and prices – an expression of the deep structural changes that have taken place in the industrialized economies – has made necessary, for the prosecution of growth, the systematic expansion of money demand; and wage increases and increases in public spending have been important sources of such an expansion. It is true that if both increases exceed certain speeds, new problems arise and new obstacles appear for the process of growth. But this is another question.

NOTES

* This paper was discussed in a meeting of the Research Group on 'Market forms, institutions and economic growth', whose activities are financed by the Ministry of Public Education. Particular thanks – not implying responsibility – are due to Salvatore Biasco, Giorgio Fuà, Paolo Savona and Mario Tonveronachi for their critical comments and suggestions.
1. The hypothesis that the production of the precious metal used as money affects the long run behaviour of prices can be taken into consideration only with reference to the time in which bank money did not exist or was of limited relevance. Things are different when convertible bank notes and deposits become the main monetary instruments (the problem disappears with inconvertible bank notes). In fact, in the last century bank money was becoming more and more important. It is true that banknotes, as a rule, were convertible and that gold reserves were putting a ceiling on their issue. But a ceiling does imply a rigid proportion; moreover, the ratio between gold reserves and banknotes was declining, since the number of people willing to use notes instead of gold coins was progressively increasing. Similar observations apply to deposits and to the reserves in banknotes that the commercial banks have to keep to insure convertibility of their liabilities. For these reasons the hypothesis that in the last century the scarcity of gold played a role in the long-run fall of prices has, at best, a very limited explanatory power.
2. The 'vertical' Phillips curve, then, is to be seen not on a purely abstract plane, but in the framework of the relations between wage changes and unemployment which can assume different forms in the course of the historical time.
3. For instance, after the Second World War in the United States money wages increased twelve times, the prices of services about ten times and consumer prices for commodities by a little more than four times. If we consider that in the tertiary sector the increase in productivity, however measured, is very low, then it is no wonder that the trend of the price of services and that of wages largely coincide.

APPENDIX I: COMMENTS ON TABLE 12.1 AND ON FIGURES 12.3–7

Table 12.1 Trend of Prices and Wages, 1800–1989

To eliminate the effects on prices and wages of the two world wars – two great shocks external to the economic system – I used the 1913 and the 1938 indices for the years 1923 and 1947. The movements of the cost of living indices diverge from those of wholesale prices of finished goods ('industrial prices') because the former include the margins related to the trade of commodities, the prices of private and public services and rents. It should be remembered that in the last century industrial commodities were much less numerous and much more homogeneous than is the case nowadays; but the relative homogeneity of commodities is precisely one of the main reasons that justify the view that in the last century competition was the prevailing market form in industry – even today it is the prevailing market form in agriculture and (with several exceptions) in mining.

As I observe in the text, the sharp rise of prices in the years 1861–4 is to be attributed to that violent external shock given by the American Civil War; that shock was felt not only in the United States, but also, with a lesser intensity, in the United Kingdom, whose textile industry in that time was to a large extent using raw cotton imported from the United States. It should be added that during the first two decades of the nineteenth century sharp rises, each of them lasting one or two years, took place in Europe in the prices of agricultural products, mainly as a consequence of bad crops, in a situation in which traffics were made more difficult and more costly owing to the Napoleonic wars.

As for the greatest fall in our century (1929–32), in the United Kingdom the fall started three years earlier than elsewhere owing to the decision to restore the gold standard at pre-war parity; this was seen as the condition for regaining the financial leadership of the pound and, thus, the role of London as the most important world financial centre. The consequences of that decision are the best illustration of the new situation discussed in this paper. In fact, to restore the pre-war parity it was necessary to determine a sharp price reduction through a credit squeeze; but such a price reduction implied a no less sharp reduction in wages. The attempt to force a wage cut in the coal industry, which in that period had a crucial role in wage determination, provoked a very long and costly strike in that industry. Eventually the workers were beaten; but it was a Pyrrhic victory. In other times, when wages and prices were flexible downward, the credit squeeze would have been far less long and painful, and the price reduction would have been achieved at a much lower cost.

It is hardly the case to emphasize that the series of national income, of industrial production and of price indices, especially when we consider very long periods, are extremely uncertain; the only justification that I can offer in using them is that – lacking evidence to the contrary – the basic trends that they show are not misleading.

Figures 12.3(a) and 3(b) United Kingdom: Industrial Prices and Raw Material Prices: 1800–1913, 1923–39, 1948–89

Until 1913 both categories of prices are flexible in both directions; in the interwar period the variability of industrial prices seems to be to a large extent a reflection of the violent oscillations in raw material prices. After the Second World War raw material prices oscillate in both directions, as in the past, whereas wholesale prices of industrial goods show a high upward flexibility, but a strong downward rigidity. So much is this the case that only once (in 1953) and only limitedly (about 1 per cent) did these prices fall, clearly a consequence of the remarkable fall in raw material prices.

Figure 12.4 United Kingdom Wages and Unemployment: 1861–1913, 1923–39, 1948–90

In the period 1861–1913 the upward flexibility of money wages is decidedly higher than their downward flexibility – which apparently was very low even in the period 1800–1860. In the period 1861–1913 variations in wages depend to a good extent on the variations of the rate of unemployment, whereas after the First World War this relation is much reduced: money wages fall very limitedly even when unemployment attains very high levels. After the Second World War money wages are completely rigid downward.

Figure 12.5 United States: Wages and Unemployment: 1890–1913, 1923–39, 1948–89

The comments on the United Kingdom apply also to the United States; see however the text for the interwar period.

Figure 12.6 Raw Material Prices and World Industrial Output: 1956–89

The correlation between raw material prices in the international markets and the world industrial output is certainly remarkable when we consider that the world industrial output is only one of the three main explanatory variables – the other two being supply and an index of the quotations of the dollar. The world industrial output represents the demand for raw materials in international markets; the flexibility of raw material prices with respect to demand, already high before 1971, became even higher after that year, as a consequence of the abandonment of the Bretton Woods agreement (see text).

Figure 12.7 United States: Industrial Prices and Raw Material Prices: 1948–89

Wholesale prices of industrial prices are rigid downward: they fall only seldom and very limitedly – in sharp contrast with the prices of raw materials. It is to be noticed, however, that the fluctuations of raw materials prices, especially those in the downward direction, are much less pronounced in the United States markets vis-à-vis raw materials prices in the international markets (Figure 12.4). This is not only because of a different composition of the indices but also because, in the United States as well as in the other industrialized countries, wages tend to rise systematically, whereas in underdeveloped countries they do not have such a tendency, and, finally, because of the measures of price support adopted in industrialized countries.

Long-Run Chances in Wage and Price Mechanisms   339

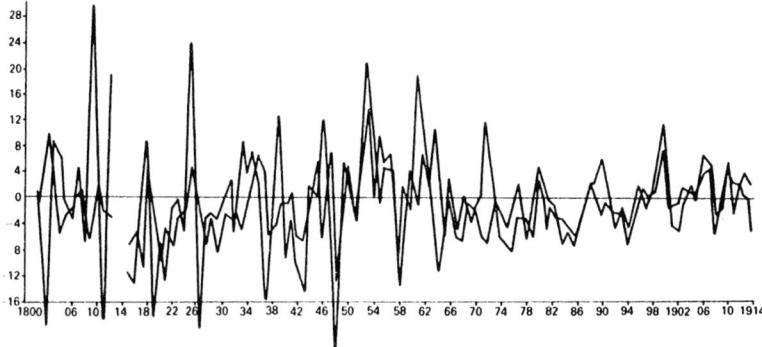

FIGURE 12.3(a) United Kingdom: industrial prices ($\hat{P}_i$) and raw material prices ($\hat{RM}$) (rates of change): 1800–1913

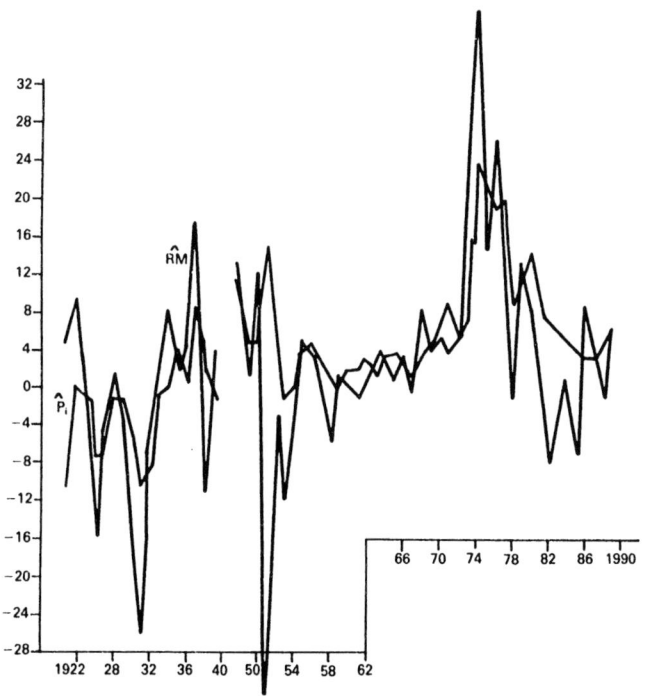

FIGURE 12.3(b) United Kingdom: industrial prices ($\hat{P}_i$) and raw material prices ($\hat{RM}$) (rates of change): 1923–39 and 1948–89

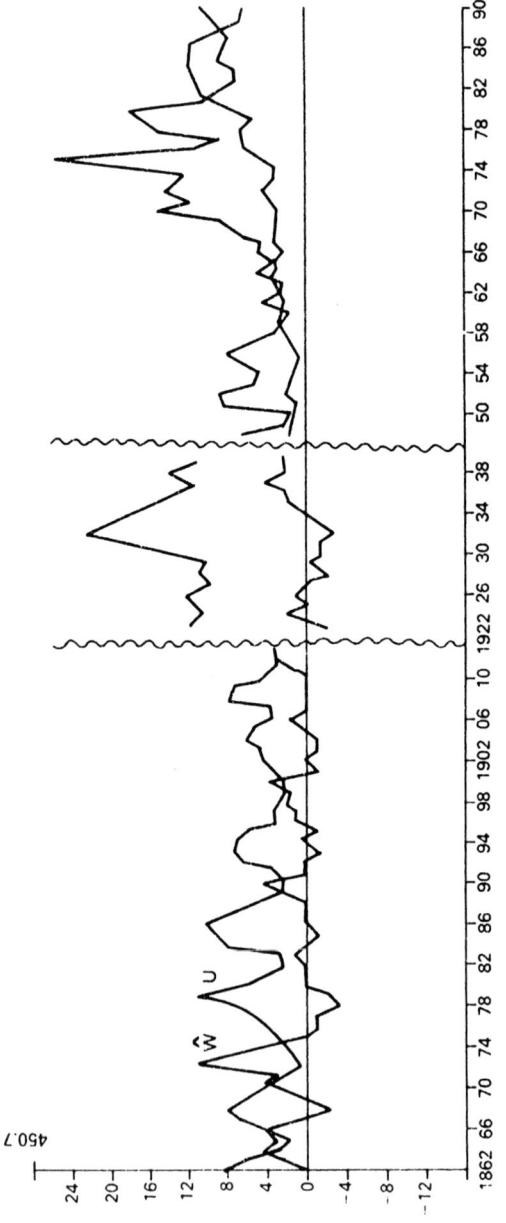

FIGURE 12.4 United Kingdom: wages (rates of change) ($\hat{W}$) and unemployment (U) three periods: 1861–1913, 1923–39, 1948–90

Long-Run Chances in Wage and Price Mechanisms   341

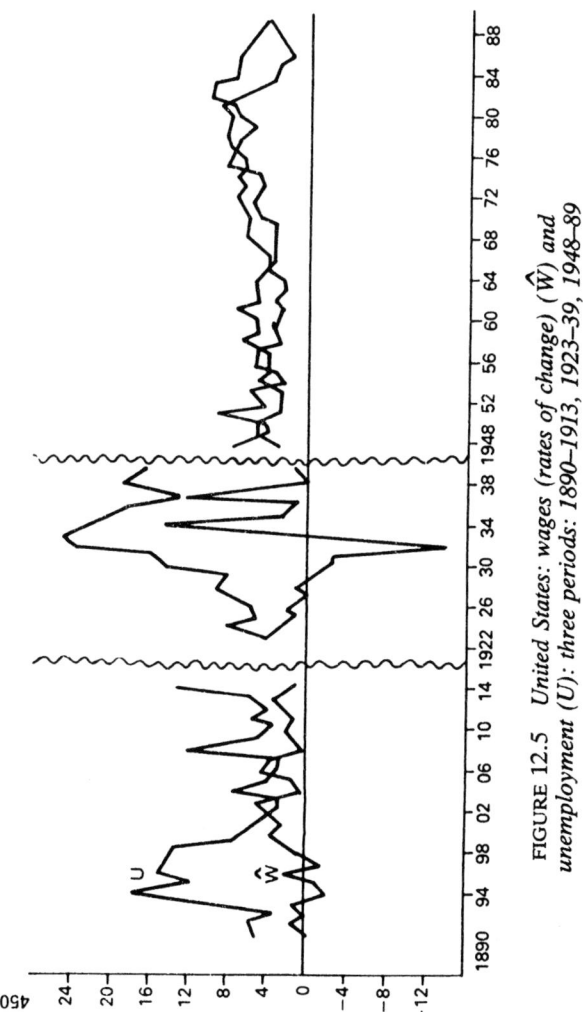

FIGURE 12.5 *United States: wages (rates of change) ($\hat{W}$) and unemployment (U): three periods: 1890–1913, 1923–39, 1948–89*

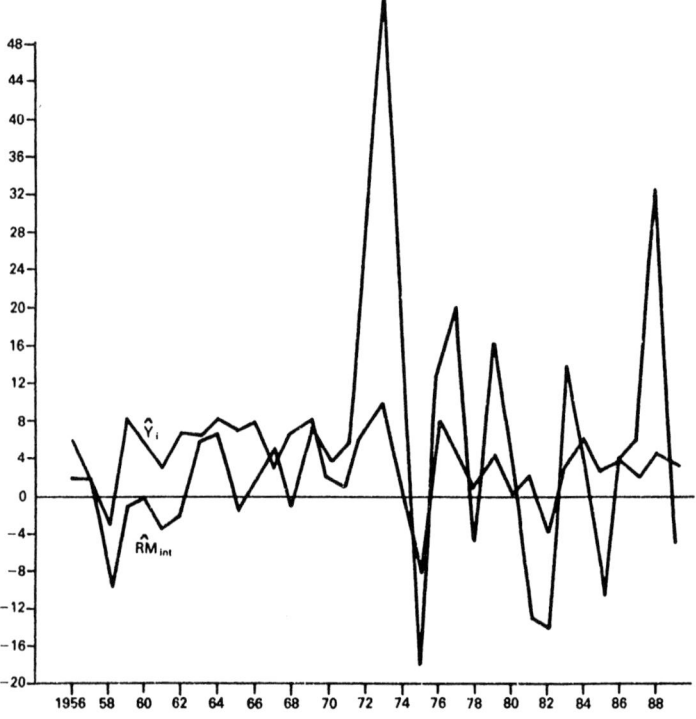

FIGURE 12.6 *Raw material prices ($\hat{RM}$) and world industrial output ($\hat{Y}_i$) (rates of change) 1956–89*

Long-Run Chances in Wage and Price Mechanisms

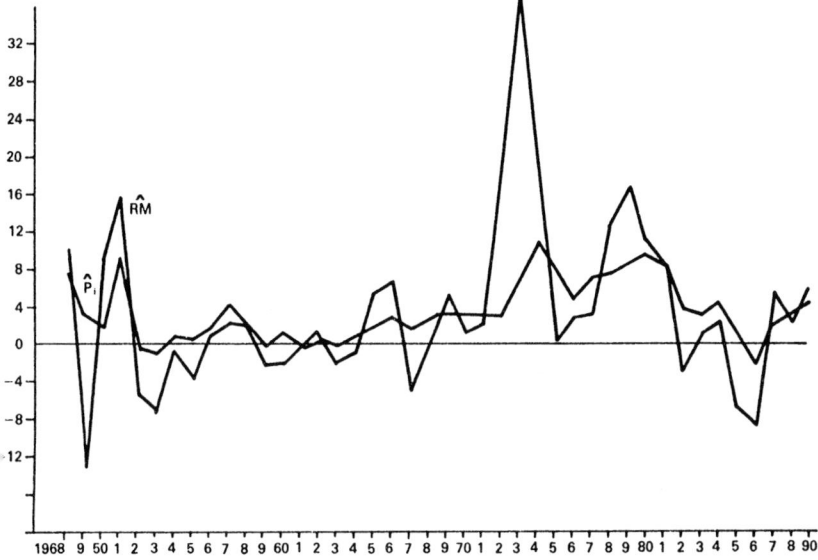

FIGURE 12.7 *United States: industrial prices ($\hat{P}_i$) and raw material prices ($\hat{RM}_i$) (rates of change) 1948–89*

SOURCES for Figures 12.3–7
In addition to the sources of the data of Table 12.1: Figure 12.3(a): *Statistical Yearbook of the United Nations* (New York: United Nations, 1990): Organization for Economic Co-operation and Development, *OECD Economic Outlook*, June 1990. Figure 12.6: Raw material prices, in dollars: *The Economist*. World industrial output: *OECD Economic Outlook: Historical Statistics 1960–88*, June 1980. Figure 12.7: *Economic Report of the President* (Washington, DC, 1990) pp. 363, 366.

APPENDIX II: UNITED KINGDOM AND UNITED STATES: INCOME, PRODUCTIVITY AND POPULATION

If we assume that the rates of increase of real wages and productivity of labour on the one side, and those of employment and of population on the other are equal, we can derive from Table 12.1 and from Figures 12.1 and 2 the rates of increase shown in Table 12.4 (the rate of increase of employment is approximately equal to the increase of income *minus* the rate of increase of productivity; all the figures indicate yearly changes).

If we admit that the share of active population in the long run varies widely, the behaviour of per capita income can give an idea of the behaviour of productivity per worker. It is worth recalling that the rate of increase of hourly productivity is greater than the rate of increase of productivity per worker; the difference between the two indicates the reduction of working hours – around 0.3–0.5 per cent per year in the two countries.

TABLE 12.4

	1800–97	*1897–1988*
United Kingdom		
National income	2.0	1.8
Population	1.0	0.9
Per capita income	1.0	0.9
United States:		
National income	3.8	3.5
Population	2.4	1.4
Per capita income	1.4	2.1

APPENDIX III: WAGE EQUATIONS IN DIFFERENT HISTORICAL PERIODS

The period 1861–1913 is taken by Phillips (1958) as the reference period for the U.K. The equation fitted is

$$\log (\hat{W} + 0.90) = 0.98 - 1.39 \log U$$

where $\hat{W}$ is the change of money wages and U the rate of unemployment.

For the said period a somewhat different equation, estimated by my colleague Paolo Palazzi, gave better results:

$$\hat{W} = -1.93 + 10.17 U^{-1} + 0.16 \hat{V} \qquad R^2 = 0.74 \qquad (1)$$
$$\phantom{\hat{W} = -1.93 + }(9.87) \qquad (2.23)$$

where $\hat{V}$ is the rate of change in the cost of living and figures below the coefficients of the variables represent t statistics.

For the period 1923–57 we have an equation fitted by Lipsey (1960), that is:

$$\hat{W} = 0.74 + 0.43 U^{-1} + 11.18 U^{-4} + 0.038 \hat{U} + 0.69 \hat{V} \quad R^2 = 0.91 \qquad (2)$$

where $\hat{U}$ is the rate of change in the rate of unemployment.

The cost of living variable, then, has become more important than in the past; in the period 1948–89 it became even more important – the coefficient rises from 0.69 to 0.81 ($R^2 = 0.70$), whereas the unemployment variable has lost much of its significance, at least in the specification that we have used. Only in the period 1973–89, which followed the abandonment of the Bretton Woods agreements and include the years of government by Mrs Thatcher, did the unemployment variable recoup some of its significance (t = 1.92) when considered together with the cost of living; $R^2 = 0.78$.

For the United States, the unemployment data are available only beginning with 1890; for the period 1890–1913 an acceptable estimate is as follows:

$$\hat{W} = 0.65 + 11.22 U^{-1} + 0.26 \hat{V} \qquad R^2 = 0.52 \qquad (3)$$
$$\phantom{\hat{W} = 0.65 + }(2.63) \qquad (1.73)$$

For the interwar period 1923–39 we do not find a systematic

relation between the rate of change of wages and unemployment. We do find, however, a certain negative relation from 1923 to 1932, as can be seen from Figure 12.3, a relation that disappears in the following years. There is, instead, a positive relation between wages and the cost of living during the whole period (1923–39). Wage movements in 1934 and 1937 are abnormal (see Figure 12.3), for the reasons explained in the text.

For the period 1948–89 an acceptable estimate of the wage equation is the following:

$$\hat{W} = 1.24 + 9.80U^{-1} + 0.50\hat{V} \qquad R^2 = 0.68 \qquad (4)$$
$$\phantom{\hat{W} = 1.24 + }(3.15) \qquad (9.30)$$

The fit improves if we introduce dummy variables or special variables in the years in which the strike activity is significantly higher than the normal level (for the period 1948–68 see Sylos Labini, 1974, p. 92).

REFERENCES

Beveridge, W. (1944, 1960) *Full Employment in a Free Society – A Report* (London: Allen and Unwin).
Clapham, J. (1951) *An Economic History of Modern Britain. Machines and National Rivalries (1857–1914), With an Epilogue (1914–1929)* (Cambridge: Cambridge University Press).
Fearon, P. (1987) *War, Prosperity and Depression. The US Economy 1917–45* (Lawrence, Kansas: The University Press of Kansas).
Hicks, J. R. (1932, 1963) *The Theory of Wages* (London: Macmillan).
Kalecki, M. (1971) *Essays on the Dynamics of the Capitalist Economies* (Cambridge: Cambridge University Press).
Keynes, J. M. (1925, 1972) 'The Economic Consequences of Mr Churchill', *The Collected Writings of J. M. Keynes*, ed. by D. Moggridge, Vol. IX (London: Macmillan).
Keynes, J. M. (1926, 1980a) 'The End of Laissez-Faire', *Collected Writings*, op. cit., vol. XI.
Keynes, J. M. (1936, 1973) *The General Theory of Employment, Interest and Money, Collected Writings*, cit., Vol. VII.
Keynes, J. M. (1980b) *Activities 1940–46: Shaping the Post-War World. Employment and Commodities, Collected Writings*, cit., Vol. XXVII.
Lipsey, R. G. (1960) 'The Relation Between Unemployment and the Rate of Change of Money Wage Rates in the United Kingdom 1862–1957: A Further Analysis', *Economica*, February.
Ohlin, B. (1937) 'Some Notes on the Stockholm Theory of Saving and Investment', *Economic Journal*, March.
Patinkin, D. (1987) 'Keynes, John Maynard', in *The New Palgrave Dictionary of Economics*, Vol. 3 (London: Macmillan).
Phillips, A. W. (1958) 'The Relation between Unemployment and the Rate of Change of Money Wage Rates in the United Kingdom 1861–1957', *Economica*, November.
Sylos Labini, P. (1954) 'Monopoli, ristagno economico e politica keynesiana', *Economia internazionale*, November.
Sylos Labini, P. (1962, 1969) *Oligopoly and Technical Progress* (Cambridge, Mass.: Harvard University Press).
Sylos Labini, P. (1970, 1974) *Problemi dello sviluppo economico* (Bari: Laterza).
Sylos Labini, P. (1974) *Trade Unions, Inflation, and Productivity* (Lexington, Mass.: Saxon House).
Sylos Labini, P. (1984) *The Forces of Economic Growth and Decline* (Cambridge, Mass.: MIT Press).
The World Bank (1981, 1989), *World Development Report* (New York: Oxford University Press).

Part VI

Institutions and Economic Structure: Human Actions and the Pure Labour Theory of Value

13 Reflections on the Significance of the Labour Theory of Value in Pasinetti's Natural System

Heinrich Bortis

THE RECEPTION OF THE NATURAL SYSTEM

Luigi Pasinetti's *Structural Change and Economic Growth* is a remarkable piece of economic theory which will have a lasting impact on the future development of political economy. Although the subtitle of this work, *A theoretical essay on the dynamics of the wealth of nations*, clearly establishes a link with Adam Smith, the main purpose of the book is to adapt David Ricardo to modern times, thus laying the analytical foundations for reestablishing the classical approach within economic theory (see on this also Roncaglia, 1988). Given this, Pasinetti (1981) is unusual both with respect to content and to method. With respect to content, because the book has grown out in a straightforward way of classical political economy and constitutes as such an unfamiliar element in a neoclassical world. The method, which is in fact Sraffa's and Ricardo's, is also unusual because of the very high degree of abstraction which brings out analytical results with great clarity; in addition, abstraction is of a particular kind in that production is put to the fore whilst exchange, considered to be secondary, is left aside. Consequently, the 'theoretical scheme of a natural economic system' (Pasinetti, 1981, p. 128) has been received with some astonishment. Among others, three features of the natural system have caused considerable surprise, i.e. the important role played by the *labour theory of value*; the fact that *production*, not exchange, constitutes the conceptual starting point in Pasinetti's system; and, finally, that this system should be a *natural* one, a term about which queries immediately arose.

The labour theory of value has, as is well known, been most severely condemned by all neoclassical economists. Thus, Schumpeter states that 'Ricardo was completely blind to the nature and the logical place in economic theory, of the supply-and-demand apparatus and that he took it to represent a theory of value distinct from and opposed to his own [labour theory of value]. This reflects little credit on him as a theorist' (Schumpeter, 1954, p. 601). And, inevitably, Schumpeter adds: 'The same applies to Marx, who took the same view without observing that his exploitation theory presupposes that demand and supply do their work' (Schumpeter, 1954, p. 601n).

However, the critique of the labour theory of value has not been confined to neoclassical quarters. J. M. Keynes never attached much importance to the problem of value although he had some sympathy for the labour theory of value. Nicholas Kaldor has always regretted that Adam Smith went wrong in the course of the fourth chapter of book one of the *Wealth of Nations* when he started to discuss the theory of value instead of going on discussing the determinants of the productive forces of an economy as he had done in the first three chapters. In addition, many Sraffian (neo-Ricardian) economists are of the opinion that Sraffa (1960) made the labour theory of value redundant, for instance Steedman (1977). Thus, outside the realm of neoclassical and socialist economics few economists are interested in value, and fewer still seem to speak about the labour theory of value: among them, however, is Luigi Pasinetti.

A second feature of the natural system has also given rise to a considerable discussion, the starting point of which has been the introduction to Pasinetti (1981) where a crucial passage reads:

> As against the pure exchange model of marginal economics, the [present] scheme [. . .] will be called a *pure production* model. All commodities considered are produced, and can be made in practically whatever quantity may be wanted, provided that they are devoted that amount of effort they technically require. To avoid unnecessary complications, scarce resources will not be considered. (Pasinetti, 1981, p. 24)

All this stands in sharp opposition to the view held by 'the marginal economic theorists [who] have chosen to look at the real world through the lens of the scarcity model' (Pasinetti, 1981, pp. 20–1). Propositions like these have given rise to the publication of an important volume (Baranzini/Scazzieri, 1986) in which exchange-oriented

The Significance of the Labour Theory of Value

and production-oriented theories are extensively discussed. In this volume, Christopher Bliss, a prominent neoclassical economist, has categorically rejected this division of economic theory:

> One cannot reasonably drive a wedge between maximization models with and without production, and claim that they are fundamentally different. In some of the best expositions of general equilibrium theory . . . equilibrium is introduced only after a discussion of both consumer and producer theory. (Bliss in Baranzini/Scazzieri, 1986, p. 372)

Thirdly, the term 'natural' itself has given rise to some queries. According to Pasinetti:

> the *natural features* of a growing economic system [. . .] are represented by (i) an evolving structure of commodity prices; (ii) an evolving structure of production; (iii) the time path of the wage rate and of the rate – or rates – of profit. [. . .]. Moreover, as a requirement for all these structural movements to take place in 'equilibrium' – by which is simply meant full employment and full capacity utilisation – two types of necessary conditions have emerged, namely: (iv) a series of *sectoral* new investment conditions, defining the evolving structure of capital accumulation; (v) a *macro-economic* effective demand condition, referring to total demand in the economic system as a whole. (Pasinetti, 1981, pp. 127–8)

From this passage, Marxists would infer that we are in a capitalist economy: there are profit rates and effective demand problems, the latter implying the possibility of economic crises. But then, equilibrium should not have any place among the basic features of such an economy; instead, conflicts about distribution and the changing size of the industrial reserve army should figure prominently, reflecting thus the internal contradictions of capitalism. Many Post-Keynesian economists would broadly agree with these remarks: 'Keynes's *General Theory* smashed up the glass house of static [equilibrium] theory in order to discuss a real problem – the causes of unemployment' (Robinson, 1969, 1st edn 1956, p.v). This proposition might raise the suspicion that, contrary to Pasinetti's claims, the natural system is not about the real world.

The neoclassical economist would, at first sight, be delighted to learn that the natural system deals with equilibrium states of economies. But he would be amazed to find out that the full employment equilibrium is not brought about by factor markets; in fact, this concept is not even mentioned. In addition, he would be surprised to learn that *prices* are not indicators of scarcity, but reflect the efforts incurred by society to produce the various goods.

The above remarks suggest that many economists, coming from most diverse quarters, hesitate to accept the natural system. Indeed, its significance, i.e. its place, in economic theory is not immediately evident. This is not surprising as economic theory has become very specialized, whereby specialization has taken place on the basis of specific approaches: neoclassical, Keynesian, Post-Keynesian and Marxian, to give examples. This has given rise to the formation of subschools which go on producing most differentiated economic theories. In many instances, for specialized economists, the assumptions and implications of their specific approach have become self-evident. Particularly, no need is felt to question the approach from which one's theory is derived and to compare it to other possible approaches. If, in such a situation, economists adhering unconditionally to some particular approach are faced with a theoretical system erected upon an alternative approach, bewilderment and mistrust sets in. This is what has happened with Pasinetti's natural system. From this fact derives the problem to be dealt with in the following pages.

PURPOSE OF THE CHAPTER AND PLAN

In the present note it is attempted to provide a rough sketch of the significance of some aspects of Pasinetti's natural system. This might contribute to eliminating some of the misunderstandings mentioned in the previous section and to situating broadly the natural system within economic theory.

The three selected features of the natural system hinted at above, i.e. the labour theory of value, the priority of production over exchange and the fact that the system is a natural one, provide a convenient starting-point for discussing the significance of the natural system. These features are closely linked and have, therefore, all to be dealt with in order to provide a sufficiently comprehensive picture of Pasinetti's framework.

The theory of value constitutes the heart of any theoretical system of economics. The choice of a particular theory of value has implications for other pieces of theory, particularly for the theory of distribution and for employment theory. Discussing, then, the role of the labour theory of value in Pasinetti's natural system amounts to sketching the *theoretical content* of the natural system which is done on pp. 364–74.

The *method* used by Pasinetti can perhaps be revealed best by clarifying the somewhat ambiguous notion of 'natural'. Pp.355–8, which, in a way, are preliminary, are devoted to this definitional problem. Starting from these preparatory remarks, issues of method will be taken up again on pp. 374–7.

The content of a theoretical system and the method used heavily depend upon the theorist's vision of the broad functioning of socioeconomic systems. As alluded to above (pp. 351–4), Pasinetti's approach to economic problems is dominated by the importance of production and by the relative neglect of exchange. On pp. 361–4, therefore, we deal with the meaning of the 'production approach' to economic problems. The significance of this approach can be brought out by considering the basic premises underlying it. This is equivalent to dealing with the social philosophy on which the natural system is erected. Pp. 358–61 are devoted to this issue. This section also deals, very broadly though, with social philosophies underlying economic theories in general so as to prepare the ground for the concluding section. Here, it is attempted to bring out the wider theoretical significance of the natural system. The place of Pasinetti's 'natural system' within economic theory can perhaps be situated best by comparing it to the neoclassical system, more specifically to the Walrasian one. While the latter certainly represents one of the summits of neoclassical theorizing, the former may, as has been hinted at the outset, be considered as a landmark of the classical line of development in economic theory initiated by Adam Smith, David Ricardo and Karl Marx in the main and partly adapted to modern requirements by Sraffa and Leontief.

SEVERAL MEANINGS OF 'NATURAL'

In various instances, Pasinetti defines 'natural' as 'a level of investigation which is so fundamental as to be independent of the institutional set-up of society' (e.g. Pasinetti, 1981, pp. xii and 127). This implies, according to him, looking at the 'natural and primary' determinants [which] are bound to make themselves felt in the long run, whatever transitory short-run deviations may be. This is something more than saying that the present analysis is long-run analysis. We have been, and we are, concerned with the norm; and the norm is always there . . . in the *short* no less than in the long run, whatever amount of temporary disturbances there may be. (Pasinetti 1981, p. 127n)

These passages evoke different associations as regarding the term 'natural'. This is not surprising as there are widely differing uses of this term as is, for instance, evident from Schumpeter (1954, ch. 2 of part II).

In order to shed some light on the significance of Pasinetti's natural system it is, indeed, convenient to distinguish between *four* different meanings of natural. All of them appear, explicitly or implicitly, in Pasinetti's work in relation to the material content of his theory or to the method used.

A first meaning of 'natural' relates to the forces of nature which are made use of by man (society) in the process of production. These comprise the productive forces of land, in agriculture or as a supplier of raw materials and, mainly, natural forces embodied in man-made means of production. The natural forces in question correspond to Marx's forces of production which embody, according to him, the relationship of man (society) to nature. It is evident that 'natural' as embracing the forces of production plays a prominent role in Pasinetti 1981: the natural system is presented as 'a pure production model' (pp. 23–5); chapter II (pp. 29–49) which brings out, in a very general way, the basic technical aspects of production: production by means of labour alone, production by means of labour and capital goods which are themselves produced. Technical progress resulting in an increased productivity of labour is equivalent to an improved mastering of the forces of nature.

A second meaning of 'natural' relates to the broad organization of society as grounded on fundamental features of human nature that are invariant or change but very slowly. In this context, it may be reminded that the word 'natural' was widely used by philosophers and students of social structures from the sixteenth to the nineteenth century. Two broad definitions of 'natural' are of some importance here.

There is, first, the view of Hobbes (1588–1679) who saw the natural state as a state of war between egoistic human beings: *homo homini lupus.* There are no institutions to protect individuals from each other. The desire for security is one of the main reasons which lead to the formation of institutions. For Hobbes, the absolutist state is the most appropriate political institution. The corresponding economic institution is 'mercantilism' where huge trade monopolies stand in the service of the absolutist state.

Another definition of 'natural' (relative to the organization of society) developed as a reaction to absolutism in the course of the late seventeenth and eighteenth centuries culminating in the intellectual framework of the Enlightenment. In the systems of Locke and Hume, but also of Montesquieu and Voltaire, a 'natural' society signifies, drastically simplified, a society organized according to the principle of reason which, in the main, means securing the 'natural' rights of the individuals making up society. In economics, François Quesnay and Adam Smith were the first to propose a comprehensive 'natural' economic system embedded in 'natural' social and political institutions. This second meaning of natural is important here because, as has already been mentioned at the outset of the present section, Pasinetti defines 'natural' as 'a level of investigation . . . which is so fundamental as to be independent of the institutional set-up of society' (pp. xii and 127). This statement is somewhat controversial, as it should be evident that Pasinetti's natural system cannot be natural in Hobbes' sense. Thus, it would, presumably, be more appropriate to say that Pasinetti's system may be compatible with or may imply different types of natural (or reasonable) institutional set-ups. This problem will be briefly considered on pp. 358–61 and 374–77 below.

The concept of a 'natural' (reasonable) organization of society leads to a third meaning of 'natural' which is also made use of in Pasinetti (1981), namely 'natural' in the sense of 'normative' implying, however, that the natural (reasonable) state of society is not brought about automatically by natural (inherent) forces which are just there, belonging to nature so to speak, as early neoclassical economists thought of market forces. The normative (natural) state has, as is implied in Pasinetti (1981), to be brought about by purposeful reformist actions of man which, in turn, implies the necessity of working out such a natural economic system in order to set a clearly defined aim for policy activities in the socioeconomic sphere. The normative aspects of Pasinetti's work will be touched upon on pp. 370–4 below.

Finally, a fourth meaning of 'natural' emerges in relation with positive economics which aims at describing and explaining reality. Description may be based upon and explanation directed to the persistent and permanent aspects of reality while neglecting rapidly changing factors as linked to the vagaries of the market in the main. For example, in neo-Ricardian economics, natural prices are said to be governed by the conditions of production and by income distribution, the former being a permanent (or slowly and regularly changing) technological and institutional factor, the latter representing a (persistent) institutional factor. 'Natural' in the sense of permanent (or slowly changing) will be dealt with on pp. 364-70 below.

SOCIAL PHILOSOPHIES AND INSTITUTIONS

In a recent paper, Luigi Pasinetti emphasized once again the basically different conceptual starting points of neoclassical economics and of what might be called neo-Ricardian economics which are, in turn, part of Post-Keynesian economics (Pasinetti, 1986, pp. 416-27). He observes 'that the theoretical choice that is implied in the formulation of the pure preference model, and with it the subjective theory of value, spring from a particular view of looking at society; it springs, so to speak, from a particular "social philosophy"' (Pasinetti, 1986, p. 419). Exactly the same conclusion is reached with respect to the pure labour model (a variant of the production model of Pasinetti, 1981) which is said to imply a social philosophy that, through division of labour, stresses the necessarily *cooperative aspects* of an organized society, (Pasinetti, 1986, p. 424). This is indeed the crucial point: behind any theoretical construction in the social sciences lies, sometimes hidden in the premises, a vision of how society broadly works and of what it is, i.e. what are the basic institutions which constitute it. This vision, if articulated analytically, is the social philosophy underlying theoretical systems in the social sciences. Among others, Schumpeter has emphasized this point: 'analytic effort is of necessity preceded by a preanalytic cognitive act that supplies that raw material for the analytic effort . . . this preanalytic cognitive act will be called *Vision*' (Schumpeter, 1954, p. 41).

In order to attempt to situate Pasinetti's natural system within economic theory, a very brief look at some systems of social philosophy is required. To avoid misunderstandings and arbitrariness as far as possible, a basic classification of social philosophies, familiar in the literature, is taken up here. Some of the terms used to characterize these systems of thought are borrowed from Lloyd (1986, p. 191).

There are, in fact, three fundamentally different groups of social philosophies, each of which is based on a different principle. Of course, only pure types are presented here. Variations and combinations of these may easily be imagined.

In the first place, there is *collectivism* (certain types of socialism or communism) which is based on the principle of *holism*. Society is seen as a tightly structured whole, like, for example, an organism or a machine, ultimately directed towards a single social (common) aim, usually the power and the splendour of a nation. Individuals are important only in so far as they carry out functions serving the social whole. History abounds with illustrations of holistic societies of which, in fact, all despotic and absolutist regimes are examples. The hallmark of a holistic society is that society is an entity of its own (a thing) which is independent of the individuals composing it. In a way individuals are not unique but exchangable and/or replacable.

A second group of social philosophies can be summarized under the heading of *liberalism*, the organizing principle being *individualism*. The aims pursued by individuals are individual aims, e.g. utility or profit maximization. Social relations come into being through explicit or implicit contracts between individuals. In this view, *exchange* (buying and selling goods or services including, of course, 'factors of production') is obviously the most important social event in the economic sphere. As regards the political sphere, some liberals have even gone as far as to claim that the state came into being through a contract between individuals (social contract). In the liberal view, then, society could be defined as a network of contracts between individuals.

In between liberalism and socialism, there is a large set of social philosophies which are of the *third-way* type. These explicitly or implicitly start from the fact that man is an individual *and* a social being and who, consequently, pursues social (common) aims requiring cooperation and individual aims. The achieving of the former is, in many instances, a precondition for pursuing the latter. For example, production is, in Pasinetti's natural system, a social process directed towards a common (social) aim, i.e. the production of the social product. Consumption, which is directed towards the achieving of individual aims, can obviously take place only if some production has taken place at all. The fact that each human being is a person who unfolds their natural potentialities only if pursuing social (in cooperation with other persons) *and* individual aims is perhaps the crucial feature of third-way social philosophies.

Now, the *persistent* pursuing of some individual or social aim may be called an *institution*. According to Veblen's excellent definition '[i]nstitutions are . . . principles of action about the stability and finality of which men entertain practically no doubt' (quoted in Roll 1973, p. 445). Institutions are thus simply standard, permanent or persistent types of action guided by some formal or informal rule.

The various institutions and their interplay constitute, broadly speaking, the *social structure*. Given this, one may say that third-way social philosophies are erected upon the principle of *structurism*. This principle implies that only part of human actions are determined by the social structure. There are, in fact, large areas of freedom mainly associated with possibilities to move within the social structure (social mobility) and with the ways in which individual and social aims are being achieved. This mirrors the real world quite well. Consequently, structurist (third-way) social philosophies, if underlying positive analyses, may be said to be linked with *social realism*. Presumably, *social democracy* would be an appropriate expression for many third-way social philosophies underlying normative systems.

The concept of 'institution' is of considerable importance here, not only because it is important in social philosophy in general and in third-way social philosophies in particular, but also because of Pasinetti's proposition that the natural system be independent of institutions (see pp. 355–8 above).

Starting from Veblen's very general definition given above and in accordance with what has been said above on social philosophies, two broad types of institutions may be distinguished. The first relates to standardized behaviour of individuals with respect to the pursuing of individual aims. First-type institutions to a large extent regulate the behaviour of individuals in the fields of, say, consumption and of culture. For instance, certain habits of eating, dressing etc. may be institutionalized in some region; a typical regional style of building would constitute a cultural institution. A second type of institution occurs if some or all individuals making up a society pursue a *common* (social) aim which isolated individuals could not achieve; each individual or group of individuals fulfills, as a rule, distinct functions within a structured entity. In this sense, football teams and choral societies are second-type institutions in the cultural sphere. The parliament and the civil service are political institutions of this type.

The Significance of the Labour Theory of Value

In the economic sphere, the process of production based upon division of labour is an institution of the second type, the same being true of enterprises and of trade-unions.

Institutions develop historically, some of them spontaneously, as the social division of labour: others are the result of purposeful human action, e.g. enterprises, trade unions, legal systems, and so on.

From the broad classification of social philosophies set forth in the present section, two associations begin to emerge. Pasinetti's natural system implies a structurist(third-way) social philosophy, while neoclassical (Walrasian) economics is clearly based upon the principle of individualism. In the subsequent sections, these propositions are to be substantiated somewhat.

A PARTICULAR VIEW OF PRODUCTION UNDERLYING THE NATURAL SYSTEM

Production is fundamental to the natural system for two main reasons. First, the theory of production is closely linked with the social philosophy implied in Pasinetti's system. Second, Pasinetti's way of conceiving of production is of decisive importance for other economic theories to be derived subsequently. This section is devoted to the first point in that the nature of the process of production underlying the natural system is broadly sketched. The next two sections then deal with the implications of this for other economic theories making up the natural system.

Even a quick glance at the natural system shows that Pasinetti sticks to the classical view of production. There is extensive division of labour (positively linked to overall labour productivity) and, consequently, production of commodities by means of commodities and labour. The process of production thus conceived is essentially a *social* process, for two related reasons. First, in participating in the process of production all workers, employees and managers taken together spontaneously pursue a social (common) aim, i.e. the production of the (gross) social product, part of which is used up in the process of production (necessary wages and intermediate products) while the remaining surplus is at society's disposal. (Of course, individual producers may not be conscious, or only more or less so, about contributing to the production of the social product which means that this social aim is automatically pursued; obviously, in a capitalist economy, most producers engage in production to realize a profit.)

Second, in the various sectors of production, the corresponding work force performs specific tasks or functions which are *complementary in an essential way*. Thus, if activities were to cease in some basic sector of production (in the Ricardo-Sraffa-Pasinetti sense), then the process of production as a whole would break down. The system of production is, therefore, something more than the sum of its parts (the sectors of production) as the parts are arranged purposefully, each one performing an essential task in the service of the economy as a whole.

The social character of the process of production shows up on *three* levels. There is, in the first place, the level of intermediate products where a tremendously complicated network of interindustry relations exist. All these relations between sectors are socially necessary, that is, they have to be established if the common (social) aim, producing the social product, is to be achieved. This is also true on a second level, i.e. on that of the final product sector where the consumption and the investment goods sector have to be in a definite relation to each other if the process of production is to function properly. The consumption goods sector delivers goods and services to the investment goods sector in order to maintain or, eventually, to expand the work force present here. Contrariwise, the investment goods sector delivers the capital goods required in order to maintain or to expand the level of activity in the consumption goods sector. The social character of these exchanges is self-evident. The exchanges taking place between the two sectors are in the service of production and are thus a means to achieve a common end. There is, finally, a third aspect of the production process, i.e. the vertical integration aspect which tells us how the original (non-produced) factors of production, land and labour, are transformed into final products. In Pasinetti's analysis land is left out of the picture for Ricardian reasons which implies that non-produced (scarce) goods are not considered. Only goods produced by direct and indirect labour are taken into the picture.

In order to be able to deal with dynamic processes properly, Pasinetti concentrates on the third aspect of the production process, i.e. he considers a vertically integrated system in that a direct link between labour and final products (the social product) as produced in the various sectors of production is established. The first and the second aspect of the production process mentioned above are *implied* in the analysis and the corresponding sectorial equilibria are taken for granted. In Chapter VI of Pasinetti (1981), however, the way in

The Significance of the Labour Theory of Value

which vertically integrated analysis and interindustry relations (input-output-analysis), i.e. the first and the third aspect of the production process mentioned above, are linked, is explicitly set out.

Pasinetti's view of the process of production as just set forth has immediate implications for the meaning of 'natural' (see pp. 355–8 above) and reveals us to some extent the social philosophy implied in the natural system.

The process of production as seen by Pasinetti implies using the term 'natural' in the first two meanings mentioned on pp. 356–7 above. In the first place, Pasinetti's theoretical framework is 'natural' in the sense that it describes, very generally, the way in which the forces of production of a society (in Marx's sense) are organized, i.e. how man is related to nature, how the forces of nature are put into the service of man. From Pasinetti's vertically integrated system it is immediately evident that man (labour) is himself the link between nature and the social product representing the result of social production activities.

In addition, Pasinetti's view of the process of production implies a certain vision as to the broad organization of society which is required by the *nature* of the process of production. This relates to the second meaning of 'natural' mentioned on p. 356 above. Production as a social process in the sense described above is a huge institution of the second type as defined on p. 360. In fact, one could speak of a macro-institution as the entire economy is involved in production. The process of production is a basic institution in the sense that the surplus coming out of it provides the material basis for establishing non-economic institutions, i.e. political, legal, social and cultural institutions. All this implies that we cannot agree with Pasinetti in defining 'natural' as a level of investigation so basic as to abstract from institutions. In the social sciences one cannot abstract from institutions entirely, as institutions make up the very essence of society. What can be done, however, is to abstract from a precise *description* of institutions as these are different from country to country and also vary over time. The basic principles according to which institutions work must, however, be included, and Pasinetti does precisely this in implicitly assuming that production is a social process which is entirely different from the neoclassical way of conceiving production which is, as will be seen, linked with a different view of the role played by institutions.

This last point gives us an important hint as to the social philosophy which is presumably implied in Pasinetti's natural system. First, the natural system cannot be based upon the principle of individualism as production is a social process in an essential way. Nor can it be based on the principle of holism, as it is to difficult to imagine that a complex production system of the classical (Sraffa-Leontief-Pasinetti) type could somehow be centrally planned. Central planning of production would be possible in a village community, for example, but not in a modern economy with extensive division of labour. This hints at the fact that it is the principle of structurism as linked with third-way social philosophies which is implied in the premises of Pasinetti's natural system, a point which will be substantiated further on pp. 377–83 below. Suffice it to state here that production is part of the social (institutional) structure which governs to some extent the behaviour of individuals.

LABOUR EQUIVALENTS AND THE REAL (POSITIVE) SYSTEM

Is the natural system as set forth in Pasinetti (1981) a piece of macroeconomics or of microeconomics? In a way it is both. It is macroeconomic in the sense that all the sectors of an economy are being considered, yet it is different from Keynesian macroeconomics where the sectorial structure of an economy is given and only global concepts, e.g. the level of employment, are taken account of. On the other hand, Pasinetti (1981) is microeconomic in the sense that it contains a theory of value. However, Pasinetti's microeconomics is different from standard microeconomics where the starting point is a certain type of behaviour of producers and households, e.g. profit and utility maximization; pricing in the natural system is a social and a macroeconomic process in that the prices of the real (positive) system depend upon the conditions of production (thus reflecting society's efforts to produce goods) and on distribution. Thus, it would not be appropriate to speak of the natural system as a macroeconomic model, nor as a microeconomic one. Instead one could call the 'natural system' a *mesoeconomic* system. Mesoeconomics deals with sectorial and structural problems and is, as such, also concerned with proportions between sectors.

The problem of the correct proportions between sectors of production has been one of the great problems of the founders of political economy. William Petty, Richard Cantillon, François Quesnay (in the standard and the extended *Tableau Economique*) and Adam

Smith (in the industry agriculture model of Book III of the *Wealth of Nations*) and Karl Marx (in the models of circulation at the end of volume II of *Das Kapital*) have all tackled the problem of sector proportions. Modern ways of dealing with this problem have been proposed by Sraffa and Leontief, but also by Keynes (the 'Fundamental Equations' of the *Treatise on Money*). Quite obviously, Pasinetti's natural system neatly fits into this line of development and completes it, by showing that sector sizes are ultimately governed by the demand for the various products, i.e. long-run Engel curves. To distinguish Pasinetti's system from conventional mesoeconomics, it is perhaps most appropriate to term the 'natural system' a system of classical mesoeconomics.

Now, once the correct proportions between sectors are determined one may take up two directions, that is, the direction of Keynesian macroeconomics and the microeconomic direction. Doing so leads Pasinetti to deal with the most important topics of economic theory which is done on two levels. Part I contains the analytical basis for primarily dealing with real world problems (the real or positive model); an important normative element, i.e. the full employment condition, is also contained in part I. However, the second part is essentially normative. Both parts thus partly overlap. In this section, the real model is briefly dealt with, whilst the next one is devoted to the normative model. Three topics are briefly dealt with here, i.e. the theories of value, distribution and employment. The natural system is complemented by a theory of the rate of interest and by a theory of international trade. These issues are, however, not considered here.

As has been mentioned above, the theory of production embodying the problem of sector proportions provides the analytical basis of the natural system. The theory of value corresponding to this view of production is represented by the price equations of the type II.6.3 in Pasinetti (1981, p. 41) if capital goods are produced by labour only or, more realistically, by equations II.7.3 (p. 44) if capital goods are produced by labour and by capital goods. Money prices basically depend upon three elements. First, upon the conditions of production as represented by the quantities of labour directly and indirectly (to produce the capital goods required to produce one unit of the consumption good considered) used up to produce a consumption good. A second element governing prices is income distribution, represented by gross profit rates. Third, there is the level of money wages which governs the absolute size of any money price. Relative prices obviously depend on the first two factors only. 'The prices thereby express a theory of value . . . which is in terms of what we may call *labour equivalents*' (Pasinetti, 1981, p. 43). For well-known reasons, it cannot be a pure labour theory as the rate of profits is positive and the ratios of direct to indirect labour are, as a rule, different in the various sectors of production.

Prices are thus determined within the spheres of production and distribution. Pasinetti's theory of prices is clearly an objective theory of prices which strictly mirrors Ricardo's theory. It is of some interest to note that in the natural system long-period prices are determined *before* goods come to the market, i.e. before exchange takes place. This does not, however, imply that demand does not play any role. In fact, consumers' demand determines the quantities of goods and services produced in the various sectors of production, a fact that is very clearly brought out by the quantity equations contained in the natural system (e.g. the equation system II.5.4 on p. 39). This is a very simple but also an extremely important feature of the natural system as set forth in Part I of Pasinetti (1981) because, first, this complements classical theory which lacks a theory of spending and thus of demand and, second, Pasinetti's natural system can be easily linked to Keynes's macroeconomic theory of output and employment determination. Obviously, this is a crucial point which we shall briefly reconsider below.

The theory of functional income distribution is but hinted at in Part I. It starts from the fact that the number of unknowns, i.e. relative prices, the real wage and the rate of profits (or the hierarchy of rates of profit), exceeds the number of price equations by one. This means that, as far as the analysis of Part I of Pasinetti (1981) is concerned, one of the variables regulating distribution, i.e. the real wage rate or the rate of profits, can be chosen from outside the production system (pp. 40–1). Thus, the first part of the natural system can be linked to any sociological or political theory of income distribution. In a capitalist system, distribution might be governed by a host of socioeconomic factors (the intensity of competition, the relative power of trade unions and of employers' associations, legal regulations, etc.) whilst in a (centrally planned) socialist system functional distribution would be largely determined by the state: the central planning authorities may fix money wages, prices, *and* the quantities of the goods to be produced.

On the macroeconomic level the analysis of Part I can, as has been hinted at above, be easily linked with a theory of employment (or unemployment) along Keynesian lines. In the real (capitalist) world,

The Significance of the Labour Theory of Value 367

there is obviously no reason why the full employment condition of the type II.2.8 (p. 32) should be fulfilled. In other words, there is no reason why full-employment income should be spent entirely on consumption and investment goods which would imply the presence of *involuntary* unemployment in Keynes's sense (see on this section II.3, pp. 33–5 in Pasinetti, 1981). Involuntary unemployment would in this case add to the structural unemployment brought about by continuous structural change going on in an economy. The latter is one of the main themes in Pasinetti's work, but the former can easily be brought in. This would, however, require the working out of a long-period theory of output and employment. Such a theory, e.g. the supermultiplier model set forth in Bortis (1984), could start from the fact that, in a capitalist economy, past capital accumulation as governed by effective demand may not have been sufficient to bring about the full employment of the available labour force. In formal terms, this means that the quantity vector $(X_1, \ldots, X_n)$ in the system (II.5.2, p. 38) for example will have to be multiplied by some scalar *smaller than unity*, e.g. 0.9, which means that 10 per cent of the labour force remain permanently unemployed. This would leave all the other properties of the natural system unchanged. A fully adjusted situation would thus coexist with permanent unemployment due to a lack of effective demand. In a way such a situation would be natural in a capitalist society if the authorities do not (or cannot, due to the foreign balance problems, for example) undertake permanent efforts to maintain full employment. It goes without saying that permanent unemployment is not natural from a normative point of point of view. This implies that the full employment requirement as is part of the natural system constitutes a normative element in part I of Pasinetti (1981). The third meaning of 'natural', natural as normative, appears for the first time in this specific context.

The possibility of combining Pasinetti's structural analysis with the Keynesian theory of output and employment determination clearly reveals the complementary nature of Ricardian and Keynesian economics. Keynes deals with the degree of 'utilization' of the labour force available in an economy as a whole; the determination of the employment scalar just mentioned would be tantamount to extending Keynes's short-period employment theory to a long-period situation, i.e. to the fully adjusted situation implied in Pasinetti's natural system. Ricardo, on the other hand, claims that the exchange relations between goods are not determined by market forces but are governed by the conditions of production (and distribution) and correspond, as such, to labour equivalents. Finally, Adam Smith clearly saw that the 'Wealth of Nations' depends on the productivity of labour which, in turn, depends upon the extent of division of labour. Labour is thus all-important in the theoretical systems just mentioned, which is equivalent to saying that classical and Keynesian economics necessarily belong together if the functioning of capitalist economies is to be understood properly. In this view, then, Luigi Pasinetti's natural system (Part I) emerges as the 'natural analytical framework' for bringing together the Classical and the Keynesian strand of economic thought.

The analysis carried out in Part I of Pasinetti (1981) is thus an appropriate theoretical basis for investigating the real-world problems which occur in capitalist economies. However, and this is of paramount importance, Pasinetti's theoretical framework may also be applied to socioeconomic systems embodying other *forms* of institutional set-ups, e.g. socialist economies. This is because the *forces* of production, as described by the production model set forth in Part I of Pasinetti (1981), may be combined with different ways of regulating the *relations* of production, mainly represented by the ownership of the produced means of production and the organization of production, and closely linked with the distribution and the use of the social product. More specifically, the relations of production are strictly linked with the way in which prices, quantities and employment levels are determined. This may be explained, for example, by considering the quantity system II.7.2 and the price system II.7.3 in Pasinetti (1981, p. 44). In a capitalist system, the private owner of the means of production may have the power, given the money wage level, to fix the prices in such a way as to achieve some satisfactory or desired rate of profit (or hierarchy of profit rates). The quantities produced are then determined by demand conditions reflecting the way in which incomes are spent by consumers. As has been mentioned above, there is no reason why past accumulation should lead to full employment, i.e. why the employment coefficient should equal unity.

In a centrally planned socialist system, on the other hand, prices (including the money wage level) and quantities may, given available labour and the means of production, be fixed by the central planning authorities. This implies that social surplus rates (the equivalents of capitalist profit rates) are also determined. With prices *and* quantities fixed, however, there is no reason why the quantities produced should correspond to the quantities demanded by households. The well-known problems of a socialist economy now emerge: some

The Significance of the Labour Theory of Value

goods cannot be sold while there are shortages of others. Given the structural rigidity of a planned system, supply cannot be adapted to demand quickly enough. Presumably, it is even impossible to plan a productive system such that the quantities produced match the demand of goods and services, the main reason being the immense complexity of a modern production system. To the structural problems just mentioned add global (macro) problems which are valid for a socialist economy taken as a whole. On the one hand, there seems to be a permanent shortage of *all* goods, implying a persistent excess of effective demand over supply. On the other hand, labour productivity is low for well-known reasons. Presumably both factors, shortages and low productivity, interact mutually (reinforce each other) as there is no incentive to work more if goods wanted by the consumer are not available in sufficient quantities and if the quality of the products which are available is low. To all this may add a lack of initiative of socialist managers with respect to introducing new and better technologies which may, in turn, partly be due to the rigidities of the plan (innovations, in fact, disturb the plan) and to an insufficient accruing of social surplus to individual enterprises.

This is not the place to go further in the analysis of capitalist and socialist economies, but it seems evident that the model of production set forth in Pasinetti (1981) may be the starting-point for a rich positive analysis. Two points should be noted in this context. First, the model describing the forces of production is such that it may be combined with different institutional set-ups regarding the relations of production. This is typical for production models of the classical-Marxian type which are of the causal type (in the sense of Pasinetti 1964–5) and can, as such, be combined at will with other causal models, to explain some given situation. Second, if Pasinetti's model of production is taken as the starting point for positive analysis, then a third meaning of 'natural' emerges. In fact, Pasinetti is not considering the whole of reality, but only its stable, slowly, regularly-changing parts, as comes out clearly from the above-quoted footnote 1 on p. 127 of Pasinetti (1981). Thus, whenever Pasinetti speaks of prices he means 'normal prices' which imply a full(normal) utilization of production capacities. In other words, Pasinetti (1981) exclusively deals with fully adjusted situations (see also pp. 127–8). These are parts of the real world only, from which short- and medium-term deviations, due to the vagaries of the market and to cyclical movements, occur at any moment of time. The (long-term) fully adjusted situation is hidden, so to speak, by short- and medium-term factors and is therefore invisible. To render the fully adjusted situation visible, temporary short-run and medium-term factors have to be removed; the rapidly changing top layers of reality have to be cleared away so as to foreground the more stable lower layers of the real world.

THE PURE LABOUR THEORY OF VALUE AND THE NORMATIVE SYSTEM

While the structural (mesoeconomic) model of Part I of Pasinetti (1981), if appropriately interpreted, provides the starting point for positive analysis, Part II, complemented by the full employment condition presented in Part I, clearly represents *normative* analysis which describes how an economic system *ought to* be organized. In this context, a fourth (and last) meaning of 'natural' appears. This term here denotes a *desirable and reasonable* state of an economic system which should be aimed at in order to secure a rational organization of economic activities. Pasinetti's normative model contains a host of fascinating insights which are immediately accessible to the theoretical economist and, intuitively, to the practitioner and the layman. This is very important as large parts of economics have, for too long, been a rather mysterious science, the secrets of which have been accessible only to some mathematically highly-trained economists. In analogy with the previous section, only the most important economic problems are dealt with here, i.e. value, distribution and employment. Some implications of Pasinetti's analysis are alluded to at the end of the present section.

Perhaps the most important normative fact, which has already been brought into the picture in Part I, is that there is '[a] central Agency entrusted with the task of keeping full employment' (Pasinetti, 1981, p. 91). In view of what has been said in the previous section, this has a double meaning: this institution has, in the first place, to take measures in order to avoid structural unemployment (see on this pp. 88–91 in Pasinetti, 1981). This type of unemployment comes into being because of the continuous structural change going on, which implies that some sectors shrink while others expand, or that there are sectors which are disappearing altogether while entirely new ones are being created. There are, then, always workers and employees who are temporarily unemployed in the shrinking or disappearing sectors and some time elapses until they find jobs in

The Significance of the Labour Theory of Value

expanding or newly-created sectors. Presumably, vocational training programmes would play an essential role in governmental attempts to avoid structural unemployment. Secondly, however, governments would have to make sure that effective demand is sufficient to ensure the full employment of the available labour force or, in other words, to avoid involuntary unemployment. This, once again, shows that Pasinetti's mesoeconomic system can and must be complemented by a long-period theory of output and employment which is essentially macroeconomic in nature. Formally speaking, appropriate policy measures would have to be derived from this employment theory in order to fix the employment scalar indicating the level of employment (defined in the previous section) as near as possible to unity.

If the 'central Agency with the task of keeping full employment' succeeds in its action, then a fully-adjusted situation including full employment of labour obtains. These are part of the natural features of a growing economy which have been quoted at the outset of the present chapter (Pasinetti, 1981, pp. 127–8). Incidentally, the very presence of the 'central agency' once again shows that, in the social sciences, it is impossible to abstract from institutions, a methodological point which will be taken up again, very briefly, in the next section.

The theory of functional income distribution (introduced in section VII.3, pp. 128–131) is a very simple one. The (net) rate of profit on capital invested in a certain sector of production must be equal to the rate of growth of the corresponding sector which, in turn, is made up of two components: the rate of growth of population plus the rate of growth of sector specific demand. In a sense, net profits have to finance investment in the long run, i.e. to pay for the amount of labour engaged in the production of new capital goods. This is very similar to the old classical view postulating a direct link between profits and growth; yet, there is an important difference:

> Total profits emerge as a kind of prior claim to share in the final national income, while total wages – by being (conceptionally) determined after profits have been determined already – emerge as a kind of a residual, or . . . as a 'surplus' that remains over and above what has been charged for profits. (Pasinetti, 1981, p. 144)

This rather surprising concept of 'surplus' could, of course, easily be modified by subtracting from it necessary consumption, i.e. minimum wages. The remaining 'surplus proper', as one might call it, would then be made up of luxury (non-necessary) consumption goods and of goods appropriated by the state. As is well known, the classical economists, mainly Ricardo, held the view that wages were determined first (Ricardo's natural wage) by a social convention and that profits were a residual, i.e. a surplus. Thus Pasinetti's approach to determine functional income distribution is basically the same as that of the classical economists; however, the way in which wages and profits are determined is reversed. This is a necessity as, in Pasinetti's natural system, the size and the evolution in time of the full employment labour force is exogenously determined. Given the techniques of production, capital accumulation has to be such that there is full employment of the given labour force in any short-run period. Capital accumulation thus passively adjusts to employment in the 'natural system'. Exactly the contrary happens in Ricardo's model. Here, the pace of capital accumulation is governed by savings, which consist of the bulk of profits, and employment (population) has to adjust to capital accumulation, all this being another way of stating Say's law. This reversal of conclusions is, of course, due to Pasinetti's taking account of Keynes's employment theory in which Say's law does not hold.

Once the natural rates of profit are introduced '[t]he theory of value implied by [the natural system] becomes . . . a *pure labour theory of value*' (Pasinetti, 1981, p. 132). This comes out clearly if prices are expressed in terms of the money wage rate, i.e. if money prices are divided by the wage rate. Prices then express labour commanded by a unit of some good; in fact,

> the price of each consumption good . . . is the sum of three *unweighted* physical quantities of *labour*: labour required directly in sector i (direct labour . . .), labour required to replace the worn-out productive capacity (*indirect labour* . . .), and labour required to expand equilibrium productive capacity (. . . *hyper-indirect labour*) (ibid, p. 132).

'Labour [thus] emerges from the very logic of the [natural system] as the only ultimate factor of production' (p. 133).

There can be little doubt that Pasinetti's objective theory of value corresponds to the theory of value Ricardo and Marx would have liked to develop had they possessed the analytical tools required. Pasinetti's pure labour theory of value reflects the essentially social character of the process of production alluded to above, pp. 361–4.

The Significance of the Labour Theory of Value

This becomes evident from two important features of the natural system.

First, Pasinetti's labour theory of value implies that each price, be it the price of an intermediate or of a final product, reflects the effort made by society in terms of direct, indirect and hyper-indirect labour in order to produce a unit of the corresponding good. Thus, if the process of production is seen as a *social* process as defined above pp. 361–4, and if natural profit rates are brought into the picture, the labour theory of value emerges as the only possible theory of value.

Second, the labour theory of value also contains a theory of personal income distribution which, however, is not brought out explicitly in Pasinetti (1981). This theory is linked to the fact that the various labour coefficients of the natural system are *not only technical*, but also *social* coefficients in the sense that they imply a wage structure. If labour is measured in labour-time, then the wage rate, w, which appears in the natural price equations must be interpreted as the money wage rate of simple (unqualified) labour. Qualified labour has to be reduced to simple labour, i.e. the reduction coefficients have to be determined somehow. For instance, one day of a tailor's labour may be equivalent to three days of unqualified labour, which means that the corresponding reduction coefficient is three. The determination of these coefficients is a complex social problem which, in sociological terms, is equivalent to determining the social status of a worker or of a group of workers. Thus, if, given the technical coefficients of production, the social esteem of a certain consumption good or of a certain type of labour increases, then the corresponding reduction coefficient would rise. One should notice that this is a 'sociological' theory of demand for labour which has no affinity with individualistic neoclassical demand theory. In fact, the determination of the reduction coefficients is a further institutional element implied in the natural system. Perhaps, a special institution, the government for example, would have to supervise workers in key sectors, to prevent them from using their power to raise their reduction coefficients above the socially acceptable level; also minimum wage levels would have to be legally fixed.

There are many highly interesting propositions that follow from the natural system presented in the key chapter (VII) of Pasinetti (1981). All of them are very simple in spite of the fact that they relate to highly complex states of affairs, which is an indication of the fact that the natural system, which has matured quite slowly, is, from an analytical point of view, fully thought out; secondary and complicating factors are left out of the picture and only principles are presented. To give a simple example of an important proposition that comes out of the natural system: 'Technical progress is ultimately revealed to be a diminuition of labour inputs [, i.e.] all technical progress is, in the end, labour saving' (Pasinetti, 1981, p. 207).

SOME METHODOLOGICAL ISSUES IMPLIED IN THE NATURAL SYSTEM

Whilst the two preceding sections have been devoted to some aspects related to the content of Pasinetti (1981), the present one takes up three methodological issues: the role played by institutions in the positive and normative part of Pasinetti (1981); general aspects of method; and two types of causal models which appear in Pasinetti's work.

There is, first, a close link between positive and normative analysis in Pasinetti (1981). In fact, as has been argued on pp. 364–70 above, Part I of this book may be considered as the mesoeconomic starting-point for a rich positive analysis aimed at explaining what is going on with respect to certain economic events in capitalist as well as in socialist economies. Out of this positive model the normative one grows out naturally by introducing requirements that would have to be fulfilled in a rationally organized society: the government must aim at avoiding structural and involuntary unemployment (in Keynes's sense). Profit rates must be natural which in turn implies a pure labour theory of value with all its desirable properties, some of which have been mentioned in the preceding section.

All this implies that the analytical skeleton of the natural system may be combined with various institutional set-ups. Part I, which constitutes the mesoeconomic starting point for positive analysis, may be combined with capitalist and socialist institutions in order to analyze real economic phenomena. The normative natural system, in turn, implies various natural institutions (which, of course, would have to be adapted to the specific socioeconomic situation in each individual country). On a very general level, there must, in the first place, be a government which has at least two important tasks: the first is to prevent the occurring of involuntary and structural unemployment. The former can be avoided by taking various measures, for example: securing, firstly, an equitable distribution of incomes so as to prevent an excess of saving over investment, a proposition based on a fundamental Post-Keynesian tenet saying that a more equitable distribution of incomes is associated with higher levels of effective demand and thus with higher employment volumes; secondly, working time has to be regulated in an appropriate way and, finally, equilibrium of the foreign balance has to be aimed at in order to prevent the leaking of effective demand abroad.

The second important task of the government is to regulate income distribution. A macroeconomically (socially) appropriate income distribution such that saving does not exceed investment is not only an important aim in itself but is, as has just been mentioned, also required to secure full employment. To bring about the natural functional distribution of income, the government would have to supervise producers in order to ensure that realized profit rates equal the natural ones. In addition, an equitable personal income distribution has to be brought about by fixing appropriate reduction coefficients, that is, an appropriate wage structure which, in turn, implies a broad social consensus concerning the level of money wages.

Once money wages and the natural profit rates are fixed, natural prices automatically obtain. If market prices persistently deviate from the natural ones, producers would have to change sector sizes in order to bring market prices into line with natural ones.

Besides the government, a second institution (or rather, a set of institutions) might be implied in the natural system. One could, indeed, imagine that each consumption good is produced by a co-operative which, in turn, may be made up of several vertically and horizontally integrated firms. Within a cooperative, firms could work together in various fields, e.g. the fixing of quality standards, research and development, the delineating of sales areas and so on. However, as alluded to above, the cooperatives in a natural system would have to be supervised: the reduction coefficients, that is, the wage structure for workers of the various cooperatives, have to be roughly fixed. Also, the government would have to make sure that gross profits do not exceed gross investment in the long run which implies that a sufficient degree of competition must prevail between firms. On these points, the government and the cooperatives may, of course, work together to find solutions.

Second, the fact that institutions are implied in the natural system has important methodological implications. First, it means that, in the long run, the most important economic variables are *directly determined by institutions other than the market*, and not by the market alone as is the case in neoclassical economics. In the positive system, prices depend upon the conditions of production and upon technology; income distribution, both functional and personal, is governed by social and political institutions. The full employment of available labour has to be secured by the government in the normative system. Second, the fact that institutions do not appear explicitly in Pasinetti's natural system is linked with his particular method which is, in fact, very similar to Sraffa's: reality is divided into layers which are ordered according to their persistence in the course of time. Then, as a first step, all the temporary factors are eliminated. Among the persistent factors, i.e. technology and institutions, political and cultural institutions are not considered, which means that the 'upper layer' institutions which are erected on the economic basis do not enter the analysis at all. Even the basic economic institutions are left in the dark, so to speak: only quantitative outcomes of economic processes are considered, whilst the working of the institutions which produce economic results are only hinted at in some places. This method obviously implies a very high degree of abstraction, the advantage being that the basic results (the nature of prices, the determination of output structures and output levels) come out with great clarity. Perhaps a disadvantage of this method is that important parts of reality, mainly institutions and their working, do not enter the picture at all. Consequently, reading is very demanding as the institutional set-ups which might be implied in the natural system have to be thought out by the reader.

Third, a remarkable methodological feature of the natural system is the explicit presence of two kinds of causality. In the first place, there is a continuous production of commodities by means of commodities and labour. Intermediate products are eliminated by using the concept of vertically integrated sectors. A direct causal link between the non-produced factor of production and final output is thus established. This type of causality could be called vertical causality: a predetermined variable (labour) exercises a causal effect on a determined variable (output) at any moment of time; in a way causality is vertical to the time axis. Causal models embodying vertical causality tell us how causality works in principle, in fact independently of time. But the way in which the causal effect is exercised may change its form as time goes by. This is taken account of by horizontal causality. Due to technical progress the amount of labour required to produce a unit of final output diminishes continuously in the course of time. In fact, past inventions (the predetermined variables) govern actual labour coefficients (the determined variables). Obviously,

The Significance of the Labour Theory of Value

causality runs horizontally along the time axis here, thus the term 'horizontal causality'.

In this context it may be noted that the modelling of vertical causality leads to the formation of theoretical models, e.g. the model describing the interindustry aspect of production (production of commodities by means of commodities) as set forth in Sraffa (1960) and Pasinetti (1977) or the model picturing the vertically integrated aspect of the process of production as is made use of in Pasinetti (1981). Horizontal causality, however, is immediately linked with the influence of the past upon the present, e.g. with historical developments. The past changes in the production coefficients of Pasinetti (1981) and the coming into being of new goods and new coefficients represent 'technical history', so to speak, which means that the vertically integrated model is particularly well suited to capture historical developments in the field of production. Pasinetti (1977 and 1981) thus establishes the analytical foundations for neatly integrating the theoretical and the historical element in economics in general, and in production in particular, as vertical and horizontal causality are both implied in his natural system. The way in which the integration of theory and history is to be carried out in the case of production is described in Chapter VI of Pasinetti (1981).

It may perhaps be recalled here that, besides the theoretical work done, the historical aspect has been strongly insisted on by the Classical economists and by Marx. The long-run tendency towards the stationary state in Ricardo and Marx's laws of capitalist development are but prominent examples of describing historical tendencies of change by making use of economic analysis.

PASINETTI AND WALRAS: PRODUCTION VERSUS EXCHANGE

Some of the threads of thought taken up in the previous sections may now be gathered together in order to bring out the wider meaning of Pasinetti's natural system. To situate the natural system broadly within economic theory, it is most appropriate to compare it with another system of pure theory, i.e. the Walrasian one, which will be briefly done in the present section. In the second place, some implications related to this comparison will be brought out.

Let us, then, first recapitulate some of the essential features of Pasinetti's natural system as briefly sketched in the foregoing sections. The starting point is production, which is essentially a social process in that there is extensive division of labour which implies that individuals active in different industries and sectors cooperate in order to reach a common (social) aim, i.e. the production of the social product which includes the surplus at society's disposal. Distribution is regulated by institutions other than the market (so-called factor markets do not exist in the natural system). Exchange stands primarily in the service of production. This is even true to a large extent of the buying of consumption goods by individuals who consume partly in order to maintain their 'productive' capacities and partly to enjoy the surplus coming out of production. Exchange relations are governed by the social effort made in order to produce one unit of some good. In the positive natural system prices correspond to labour equivalents while in the normative natural system a pure labour theory of value emerges. Both systems imply a theory of personal income distribution as reduction coefficients will have to be determined through complex social processes.

The positive system may easily be completed by a long-run theory of employment. In a further step, money might be brought in with relation to the (speculative) behaviour of individuals acting within historically grown structures, i.e. technology and institutions. The normative natural system would have to be completed by a careful description of the natural institutions, i.e. the state and its role and the tasks of producers' cooperatives.

The broad content of the Walrasian system can be brought out best by having a quick look at the structure of Walras's *Eléments* (Walras, 1952, first edn 1874). Clearly, *the starting point is exchange* (ibid., Sections II and III, pp. 43ff.) Individuals are endowed with certain quantities of goods; tastes are given. Now, exchange starts, the behaviour of each individual being guided by the aim of utility maximization. This leads to a new allocation of goods which is a social optimum in the sense that it is not possible to increase the well-being of one or several individuals without diminishing the well-being of others. In a second step, production is introduced (Section IV, pp. 175ff.). The problem is to allocate given (or variable) quantities of factors of production in a way that each producer maximizes his profit. It is of crucial importance to note that production is regulated by exchange which takes place on 'factor markets'. In Section V capital accumulation is brought in. Again, equilibrium on the market for new capital goods is brought about by exchange ('Courbes d'achat et de vente des capitaux neufs', pp. 289–90).

The Significance of the Labour Theory of Value

Finally, in Section VI the determination of absolute (money) prices is considered, while parts of Section VII are devoted to some issues of development in the long run. Comparing the systems of Pasinetti and of Walras in the light of what has been said in the preceding sections of this note brings out some important implications which can, of course, only be hinted at here (for a more extensive development of many issues related to production and exchange see Baranzini and Scazzieri, 1986).

First of all in Pasinetti's natural system production is clearly the starting point for analysis while exchange, in its being in the service of production, plays a secondary role. The contrary holds in Walras's system. Here, exchange between individuals dominates everything; production is, in fact, an application of the principle of exchange: on factor market exchange links demand and supply of productive services so as to bring about an optimal allocation of disposable resources. This is not to say that in Pasinetti's natural system there is no optimal allocation of resources. Here, however, allocation is regulated by a different principle: given the (long-run) prices of production, that is, the natural prices, it is demand which regulates sector sizes and thus the allocation of resources, i.e. labour; the natural prices, in turn, may be associated with 'optimal' techniques of production (on this, see Pasinetti, 1977, pp. 151ff.).

Second, different social philosophies are behind both systems. In Pasinetti's natural system technology and institutions (which are implied) form a structure which to some extent determines the behaviour of individuals. For example, the prices of production depend upon the conditions of production which are the result of past capital accumulation and upon distribution which is governed by a set of institutions which have developed historically. Competition now brings about a tendency to sell goods and services at the prices of production. The objective factors governing the latter thus force producers to act in a certain way. Because of the importance of technological and social structures Pasinetti's natural system may said to be based upon the principle of 'structurism' (see on this Lloyd, 1986, pp. 148ff.). To some extent the behaviour of individuals is thus governed by objectively given structures which have developed historically; determinism is (as has been alluded to above) mainly occuring in the sphere of production. Within given structures there are, however, areas of freedom for individuals, above all in the sphere of consumption or, more generally, in relation with the use of the surplus; in addition, the possibility to move within structures (social mobility) may also constitute an important element of freedom. If the normative part of Pasinetti's natural system is considered, the relationship between structures (as linked with determinism) and free choice comes out most clearly: structures stand, so to speak, in the service of individuals, permitting them to unfold their potential individual capacities. This point which, of course, is also implied in classical (and Marxian) political economy, can best be brought out by considering the production and the use of the surplus. Production of the national product and thus of the surplus provides the material basis for a higher social and individual life which is linked to the various possible uses of the surplus (political and cultural institutions, and non-necessary consumption for example).

The Walrasian system, however, is clearly based upon the principle of individualism. In the economic sphere there is free choice (within budget constraints of course) and the market is supposed costlessly to coordinate the profit and utility maximizing behaviour of individuals. Structural constraints appear outside the economic sphere only: political and legal institutions provide a structural framework which enforces certain types of behaviour. All the important economic problems, i.e. value, distribution, employment and so on, are, however, solved by the natural economic institution of neoclassical economics, that is, by the market.

From the different social philosophies implied in the systems of Pasinetti and Walras a related third point immediately emerges, namely the different role played by institutions in both systems. In Pasinetti's natural system (economic and non-economic) institutions *directly* govern the outcome of economic events. For example, the natural prices depend on the conditions of production and upon the institutions regulating income distribution. In the Walrasian system, however, all important economic problems are solved by just one natural (i.e. not man-made) institution, namely the market. Institutions created by human beings (political, legal and social institutions) exercise an *indirect* effect upon economic events only. In a neoclassical (Walrasian) view, these institutions act through the market by shifting demand and supply curves. For instance, trade-unions may bring about a leftward shift of the supply curve of labour, thus pushing up wages and, consequently, diminishing the volume of employment. The direct economic relevance of non-economic institutions is perhaps the main reason why Pasinetti's natural system if seen together with the Keynesian principle of effective demand form a system of *political economy* while the Walrasian system is a piece of

The Significance of the Labour Theory of Value

economics; in a way one could even speak, as Walras does, of pure economics.

Fourthly, Walrasian economics is clearly normative in nature: the *Eléments d'économie politique pure* tells us how an ideally functioning liberal economic system ought to look like. Reality is then interpreted in terms of deviations from the ideal which frequently appear in the form of imperfections which, of course, include market failures. Pasinetti's natural system, however, is both positive and normative (see pp. 364–74). The normative natural system is, however, normative in a special way in that it is not very far away from reality as is the case with the liberal Walrasian system (and with centrally planned socialist economies). The 'state of the world' implied in Pasinetti's normative natural system might be reached by institutional reforms. As such it resembles very much Quesnay's system embodied in the *Tableau économique* which describes a reasonable (natural) situation of the French economy as opposed to the chaotic heritage left by mercantilist economic policy. Normative models of the Quesnay-Pasinetti type could be termed 'moderately normative'. To approach some desirable situation parts of the actually existing situation may be preserved while others have to be changed through reforms. This is entirely different in 'extreme' normative models, that is the liberal or the central planning model, which may require thoroughgoing changes of historically grown situations. In this process valuable institutions that have stood the test of time may eventually be partly or entirely destroyed.

Fifth, the fact that in the positive natural system no automatic tendency towards a full employment situation exists requires its complementing by a macroeconomic model of the Keynesian type (see pp. 364–70 above). There is, however, no need for a macroeconomic complement in a Walrasian model. Here the market is supposed to solve the employment problem, in the long run at least.

Finally, in the introductory chapter to his book Luigi Pasinetti presents some distinctions, two of which have given rise to particularly heated discussions. At some stages, he associates neoclassical (Walrasian) economics with 'optimatization' (rationality, rational allocation of resources) and with dealing with 'scarce' goods only; while his own classical approach to economic problems emphasizes 'learning' and takes account exclusively of goods that can be produced without limit, that is reproducible goods or commodities of the production type. There seems to be a misunderstanding here. It is of course true that neoclassical economics *starts* from individual optimization and the fact that economic goods are always scarce, i.e. are not 'free' goods. However, neoclassical economics allows the additional production of goods if there are increases in demand; also learning (technical progress) may be brought in. On the other hand, as is indeed hinted at on p. 24 of Pasinetti (1981), the natural system contains an 'optimization' aspect in that, given profit rates, money wages and sufficient competition, producers aim at choosing cost-minimizing techniques of production, behaviour which, on the macro level, corresponds to maximizing the surplus if the employment level is given. Furthermore, the scarcity aspect may be brought into Pasinetti's natural system in the same way as Ricardo did for agriculture and mining. The prices of the corresponding goods increase if the conditions of production become more and more unfavourable. It does not seem appropriate, then, to state that neoclassical models deal with some problems while neglecting others and vice versa for classical-Keynesian models. Both approaches are capable of dealing with *all* economic problems. However, the *way* in which problems are tackled are completely different, which in turn is due to an entirely different outlook on real world problems, that is, to different ways of perceiving the broad functioning of socioeconomic systems. In other words, it is social philosophies and the (Schumpeterian) visions derived therefrom which are different.

Given this, how can an economist make a choice between entirely different socioeconomic theories such as the Walrasian model and Pasinetti's natural system? The only possibility seems to be the acquiring of what might be called theoretical and practical experience. One must persist in asking which approach underlying the theories in question is more satisfactory both from a theoretical and empirical point of view. Or, more specifically, which theory allows us to deal with important problems (value, distribution, employment, technical progress etc.) in a more plausible way? That is, one has to form an opinion based upon comprehensive experience. It is our conviction that, in doing so, most economists will find Pasinetti's natural system, complemented by the Keynesian model in an appropriate way, far more satisfactory than the neoclassical equilibrium model. This brings us back to the outset of these notes, where it has been stated that the 'natural system' will have a lasting influence upon the future development of economic theory, the main reason being, of course, that the great classical economists (including Marx) and Keynes simply cannot be ignored if we are attempting to explain what is going on in the real world. Providing the analytical foundations for the bringing together of Ricardo and Keynes in a great synthesis of Post-Keynesian political economy is indeed the principal achievement of Luigi Pasinetti's natural system.

REFERENCES

Baranzini, M. and Scazzieri, R. (eds) (1986) *Foundations of Economics: Structures of Inquiry and Economic Theory* (Oxford and New York: Blackwell).
Bliss, C. (1986) 'Progress and Anti-Progress in Economic Science', in Baranzini and Scazzieri (eds) (1986), pp. 363–76.
Bortis, H. (1984) 'Employment in a Capitalist Economy', *Journal of Post-Keynesian Economics*, 6, pp. 590–604.
Lloyd, C. (1986) *Explanation in Social History* (Oxford: Basil Blackwell).
Pasinetti, L. (1977). *Lectures on the Theory of Production* (Macmillan: London and Basingstoke).
Pasinetti, L. (1981) *Structural Change and Economic Growth: A Theoretical Essay on the Dynamics of the Wealth of Nations* (Cambridge: Cambridge University Press).
Pasinetti, L. (1986) 'Theory of Value: a Source of Alternative Paradigms in Economic Analysis', in Baranzini and Scazzieri (eds) (1986), pp. 409–31.
Roncaglia, A. (1988) 'The Sraffian Schools', unpublished mimeo, Università di Roma, 'La Sapienza'.
Schumpeter, J. A. (1954) *History of Economic Analysis* (London: Allen and Unwin).
Sraffa, P. (1960) *Production of Commodities by Means of Commodities* (Cambridge: Cambridge University Press).
Steedman, I. (1977) *Marx after Sraffa* (London: New Left Books).
Walras, L. (1952, 1st edn 1874) *Eléments d'Economie Politique Pure ou Théorie de la Richesse Sociale* (Paris: Librairie Générale de Droit et de Jurisprudence).

14 Rationality and Economic Behaviour
Siro Lombardini

THE ROLE OF INDIVIDUALS AND OF INDUSTRIES (MARKETS) IN ECONOMICS

Economists are looking for microfoundations of macroeconomics. Since an individual's choices are constrained by decisions that cannot be interpreted as resulting from aggregation of individual preferences, we can also set the problem of what are the macrofoundations of microeconomics. There is a level of analysis that may help to solve both problems. It is the analysis of the interrelations between industry and markets as it has been carried out by Pasinetti (1981) in his *Structural Change and Economic Growth*. Some additional help to the understanding of these problems can come from a critical assessment of the rationality assumption that is usually made about individuals' behaviour in microeconomics. In this chapter I shall try to move in this direction, by showing why rationality criteria for the system cannot be reduced to individual rational criteria as they have been defined in the context of utilitarianism. Our analysis suggests that the two problems are interlinked.

In other fields as well scientists are starting to realize that local laws do not allow us to understand the working of the global system. When the global system is considered as a whole, the need arises to study afresh the problem of how to explain the behaviour of the elements of the system itself. (In fact there is an even more fundamental problem: are there entities, which can be considered as elements of the system, that cannot be factored into more elementary units?)

The criterion of individual rationality is defined by neo-classical economists by referring to an equilibrium that is analogous to the mechanical equilibrium of physics. Such an equilibrium cannot account for the evolution of the system. In this paper we shall confine ourselves to an analysis of the link between equilibrium and rationality in order to open the way to an analysis of the relationship between individual rationality and system rationality.

RATIONALITY AND EQUILIBRIUM

Rationality has been associated with the concept of order, namely with the assumption that the system under examination is structurally stable. According to the Newtonian conception of science, a system may be explained only if it is structurally stable. Then a model can be associated with it and a theory built up in the language of mathematics. Man's behaviour is rational if it results in some kind of social order. It is the theory of celestial mechanics that has led economists to identify social order with equilibrium in the mechanical sense. In fact – as Hayek has shown – the concept of social order is weaker than that of equilibrium.

In any case, when we talk of social order we assume that some essential features of society can be foreseen. The concept of rationality is thus linked with that of certainty. Certainty may be provided either by causal laws or by functional associations that are established among the relevant events. 'If A then P, the reverse statement being meaningless': this is a paradigm of a causal law. When A is always associated with B and *vice versa*, we can talk of a functional law. The Pareto concept of mechanical equilibrium has freed economics of all causal laws. Evolution is not the result of internal laws, but of the adaptation of the system to external changes. Then only partial certainty is assured to individuals: they can know how the system will react to the external factors which are the cause of evolution. In fact the evolution of the system depends not only upon the process of adjustment which may be explained by the functional laws constituting the theory of general equilibrium. It depends also upon exogeneous factors (like population growth, technical progress, etc.) inducing changes in the state of equilibrium. As we shall see in a moment, partial certainty endangers the rationalistic foundations of the neo-classical approach.

Rational behaviour has been identified with optimizing behaviour. For this approach to be acceptable, we must assume that individuals' optimizing behaviour can occur simultaneously and be compatible with one another. If individuals' decisions depend not only on the initial conditions and on the information provided by the market (prices) but also on their expectations, optimizing behaviour can no longer be considered as rational if rationality is defined as the search for the actions that enable individuals to reach their goals in the most efficient way. Thus the fundamental theorem that individuals' rational behaviour brings the system to equilibrium seems to loose its traditional ground.

In order to revitalize it we must make two assumptions:

(i) Expectations are rational and information is adequate (and symmetrical).
(ii) Markets can be cleared instantaneously.

Both assumptions are made by the new neo-classical economists. Their approach cannot provide satisfactory grounds for the link that has been established between equilibrium and rationality.

In making the assumption of adequate information, rational-expectations economists do consider as relevant those external events that are produced by the decisions of the state. Thus for the first condition to be granted it is sufficient that the state announces its decisions on economic policy in time. In fact such a condition is never satisfied because government actions do not pursue a coherent set of goals on the basis of objective evaluations. Even if economic policy is foreseeable, information cannot be adequate since relevant for individuals' behaviour are not only economic policy decisions. Many other events of a different kind may change the perspectives of the economy. Therefore, even in case of a coherent economic policy announced in time, the future values of many exogenous variables would be uncertain.

In fact, in a dynamic context there are additional reasons for individuals' expectations to diverge. People have different opinions not only about the process of adjustment and its speed, but also on the way the growth factors operate. All individuals may agree that a certain technical innovation is forthcoming and yet they may differ on the date of such a future event.

Divergencies in expectations are not only inevitable: they are also necessary for the economy to develop. Uniformity of expectations are incompatible with entrepreneurs being innovators. Speculation is possible because people have different expectations.

As Hayek (1937) has pointed out, the market system is a necessary mechanism for efficiency (more precisely for some conditions for efficiency) just because the knowledge division can be exploited.

Let us now turn to the second assumption which is required to link rationality to equilibrium. We do not need to spend many words to prove why such an assumption is untenable. We need only to remember what happened in the Wall Street crisis of 17 October 1987, when the agents' rational decisions (rationality being helped by computers!) caused the market to collapse, the Federal Reserve being forced to behave in just the way that monetarism deems irrational.

When we drop the assumption of instantaneous clearance of the markets, a more general and relevant problem arises: i.e. the problem of rationality. As Simon (1976) has shown, we can no longer adhere to the substantive rationality approach; we must adopt a conception of procedural rationality. Procedural rationality no longer assures that individual rational decisions are consistent with each other. Speculative activity is based on the assumption that they are not.

A WEAKER DEFINITION OF RATIONALITY

Popper (1987, p. 145) has suggested a weaker concept of rationality. According to him, we can talk of rational behaviour in so far as we assume that 'individuals always behave in the way that fits better to the situations in which they find themselves'. Popper, who does not adhere to the instrumentalistic approach as it has been actually applied to economics by Friedman, thinks that also for the postulates (assumptions) a refutability problem can arise. In fact the rationality postulate is refuted: it is easy to find instances of behaviour that cannot be qualified as rational in Popper's sense. In spite of that, according to Popper, the rationality postulate must be accepted as a methodological principle required, in economics, to produce theoretical models that can be framed in such a way as to be refutable. In fact, in Popper's opinion, there is no alternative principle that allows us to arrive at a scientific explanation of social activities.

Popper's principle of rationality covers both Pareto's logical actions as well as the non-logical action, if by the term 'situation' we consider not only individuals' tastes and their resources, but also their beliefs, expectations, psychological and sociological propensities, their information and capacity to perceive and to evaluate objective data. Then the principle, contrary to what has been stated by Popper himself, appears as an *a priori* principle (similar to Kant's *a priori* synthetic truths, such as the causality principle); namely a principle that reason has to be equipped with in order to understand social behaviour. In fact we must start from some preanalytical knowledge that includes also general paradigms enabling us to build specific models (in Kuhn's sense) applied in the various scientific fields. With reference to these general paradigms the problem is not how to make and evaluate a refutability test, but how to argue in order to find possible alternatives.

ACTION AND CHOICE

Rationality, both in Pareto's conception and in Popper's weaker one, presupposes the concept of free will, or, to say it in Hayek's terms, intentional actions. The *a priori* principle of rationality needs to be associated with another *a priori* principle. In fact, as Ryle has stressed, volition is an 'artificial concept' to which we must refer when we want to explain how ideas are converted into facts. I think that the free choice premise to the analysis of rational behaviour may be grounded only on the basis of our psychological experience as has been substantially asserted by the Austrian economists (Hayek in particular). When I make up my mind about the restaurant where I shall have my lunch today, I feel that I can choose. I shall not feel free if I am obliged by somebody else to go to a particular restaurant. That corresponds to the concept of freedom outlined by Ayer (1984, p. 12). Psychologists will try to explain my behaviour; perhaps they will find a certain number of factors that can account for my choice. Yet to understand human actions we must visualize the problems that individuals want or need to solve. The problems become relevant (and need to be solved) when certain conditions occur; the way a problem is framed (and is perceived) depends on the information available to the individual. Some of the factors accounting for the action can be considered as initial conditions. The fact that a psychologist can find another set of conditions (factors) that, added to the initial conditions, can produce a unique explanation of the individual's choice does not invalidate the approach aiming at explaining the action as an intentional action.

What we can say is that we have two different paradigms in order to understand human behaviour:
– a descriptive one that may offer an *ex-post* explanation and, possibly, can help in forecasting what an individual having particular features will do in specified conditions,

– a normative one that may help us to visualize how an individual, being rational, will operate in given conditions.

Each paradigm has its own shortcomings. When we apply the first we can never be sure that the underlying theory is adequate to explain individual behaviour. In fact behaviour that is considered anomalous, according to some specific theory, is rather frequent. What the sociologist aims at discovering is how the majority of individuals act in given conditions.

The second paradigm also has its shortcomings. We must first of all isolate a certain problem (my choice of the restaurant) from others. In fact the individual problem that economists want to explain is interlinked with other problems; the way it is perceived depends also on these specific connections.

If we consider some of these connections it may be difficult to isolate a number of problems. Hubert L. Dreyfus and Stuart E. Dreyfus (1975, v. 1, p. 120) have shown that when individuals (who may choose among different combinations of possible outcomes with different probabilities) have strong feelings about risk or are seriously concerned about equity, 'optimal decision should be arrived at holistically and not by decision analysis'.

Even if we disregard the effects that some of the individual's feelings may have on the perception of the problem, the rationality principle cannot be deemed sufficient to make it possible to foresee individual behaviour. In fact, the result of the choice depends not only on the rationality principle that has been applied, but also on the information and on the expectations of individuals. Since we have not sufficient information about the information available to the individuals and we cannot know their expectations in advance, it is difficult both to prove and to refute, on the basis of the result of the individual actions, whether a certain rationality principle has been applied or not (see Anscombe, 1957).

If we assume, according to the view of the rational expectation economists, that people, having definite goals and adequate and certain information, act in order to maximize some pre-established objective function, the concept of free will loses its sense. Man will act as a goal-pursuing robot. Yet, as Harsanyi has remarked:

> To be sure, while we could at least conceive of a perfectly well-constructed goal-pursuing robot, completely consistent and completely single minded in working for his pre-established goal,

human beings are seldom that consistent. In some situations, they will be deflected from their objective by Freudian-type emotional factors, while in others they will fail to pursue any well-defined objective altogether. (Harsanyi, 1986, p. 84; first edn 1977)

PROBABILITY AND ECONOMIC BEHAVIOUR

In many models of rational choice, devices have been found to reduce uncertainty to a sophisticated certainty context. The essential algorithm is the probability calculus. Probability is defined as a property of subjective evaluations. I shall confine myself to games with incomplete information: each player does not know what kind of rivals he has to face, and, possibly, what their payoff functions are, the strategical possibilities available to them and the amount of information they have on the game. Harsanyi (1967–8) has produced a model to deal with this kind of game. The model is based on the assumption that the players' subjective probability distribution over all possible types of other players are sufficiently consistent to be expressible in terms of one basic probability matrix. As Harsanyi explains 'What this model does is to reduce the original game with incomplete information . . . to an artificial constructed game with complete information' (Harsanyi, 1967–8, p. 91).

As we have seen above, the consistency hypothesis is disputable in a certainty context. It is much more difficult to accept when we talk about subjective probabilities: the assumption is indeed heroic when consistency is required for the probabilities of all players in order for their expectations to be mutually consistent.

In very few situations may subjective probabilities be grounded on objective information. In general they reflect not only the information available to the player but also some of their psychological and sociological features, their interest in the game and their feelings about the other players. Because of their nature, it is reasonable to assume that the players' expectations are mutually inconsistent and are adjusted through a learning process. Such an assumption is in line with a number of remarks by Wiener.

The probability algorithm is used to reduce uncertainty to some kind of certainty equivalent also in model building, after Haavelmo's (1944) fundamental contribution. Such an approach is open to serious objections. In thermodynamics – as well as in quantum theory – the probability algorithm is used as a scientific paradigm. In other fields (as in biology) it can be considered as a tool to describe states of nature that resemble the logical model of an urn containing balls differing from one another only in colour (in situations arising for instance in the field of biology). By using the probabilistic approach in medicine we can produce informations that may be considered valid in a instrumentalistic context. In economics we cannot consider the probability model as specific scientific paradigms (in fact they are intended to translate uncertain contexts into certainty-equivalent ones). Neither we can assume that the situations we are dealing with resemble the ideal ones interpreted by the urn model. There is the risk that the probability model has in fact the role of increasing the probability of the model being confirmed by facts. Such an advantage (but is it really?) is paid by the loss of relevance of the results obtained by the applications of the model.

When we apply the probability algorithm to the analysis of individual choice, probability assignments reflect only subjective evaluations and propensities. For such applications we must assume that the individual is capable of translating all perspectives into sets of different states of nature, each set comprising states that are mutually exclusive, and the sum of the probabilities of the various states must amount to unity.

In 1953, in a paper on 'Uncertainty in economic theory', I opposed the generally held view of complete knowledge of alternatives by the more realistic assumption that an agent has incomplete knowledge (cf. Lombardini, 1953, pp. 25–57). An individual always has the feeling that something that he cannot perceive may happen, this changing the perspectives as they appear from the alternative he can visualize. This means that if the agent is consistent in his evaluation of the alternatives individually perceived, the sum of the probabilities assigned to them is less than unity. The difference between unity and such a sum may be considered as a measure of what I called residual uncertainty. In a contribution of mine to the monopoly theory, in 1954 (see Lombardini, 1954, p. 403), I applied such a notion to the analysis of the process by which a monopolist arrives at his conjectured demand curve: the curve has a kink at the point corresponding to the current sales. Meade (1970, p. vii) later utilized my notion of residual uncertainty to clarify the reasons for indicative planning.

SUBSTANTIVE AND PROCEDURAL RATIONALITY. THE COMPLEX PROCESS OF DECISIONS

Uncertainty is an inescapable context – and, indeed, a favourable one – for human action.[1] Then optimizing behaviour as it has been defined in the context of the general equilibrium theory cannot be deemed a rational criterion for action. Simon has suggested a move from such a conception of rationality (substantive rationality) to a concept of procedural rationality.

> As economics becomes more concerned with procedural rationality, it will necessarily have to borrow from psychology or build for itself a far more complex theory of human cognitive process than it has had in the past. Even if our interest lies in normative rather than descriptive economics, we will need such a theory. (Simon, 1979, p. 81; first edn 1976)

I am definitely in favour of the second of the two approaches suggested by Simon. One must realize that the decision process is a complex one. A fundamental role is played by expectations that cannot be explained either on the basis of the the rational expectation approach or of the adaptive expectation one. The decision process is complex because it entails assessments that resemble those of the optimizing behaviour model as well as evaluations that are proper of procedural rationality.

A few considerations may be useful on the links between the various mechanisms that enable us to define the individual decision problem. They are essentially:

An Optimization Model

To be rational an individual must operate in order to reach the goals he is pursuing in the most efficient way. In an uncertain context there may be some difficulties even in defining the individual's goals. In fact for a firm one strategy may be preferable to another that is more profitable if the former is likely to make easier the adjustment of its structure to unforeseeable changes, namely if it entails a higher degree of *flexibility*. The goals are not decided once and for all. As we shall say below, they will be adjusted after the experience acquired during the process.

A Model for the Formation of Expectations

Individuals have to utilize all available informations to estimate some of the variables entering the optimization model. Such an operation is performed according to the models that individuals have built in their minds, more or less consciously.

A Mechanism of Learning

In the process individuals acquire experiences and information that enable them to revise:

(i) the optimization model (the goals may be revised: for instance the flexibility requirements may increase or decrease);
(ii) the set of facts that are deemed to be relevant and the mechanism by which they are utilized for the formation of expectations and for the acquisition of experience (process of learning);
(iii) the model for the formation of expectations;
(iv) the mechanisms of learning.

A Model for Error Correction

When expectations are not realized (when for instance stocks increase faster than was expected) individuals have to make some corrections in their expectations or in the models in which the problem is framed. The model for error correction establishes some links with the other models.

It is usually assumed that the analysis of decision process leads to continuous relations among the relevant variables. Discontinuities are usually associated with decisions of economic policies. In fact – as Goodwin (1951) has shown – discontinuities may result also as a consequence of market decisions. Even at the individual level, there may be reasons for having discontinuities. When some inequalities (between the rate of assets rentability and the rate of interest) are reversed, individuals may find it convenient to change their behaviour abruptly (for instance to stop purchasing assets and to increase their money funds).

Up to now we have assumed that individuals are autonomous and act independently from one another. Even in this case – and even in the context of the theory of equilibrium – the aggregation of the relations explaining their behaviour raises difficult problems if individuals are not the same under those aspects that are relevant for the process of aggregation. The difficulties increase tremendously if interactions among individuals are taken into account.

A first set of difficulties arise with regard to the same choice criteria. As McClennen (1975) has proved, the expected-utility principle, as a basic criterion of rational behaviour, looks less plausible than is usually thought.

A second set concerns the learning mechanism. As Bjierring has remarked:

> Sometimes we 'know' our opponent and sometimes we don't. Exactly what is involved in 'knowing' our opponent is a large issue . . . In short 'knowing' an opponent means that every particular interaction with him should be viewed as one in a *series* of interactions; and that series itself has an important unity overlooked by traditional game theory. (Bjierring, 1976)

A third specific set of difficulties concerns the strategy that the various individuals have to adopt concerning the interrelation between their decisions. The analysis of situations like the prisoner's dilemma, to which the von Neumann criteria are not applicable, leads Burns and Meeker to state that:

> Knowledge of the action structure is not sufficient. Also necessary are procedures capable of coordinating decision-making. This may pose obvious difficulties in the case of social action. For instance, chlorination generally requires certain opportunities for implicit or explicit communication among the actors involved. Even if the conditions for a 'cooperative game' – possibly for communication and making 'binding agreements' obtain – the social relationships between the actors may be such as to preclude or inhibit utilization of available opportunities. (Burns and Meeker, 1978, p. 107)

Even in the context of von Neumann and Morgenstern's theory of games, if we want to make the result of the model manageable, we have to make some assumptions about the social relations among actors, as Luce and Raiffa (1957) have shown.

There has recently been considerable research work on the microeconomic foundations of macroeconomics. As we have remarked, there is also a problem of macroeconomic foundations of microeconomics. Some of the rational expectations economists are right when they stress the possible changes in individuals' behaviour produced by changes in economic policy. Such a remark ought however to be generalized. The economy is a system whose global behaviour may change also because of its connections with the social system. Such changes are bound to affects individuals' behaviour.

ACTIONS, OUTCOMES AND PROBABILITIES

In the analysis of economic behaviour so far considered, economic behaviour is the result of the individual's choice. The individual is conceived of as a goal-pursuing agent. Such a conception is inadequate when we consider various economic operators for whom goals are simply results of actions: the results having a certain degree of desirability. In Schumpeter's thought, the entrepreneur is such an operator. In fact in his opinion, entrepreneurs are different from the kind of agent that make the choice for the firm according to neoclassical theory. Entrepreneurial activity has a value in itself. It aims at power. Money, as was noticed by Smith, is power. In fact profits measure the success of entrepreneurial activity. But power cannot be reduced to the economic utility of having a certain quantity of money at our disposal. The entrepreneur is not the same kind of animal as the rentier. Weber would say that business is different from finance.

On a logical plane, Savage has, in a certain sense, reversed the paradigm underlying the neoclassical analysis of rational behaviour. The structure of the neo-classical paradigm can thus be stated: we start from the individual's goals summarized by an objective function; we then assume that the individual has certain means to reach them. The problem is a 'choice problem': the choice of the means that maximize the objective function. According to Savage, we need to start from action and think of those consequences of action that are judged desirable by the operator (instead of the goals assumed as given *a priori* in the neoclassical paradigm).

Gibbard and Harper (1978) have started from Savage's approach and distinguished two kinds of expected utility: one is the sum of the probabilities that the various actions will produce specific results to which we can attach a magnitude expressing the degree of desirability; the other is the Bayesian expected utility, i.e. the sum of the probabilities of the various outcomes that will be obtained (given the various actions), the desirability measure being attached to every single outcome. The two kind of expected utility are by no means necessarily equal; the two authors examine the case where the two differ. They diverge, in fact, when a common factor is believed to affect both behaviour and outcome. The Schumpeterian definition of entrepreneurial activity seems to offer an interesting instance of such a case.

When we consider actions we cannot assume that they represent a coherent and ordered set for the individual. Action A may be perceived as the one that produces the more favourable results in the present period; other actions (B) being available such that, by causing limited damage now, can produce great advantages in the future. Individuals may be well aware that a rational trade off will suggest taking action B and yet may actually choose action A. It is relevant to quote the Latin poet Lucrezio: *Video meliora proboque, sed deteriora sequor* (I see what is better and I approve it, but I choose what is worst). Thus for a rational action individuals have to abide by a moral precept. Single individuals will thus find themselves in situations similar to those that can occur when the whole society is considered, as we shall see in a moment.

AGGREGATION AND RATIONALITY

So far we have been concerned with single individuals; rationality has been defined in normative terms, in the hope of being able to predict their behaviour. In fact economists seldom apply their theories to forecast the behaviour of a single individual. What they want to explain is the behaviour of a sufficiently large set of individuals who are supposed to be solving similar problems (families purchasing certain commodities, firms of a certain industry deciding the level of investment, and so on). When we aggregate individuals the problem of rationality needs to be faced afresh for three reasons:

(i) If we assume that the individual's tastes reflect his autonomy and apathy, namely that there is no envy nor philanthropy, the choice of any individual is independent from the choice made by other individuals. The society may be interpreted as a set of individuals. On this assumption Pareto has proposed a rationality principle, for the society as a whole, that is coherent with methodological individualism. In fact sentiments of envy and of benevolence are largely diffused. If we disregard such sentiments we can find situations in which changes in the structure of the economy can make some people better off, the other being unaffected by the change. Pareto's optimality criterion tells us that we must move towards such situations. Yet if envy for people that benefit from the change is rather diffused we cannot tell whether the change entails greater welfare for the society. Pareto has denied the possibility of making comparison between different situations which are rational according to his criterion (Pareto optima). Yet if sentiment of benevolence towards certain strata of society are diffused, a change from a Pareto optimum to another that improves the welfare of these strata may be welcomed also by those whose situation would have to be considered worse, should they be indifferent towards the effects of the change.

(ii) For economists two kinds of social aggregation are relevant: that revealed by the market and that occuring in the political system where decisions are based on polls. The first kind of social aggregation is assumed to be sufficient to explain productive activities and consumption. We are becoming more and more aware that there are some goods (public goods, as, for instance, the environment) that cannot be produced after an aggregation of the first kind. Political decisions are required. Two specific problems then arise: what are the alternatives among which to choose and how are collective decisions arrived at? The two kinds of social aggregation can no longer be considered separate from each other; there are interrelations between them that cannot be ignored by economists.

(iii) Individuals by their choice can alter the conditions under which other individuals make their own. Thus two possibilities arise. Either we assume that individuals can and will take account of such interdependences in framing their own action (oligopoly) in such a way as to produce an optimum for the system, or we ought to expect a link to be established between the two kinds of social aggregation we have mentioned above. The theory of games has been devised to deal with these interdependences. Yet their analysis is still largely unsatisfactory (see, in particular, Bjierring, 1978; Burns and Meeker, 1978). We have hinted above at some of the difficulties which arise when we dealt with interdependence between the individual's actions.

INDIVIDUAL OR SYSTEM RATIONALITY?

In the past economists have associated self-interest with individual action. Situations may indeed arise where self-interest can be pursued only through collective action (political decisions). Let us consider the problem of pollution which is getting more and more serious. If people damaged by other people's behaviour are few, we can conceive of some kind of negotiation that can bring about an efficient state of the economy, provided that what we are interested in is a structure of the system which is rational according to the Pareto principle. On the contrary, if damaged people are numerous, private negotiations are practically impossible. A general operator (the state) has to visualize the state being rational according to the Pareto criterion and induce all individuals to behave in such a way as to make it possible to bring the economy to such a state by some specific political decisions.

A philosophical-political problem arises at this point: how can we be sure that the political mechanism will produce decisions capable of bringing the system to a Pareto optimum condition? For this problem to make any sense, we must assume that the state can visualize ex-ante the Pareto optimum condition. In general there is not a unique Pareto-optimum condition even if the initial condition, being the one that the choices autonomously made by individuals tend to produce, is unique. The possible Pareto optimum conditions to which the state can bring the economy may differ because of different income distributions. Then again a problem arises: on the basis of what criteria can the state choose among these various conditions? Such a question is a specific instance of a more general question. In fact society has to choose one of the possible set-ups which are required to allow individuals to be capable of making their choices. The individuals' behaviour on the market presupposes a social context which cannot be the result of individual choice.

We are then left with two alternatives. Either we assume as given the institutional set-up or we must have rationality criteria which are not the same as those by which individuals evaluate the alternatives that, given the set-up, are offered to them. This has been clearly stated by Arrow who, having reminded us that in a market economy 'any social action is thought of as being factored into a sequence of individual actions' points out that

> the partition of a social action into individual components, and the corresponding assignment of individual responsibility, is not a datum. Rather, the particular factoring in any given context is itself the result of a social policy and therefore already the outcome of earlier and logically more primitive values. (Arrow, 1979, p. 114)

Pareto was quite aware that an assessment of the structure of society cannot be made on the basis of the mere criterion of ophemility. He speaks in fact of a calculus of utility that science is not able to perform. What can be said is that social values cannot be reduced to individuals' utility assessments.

Let us assume that individuals of both present and future generations are very similar to each other and let us associate with each action taken by the state a set of magnitudes expressing all direct and indirect effects that, by knowing how individuals will react, we can foresee. Actions by the state can either produce public goods or change the institutional set-up and the economic conditions affecting individual choices on the markets. Every individual will evaluate each effect on the prospect of being the one that will benefit from it (if the effect is positive) or be damaged by it (if negative). Having assumed that individuals are similar we can suppose that their evaluations are identical. We may distinguish three cases:

(i) some actions A entail effects that individuals deem unbearable and that could be avoided by taking different actions (Rawls' constraint);
(ii) some actions B entail effects that are considered no more positive than those associated with other actions, some of the latter being deemed more positive (Pareto constraint);
(iii) there are actions C that will produce radical changes in the situation such as to make individuals no longer similar (incomparability constraint).

Let us exclude actions A, B and C. We are left with a set of actions whose effects individuals can bear. For the effects associated with each admissible action, individuals will determine weights in such a way as to make possible a comparison between actions in the prospect of having an equal chance of being the ones that will benefit from the positive effects and that will be damaged by the negative ones.

In this way social values can be expressed on the basis of a generalized Kant morality principle.[2] Having postulated individuals sufficiently similar to one another, we can assume that this principle works. Such a principle makes it possible to evaluate as non-moral a set of actions (A and B). It enables us to produce a moral assessment of action C.

The social values that can be produced on the generalized Kant morality principle are in fact a first-level definition of social values. We must recall that, as we have already mentioned, the assumption that men are similar disregards some essential features of the human person. Even if we imagine conditions, through a logical process, at the beginning of man's history, we must allow for differences among individuals. It is because of these differences, which may pre-exist or may be induced by some action, (C), that the generalized Kant principle is not sufficient to produce social values. In particular, individuals of the present generation have the power to induce the state to take specific actions for their benefit; a power that individuals of future generations do not have. Then action capable of producing serious damage to future generations may be taken, even if the interests of some individuals of these generations are, to some extent, taken care of by the present agents.

Having found it impossible to ground social values on individual utility assumptions and having proved that the Kant generalized morality principle is not sufficient to produce a complete set of social values for all prospective situations, we are left with the problem of how to find the ethical criteria which are necessary in order to judge the rationality of state action and, thereby, the efficiency of the economy as a whole. As we have shown above, ethical criteria are required also to have a complete rationality criterion for the individual, namely a criterion capable of determining optimum choice also when feasible actions do not constitute a coherent and ordered set.

NOTES

1. To justify such a statement let me invite the reader to think about the effects that would be produced should God tell us all what will happen to us from now to our death. We shall acquire complete certainty. Just because of that life will become unbearable!
2. I think we can talk of a generalized Kant morality principle in so far we assume that all effects – as may occur in the particular situations considered – are taken into account. A lie may not be immoral if the consequence of telling the truth is the death of a man.

REFERENCES

Arrow, K. J. (1979), 'Valued and Collective Decision Making', in F. H. Hahn and M. Hollis (eds) *Philosophy and Economic Theory* (Oxford: Oxford University Press).

Anscombe, G. E. M. (1957), *Intention* (Oxford: Basil Blackwell).
Ayer, A. J. (1984), *Freedom and Morality and Other Essay* (Oxford: Clarendon Press).
Bjierring, A. K. (1978), 'The 'Tracing Procedure' and a Theory of Rational Interaction', in C. A. Hooker, J. J. Leach and E. F. McClennen (eds), (1978).
Burns, T. R. and Meeker, D. (1978), 'Conflict and Structure in Multi-Level Multiple-Objective Decision-Making Systems', in C. A. Hooker, J. J. Leach and E. F. McClennen (eds), (1978).
Dreyfus, H. L., and Dreyfus, S. E. (1978), 'Inadequacy in the Decision Analysis Model of Rationality', in C. A. Hooker, J. J. Leach, E. F. McClennen (eds), (1978).
Gibbard, A., and Harper, W. L. (1978), 'Counterfactuals and Two Kinds of Expected Utility', in C. A. Hooker, J. J. Leach and E. F. McClennen (eds.), (1978).
Goodwin, R. M. (1951), 'The Nonlinear Accelerator and the Persistence of Business Cycles', *Econometrica*, January.
Haavelmo, T. (1944), 'The Probability Approach in Econometrics' *Econometrica*, Supplement.
Harsanyi, J. C. (1986) 'Advance in Understanding Rational Behaviour' in R. E. Butts and J. Hintikka (eds) *Foundational Problems in the Social Sciences*, (Dordrecht: Reidel, 1977) reprinted in Jon Elster, *Rational Choice* (New York: City of New York University Press).
Harsanyi, J. C. (1967-8), 'Games with incomplete information played by "Bayesian players"', *Management Science*.
von Hayek, F. A. (1937), 'Economics and Knowledge', *Economica*.
von Hayek, F. A. (1967) *Studies in Philosophy, Politics and Economics (Notes on the Evolution of Systems of Rules of Conduct)* (Chicago: Chicago University Press).
Hooker, C. A., Leach, J. J. and E. F. McClennen (eds) (1978) *Foundations and Applications of Decision Theory*, Vol. I (Boston: Reidel).
Lombardini, S. (1953), 'L'incertezza nella teoria economica', *Studi in memoria di Gino Borgatta* (Bologna: Il Mulino) pp. 25–57.
Lombardini, S. (1954), 'Monopolies and Rigidities in the Economic System', in E. H. Chamberlin (ed.) *Monopoly and Competition and Their Regulation* (International Economic Association) (London: Macmillan).
Lombardini, S. (1983), *Il metodo della scienza economica: passato e futuro* (Turin: UTET).
Lombardini, S. (1989), 'Market and Institutions', in T. Shiraishi and S. Tsuru (eds) *Economic Institutions in a Dynamic Society* (International Economic Association) (London: Macmillan).
Luce, R. D. and Raiffa, H. (1957), *Games and Decision* (New York: Wiley).
McClennen, E. F. (1978), 'The Minimax Theory and Expected-Utility Reasoning', in Hooker, C. A., Leach, J. J. and E. F. McClennen (eds.), (1978).
Meade, J. E. (1970), *The Theory of Indicative Planning* (Manchester: Manchester University Press).
Pasinetti, L. L. (1981), *Structural Change and Economic Growth. A Theoretical*

Essay on the Dynamics of the Wealth of Nations (Cambridge: Cambridge University Press).

Popper, K. (1987), 'La rationalité et le statut du principe de rationalité', in E. Classen (ed.) *Les fondaments philosophiques des systèmes économiques* (Paris: Payot).

Simon, H. A. (1976), 'From Sustantive to Procedural Rationality', in S. Latsis (ed.) *Method and Appraisal in Economics* (Cambridge: Cambridge University Press) reprinted in F. Hahn and M. Hollis, *Philosophy and Economic Theory* (Oxford: Oxford University Press, 1979).

Bibliography of the Works of Luigi Pasinetti

BOOKS

1963, *A Multi-sector Model of Economic Growth*, King's College, Cambridge, July 1963, pp. 59 (for limited circulation).

1966, *Analisi delle interdipendenze industriali*, as part I of *Lezioni di Econometria*, Università Cattolica del S. Cuore, 1966–67, pp. 98 + A66, notes for students (for limited circulation).

1974, *Growth and Income Distribution – Essays in Economic Theory* (Cambridge: Cambridge University Press) pp. X + 151.

ITALIAN VERSION: *Sviluppo Economico e distribuzione del reddito – Saggi di teoria economica* (Bologna: Il Mulino, 1977) pp. 203.

SPANISH TRANSLATION: *Crecimiento económico y distribución de la renta – Ensayos de teoría económica* (Madrid: Alianza Editorial, 1978) pp. 178.

PORTUGUESE TRANSLATION: *Crescimento e Distribuição de Renda – Ensaios de Teoria Econômica* (Rio de Janeiro: Zahar Editores, 1979) pp. 179 + XI.

JAPANESE TRANSLATION: publisher Iwanami Shoten, Tokyo, 1985, pp. XII + 209.

1975, *Lezioni di teoria della produzione* (Bologna: Il Mulino) pp. XIV + 339; 2nd edition (Bologna: Il Mulino, 1981) pp. XVI + 378; 3rd edition (Bologna: Il Mulino, 1989) pp. XVII + 417.

ENGLISH VERSION: *Lectures on the Theory of Production* (New York: Columbia University Press; London: Macmillan, 1977) pp. XIV + 285.

JAPANESE TRANSLATION: publisher Orion Press, Tokyo, 1979, pp. 341 + XVI.

SPANISH TRANSLATION: *Lecciones de teoría de la producción* (Madrid: Fondo de Cultura Económica, 1983; Mexico City, 1984) pp. 373.

FRENCH TRANSLATION: *Leçons sur la théorie de la production* (Parigi: Bordas/Dunod, 1985) pp. XVII + 302.

GERMAN TRANSLATION: *Vorlesungen zur Theorie der Produktion* (Marburg: Metropolis Verlag, 1988) pp. 313.

1977, (as editor), *Contributi alla teoria della produzione congiunta* (Bologna: Il Mulino) pp. 327.

ENGLISH VERSION: *Essays on the Theory of Joint Production* (London: Macmillan; New York: Columbia University Press, 1980) pp. XVII + 243.

SPANISH TRANSLATION: *Aportaciones a la teoría de la producción conjunta* (México City: Fondo de Cultura Económica/Serie de Economía, 1986) pp. 286.

JAPANESE TRANSLATION: publisher Nihon Keizai Hyôronsha, Tokyo, 1989, pp. 338 + XII.
1981, *Structural Change and Economic Growth – A Theoretical Essay on the Dynamics of the Wealth of Nations* (Cambridge: Cambridge University Press) pp. XV + 281.
JAPANESE TRANSLATION: publisher Nihon Keizai Hyôronsha, Tokyo, 1983, pp. XII + 340.
ITALIAN VERSION: *Dinamica strutturale e sviluppo economico – Un'indagine teorica sui mutamenti nella ricchezza delle nazioni* (Torino: UTET, 1984) pp. XIX + 326.
SPANISH TRANSLATION: *Cambio estructural y crecimiento económico* (Madrid: Ediciones Pirámide, 1985) pp. 270.
1986, (as editor) *Mutamenti strutturali del sistema produttivo – Integrazione tra industria e settore terziario* (Bologna: Il Mulino) pp. 129.
1987, (as editor, with Peter Lloyd) *Structural Change and Adjustment in the World Economy*, volume III of *Structural Change, Economic Interdependence and World Development*, (Proceedings of the Seventh World Congress of the International Economic Association, Madrid, Spain, September 1983) (London: Macmillan) pp. XIV + 578.
1989, (as editor) *Aspetti controversi della teoria del valore* (Proceedings of the XXVIII Annual Scientific Meeting of Società Italiana degli Economisti, Rome, 29–30 September 1987) (Bologna: Il Mulino) pp. 270.

ARTICLES

1955, 'La funzione del consumo in alcuni modelli econometrici applicati ai cicli economici', *Rivista Internazionale di Scienze Sociali*, LXIII, pp. 397–421.
1956, 'La funzione degli investimenti in alcuni modelli econometrici applicati ai cicli economici', *Rivista Internazionale di Scienze Sociali*, LXIV, pp. 125–51.
1956, 'Gli indicatori congiunturali dell' "Ifo Institut" di Monaco e le previsioni economiche', *Rivista Internazionale di Scienze Sociali*, LXIV, pp. 397–428.
1956, 'Lo sviluppo economico e le aree arretrate', *Rivista Internazionale di Scienze Sociali*, LXIV, pp. 519–27.
1957, 'Un nuovo modello econometrico per la rappresentazione del sistema economico statunitense', *Rivista Internazionale di Scienze Sociali*, LXV, pp. 57–62.
1957, 'Nota intorno alle relazioni tra salari, profitti e occupazione in un processo di accumulazione di capitale', *Rivista Internazionale di Scienze Sociali*, LXV, pp. 359–65.
1958, 'La presente recessione negli Stati Uniti d'America', *Rivista Internazionale di Scienze Sociali*, LXVI, pp. 321–7.
1958, 'Il recente modello di sviluppo di J. Robinson e la teoria neoclassica del capitale: alcune osservazioni', *Rivista Internazionale di Scienze Sociali*, LXVI, pp. 429–44.
1959, 'On Concepts and Measures of Changes in Productivity', *The Review*

of Economics and Statistics, XLI, pp. 270–82, with 'Comment' by Robert M. Solow, pp. 282–5, and 'Reply' by author, pp. 285–6.

1960, 'A Mathematical Formulation of the Ricardian System', The Review of Economic Studies, 1959–60, XXVII, pp. 78–98.

1960, 'Fluttuazioni cicliche e sviluppo economico', L'industria, 1, pp. 18–50.

1960, 'Cyclical Fluctuations and Economic Growth', Oxford Economic Papers, 12, pp. 215–41.

1960, (with Luigi Spaventa), 'Verso il superamento della modellistica aggregata nella teoria dello sviluppo economico', Rivista di Politica Economica, L, pp. 3–35.

1961, 'Cyclical Fluctuations and Economic Growth: A Reply to Mr. Neisser', Oxford Economic Papers, 13, pp. 222–3.

1961, 'Criteri per la valutazione degli aumenti di produttività', AA. VV., Il progresso tecnologico e la società Italiana – Aspetti di teoria e politica economica, (proceedings of an International Conference held in Milan, 1960, by Centro Nazionale di Prevenzione Sociale), Giuffré, Milano, pp. 377–89; republished in Progresso tecnico e sviluppo economico, (Milan: Vita e Pensiero, 1962) pp. 49–66.

1961, 'Ciclo economico', entry in Enciclopedia Italiana (Treccani) 1949–1960, app. III, vol. 1 (Rome: Istituto della Enciclopedia Italiana) pp. 371–373; republished in: Rivista Internazionale di Scienze Sociali, 1962 (V), pp. 485–91.

1961, 'Produttività', entry in Enciclopedia Italiana (Treccani) 1949–1960, app. III, vol. 2 (Rome: Istituto della Enciclopedia Italiana) pp. 493–4.

1962, 'Rate of Profit and Income Distribution in relation to the Rate of Economic Growth', The Review of Economic Studies, 1961-2, XXIX, pp. 267–79.

1964, 'A Comment on Professor Meade's "Rate of Profit in a Growing Economy"', The Economic Journal, LXXIV, pp. 488–9.

1965, 'Causalità e interdipendenza nell'analisi econometrica e nella teoria economica', Annuario dell'Università Cattolica del S. Cuore, 1964–65, Vita e Pensiero, Milano, pp. 233–50.

1965, 'A New Theoretical Approach to the Problems of Economic Growth', in Pontificiæ Academiæ Scientiarum Scripta Varia, n. 28; Proceedings of a Study Week on "The Econometric Approach to Development Planning", Vatican City, 1965; reprinted by: North Holland Publ. Co., Amsterdam, 1965, pp. 572–696.

1966, 'The Rate of Profit in a Growing Economy: a Reply', The Economic Journal, LXXVI, pp. 158–60.

1966, 'New Results in an Old Framework: Comment on Samuelson and Modigliani', The Review of Economic Studies, XXXII, pp. 303–6.

1966, 'Changes in the Rate of Profit and Switches of Techniques' (leading article in 'Paradoxes in Capital Theory: A Symposium'), The Quarterly Journal of Economics, LXXX, pp. 503–17.

1967, 'Nota sul tema dei rapporti commerciali internazionali', in AA.VV., I problemi dell'economia mondiale alla luce della "Populorum Progressio", Vita e Pensiero, Milano, pp. 111–18.

1969, 'Switches of Techniques and the "Rate of Return" in Capital Theory', *The Economic Journal*, LXXIX, pp. 508–31.
1970, 'Again on Capital Theory and Solow's "Rate of Return"', *The Economic Journal*, LXXX, pp. 428–31.
1972, 'Reply to Mr. Dougherty', *The Economic Journal*, LXXXII, pp. 1351–2.
1972, 'I problemi dello sviluppo economico e i paesi del "Terzo Mondo"', *Rivista Internazionale di Scienze Sociali*, LXXX, pp. 599–616.
1973, 'The Notion of Vertical Integration in Economic Analysis', *Metroeconomica*, XXV, pp. 1–29; reprinted in: L. Pasinetti (ed.), *Essays on the Theory of Joint Production* (London: Macmillan; New York: Columbia University Press, 1980) pp. 16–43;
ITALIAN TRANSLATION: 'La nozione di settore verticalmente integrato nell'analisi economica', in L. Pasinetti (ed.), *Contributi alla teoria della produzione* (Bologna: Il Mulino, 1977) pp. 37–74.
1973, 'La teoria de Cambridge sobre la tasa de beneficio y sus precedentes teoricos', *Cuadernos de Economia*, I, pp. 221–34.
1974, 'A Reply of Dr. Nuti on the Rate of Return', *Kyklos*, pp. 370–3.
1975, 'Determinatezza del saggio di profitto nella teoria Post-Keynesiana: risposta al Professor Campa', *Giornale degli Economisti e Annali di Economia*, XXXIV, pp. 639–47.
1977, 'Reply to Stiglitz', contained in: Morishima, Michio 'Pasinetti's "Growth and Income Distribution" Revisited', *The Journal of Economic Literature*, XV, pp. 57–8.
1977, 'Le choix des techniques et les théories du capital, des prix et de la répartition du revenu', *Revue d'économie politique*, LXXXVII, pp. 244–81.
1977, 'On "non-substitution" in production models', *Cambridge Journal of Economics*, I, pp. 389–94.
1977, 'Contributi alla teoria della produzione congiunta: Introduzione', in L. Pasinetti (ed.), *Contributi alla teoria della produzione congiunta* (Bologna: Il Mulino) pp. 9–16.
1977, 'Nota sulle merci base, le merci non-base e la produzione congiunta', in L. Pasinetti (ed.), *Contributi alla teoria della produzione congiunta* (Bologna: Il Mulino) pp. 85–9.
1978, 'Wicksell Effects and Reswitchings of Technique in Capital Theory', *The Scandinavian Journal of Economics*, LXXX, pp. 181–9.
1978, 'La teoria di Keynes ed i problemi del nostro tempo', *Annali della Facoltà di Economia e Commercio*, 5 (new series), 1977–8, Università degli Studi di Perugia, pp. 87–114; reprinted in: Caravale Giovanni (ed.), *La crisi delle teorie economiche* (Milano: Franco Angeli Editore, 1983) pp. 254–75.
1979, 'The Unpalatability of the Reswitching of Techniques – A comment on Burmeister, Krelle, Nuti and von Weizsäcker' and 'The "Unobtrusive Postulate" of Neo-classical Economic Theory – A Rejoinder to Professor Burmeister', as part of 'Exchanges et Controversies', *Revue d'économie politique*, pp. 637–42 and pp. 654–6.
1979, 'Kaldor, Nicholas', entry in *International Encyclopedia of the Social*

Sciences, Biographical Supplement, 18 (New York: The Free Press) pp. 366–9.
1979, 'Sraffa, Piero', entry in ibid., pp. 736–9.
1980, 'The Rate of Interest and the Distribution of Income in a Pure Labour Economy', *Journal of Post-Keynesian Economics*, Winter 1980–1, III, pp. 170–82.
1980, 'Joint Production – An Introductory Note', in L. L. Pasinetti (ed.), *Essays on the Theory of Joint Production* (London: Macmillan) pp. XII–XVII.
1980, 'A Note on Basic, Non-Basic and Joint Production', in ibid., pp. 51–54.
1981, 'On the Ricardian Theory of Value: A Note', *The Review of Economic Studies*, (XLVIII), pp. 673–5.
1981, 'Inflazione e sviluppo economico', pp. 41–73, and 'Repliche agli interventi', pp. 114–118, in AA.VV. *L'inflazione oggi: distribuzione e crescita* (Proceedings of the XXth Scientific Meeting of Società Italiana degli Economisti, Rome, 6–7 November 1979) (Milan: Giuffré Editore) p. 141.
1982, 'A Comment on the "New View" of the Ricardian Theory', pp. 240–2, in Mauro Baranzini (ed.), *Advances in Economic Theory*, (Oxford: Basil Blackwell) pp. X + 231.
1983, 'Il principio della domanda effettiva di J. M. Keynes', in: *Keynes*, special issue of *Piemonte Vivo Ricerche, Rivista della Cassa di Risparmio di Torino*, pp. 31–8.
1983, 'Conditions of Existence of a Two Class Economy in the Kaldor and More General Models of Growth and Income Distribution', *Kyklos*, XXXVI, pp. 91–102.
1983, 'Nicholas Kaldor: a Few Personal Notes', *Journal of Post Keynesian Economics*, Spring 1983, V, pp. 333–40.
1983, 'The Accumulation of Capital', *Cambridge Journal of Economics*, VII, pp. 405–11.
1983, 'Piero Sraffa e la scienza economica', *Il Dovere*, daily, Bellinzona, Canton Ticino, 10 December 1983.
1984, 'Preface' to: Cristian Bidard (ed.), *La Production Jointe* (Paris: Economica) pp. V–VII.
1984, (with Roberto Scazzieri), 'Dinamica economica strutturale', in *Scienza e Tecnica*, Updating Bulletin of *Enciclopedia della Scienza e della Tecnica* (Milan: Mondadori) pp. 357–60.
1984, 'The Difficulty, and yet the Necessity, of aiming at Full Employment: a Comment on Nina Shapiro's Note', *Journal of Post Keynesian Economics*, Winter 1984–5, VII, pp. 246–8.
1985, 'Technical Progress and the Wealth of Nations', in Heinrich Bortis and Louis Bosshart (eds), *Technologischer Wandel in Wirtschaft und Gesellschaft (Technological Change in Economy and Society)* (Freiburg: Universitätsverlag) pp. 47–66.
1985, 'In memoria di Piero Sraffa: economista italiano a Cambridge', *Economia Politica*, II, pp. 315–31.
FRENCH TRANSLATION: 'A la Mémoire de Piero Sraffa, économiste

Italien à Cambridge', in Richard Arena (ed.), *Sraffa Trente ans après* (Paris: Presses Universitaires de France, 1990) pp. 3–18.
1985, 'Piero Sraffa (1898–1983): breve saggio bio-bibliografico', in *Economia Politica*, II, pp. 333–41.
1985, 'La ricchezza delle nazioni' (Lecture delivered at Istituto Universitario di Magistero 'Suor Orsola Benincasa', Napoli, 13 April 1984) (Napoli: Guida Editori) pp. 35.
1986, 'Theory of Value – A Source of Alternative Paradigms in Economic Analysis', in Mauro Baranzini and Roberto Scazzieri (eds), *Foundations of Economics – Structure of Inquiry and Economic Theory* (Oxford: Basil Blackwell) pp. 409–31.
1986, 'Sraffa's Circular Process and the Concept of Vertical Integration', in *Political Economy – Studies in the Surplus Approach*, (I), pp. 3–16.
1986, 'Nicholas Kaldor – An Appreciation', *Cambridge Journal of Economics*, 10, pp. 301–3.
1987, 'Economic Growth with Structural Change: an Introduction', in Luigi Pasinetti and Peter Lloyd (eds), *Structural Change and Adjustment in the World Economy*, vol. 3 of: *Structural Change, Economic Interdependence and World Development* (Proceedings of the Seventh World Congress of the International Economic Association, Madrid, Spain, Sept. 1983) (London: Macmillan) pp. 7–12.
1987, '"Satisfactory" versus Optimal Economic Growth', in *Rivista Internazionale di Scienze Economiche e Commerciali*, XXXIV, pp. 989–1000 (Proceedings of a Study Meeting of Italian and Soviet Economists on 'Theoretical Issues in Economics for both Market and Centrally Planned Economies', Milano, 16–17 March 1987).
1987, 'Kahn, Richard Ferdinand', item in *The New Palgrave Dictionary of Economics*, (London: Macmillan) vol. III, pp. 1–3.
1987, 'Robinson, Joan Violet', item in ibid., vol. IV, pp. 212–17.
1987, (with Roberto Scazzieri) 'Capital Theory: Paradoxes', item in ibid., vol. I, pp. 363–8.
1987, (with Roberto Scazzieri) 'Structural Economic Dynamics', item in ibid., vol. IV, pp. 525–8.
1988, 'La centralità del lavoro nei sistemi economici industriali', in *Una repubblica fondata sul lavoro* (Proceedings of a Meeting of the Association 'Città dell'uomo' on 'L'Italia, repubblica democratica fondata sul lavoro', Milan, 12–13 December 1986), (Rome: Editrice Ave) pp. 79–95.
1988, 'Growing Sub-systems, Vertically Hyper-integrated Sectors and the Labour Theory of Value', *Cambridge Journal of Economics*, XII, pp. 125–34.
1988, 'Sraffa on Income Distribution', *Cambridge Journal of Economics*, XII, pp. 135–8.
1988, 'La théorie de la croissance et son avenir', in *Revue européenne des Sciences Sociales – Cahiers Vilfredo Pareto*, (XXVI), n. 81, Librairie Droz, Geneva, pp. 5–18.
1988, 'Nicholas Kaldor. Profilo biografico', in: Nicholas Kaldor, *Economia senza equilibrio*, (Italian translation of *Economics without Equilibrium*) (Bologna: Il Mulino) pp. 9–21.

1988, 'Technical Progress and International Trade', *Empirica*, XV, pp. 139–47.
1988, '"Prezzi tipo" e linearità della relazione consumi/investimenti', in S. Lombardini, G. Melzi and P. C. Nicola (eds), *Rendiconti del Seminario Matematico di Brescia – Saggi in onore di Carlo Felice Manara* (Milan: Vita e Pensiero) pp. 145–59.
1989, (jointly with G. Gambetta), 'Econometria', item in *Enciclopedia del Novecento*, Istituto della Enciclopedia Italiana, vol. VIII, pp. 313–22.
1989, 'Ricardian Debt/Taxation Equivalence in the Kaldor Theory of Profits and Income Distribution', *Cambridge Journal of Economics*, XIII, pp. 25–36.
1989, 'La teoria del valore: introduzione', in Luigi Pasinetti (ed.), *Aspetti controversi della teoria del valore* (Proceedings of the XXVIII Annual Scientific Meeting of Società Italiana degli Economisti, Rome, 29–30 October 1987) (Bologna: Il Mulino) pp. 9–10.
1989, 'La teoria del valore come fonte di paradigmi alternativi', in ibid., pp. 231–54.
1989, 'Una nota sulla valutazione dei disavanzi pubblici: al netto o al lordo degli interessi?' in *Moneta e Credito*, XLII, pp. 165–73.
ENGLISH VERSION: 'A Note on the Evaluation of Public Deficits: Net or Gross of Interest?', *Banca Nazionale del Lavoro Quarterly Review*, 170, pp. 303–11.
1989, 'Address' at Richard Ferdinand, Baron Kahn of Hampstead's Memorial Service, leaflet of King's College, Cambridge, 21 October 1989, pp. 6–11.
1989, 'Growing Subsystems and Vertically Hyper-integrated Sectors: a Note of clarification', *Cambridge Journal of Economics*, XIII, pp. 479–80.
1989, 'Government deficit spending is not incompatible with the Cambridge theorem of the rate of profit: a reply to Fleck and Domenghino', *Journal of Post Keynesian Economics*, pp. 641–7.
1990, 'Sraffa's Circular Process and the Concepts of Vertical Integration', pp. 229–60, and 'Appendix: Growing (or hyper-) subsystems and vertically hyper-integrated sectors', pp. 239–49, in Krishna Bharadwaj and Bertram Schefold (eds), *Essays on Piero Sraffa* (London: Unwin Hyman).
1990, 'Normalised General Coordinates and Vertically Integrated Sectors in a Simple Case', in Kumaraswamy Velupillai (ed.) *Nonlinear and Multi-Sectoral Macrodynamics – Essays in Honour of Richard Goodwin* (London: Macmillan) pp. 151–64.
1990, 'Structural Change and Unemployment', in *Structural Change and Economic Dynamics* (Oxford: Oxford University Press) Vol. 1, pp. 7–13.
1990, *Introduction* to a meeting organized by the Società Italiana degli Economisti and by the Economics Department of Università Cattolica del S. Cuore, in 'Fare l'economista oggi: contenuti, metodi, strumenti', (Milan, 21 March 1989), July, pp. 7–18 (a publication by the Società Italiana degli Economisti, limited circulation).

1990, 'Mutamenti strutturali in un processo di crescita economica: una caratteristica inevitabile', in Mario Amendola (ed.) *Innovazione e progresso tecnico* (Bologna: Il Mulino) pp. 35–42.
1990, 'Vertical Integration and Capital Theory', *Journal of Post Keynesian Economics*, 13, Fall 1990–1, pp. 65–70.
1990, 'Richard Ferdinand Kahn: 1905–1989', in *Proceedings of the British Academy*, 76, '1990 Lectures and Memoirs', pp. 423–43.
1991, 'At the Roots of Post-Keynesian Thought: Keynes' Break with Tradition', in W. L. M. Adriaansen and J. T. J. M. van der Linden (eds) *Post-Keynesian Thought in Perspective* (Utrecht: Wolters-Noorhoff) pp. 21–9.
1991, 'Dal Treatise on Money alla General Theory: continuità o rottura?' in Jan Kregel (ed.), *Nuove interpretazioni dell'analisi monetaria di Keynes* (Proceedings of the XXXth Annual Scientific Meeting of Società Italiana degli Economisti, Rome, 26–7 October 1989) (Bologna: Il Mulino) pp. 43–51.

COMMENTS AND DISCUSSIONS AT CONFERENCES

1968, Discussion of: M. Bronfenbrenner, 'Neo-classical Macro-distribution Theory', in: J. Marchal and B. Ducros (eds), *The Distribution of Income*, Proceedings of a Conference of the I.E.A. (Palermo, 1964) (London: Macmillan) pp. 501–3.
1973, Various contributions to the discussion, in: J. A. Mirrlees and N. H. Stern, *Models of Economic Growth*, Proceedings of a Conference of the I. E. A. (Jerusalem, 1970) (London: Macmillan) esp. pp. 163–6, 366–7, et. al.
1982, Discussion of: Lawrence R. Klein, 'Economic Theoretic Restrictions in Econometrics', Proceedings of a Conference of the Econometric Society (Pisa, 1980), in: Gregory Chow and Paolo Corsi (eds), *Evaluating the Reliability of Macro-economic Models* (New York: Wiley, 1982) pp. 38–42.
1983, Comment on: Axel Leijonhufvud, 'What would Keynes have thought of Rational Expectations?' in: David Worswick and James Trevithick (eds), *Keynes and the Modern World*, Proceedings of the Keynes Centenary Conference (King's College, Cambridge, 1983) (Cambridge: Cambridge University Press) pp. 205–11.
1984, Contribution to the discussion in: Richard Kahn, 'The Making of Keynes' General Theory', Raffaele Mattioli Lectures (Milan, 1978) (Cambridge: Cambridge University Press) pp. 222–5.
1984, Discussion of: S. M. Nikitin, 'Trends in Relative World Market Prices', in: Bèla Csikos-Nagy, Douglas Hague and Graham Hall (eds), *The Economics of Relative Prices*, Proceedings of a Conference of the I. E. A. (Athens, 1981) (London: Macmillan) pp. 297–9.
1985, Comment on: Edmond Malinvaud, 'The Identification of Scientific Advances in Economics', in: T. Hägerstrand (ed.), *The Identification of Progress in Learning*, Proceedings of a Conference of the Euro-

pean Science Foundation (Colmar, 1983) (Cambridge: Cambridge University Press) pp. 183–6.
1986, Contribution to the discussion, in: Franco Modigliani, 'The Debate over Stabilization Policy', Raffaele Mattioli Lectures (Milan, 1977) (Cambridge: Cambridge University Press) pp. 184–7.
1986, 'Comment' presented at the Commemoration of Ezio Vanoni, on the occasion of the Conference 'Territorial Disequilibria and Regional Policies' ('Gli squilibri territoriali e le politiche regionali'), 5th European Symposium of the 'Confederation of European Economic Associations', Bormio, 5–7 June 1986, *Economia Internazionale*, XXXIX, 1986, 2, pp. 62–3.
1986, 'Il difficile equilibrio fra sviluppo economico e solidarietá', ed. by Giancarlo Botti, in *Terra Ambrosiana*, Diocesi di Milano, May-June, pp. 16–19.
1988, 'Foreword' to the volume: *Richard F. Kahn: un discepolo di Keynes*, by Cristina Marcuzzo (ed.), (Milan: Garzanti) pp. 7–11.
1988, 'Interventi' to the international meeting 'Chimica e Ambiente' (Rome, 8–9 October 1987), in: *Atti del convegno internazionale "Chimica e ambiente"*, Enichem, p. 15 and p. 34.
1989, 'Interventi' to an Italo-Sovietic meeting organized by the Bank of Italy (Perugia, 9–11 June 1988), in A. G. Aganbegjan, P. Ciocca, P. Sylos-Labini, V. S. Zacharov (eds), *Perestrojka e ristrutturazione produttiva* (Bologna: Il Mulino) p. 44 and pp. 222–227.
1989, 'Intervento' at the meeting organized by Istituto di economia politica of Università Bocconi (22 January 1988) in *Piero Sraffa e l'Economia Politica degli anni 80*, Università Bocconi, Milan, pp. 9–14.
1989, Comment on: Wilfred Beckerman, 'Inflation and Growth', in Victor Urquidi (ed.), *Incomes Policies*, Proceedings of a Conference of the International Economic Association, Mexico City, September 1985 (London: Macmillan) pp. 61–4.
SPANISH TRANSLATION: 'Comentario al ensayo de Wilfred Beckerman: "La opción entre inflación y desempleo"', in Victor Urquidi (ed.), *Política de ingresos, El trimestre Económico*, pp. 73–6.
1989, 'Sulla dinamica strutturale dei sistemi economici; colloquio con Luigi Pasinetti', edited by Giangiacomo Nardozzi, *Rivista di storia economica*, 3, October 1989, pp. 359–67.
1990, Comment on: Massimo Pivetti 'On the Monetary Explanation of Distribution', in Krishna Bharadwaj and Bertram Schefold (eds), *Essays on Piero Sraffa – Critical Perspectives on the Revival of Classical Theory* (Proceedings of a Conference held in Florence, August 1985) (London: Unwin Hyman) pp. 460–2.
1990, Interview on *Debito pubblico, emergenza nazionale* (Public Debt: National Emergency), in 'La discussione', 9 (3 March), pp. 13–14 and 13 (31 March), p. 27.

Bibliography of the Works of Pasinetti

BOOK REVIEWS

1961, *Ricardo on Taxation*, by C. C. Shoup (New York: Columbia University Press; London: Oxford University Press, 1960) pp. 285; in *The Economic Journal*, 1961, LXXI, pp. 388–390.

1962, *Econometrie per Dirigenti d'Azienda*, by Pietro Castiglioni, (Padua: Cedam, 1959) pp. IX + 288; in *Econometrica*, 1962, XXX, p. 391.

1963, *Essai sur les problèmes d'investissement en pays sous-développés*, by G. Abraham-Frois (Paris: SEDES, 1962) pp. 344; in *The Economic Journal*, 1963, LXXIII, pp. 300–1.

1972, *Monetary and Fiscal Policy in a Growing Economy*, by Duncan K. Foley and Miguel Sidrauski (London: Collier-Macmillan; New York: Macmillan, 1971) pp. XII + 304; in *The Journal of Economic Literature*, 1972, X, pp. 454–5.

1978, *The Megacorp and Oligopoly: Micro Foundations of Macro Dynamics*, by Alfred S. Eichner (Cambridge: Cambridge University Press, 1976) pp. XIII + 365; in *Challenge – The Magazine of Economic Affairs*, January–February 1978, XX, pp. 64–5.

1982, *Capital Theory and Dynamics*, by Edwin Burmeister (Cambridge: Cambridge University Press, 1980) pp. IX + 330; in *Journal of Money, Credit and Banking*, Nov. 1982, XIV, I, pp. 555–7.

1984, *Macroeconomics*, by Wynne Godley and Francis Cripps (Oxford and London: Oxford University Press, 1983) pp. 315; in *Contributions to Political Economy*, III, 1984, pp. 108–12.

1985, *Le forze dello sviluppo e del declino*, by Paolo Sylos-Labini (Bari: Editore Laterza, 1984) pp. XIV + 290; in *Moneta e Credito*, Rivista Trimestrale della Banca Nazionale del Lavoro, XXXVIII, 1985, pp. 331–5.

Names Index

Abraham-Frois, G., 412
Adriaansen, W. L. M., 410
Aganbegjan, A. G., 411
Allen, R. F., 166, 170
Amadeo, E. J., xii, 30, 31, 181, 201, 203, 204
Amendola, M., 243, 410
Amsden, A., 292, 296
Ando, A. K., 242, 243
Anscombe, G. E. M., 389, 401
Anstey, V., 278, 295, 296
Archibald, G. C., 158, 170
Arena, R., 408
Arestis, P., 38–40
Arndt, H., 277, 278, 295, 297
Arrow, K. J., 158, 164, 168, 170, 252, 254, 268, 269, 282, 292, 295–7, 398, 400
Ashley, W. J., 55–7, 61, 66–8
Asimakopulos, A., 201–3
Ayer, A. J., 388, 401

Bacha, E., 120, 122
Bagehot, W., 65, 68
Baldone, S., 31, 229–31, 243
Balestra, P., 14, 39, 202, 203
Ball, R. J., 202, 203
Baranzini, M., xi, xii, 1, 13, 14, 16, 17, 38, 39, 41, 42, 70, 93, 145, 146, 171, 202, 203, 224, 243–5, 270, 352, 353, 379, 383, 407, 408
Barbour, 59, 67
Becattini, G., 266, 269
Beckerman, W., 411
Bell, D., 171
Belloc, B., 31, 243
Bendixson, 301
Bentham, J., 65
Beveridge, W. H., 330, 347
Bhaduri, A., xii, 30, 175, 180, 228, 243
Bhagwati, J. N., 283, 296, 297
Bharadwaj, K., 38, 64, 68, 409, 411
Biasco, S., 346
Bidard, C., 118
Birkhoff, G. D., 300, 301, 309
Bjierring, A. K., 394, 397, 401
Blakley, G. R., 242, 243
Blaug, M., 38, 39, 120, 122, 161, 166, 170

Bliss, C. J., 4, 8, 12, 39, 158, 161, 168–70, 353, 383
Boeke, J. H., 277, 295, 297
Böhm-Bawerk, E. von, 53, 154, 166, 170
Bonar, J., 48, 49, 52, 54, 58, 61, 64, 68
Bortis, H., xii, 35, 351, 367, 383, 407
Boskin, M. J., 205
Bosshart, L., 407
Botti, G., 411
Brahmananda, P. R., 297
Braithwaite, R. B., 270
Brechling, F. P. R., 171
Bronfenbrenner, M., 410
Broome, J., 120, 122, 179, 180
Brower, L. E. J., 254, 259, 268, 269
Brown, J. A. C., 245
Brown, M. B., 166, 170
Buchanan, D. A., 86
Burgstaller, A., 129, 141–5
Burmeister, E., 10, 39, 120, 122, 412
Burns, T. R., 394, 397, 401
Butts, R. E., 401

Cairns, J. E., 286, 296, 297
Camargo, J. M., 201, 203
Candela, G., 92
Cannan, E., 66, 68, 94
Cantillon, R., 364
Carabelli, A., 201, 203
Caravale, G. A., 126, 141, 145, 244, 406
Carneiro, D., 120, 122
Casarosa, C., 29, 126, 127, 141, 142, 144, 145
Castiglioni, P., 412
Chakravarty, S., xii, 32, 33, 235, 242, 243, 275, 295–7
Chamberlin, E. H., 401
Champernowne, D. G., 2
Chick, V., 201, 203
Chow, G., 410
Ciocca, P., 411
Clapham, J. H., 317, 347
Clark, J. B., 12, 47, 67, 154, 159, 166, 170, 243
Classen, E., 402
Cohen, A. J., xii, 29, 149, 164, 166, 169, 170

413

Names Index

Cohen, J. S., 165, 166, 169, 170
Cohen, R., 9
Colson, L. C., 47
Condillac, E. B. de, 79
Corsi, P., 410
Cournot, A. A., 63, 251, 268, 269
Craven, J., 12, 39
Cripps, F., 412
Crowther, G., 312
Csikos-Nagy, B., 410

D'Agata, A., 118
Dahmen, E., 240, 243
Daire, E., 93, 94
Dardi, M., 62, 68
Darity, W. A., 203
Dasgupta, A. K., 284, 296
Datta, B., 278, 297
Davenant, C., 264
Davidson, P., 38, 201, 203
De Marchi, N., 165
Debreu, G., 252, 254, 268, 269
Denicolò, V., 15, 39
Di-Marco, L. E., 298
Dixit, A., 12, 39
Dobb, M. H., 2, 46, 62, 69, 70, 92, 123, 150, 170, 179, 180
Domar, E. D., 13, 177, 180
Domenghino, C.-M., 15, 39
Dore, M., 242, 243
Dougherty, C. R. S., 12, 39
Dreyfus, H. L., 389, 401
Dreyfus, S. E., 389, 401
Ducros, B., 410
Dunbar, C. F., 65, 69
Dupriez, L. H., 243
Dupuit, A. J., 251, 268, 269
Dussard, H., 93, 94
Dutt, A. K., xii, 30, 31, 165, 181, 201–4

Eatwell, J. L., 38, 120, 122, 123, 203
Edgeworth, F. Y., 251, 268, 269
Eichner, A. S., 38, 202, 204, 412
Ellis, H. S., 298, 299
Elster, J., 401
Eltis, W. A., 166, 170
Engel, E., 17, 23, 211, 259, 365
Engels, F., 93, 276, 295, 298
Enriques, F., 268, 269

Faliva, M., 245, 264, 268, 269
Fano, E., 324
Fay, C. R., 60, 69
Fazi, E., 202, 204

Fearon, P., 324, 347
Feldman, G. A., 177
Ferguson, C. E., 156, 166, 168, 170
Fey, J. C., 285
Findlay, R., 141, 144, 145
Fisher, F. M., 242, 243
Fisher I., 8, 10–12
Flaschel, P., 113, 118, 121, 123
Fleck, F. H., 15, 39
Foley, D. K., 412
Foxwell, H. S., 64
Frank, A. G., 276
Freud, S., 390
Friedman, M., 387
Frisch, R. A. K., 33, 263, 264, 300, 301, 309
Frobenius, G., 258
Fuà, G., 263, 346

Gadgil, D. R., 284
Gaffard, J. L., 243
Gale, D. M., 254, 268, 269
Gambetta, G., 268, 270, 409
Ganguli, B. N., 278, 286, 295–7
Garegnani, P., 38, 50, 69, 118, 119, 123, 155, 167, 169, 170
Gehrke, C., 234, 244
Gelderen, J. van, 277, 295, 299
George, H., 49
Gibbard, A., 395, 401
Godley, W., 412
Gonner, E. C. K., 65, 66, 69
Goodwin, R. M., x, xii, 2, 25, 31–4, 210, 221, 222, 242, 243, 300, 309, 393, 401
Gordon, R. A., 309
Gossling, W. F., 220, 242, 243
Gram, H., 150, 172
Greaves, I., 277
Groenewegen, P., xii, 26, 27, 45
Guillebaud, C. W., 58, 69

Haavelmo, T., 390, 401
Haberler, G., 64, 69
Hagemann, H., 165, 234, 244
Hagen, E. E., 283, 296, 297
Hägerstrand, T., 410
Hague, D. C., 123, 410
Hahn, F. H., 157, 158, 160, 161, 164, 166, 168, 170, 171, 400, 402
Haken, H., 310
Hall, G., 410
Hamouda, O. F., 38, 40, 201, 204
Hands, W., 165

Names Index

Harcourt, G. C., xi, xii, 1, 12–14, 16, 38, 40, 118, 161, 165, 169, 171, 201, 202, 204, 211, 244
Harper, W. L., 395, 401
Harrod, R. F., 13, 117, 118
Harsanyi, J. C., 389, 390, 401
Hawkins, D., 234
Hayashida, H., 87
Hayek, F. A. von, 385, 386, 388, 401
Heckscher, E. F., 29, 140, 144, 283
Hermann, F. B. W. von, 64
Hicks, J. R., 29, 31, 50, 69, 117, 118, 126, 127, 141, 142, 144, 145, 154, 166, 171, 210, 225–8, 241, 242, 244, 316, 347
Hintikka, J., 401
Hirschman, A. O., 277
Hishiyama, I., xiii, 26, 27, 71, 87–9, 92, 93
Hobbes, T., 291, 356, 357
Hollander, J., 49, 64, 66, 68, 69
Hollander, S., 29, 63, 66–9, 126, 127, 141–5
Hollis, M., 400, 402
Hooker, C. A., 401
Hopkins, S. V., 312
Hume, D., 357
Huncke, G. D., 170
Hunt, E. K., 123
Hurwitz, L., 292, 297
Hutchison, T. W., 66, 69

Imlah, A., 312
Intriligator, M. D., 252, 268, 269

Jaffe, W., 172
Jevons, W. S., 49, 52–4, 64
Jorgenson, D. W., 285
Jossa, B., 118
Juglar, C., 300

Kahn, R. F., x, 1–4, 25, 38, 282, 295, 297, 410
Kakutani, S., 254, 268, 269
Kaldor, N., x, 1–3, 5, 9, 13–16, 22, 25, 30, 38, 40, 124, 145, 181, 182, 200–2, 204, 287–90, 293, 296, 297, 352, 408
Kalecki, M., 13, 38, 184, 186–8, 200, 202, 204, 256, 278, 281, 295, 297, 330, 347
Kamiya, T., 87
Kant, I., 387, 399, 400
Kenyon, P., 16, 40, 202, 204
Kerr, I., 165

Kerr, P., 40, 171
Keynes, J. M., x, 2–4, 7, 12–18, 22–6, 30, 31, 33, 35–8, 40, 46, 47, 58, 63–5, 69, 173, 176, 181–7, 194, 200–4, 256, 262, 266, 269, 278, 279, 281, 287, 289, 293–8, 326, 328–30, 333, 347, 352–4, 358, 364–8, 372, 374, 375, 380–3
Kindleberger, C. P., 285, 296, 298
King, G., 264
Kishimoto, S., 92
Kitchins, 300
Klein, L. R., 122, 309, 410
Knies, K., 276
Kondratieff, N. D., 34, 300, 304, 309, 310
Koopmans, T. C., 268, 269
Kregel, J. A., 123, 141, 145, 201, 204
Kristol, I., 171
Krüger, M., 309
Kubota, A., 71, 87, 93
Kuczynski, M., 93
Kuhn, H. W., 269, 388
Kuroki, R., 87
Kurz, H. D., xiii, 26–8, 95, 111, 118, 120, 123
Kuznets, S., 263, 277, 291

Laing, N. F., 14, 40, 202, 204
Landesmann, M. A., xiii, 31, 209, 223, 243–5
Latsis, S. J., 402
Lawson, T., 165, 201, 204
Layton, W. T., 312
Le Corbeiller, P., 301, 309
Le Trosne, J.-F., 79, 89, 91, 93
Leach, J. J., 401
Leijonhufvud, A., 410
Leon, P., 244
Leontief, W. W., 225, 244, 256, 257, 260, 262, 268, 269, 355, 364, 365
Levhari, D., 9, 10, 38, 40
Levy, A., 313
Lewis, W. A., 284–7, 289, 291, 293, 296, 298
Linden, J. T. J. M. van der, 410
Lipsey, R. G. 322, 345, 347
List, F., 275, 276, 288, 295, 298
Lloyd, C., 359, 379, 383
Lloyd, P., 404, 408
Loasby, B. J., 62, 69
Locke, J., 59, 357
Lombardini, S., x, xiii, 35, 36, 246, 262, 268, 269, 384, 391, 401, 409
Longfield, S. M., 286, 296, 298

Lowe, A., 150, 163, 171, 225, 233, 234, 244, 290
Luce, R. D., 394, 401
Lucrezio Caro, T., 396
Lutz, F. A., 123

Macleod, H. D., 53
Magnan de Bornier, J., 244
Mahalanobis, P. C., 177, 180, 242, 244, 290
Malinvaud, E., 153, 154, 156, 158, 161, 165, 168, 169, 171, 264, 268, 269, 410
Malthus, T. R., 8, 48, 49, 53, 54, 64, 66, 67, 101, 102, 106, 141, 143, 165, 256
Manara, C. F., 245, 246, 261, 268, 269
Mandelbaum, K., 280, 283, 296, 298
Maneschi, A., xiii, 26, 28, 29, 124, 127, 141, 142, 145
Manoilesco, M., 278, 282, 295, 298
Marchal, J., 410
Marcuzzo, M. C., 96, 123, 411
Marglin, S. A., 16, 40, 201, 204
Marris, R. L., 16, 38, 40
Marshall, A., 26, 27, 45–69, 152, 153, 162, 168, 171, 250, 251, 254, 267–9, 276, 278, 283, 285, 292, 295, 296, 298
Marshall, M. P., 48, 69
Martin, K., 312
Marx, K., 10, 22, 33, 49, 87, 93, 118, 182, 275, 276, 291, 292, 294–6, 298, 352–6, 363, 365, 369, 372, 377, 380, 382
Massaro, V. G., 211, 244
Mathur, G., 235, 244
Matteuzzi, M., 15, 39
McClennen, E. F., 394, 401
McCulloch, J. R., 48, 49, 58, 64, 65, 69, 99–101, 104, 119
McKenzie, L. W., 254, 268, 269
Meade, J. E., 15, 16, 40, 391, 401
Medio, A., 120, 123
Meek, R. L., 93, 150, 171
Meeker, D., 394, 397, 401
Melzi, G., 409
Menger, C., 53
Menger, K., 271
Metzler, L. S., 298
Milgate, M., 38, 122, 123, 169, 171, 203
Mill, J., 49, 65, 143, 165
Mill, J. S., 46–8, 55, 56, 60, 61, 63–5, 67, 101, 143
Minsky, H., 38, 201, 202, 204
Mirrlees, J. A., 172, 410

Mitchell, B. R., 312
Mitchell, W. C., 277
Miyao, T., 122, 123
Miyazaki, K., 16
Modigliani, F., 15, 16, 42, 411
Moggridge, D. E., 40, 204, 298, 347
Mongiovi, G., 165
Montesquieu, C. de Secondat, 357
Moore, B. J., 40, 202, 204
Morgenstern, O., 271, 394
Morishima, M., 40, 242, 244, 406
Myrdal, G., 276, 277, 295, 298

Nardini, F., 228, 244
Nardozzi, G., 411
Nei, M., 87
Nerlove, M., 122
Neumann, J. von, 210, 221, 222, 236, 238, 241, 242, 244, 252, 254, 256, 258, 259, 268, 270, 271, 310, 394
Newman, P. K., 122, 123, 203
Newton, I., 385
Nicola, P. C., 252, 267–70, 409
Nikaido, H., 254, 268, 270
Nikitin, S. M., 410
Nobel, A. B., 3, 252, 285
Nurkse, R., 278, 280–3, 295, 296, 298
Nuti, D. M., 244

Ohlin, B. G., 29, 140, 144, 283, 330, 347
Oncken, A., 71, 87, 93
Ong, N.-P., 123

Pacault, A., 310
Palazzi, M., 92
Palazzi, P., 345
Panico, C., 118, 185, 204
Pantaleoni, M., 249, 250, 267, 270
Pareto, V., 157, 251, 255, 268, 270, 282, 385, 387, 388, 396–9
Parker, W. N., 172, 270
Pascal, B., 261
Pasinetti, L. L., x, 1–27, 29–32, 35–8, 41, 45, 46, 54, 60–3, 69, 70, 87, 93, 124–7, 132, 134, 141–3, 145, 146, 155, 163, 165, 171, 176, 177, 179–82, 185, 200, 202, 204, 205, 211–17, 220, 224, 225, 240, 241, 244–6, 256, 258–60, 267–70, 296, 351–74, 376, 377, 379–84, 401, 403–12
Patinkin, D., 330, 347
Pellizzari, F., 245
Perron, O., 258

Names Index 417

Pesaran, M. H., 265, 268–70
Petty, W., 27, 64, 97, 255, 264, 364
Phelps Brown, E. H., 312
Phillips, A. W. H., 321, 345, 347
Physiocrats, 48
Pigou, A. C., 47, 52, 53, 61, 64–7, 69, 70, 267, 270
Pivetti, M., 185, 205, 411
Poincaré, H., 301, 310
Pol, B. van der, 301, 310
Popper, K., 387, 388, 402
Prebish, R., 285, 296, 298
Price, L. L., 65
Punzo, L. F., 309

Quadrio-Curzio, A., xiii, 31, 32, 42, 229, 230, 235, 238, 242, 245, 246, 267–70
Quesnay, F., 27, 48, 71–84, 86–93, 255, 357, 364, 381

Raiffa, H., 394, 401
Ramaswami, V. K., 283, 296, 297
Ramsey, F. P., 154, 171, 252, 268, 270
Ranade, M. G., 276, 295, 298
Ranis, G., 285, 299
Rawls, J., 399
Reagan, R. W., 329
Ricardo, D., x, 7, 8, 11, 13, 22, 26–30, 35, 38, 43, 45–68, 70, 71, 84–6, 89–91, 93, 95–107, 112–21, 123–7, 129, 130, 132, 134, 138–44, 146, 149–53, 156, 157, 159, 164–6, 171, 175, 177, 179, 180, 222, 230, 238, 241, 256, 258, 285, 289, 294, 319, 351, 352, 355, 358, 362, 366, 367, 372, 377, 382, 383
Robertson, D. H., 284, 296, 298
Robinson, E. A. G., 40, 64, 70
Robinson, J. V., x, 1–4, 10, 13, 25, 38, 141, 146, 161, 169, 181, 201, 202, 205, 281, 294, 295, 298, 353
Roll, E., 360
Roncaglia, A., 118, 120, 123, 351, 383
Roosevelt, F. D., 322
Roscher, W., 47, 51
Rosenstein-Rodan, P. N., 280–2, 295, 299
Rosselli, A., 96, 123
Rössler, O. E., 33, 34, 301, 303, 310
Rousseas, S., 202, 205
Rowthorn, B., 201, 202, 205
Rutherford, R. P., 141, 146
Rybczynski, T. M., 144, 146

Salvadori, N., xiii, 26–8, 95, 111, 118, 120, 123, 202, 204
Salvati, M., 38
Samuelson, P. A., 9, 10, 15, 16, 29, 40, 42, 120, 123, 132, 141, 146, 149, 154–6, 159, 160, 163, 164, 166, 167, 169, 171, 172
Sato, K., 170
Savage, L. J., 395
Savona, P., 318, 346
Sawyer, M. C., 38, 39
Say, J.-B., 372
Scazzieri, R., xiii, 9, 17, 24, 31, 32, 39, 41, 42, 70, 93, 171, 209, 223, 224, 241, 243–5, 267, 268, 270, 352, 353, 379, 383, 407, 408
Schacht, H., 330
Schefold, B., 113, 118, 123, 409, 411
Schelle, G., 94
Schultz, P. T., 299
Schultz, T. W., 284, 294, 296, 299
Schumpeter, J. A., 33, 46, 61, 70, 89, 94, 143, 146, 166, 169, 263, 294, 300, 301, 309, 310, 330, 352, 356, 358, 382, 383, 395, 396
Schwartz, J. G., 123
Scitovsky, T., 280, 281, 295, 299
Sen, A. K., 166, 172
Shackle, G. L. S., 201, 205
Shaw, G. B., 25
Shiraishi, T., 401
Shoup, C. C., 412
Shove, G. F., 46, 52, 58, 70
Sidgwick, H., 65
Sidrauski, M., 412
Simon, H. A., 234, 242, 243, 387, 392, 402
Singer, H. W., 285, 299
Skinner, A. S., 275, 299
Skott, P., 185, 205
Skouras, T., 40
Smith, A., 20, 22, 27, 48, 51, 62, 65, 66, 71–3, 77–87, 89–92, 94, 97, 151, 165, 239, 245, 256, 275, 289, 313, 318, 351, 352, 355, 357, 364, 365, 368, 395
Solow, R. M., 4, 11, 12, 42, 154, 155, 163, 165, 172, 284, 296, 405
Spaventa, L., 405
Sraffa, P., x, 1–3, 5, 9–11, 17, 19, 22, 25, 26, 28, 30, 35, 38, 45, 49, 63, 65, 67, 70, 93–6, 100, 103, 106–18, 120–3, 125, 126, 141, 146, 167, 171, 175, 177, 179, 180, 185, 205, 211, 212, 219, 220, 222, 240, 242, 245, 256–60, 262, 268,

270, 351, 352, 355, 362, 364, 365, 376, 377, 383
Steedman, I., 15, 42, 117, 118, 123, 352, 383
Steindl, J., 189, 202, 205
Stern, N. H., 172, 410
Steuart, J. D., 275, 295, 299
Stigler, G. J., 29, 46, 64, 66, 68, 70, 149–53, 156–8, 164, 165, 167, 172
Stiglitz, J. E., 166, 169, 172
Stolper, W. F., 299
Stone, J. R. N., 2, 245, 268, 270
Swan, T. W., 284
Sylos-Labini, P., xiii, 6, 32, 34, 35, 263, 268, 270, 311, 313, 318, 320, 323–6, 346–8, 411, 412

Taniguchi, K., 14, 42
Targetti, F., 16, 42
Tarshis, L., 201, 205
Taylor, B., 141
Taylor, L. D., 120, 122, 185, 201, 202, 205
Thackeray, F. G., 312
Thatcher, M., 345
Theil, H., 264, 268, 270
Thünen, J. von, 64
Thweatt, W. O., 141, 145, 146
Tobin, J., 16, 42
Tonveronachi, M., 346
Tooke, T., 60
Torrens, R., 101, 119
Tosato, D. A., 126, 141, 145
Toynbee, A., 65, 70
Trevithick, J. A., 410
Trower, H., 49, 64
Tsiang, S.-C., 122
Tsuru, S., 401
Tucker, A. W., 269

Turgot, A.-R. J., 27, 71, 79, 80, 89, 94
Turnovsky, S. J., 10, 39

Urquidi, V., 411

Vaggi, G., 71, 87, 88, 94
Vanoni, E., 411
Veblen, T. B., 33, 46, 294, 360
Velupillai, K., 409
Vercelli, A., 309
Vidal, C., 310
Viner, J., 64, 70, 283, 295, 299
Voltaire (Arouet, F. M.), 357

Wald, A., 252, 254, 268, 271
Walras, L., 35, 53, 153, 165, 168, 172, 251, 254, 255, 268, 271, 355, 361, 377–83
Walsh, V. C., 141, 146, 150, 172
Weber, M., 395
Weintraub, S., 38, 201, 205
Weizsäcker, C. C. von, 161, 162
Wertheim, W. F., 277, 297, 299
West, E., 143
Whitaker, J. K., 46–8, 50, 51, 61, 64, 70
Wicksell, K., 285
Wiener, N., 390
Wieser, F. von, 53, 280
Wood, A. J. B., 16, 38, 42, 202, 205
Wood, J. C., 69
Woods, J. E., 121, 123
Worswick, D., 410

Young, A. A., 287

Zacharov, V. S., 411
Zarembka, P., 170
Ziber, N. I., 218, 241, 245

Subject Index

absolute value, 100–4
accumulation process, 6, 15–16, 21, 189–202, 287
action and choice, in economics, 388–90
aggregate
   demand, 325–6, 396–7
   production function, 153–62, 166
aggregation process, 396–7
aggregative economic system, 308
agricultural goods, in physiocracy, 71–86
American Civil War, 311
axiomatic method, 261

'backward countries', 275
basic and nonbasic sectors, 125
basic products, 107, 111
Bayesian
   expected utility, 395
   inferential procedures for econometric estimation and prediction, 265
Birkhoff's ergodic theory, 301
blockages, of the unequal expansion of different subsystems, 237
bon prix, 75
Bullion Controversy, 96–7

Cambridge (England)
   capital theory controversy, 9–12, 149–72
   Equation, 13–14
   tradition, 200
capacity utilization, 188–91, 200, 203
capital
   accumulation, 21, 125, 127, 142, 154, 256, 353
   fixed and circulating, 150–3
   goods, 149–72
   goods industries, 291
   output ratio, 11, 13, 19–21, 177–9, 290
   reversing, 9–10
   theory, 9–12
   using economy, 216
capitalists' savings, 176–9
Catholic University of Milan, x
causal models, 376–7
causality in economics, 159–64, 246
Central Bank, 185, 187, 201
centrally planned economies, 276

chaotic
   growth oscillator, 300–9
   models, 307
circular models, 255
'circularity' in economic theory, 5, 20
class conflict, 182
classical
   economists, 124, 141–4
   political economy, 86, 351, 364–9
   theory of value, 149–53
collective bargaining, 316–19
commodity flows and productive subsystems, 209–40
comparative advantage
   in open Ricardian economies, 142
   in Ricardo's *Principles*, 124, 138, 142, 143
   in stationary state, 133, 137–9
   principle, 284
comparisons
   interspatial, 96–107
   intertemporal, 96–107
composite
   commodity, 18
   technologies and the separation of circular sub-systems, 238–9
consumption, 397
contracting and expanding subsystems, their complementarity on a structural change path, 234–9
control theory, 265
Corn Laws, 127, 139
corn model, 106–7, 112
CRANEC, xi
cycles, Kitchins, Juglar, Kondratieff, 300

decision
   makers, 183–5, 202
   process, 392–5
decolonization, 276
decomposition
   of an economic system into circular subeconomics, 228–34
   of an economic system into partially overlapping subsystems along the time dimension, 225–8
   of an economic system into vertically integrated subsystems, 217

Subject Index

demand, 58–63, 160, 319, 353
development
  blocks, 240
  economics, 275–95
  and patterns of growth, 280–92
  planning, 295
  theorizing in economics, 275
'disguised unemployment', 281
distribution, 353–4, 370–4, 377–83
  post-Keynesian School of, 12–17
distributive dynamics and the 'uniform proportion' system, 219–20
duo-economics, 277
dynamic
  control, 301
  feasibility
    and the mutual compatibility of given rates of expansion and contraction of different subsystems, 234
    of transitional paths, 233–4
dynamics of a cycle, 302–9

Econometric Society, 263–4
econometrics, 248, 261–6
economic
  behaviour, 384–400
  growth, 45
  science, 246–67
    its tools, 246–67
    object and method of, 246–9
    theories, theorems, models, 249–50
    use of mathematics in, 251–3
effective demand, 287, 353, 367
efficiency, 392–3
elasticity of demand, 57
empirical
  criticism, 262–3
  method, 261–6
employment, 370–3
Engel's Law, 17, 23, 211, 259
England (Britain), 51, 127, 139, 143
entrepreneurial activity, 395–6
equilibrium, 138, 353
  analysis, 182–5
  and rationality, 385–8
  properties, of the post-Keynesian model of distribution, 177–9
  temporary, 131–2
exchange, 351, 352, 354, 359, 377–83
  model, 153–7, 253–5
expectations, 392–5
  about the future, 182
  formation, 393
expected utility principle, 394

factor prices, 159
factors of production, 359
factual-theoretical methods, 261–6
fiscal policies, 327–9
'fix-wage' system, 126, 144
flow input-flow output of structure of the production process, 227–8
fluctuations of the economy, 300–9
formalization in economics, 251
full-employment, 12–17, 22–3, 182–3, 201, 279

general equilibrium model, 157–9, 253–5, 265, 283, 287
global factors and structural dynamics, 210–11
'global technology', 230
gold, role of, 313
Gonville and Caius College, Cambridge, 1
Great Depression, 311, 321
growth, 311–35
  and price mechanism, 311–35
  and wage mechanism, 311–35
  balanced, 280
  unbalanced, 280

Heckscher-Ohlin model, 140, 144–5
Hicks, J. R., on Marshall, 50
horizontal decomposition and traverse analysis, 232–4

imperfect competition, 314
income distribution, 12–17, 28–9, 98–107, 175–80, 256, 259
  and redistribution, 182–5, 191, 193, 200
individual rationality, 384–400
inflation, 182, 184–5, 189–90, 196–7, 200, 311–35
  long-run trend, 311–13
innovational productive capacity, 309
input-output analysis, 5, 19, 22, 256–8
institutional
  changes, 327–9
  set-up, 6–7, 21, 279, 292, 327–9
institutions, 52, 358–61, 374–9
interdependence in economics, 159–64, 246, 255
internal
  feasibility of a technological traverse, 233–4
  rates of accumulation of individual subsystems, 236
international trade
  distributional implications, 132–3, 139–40

Subject Index

dynamic gains, 124, 127, 132, 139–41
dynamic losses, 132, 139–41
  in Ricardo, 60
  static gains, 132, 139–41
investment
  capital stock ratio, 190–1
  decisions, by firms, 184–5, 202–3

Jesus College, Cambridge, x–xi

Kaldor's foreign trade multiplier, 290
Kaldor/Pasinetti model, 9, 12–17, 176, 182–3, 200–1
Kalecki's distribution theory, 184, 186, 188, 200
Keynes' *General Theory*, 278–9, 293
Keynesian
  economics, 353, 354, 367
  literature, 181, 194, 200
  policy, 281
  revolution, 4
  theory, 329–33
King's College, Cambridge, x, 1

labour
  analytical and empirical, 152–3
  commanded, 6, 21
  economy, 21
  embodied, 6, 21
  requirements, 18
labour theory of value, 149–72
  and vertically hyper-integrated labour coefficient, 19–20
  in Ricardo, 149–72
  pure, 19
laissez-faire, 279, 293
law of value, 106
learning process, 21, 393
Leontief/Sraffa model, 262–3
long-run, 189–91, 356

macro-foundations of micro-economics, 384, 394
Malthus' theory of value, 48
Malthusian
  population hypothesis, 143
  principle of population, 8
manufactured good, in physiocracy, 71–86
marginal products, 157–9
Marginalism (neoclassical economics), 46, 157, 168, 182–3, 201, 352–3, 382
mark-up, and desired wage-rate, 184

market, 384–5
  clearing, 386
  system, 385
  value, in physiocracy, 72–86
Marshall
  on Ricardo, 45–63
  Principles of Economics, 48
  The Economics of Industry, 48
Marxian economics, 354
mathematical modelling, 183
mathematics, language of, 385
maximum growth rates and circular subsystems, 234–9
measure of value, 95–118
  and absolute value, 100–4
  and changing distribution of income, 98–107
  and law of value, 106
  and medium between extremes, 104–5
  and technical environment, 98–107, 112–13
  and time, 105
  gold, 98–9
  Ricardo's invariable measure of value, 96–107, 112–17
  Sraffa's Standard commodity, 107–17
Mercantilism, 357
micro-foundations of macro-economics, 15, 384, 394
Mill's Principles of Political Economy, 46
monetary
  policy, 185–205, 327–9
  and rate of interest, 184–5
  system, 313
money, 14, 181–205
  supply, 185, 190
mono-economics, 277
monopoly, 391

natural, 353–8, 374–7, 382
  prices and vertically hyper-integrated subsystems, 213–14
'natural'
  rate of interest, 5, 18, 21, 24
  rate of profits, 24
  system, 5, 24, 351, 354–8, 374–7, 382
  wage, 8
Neo-Ricardians, 157, 159
neoclassical
  economics, 46
  model, 182–3, 201
  theory of distribution, 157, 168
net product, 71–86, 255
  accumulation and non proportional dynamics, 234–9

Subject Index

Neumann's model, von, 258–9
non-basic products, 107, 111
non-proportional dynamics, 211–17, 225–8
normative
 aspects, 370, 378, 381, 389
 economics, 247, 266
 theoretical models, 266
Nuffield College, Oxford, x, 1

offer curve, 132–4
oligopoly, 314–16
optimizing behaviour, 385
'ordinary price', 80

Pareto
 equilibrium, 385, 397
 optimum, 397, 398
Pasinetti, L. L.
 a short biography, 1–2
 Kaldor/Pasinetti model, 9, 12–17, 176, 182–3, 200–1
 on Ricardo, 45–6
 'senior' heir of the post-Keynesian School, 2–7
 structural dynamics theory, 7, 17–19, 211–17
 Theorem, 9, 12–17, 176, 182–3, 200–1
Perron-Frobenius Theorem, 111
Phillips curve, 321–2
physiocratic dichotomy, in price determination, 71–86
political arithmeticians, 264
Popper's concept of rationality, 387
population growth, 260
portfolio choice, 14
post-Keynesian
 economics, 354, 375
 School, x, 2–7, 12–17, 175–205
  and income distribution, 191, 193, 199, 200
  and theory of growth, 181–205
  and theory of money, 181–205
  its micro-foundations, 15
price, 354, 369, 386
 determination, 71–86
  and physiocratic dichotomy, 71–86
 level, 184–5
 mechanisms, 311–35
 system of, 23
 system, in physiocracy, 71–86
 various definitions, 71–86
primitive circular structure of an economic system, 222–3

probability
 and economic behaviour, 390, 395–6
 subjective, 390
process of growth, 311–35
 and aggregate demand, 325–6
production, 45, 351, 353, 355–8, 362–5, 368, 377–83
 function, 187
 function models, 153–7, 159–60
 model, 255–9
 processes, 259
productive
 funds and structural dynamics, 214–15
 subsystems, 209–40
  and structural change, 223–4
  circular subsystems, 217–23
  net product subsystems, 209–17
  partially overlapping, and traverse analysis, 225–8
productivity, *see* technical progress
 growth, 309
 increase, 322–35
produit net, *see* net product
profit rate, corn, 128–30, 139–41
public
 expenditure, 329–33
 goods, 397
 sector, 15
pure
 labour economy, 214–17
 labour theory of value and vertically hyper-integrated subsystems, 213–17
'pure ratio' method, 175–80
 in classical economics, 175
 in post-Keynesian economics, 176–9

Quadrio-Curzio's model, 229, 235, 238–9
Quesnay's economics, 71–86

random shocks, 301
ratchet effects, 194
rate
 of growth, 12–17, 177–9
 of interest, 9–17, 24, 184–5, 191
  and Central Bank policy, 184–5, 187
  and demand for liquidity, 184–5
 of profits, 9–17, 24, *see also* rate of interest, 175–9
 in Ricardo, 175
rational expectations, 394

Subject Index

rationality, 384–400
raw materials, 318–21
realistic causal analysis
  and the relationship between
  macro-concepts and concepts
  appropriate to the process
  of transformation (Dahmen),
  239–40
relative prices, 150, 175
rent
  of land, 106
  theory of, 84–6
residuals of produced commodities, 237
retention rate, 202
returns to scale, 288
Ricardian
  diminishing returns
    and the 'composite technology'
    representation of production
    processes, 234–9
    and the 'global technology'
    representation of production
    processes, 229–30
  system, 7–9, 48–9, 52–63, 125, 138
  mathematical formulation, x, 7, 45
  monetary theory, 52–3
  'New View', 126, 141, 144
  open-economy, 127–32
  Pasinetti's model of, 45, 61, 63,
    125–6, 132–3
  Pasinetti-Sraffa view, 126
  theory of value, 8
  theory of value, 71–86
  'vice', 143–4
Ricardo's
  Labour theory of value, 149–72
  Principles, 85
richesse, in physiocracy, 71–86
Rössler's
  band, 303
  chaotic attractor, 301–2

savings function, classical, 128
scarce resources, 153–9, 253–5
scarcity, 253–5, 354
  theory of value, 153–7
    analytical theory, 156
    empirical theory, 156
Schumpeter analysis, 300
'scope and method' of analysis, 6
self-replacement of circular subsystems, 235
share of profits, 177–9
short- and long-period, of the model of
  distribution, 189–91
short-run, 356
shortening and lengthening of the
  construction or utilization phase in
  vertically integrated processes, 226
Smith's theory of value, 81–4
  Wealth of Nations, 80, 83
social
  learning, 21
  and technical progress, 21
  philosophy, 358–61
  rate of return on investment, 11
  sciences, and natural sciences, 251
specialization, resulting from trade,
  129–30, 132, 135–41, 143–4
splitting coefficients
  and the dynamics of productive
    subsystems, 228–34
  and the 'global technology'
    representation of the productive
    system, 229–30
  and the speed of reproduction of
    individual subsystems, 231–2
  defined, 229–30
Sraffa's model, 256–8
Sraffa/Leontief/Pasinetti, model of, 364, 365
stability analysis, of post-Keynesian
  model, 190–1
Standard commodity, 107–18, 175
  a physical analogue?, 111–12
  a purely auxiliary construction,
    116–17
  a tool of analysis, 111, 116–17
  and 'critical proportion', 112–15
  and 'deficit' and 'surplus' industries, 113
  and labour commanded, 116–17
  and maximum rate of profits, 109, 115
  and proportion of labour to means of
    production, 112–15
  and Ricardo's search for an
    'invariable measure of value',
    112–15
  and Standard national income, 111
  and Standard ratio, 111
  and Standard system, 111
  and wage-profit relation, 111–12
  not a measure of real wages, 111–12
stationary state
  approach to, 125–7, 139
  characterization of, 124–5, 132–6, 141
  gains (losses) from trade in, 132, 139–41

land rent in, 126, 133–4, 138–41
population (labour force) in, 133–41
rate of profits in, 126, 138
Ricardo's attitude towards, 139–41, 143
terms of trade in, 132–41
trade pattern in, 132–9
trajectory towards, 125–6, 128–9
steady state, in Pasinetti, 176–7
structural
  change, 45, 46
  economic dynamics, 7, 17–19, 258–61
structure, 143, 353–4, 360–4
'stylized facts', 247, 259, 263
subsistence wage, in Ricardo, 8
subsystems, see productive subsystems
supply and demand, 51, 53, 54, 57, 160, 319
surplus product, 113
switching of techniques, 9–12
system rationality, 397–400

Tableau économique, 72–86, 381
technical progress, 5–21, 260
technological
  change
    Harrod-neutral, 117–18
    Hicks-neutral, 117–18
  matrix, 257
technology, in production models, 165, 256
terms of trade, 130, 133, 142–4
theory of value, 149–72
time, 105
  connectedness of productive activities on a structural change path, 234–9
  series analysis, 264
trade
  cycle, 300–1, 306
  unions, 313–16, 323–5
traverse, 15, 225–8
Turgot's economics, 79–81
two-sector model, 177–9

uncertainty, 390–1, see also portfolio choice
  in a growth model, 181–205
  in economic theory, 391
under-employment, 279, 281
under-investment, 292
unemployment, 182, 322–35
University of Fribourg, xi
University of Verona, x
unproductive consumption, 125
unstable aggregate system, 302–7
use value, in physiocracy, 72–86

value, see also measure of value
  labour theory of, 351–4, 372
  supply-and-demand theory of, 353
  theory of, 52–3, 55–60, 62–3, 149–72
vertical integration, 17–19, 21
  and productive subsystems (Pasinetti), 211–17
  and the time structure of production (Hicks), 225–8
vertically
  hyper-integrated productive capacity, 213
  hyper-integrated sectors, 213–14
vision (Schumpeterian), 358, 382

wage
  flexibility, 312–13, 316–19, 322–35
  fund, 129–30, 141, 144–5
  mechanisms, 311–35
  rate, 186–90
    market and natural, 125–6, 128–30, 141–3
    natural, 135–7, 141
    subsistence, 126, 138–9
wages
  and prices, 322–35
  in Ricardo, 58–9
wave system, long and short, 304
wealth 46, 187
Wealth of nations, dynamics of, 46
workers' savings, 176–9
world industrial output, 319–21